INFORMATION TECHNOLOGY RISK MANAGEMENT IN ENTERPRISE ENVIRONMENTS

INFORMATION TECHNOLOGY RISK MANAGEMENT IN ENTERPRISE ENVIRONMENTS

A REVIEW OF INDUSTRY PRACTICES AND A PRACTICAL GUIDE TO RISK MANAGEMENT TEAMS

Jake Kouns
Daniel Minoli

A JOHN WILEY & SONS, INC., PUBLICATION

Copyright © 2010 by John Wiley & Sons, Inc. All rights reserved.

Published by John Wiley & Sons, Inc., Hoboken, New Jersey.
Published simultaneously in Canada.

No part of this publication may be reproduced, stored in a retrieval system, or transmitted in any form or by any means, electronic, mechanical, photocopying, recording, scanning, or otherwise, except as permitted under Section 107 or 108 of the 1976 United States Copyright Act, without either the prior written permission of the Publisher, or authorization through payment of the appropriate per-copy fee to the Copyright Clearance Center, Inc., 222 Rosewood Drive, Danvers, MA 01923, (978) 750-8400, fax (978) 750-4470, or on the web at www.copyright.com. Requests to the Publisher for permission should be addressed to the Permissions Department, John Wiley & Sons, Inc., 111 River Street, Hoboken, NJ 07030, (201) 748-6011, fax (201) 748-6008, or online at http://www.wiley.com/go/permission.

Limit of Liability/Disclaimer of Warranty: While the publisher and author have used their best efforts in preparing this book, they make no representations or warranties with respect to the accuracy or completeness of the contents of this book and specifically disclaim any implied warranties of merchantability or fitness for a particular purpose. No warranty may be created or extended by sales representatives or written sales materials. The advice and strategies contained herein may not be suitable for your situation. You should consult with a professional where appropriate. Neither the publisher nor author shall be liable for any loss of profit or any other commercial damages, including but not limited to special, incidental, consequential, or other damages.

For general information on our other products and services or for technical support, please contact our Customer Care Department within the United States at (800) 762-2974, outside the United States at (317) 572-3993 or fax (317) 572-4002.

Wiley also publishes its books in a variety of electronic formats. Some content that appears in print may not be available in electronic formats. For more information about Wiley products, visit our web site at www.wiley.com.

ISBN   978-0-471-76254-6

Library of Congress Cataloging-in-Publication Data is available.

Printed in the United States of America

10 9 8 7 6 5 4 3 2 1

Jake:

I would like to dedicate this book to all of the volunteers that have supported the Open Security Foundation. To my friends and colleagues over the years. To my parents, Barry and Roxanne, for their continued support and to Jill and Elora for their unending love and patience.

Dan:

For Anna

CONTENTS

PREFACE

Well-documented studies show that cyber attacks continue to remain a substantial threat to organizations of all types and their information technology (IT) assets. It has been forecasted that in 2010 around 10,000 new vulnerabilities will be discovered in software applications in that year alone; this will force companies to assess and mitigate one new risk every hour each day of the year. Considering that each vulnerability instance has the potential to disrupt or bring a company's business to a complete halt, organizations must take risk assessment seriously and determine how each risk will be handled. The increased number of vulnerabilities being discovered also drives up the number of security incidents worldwide, and it will increase to a point where hundreds, if not thousands, of incidents per month will affect organizations that have not properly addressed and mitigated their risks.

Risk is a quantitative evaluation of the potential damage caused by an attack, a vulnerability, or an event impacting the set of company IT assets. A vulnerability (or weakness) is a lack of a safeguard, which may be exploited by a threat, causing harm to the information systems; specifically it can be a software flaw that permits an exogenous agent to use a computer system without authorization or use it with authorization in excess of that which the system owner specifically granted said agent. Risk-generating events and vulnerabilities are implicitly related in the context of this discussion in the sense that (we postulate that) a vulnerability is ultimately caused by some subtending event, malicious or nonmalicious. For example, in a so-called "non-malicious event," a flaw may be introduced in some software release by its designers, and then the event of having the IT group load and distribute that software throughout the enterprise creates a predicament where risk ensues. A "malicious" event may be a direct attack on the organization firewall, router, website, or database platform.

Corporate information security has become the fiduciary concern of the CEO, the CSO, the CFO, the CIO, and the COO of the organization. If a company were to lose its IT (computer and/or voice/data networking) resources (assets) for more than a day or two, the company may well find itself in financial trouble. Obviously brokerage firms, banks, airports, critical infrastructure, medical establishments, and homeland security concerns would be impacted faster than, say, a manufacturing firm or a book publishing firm. However, the general concern is universal. If a company is unable to conduct business for more than a week, the company may well be permanently incapacitated. Therefore, a clear need arises to protect the enterprise from random, negligent, malicious, or planned attacks on its IT assets. It is critical, therefore, for companies to develop ready-to-go technological and human resources within the organization, to handle vulnerabilities and events that likely will impact the organization in the years to come. Some have called these teams *risk management* or *risk assessment* teams. The job function of a risk management team is to assess the risk that ensues from vulnerabilities and/or from risk-generating/causing events and to identify and ensure that risk mitigation solutions are implemented.

As more and more companies send their IT business abroad because of "outsourcing" or near-shoring, the potential IT (and, hence, corporate) risks are arguably growing at a geometric pace; these risks can have ultimate negative implications, particularly in view of cumulative exposures to risks that, in the aggregate, do not take on a trivial probability and, thus, risk.

This book aims at surveying industry approaches, best practices, and standards for how an organization can position itself to properly handle this ever-increasing and perennially mutating tsunami of risks to their business-critical IT assets. The book has two major sections. Part 1 reviews industry practices in the area of risk assessment and mitigation. The aim is to provide an overview of the well-known risk management approaches and methodologies. Part 2 focuses on helping an organization to develop a repeatable program that will address technological issues and human resources within the organization, to effectively undertake the risk assessment and mitigation function. It looks at the best use of IT resources, procedures, tools, and preparedness, and it places emphasis on implementing a risk assessment team that can properly foresee, prevent, and/or rapidly remediate potential infractions. This text is intended to be used by information security managers, security analysts, systems developers, auditors, consultants, and students, among others.

JAKE KOUNS
DANIEL MINOLI

ABOUT THE AUTHORS

Jake Kouns is a business-focused technology and information security executive with an extensive knowledge base and international experience. He focuses on the application of security concepts across a broad range on information technology areas including data communications, network design, operations, database structures, operating systems, application development, and disaster recovery. He holds both a Bachelor of Business Administration and a Master of Business Administration with a concentration in Information Security from James Madison University. In addition, he holds a number of certifications including ISC2's CISSP and ISACA's CISM, CISA, and CGEIT. Mr. Kouns is currently the Senior Director of Technology for Markel Corporation, a specialty insurance company. Prior to his current role, he was Senior Network Security Manager for Capital One Financial, a Fortune 200 financial institution where he was responsible for the day-to-day global security management of a large complex firewall environment, intrusion detection, and risk assessment.

Mr. Kouns has twice presented for Check Point Software Technologies as an expert in global firewall management and intrusion detection. In recent years, Mr. Kouns' main focus has been spent redefining the information security vulnerability industry, and he has presented on the topic at many well-known security conferences including CanSecWest and SyScan. He is the co-author of the book *Security in an IPv6 Environment*, Taylor and Francis, 2009, and he has also been interviewed as an expert in the security industry by *Information Week, eWeek, Processor.com, Federal Computer Week, Government Computer News*, and *SC Magazine*.

Mr. Kouns is the co-founder, CEO, and CFO of the Open Security Foundation (OSF), a nonprofit organization that oversees the operations of the Open Source Vulnerability Database (OSVDB.org) and the DataLossDB. Mr. Kouns' primary focus is to provide management oversight and define the strategic direction of the projects. Both projects are independent and open source databases that provide detailed and unbiased technical information on security vulnerabilities and data loss incidents worldwide. Mr. Kouns has also has participated in Google's Summer of Code and volunteered time to mentor students during the 2006, 2007, and 2008 programs.

Daniel Minoli has extensive technical-hands-on and managerial experience in security, networking, telecom, wireless, video, and Enterprise Architecture for global Best-In-Class carriers and financial companies. He has worked at financial firms such as AIG, Prudential Securities, and Capital One Financial and at service provider firms such as Network Analysis Corporation, Bell Telephone Laboratories, ITT, Bell Communications Research (now Telcordia), AT&T, Leading Edge Networks Inc., and SES Engineering, where he is Director of Terrestrial Systems Engineering (SES is the largest satellite services company in the world).

At SES Mr. Minoli has been responsible for the development and deployment of IPTV systems, terrestrial and mobile IP-based networking services, and IPv6 services over satellite links. He also played a founding role in the launching of two companies through the high-tech incubator Leading Edge Networks Inc., which he ran in the early 2000s: Global Wireless Services, a provider of secure broadband hotspot mobile Internet and hotspot VoIP services; and, InfoPort Communications Group, an optical and Gigabit Ethernet metropolitan carrier supporting Data Center/SAN/channel extension and Grid Computing network access services. He is also the Founder and President Emeritus of the IPv6 Institute, the premiere leading certification organization for IPv6 networking technology, IPv6 global network deployment, and IPv6 security (www.ipv6institute.org). For several years he has been Session, Tutorial, and now overall Technical Program Chair for the IEEE ENTNET (Enterprise Networking) conference. ENTNET focuses on enterprise networking requirements for large financial firms and other corporate institutions.

Mr. Minoli has done important work in security, including leading-edge work such as security in an IPv6 environment (results documented in the first text on the topic of *Security in an IPv6 Environment*, Taylor and Francis, 2009, co-authored), security for IPTV systems, particularly encryption and Conditional Access (approaches documented in his text *IP Multicast with Applications to IPTV and Mobile DVB-H, Wiley, 2008*), and basic security work as documented in the *Minoli–Cordovana Authoritative Computer and Network Security Dictionary* (Wiley, 2006, co-authored).

Mr. Minoli has also written columns for *ComputerWorld, NetworkWorld*, and *Network Computing* (1985–2006). He has taught at New York University (Information Technology Institute), Rutgers University, and Stevens Institute of Technology (1984–2006). Also, he was a Technology Analyst At-Large for Gartner/DataPro (1985–2001); based on extensive hands-on work at financial firms and carriers, he tracked technologies and wrote CTO/CIO-level technical scans in the area of telephony and data systems, including topics on security, disaster recovery, network management, LANs, WANs (ATM and MPLS), wireless (LAN and public hotspot), VoIP, network design/economics, carrier networks (such as metro Ethernet and CWDM/DWDM), and e-commerce.

Over the years he has advised Venture Capitals for investments of $150M in a dozen high-tech companies. He has acted as Expert Witness in a (won) $11B lawsuit regarding a VoIP-based wireless Air-to-Ground communication system, and he has been involved as a technical expert in a number of patent infringement proceedings.

PART I

INDUSTRY PRACTICES IN RISK MANAGEMENT

CHAPTER 1

INFORMATION SECURITY RISK MANAGEMENT IMPERATIVES AND OPPORTUNITIES

1.1 RISK MANAGEMENT PURPOSE AND SCOPE

1.1.1 Purpose of Risk Management

This text deals with information technology (IT) risk management (ITRM), which, given the context of this text, we also just refer to as risk management.[1] Concerns about the possibility of compromise and/or the loss of proprietary information have reached critical levels in many organizations in recent years as a barrage of news bulletins reporting on infractions and product defects, staff's shortfalls and shortcomings, functions' outsourcings and offshorings, political instabilities in a number of countries and in wider regions, and management's emphasis on short-term financial breakeven has become all too frequent. Cyber attacks continue to be a source of significant exposure to organizations of all types, and, as a consequence, potential damage, potential impairment, and/or potential incapacitation of IT assets have become fundamental business viability/continuity issues.

Information Security[2] is recognized at this juncture to be a key area of IT management by a majority of government, commercial, and industrial organizations. Information Security is defined as the set of mechanisms, techniques, measures, and administrative processes employed to protect IT assets from unauthorized access, (mis)appropriation, manipulation, modification, loss, or (mis)use and from unintentional disclosure of data and information embedded in these assets. Some organizations have individuals on staff with a plethora of security certifications, yet these organizations continue to be afflicted with security

---

[1]Some also refer to ITRM as "information security risk management (ISRM)."
[2]Some also use the terms "infosecurity," and/or "INFOSEC," and/or "information systems security (ISS)," and/or "information security management (ISM)."

Information Technology Risk Management in Enterprise Environments: A Review of Industry Practices and a Practial Guide to Risk Management Teams, by Jake Kouns and Daniel Minoli
Copyright © 2010 John Wiley & Sons, Inc.

breaches on a fairly routine basis and continue to be exposed to risk; this implies that perhaps other approaches to information security are needed. Practitioners of information security are all well aware that exposure to risk is ever-changing and that it is also hard to assess; therefore, what is needed to manage and minimize risk in organizations is a diversified, versatile, and experienced IT/networking staff along with a solid set of policies, processes, and procedures that create a reliable information security program. This approach is typically much more successful as compared to the case where an organization just attempts to rely on ultra-narrow staffers with cookbooks of perishable memorized software commands specific to a given version of a given program of a given vendor to produce results, where the organization seems to be assuming that the real-life information security issues are similar to an academic pre-canned rapid-fire test for abstract scholastic grades, and simply believes that an alphabet soup of tags following one's name is sufficient (or necessary) to address incessant IT security threats.

Risk is a quantitative measure of the potential damage caused by a threat, by a vulnerability, or by an event (malicious or nonmalicious) that affects the set of IT assets owned by the organization. Risk exposure (that is, being subjected to risk-generating events) leads to potential losses, and risk is a measure of the "average" (typical) loss that may be expected from that exposure. Risk, therefore, is a quantitative measure of the damage that can incur to a given asset even after (a number of) information security measures have been deployed by the organization. Obviously, when the risk is high, an enhanced set of information security controls, specific to the situation at hand, needs to be deployed fairly rapidly in the IT environment of the organization. See Table 1.1 for some risk-related definitions, loosely modeled after [HUB200701]. The term "information asset" refers here to actual data elements, records, files, software systems (applications), and so on, while the term "IT asset" refers to the broader set of assets including the hardware, the media, the communications elements, and the actual IT environment of the enterprise; the general term "asset," refers to either "information asset" or "IT asset;" or both, depending on context. Typical corporate IT assets in a commercial enterprise environment include, but are not limited to, the following:

- Desktops PCs and laptops
- Mobile devices and wireless networks (e.g., PDAs, Wi-Fi/Bluetooth devices)
- Application servers, mainframes
- Mail servers
- Web servers
- Database servers (data warehouses, storage) as well as the entire universe of corporate data, records, memos, reports, etc.
- Network elements (switches, routers, firewalls, appliances, etc.)
- PBXs, IP-PBXs, VRUs, ACDs, voicemail systems, etc.
- Mobility (support) systems (Virtual Private Network nodes, wireless e-mail servers, etc.)

TABLE 1.1. Uncertainty, Probability, and Risk

Uncertainty	The lack of complete certainty, that is, the existence of more than one possibility for the outcome. The "true" outcome/state/result/value is not known.
Measurement of uncertainty	A set of probabilities assigned to a set of possibilities (specifically for risk events, threats, and/or vulnerabilities).
Risk exposure (also, liability)	A state of uncertainty where some of the possibilities (also colloquially called "risks") involve a loss, catastrophe, or other undesirable outcome. An environment exposed to risk events, threats, and/or vulnerabilities. Each new risk event, threat, and/or vulnerability gives rise to new risk exposure.
Measurement of risk	A set of possibilities, each with quantified probabilities and quantified losses.
Risk (singular)	The expected loss. Namely, the aggregation (summation) of the possibilities, their probabilities, and the loss associated with each possibility.
Risks (plural) (colloquial)	Individual possibilities (risk events) that are encountered with risk exposures.
Risk-exposing event (also called risk event)	Any changes in the state of the environment that have the potential of creating a new state where there is nonzero risk.

- Power sources
- Systems deployed in remote/branch locations (including international locations)
- Key organizational business processes (e.g., order processing, billing, procurement, customer relationship management, and so on)

Continuing with some definitions, a security threat is an occurrence, situation, or activity that has the potential to cause harm to the IT assets. A vulnerability (or weakness) is a lack of a safeguard that may be exploited by a threat, causing harm to the IT assets; specifically, it can be a software flaw that permits an exogenous agent to use a computer system without authorization or use it with an authorization level in excess of that which the system owner specifically granted to said agent. Risk-exposing events (also called risk events) are any changes in the state of the environment that have the potential of creating a new state where there is nonzero risk. Risk events and vulnerabilities are implicitly related in the context of this discussion in the sense that a vulnerability is ultimately given an opportunity for harm by some subtending event, malicious or nonmalicious. For example, in a so-called "nonmalicious event," a flaw may be inadvertently introduced in some software release by its designers; the event of having the IT group load and distribute that software throughout the enterprise creates a predicament where risk ensues. A "malicious" event may be a direct attack on the organization's firewalls, routers, website(s), or data warehouse.

> **Note:** Some people use the term "risk" (singular) more loosely than defined above to mean a potential threat, vulnerability, or (risk) event; we endeavor to avoid this phraseology, and we use the term risk to formally describe the quantitative (numerical) measure of the underlying damage-causing issues, and not the issues themselves.
>
> We acknowledge that the term "risks" (plural) is used colloquially to describe the set of individual possibilities (risk events) that are encountered with risk exposures. We occasionally use this phraseology.

Information security spans the areas of *confidentiality, integrity, and availability*. Confidentiality is protection against unauthorized access, appropriation, or use of assets. Integrity is protection against unauthorized manipulation, modification, or loss of assets. Availability is protection against blockage, limitation, or diminution of benefit from an asset that is owed. The Computer Crime and Intellectual Property Section (CCIPS) Computer Intrusion Cases of the U.S. Department of Justice defines these terms (and considers respective infractions as crimes) as follows:

- *Confidentiality.* A breach of confidentiality occurs when a person knowingly accesses a computer without authorization or exceeding authorized access. Confidentiality is compromised when a hacker views or copies proprietary or private information, such as a credit card number or trade secret.
- *Integrity.* A breach of integrity occurs when a system or data has been accidentally or maliciously modified, altered, or destroyed without authorization. For example, viruses and worms alter the source code in order to allow a hacker to gain unauthorized access to a computer system.
- *Availability.* A breach of availability occurs when an authorized user is prevented from timely, reliable access to data or a system. An example of this is a denial of service (DoS) attack.

At this point in time, the practical challenges for enterprises are how to organize and run an efficient and effective information security program for persistent, high-grade protection and, in turn, how to actually (i) identify risk events, (ii) assess the risk, and (iii) mitigate ("manage") the environment to reduce risk. IT risk management (information security risk management) is the process of reducing IT risk (a process is a well-defined, repeatable sequences of activities.) Risk management is a continuous process. IT risk management encompasses five processes (also see Table 1.2 and Figure 1.1):

1. (Ongoing) identification of threats, vulnerabilities, or (risk) events impacting the set of IT assets owned by the organization

TABLE 1.2. Risk Management Processes

Risk identification	The process of identifying threats, vulnerabilities, or events (malicious or nonmalicious, deterministic/planned, or random) impacting the set of IT assets owned by the organization.
Risk assessment	The process of calculating quantitatively the potential damage and/or monetary cost caused by a threat, a vulnerability, or by an event impacting the set of IT assets owned by the organization. Identification of the potential damage to the IT assets and/or to the business processes based on previous internal and external events, input from subject matter experts, and audits. Specifically, this entails (a) quantifying the potential damage, and (b) quantifying the probability that damage will occur.
Risk mitigation planning	Process for controlling and mitigating IT risks. It typically includes cost–benefit analysis, and the selection, implementation, test, and security evaluation of safeguards. This overall system security review considers both effectiveness and efficiency, including impact on the mission and constraints due to policy, regulations, and laws [STO200201].
Risk mitigation implementation	Deploying and placing in service equipment and/or solution identified during the risk mitigation planning phase, or actuating new corrective processes.
Evaluation of the mitigation's effectiveness	Monitoring the environment for effectiveness against the previous set of threats, vulnerabilities, or events, as well as determining if new/different threats, vulnerabilities, or events results from the modifications made to the environment.

2. Risk assessment (also called risk analysis by some, especially when combined with Step 1)
3. Risk mitigation planning
4. Risk mitigation implementation
5. Evaluation of the mitigation's effectiveness

When the term risk management (or information security risk management) is used in this text, all five of these processes are implied. Risk management is a fundamental, yet complex, element of information security. Figure 1.2, contained in the International Organization for Standardization (ISO) 27002 standard, depicts the macrocosms of information security management (ISM), including risk management. The National Institute of Standards and Technology (NIST) defines risk management (in their recommendation NIST SP 800-30) as the process that allows IT managers to balance the operational and economic costs of protective measures and achieve gains in mission capability by protecting the IT systems and data that support their

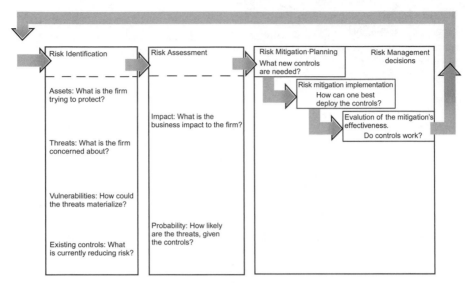

FIGURE 1.1. Risk management process as defined in this text.

FIGURE 1.2. A view of information security management, as conceived in ISO 27002.

organizations' missions. Figure 1.3 provides a graphical view of the (assessment) process of NIST SP 800-30. Figure 1.4 depicts the ISO 31000 view of risk management. Figure 1.5 depicts the view in the Australian/New Zealand Standard AS/NZS 4360:2004. Figure 1.6 shows a vendor-based approach, specifically from Microsoft. Finally, Figure 1.7 depicts the view taken by OCTAVE (Operationally Critical Threat, Asset, and Vulnerability Evaluation), a risk-based strategic assessment and planning technique for security, developed by CERT (Carnegie Mellon University's Computer Emergency Response Team).

A recent confluence of technical and geopolitical factors has sensitized decision-makers about the business and legal consequences of cyber intrusions and risk exposures to an organization's IT assets, both at the corporate level as well as at the national security level. As a result of these developments, legislature has been introduced in a number of countries (e.g., Sarbanes–Oxley Act in the United States) that, in the final analysis, forces information security and privacy issues to be assessed rigorously and with fiduciary oversight by company executives and officials. In an effort to achieve business continuity and protect the enterprise from random, negligent, malicious, or planned security attacks, the organization must have a clear top-down understanding of its IT-supported business operations at a fundamental and comprehensive level. There must be an understanding of (a) what IT assets the company has deployed across its entire functional landscape, (b) how the resources are being used; and (c) who could attack these resources and the manner of such attacks.

IT security measures are intrinsically (and unfortunately) limited in their total effectiveness, therefore, organizations must equip themselves to manage risk. The following is an honest observation about the state of affairs from industry observers [MAR200601]:

> Even though serious responsibilities for complying with the organization's objectives have been placed in the hands of information systems, doubts about their security continue to arise. Those affected, often not technicians, wonder if they can place their trust on these systems. Each failure lowers the trust on information systems, especially when the investments made in defending the means of work do not rule out failures . . . The matter is not as much the absence of incidents, but the confidence that they are under control.

The convergence of IT networks and mobile communications (including "mobility solutions"), increases the number of potential threats, including unauthorized access, exploitable vulnerabilities, malicious attacks, viruses, worms, and DoS attacks to both wired and wireless corporate systems. Press time studies by the *IT Policy Compliance Group*[3] have shown that the primary business and financial liabilities from the use of IT are directly related to how well, or poorly,

---

[3]The IT Policy Compliance Group conducts benchmarks that are focused on delivering fact-based guidance on the steps that can be taken to improve results. Benchmark results are reported through www.itpolicycompliance.com for the benefit of members.

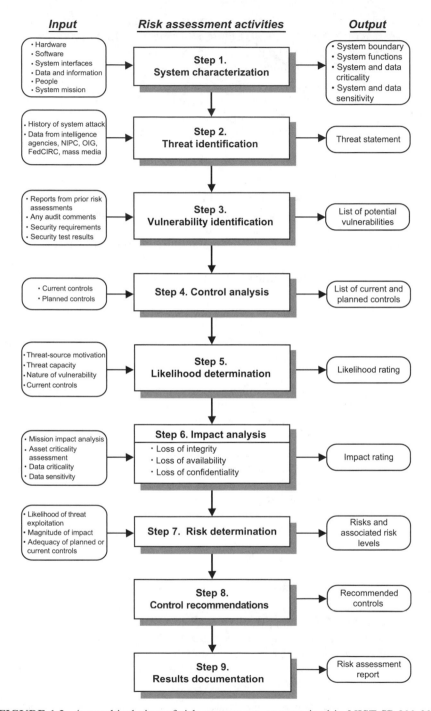

FIGURE 1.3. A graphical view of risk assessment, as conceived in NIST SP 800-30.

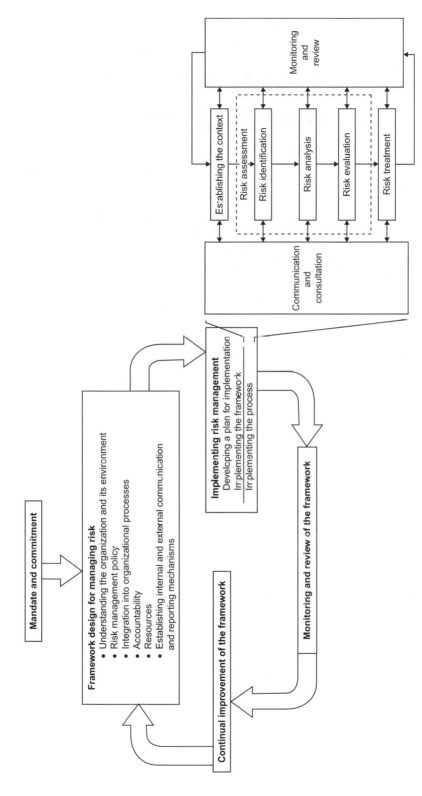

FIGURE 1.4. Framework for managing risk per (Draft International Standard) ISO/IEC 31000.

11

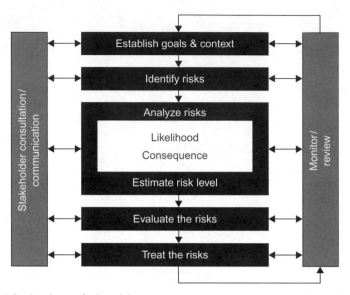

FIGURE 1.5. A view of the risk management process, as conceived in AS/NZS 4360:2004.

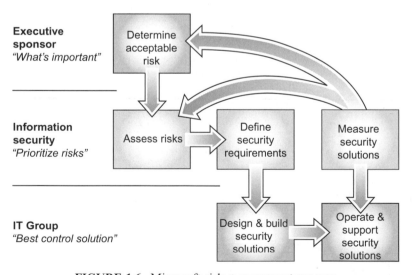

FIGURE 1.6. Microsoft risk management process.

organizations are managing the confidentiality, integrity, and availability of information and IT assets. These are, in turn, directly related to the controls and procedures implemented to protect sensitive information, maintain the integrity of information and audit controls, and the availability of IT services. The

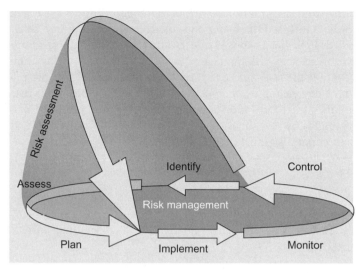

FIGURE 1.7. OCTAVE risk management/risk assessment.

primary business and financial liabilities are due to losses, or lapses that are occurring in three areas [ITP200901]:

- Confidentiality, or protection, of sensitive information
- Integrity of information, assets, and controls in IT
- Availability of IT services

These three—the loss of confidentiality, integrity, and availability—are ranked as the top business liabilities by organizations, well ahead of other possible concerns, including those from outsourced IT projects, systems, and information; delays to critical IT projects; and shortages of IT skills. Measured across almost 500 organizations surveyed, the findings reveal that the top business liabilities include:

1. Loss or theft of customer data
2. Business disruptions from IT failures and disruptions
3. Loss of integrity for critical IT assets and information

Specifically, in this 2009 study, the theft or loss of customer data was rated as the highest business risk by more than 72% of organizations while business disruptions and the loss of integrity were rated as posing the most business risk by 64% and 61% of organization, respectively. After the top three, theft or fraud related to IT assets and information and Internet security threats pose similarly high business liabilities. These highest-ranked business liabilities are followed by shortages of critical IT skills, delays to IT projects, and outsourced *importance of data loss Prevention solution* (handwritten margin note)

IT capabilities and information [ITP200901]. According to the Open Security Foundation's DataLossDB (http://datalossdb.org), as of early 2009 over 358 million records have been exposed due to data loss incidents since January 2005.

Information security risk management seeks to reduce and/or minimize risk. It is unlikely that the risk can be reduced to zero; however, proper intervention should aim at decreasing it, and such goals are achievable when risk management techniques (methods and tools) are properly applied. If an organization has any of the following, then it is highly advisable, if not critical, that a risk management capability must be put in place:

- Has IT assets
- Has data
- Has proprietary information
- Keeps customer credit card, financial data, personal information or medical data
- Requires formal documentation and policies
- Is required to adhere to legal requirements, Sarbanes–Oxley (SOX), Health Insurance Portability and Accountability Act (HIPAA), ISO 27000, and so on or
- Has a fiduciary responsibilities to stockholders

Of course, information security risk management is part of an overall business risk management continuum, as depicted in Figure 1.8.

There is no doubt that security threats are an ever-moving target, and, therefore, no definitive formula-based-solution is in sight at this juncture. Many books have been written in the past quarter century on the issue of information security and on general mechanisms that, at face value, address the

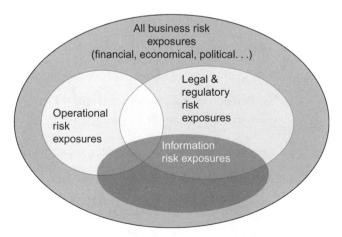

FIGURE 1.8. Risk management continuum.

underlying technical issues. However, sadly, the complex issue of security and risk management is often reduced to a discussion about network security (in any event, when most people say "network security," they really mean "perimeter security" and not security of the network itself—that is, security of the network elements, transmission facilities, network management and/or provisioning system, and so on). It ought to be self-evident from recent history that for all intents and purposes, bookshelves of books that simply "blame" the network or hold it responsible for all sorts of security infractions to corporate IT assets is just a nonstarter for corporate officers under stringent regulatory mandates to demonstrate assured integrity.[4-6] It can be argued that there are clear benefits from implementing network or perimeter security, but it cannot be the only major control relied on as part of an information security program. A few years ago the concepts of "host security" and "network security" (perimeter security) were topics of "equal" treatment; today the concept of "host security" has almost exited the parlance even though some security vendors are now advocating endpoint security solutions, at least as documented by a book search on Google (see Appendix 2A, Section 2A.2). (There may be an "explanation" for this: After all, there is "something" that can be done for perimeter security: Having scripts to block Transmission Control Protocol (TCP) port i used by protocol ı, block TCP port j used protocol φ, block TCP port k used protocol k, block TCP port l used protocol λ, block TCP port m used protocol μ, and so on; the issue is that there may be rather scant science on the topic of host security for host A, or B, or C, even though these security measures would be of critical importance—focusing excessively on network/perimeter security obfuscates the critical fact that host security is of equal or even greater importance. The coming increased deployment of mobile devices and IPv6 will greatly increase this need for host/endpoint security in the near future.) Unfortunately, stories like the one that follows seem to be *a routine occurrence* at some U.S. organization: In February 2009, hackers broke into the Federal Aviation Administration's computer system, accessing the names and

[4]Perimeter and host security (including endsystems) need emphasis instead—networks are just "pipes." We do not blame the interstate highways, county roads, bridges, intercostals canals, airlines, railroads, pedestrian white stripes, or bicycle lanes when there is a physical break-in at a local bank or at someone's home, so why blame the network for the theft of a file of credit card accounts or for the disclosure of some memo on a server?

[5]We take encryption to be, optimally, a host's responsibility. For example if two polyglot individuals wanted to communicate in public but in a semi-secure manner in a place where the prevalent language might be A, then they could switch to language B; it would not be the responsibility of the "air" (the communication channel) to provide security—naturally these issues could be debated at infinitum, but we argue that perhaps one way to move the discourse along is to re-focus the security issue less on the network and more on the host/perimeter/bastion. We take perimeter security (including firewalls) to be a form of host-level security and not an intrinsic long-haul network issue per se. While the network could be enhanced to provide link-level encryption, why would the host be relieved of this responsibility?

[6]While the majority of the infractional code often arrives to the IT resource over the network, we take the position that the responsibility of blocking such threats lies with the perimeter defense mechanism and ultimately with the host/server and/or application.

Social Security numbers of 45,000 employees and retirees. "These government systems should be the best in the world and apparently they are able to be compromised," said an FAA contracts attorney. *"Our information technology systems people need to take a long hard look at themselves and their capabilities. This is malpractice in their world"* [LOW200901].

A more inclusive, systematic view of security is needed. Even then, what is required by organizations is more than just an intellectual recognition that security is a critical area of IT: What is needed is the establishment of a reliable and repeatable plan on how to reduce risk and how to comply with the regulatory mandates in a cost-effective manner. Risk management is a facet of regulatory compliance. Risk management encompasses the establishment of processes for risk assessment, processes for risk mitigation planning, processes for risk mitigation implementation, and processes for effectiveness evaluation and assessment. Furthermore, it must be recognized at the outset that given the fragmented state of the field of security, *people* are the key line of defense for managing exogenous and endogenous security events and to mitigate the ensuing risk exposures. As a point of reference, institutional spending on IS security was at $30 billion in 2005, yet, in spite of these investments, losses in excess of $15 billion were thought to occur because of security breaches. While the industry is seeing the emergence of new technologies for security control and compromise detection, there is, according to observers "a relative dearth of insights that help firms to understand the socio-organizational challenges of managing the deployment and use of these tools to prevent IS security compromises" [BEA200801]. Tools do not run themselves; therefore, experienced professionals operating in viable, well-supported teams are required. People are almost invariably the largest cost component over time of any IT initiative; hence, optimization of the human capital is the first precept for establishing an information security program that deals effectively and reliably with risk management. Our focus in this text, therefore, includes the people, teams, and human resources needed to carry out these tasks.

It is critical, therefore, for organizations and enterprises to develop

(i) Technological and procedural information security and risk management capabilities and
(ii) "Ready-to-go" human resources

to (a) address vulnerabilities and risk exposures that likely will impact the organization in the years to come and (b) be able to deal with information security and risk management in an effective manner. The fundamental goal of the risk management process, and of the team that owns this responsibility, is to protect the organization's ability to perform its mission, not just to protect its IT assets. It follows that the risk management process should not be treated primarily or exclusively as a technical function carried out by the IT or packet-level experts who operate and manage the IT system, or some perimeter firewall, but as an essential management function of the organization at senior levels [STO200201].

We show later in the book (Chapter 8) that some heuristic/empirical guidelines are as follows:

- For low probability of risk exposure the company revenue must be at around \$4B/year, before one full time equivalent (FTE) dedicated to risk management is justified. For revenue of \$16B/year, 2–3 FTEs are justified.
- For a relatively high probability of risk exposure the company revenue must be at around \$1B/year, before one FTE dedicated to risk management is justified. For revenue of \$16B/year, a team of 8–11 FTEs is justified.

These observations provide a rough order of magnitude (ROM) estimate for a risk management/assessment team that is sized to "pay for itself" in terms of remediated risk to the organization. Again, these are just guidelines, however, they provide some critical insight to the challenge an organization will face to justify the resources required to implement a risk management team. Many smaller companies will still need an employee serving in the risk assessment function even if the guidance does not quite add up. It is also important to note that many security practitioners in organizations often wear many hats and do not focus solely on risk management. The estimates provided are for FTE that are completely dedicated to fulfilling the risk management function.

1.1.2   Text Scope

With these observations as a backdrop, this book identifies risk management techniques and standards. It then discusses how to best assemble and maintain the *team of people* that will make effective, proactive, reliable, and on-target use of the available security framework mechanisms and tools to establish a risk-minimized IT environment. Some people have called these teams risk assessment teams (RATs); however, the term risk management team (RMT) or risk assessment and management team (RAMT) or even risk management and assessment team (RMAT) may be more appropriate and/or inclusive.[7] For the purposes of this text we will refer to the risk management team. The job function of a risk management team is to (a) assess the risk that ensues from vulnerabilities and/or from risk events and (b) identify and implement risk mitigation solutions. Some large organizations may have a team focused just on risk assessment and a separate team for risk mitigation. Smaller firms may have a small team of people (perhaps as small as one person) to handle the entire risk management function. The focus of this book is on deploying *risk management capabilities and the supportive team* within the organization.

---

[7]Just assessing a risk exposure may be of limited utility for an organization; preferably, one wants to assess and then correct/mitigate these risk exposures.

We observe yet again that risk management teams are much more than a collage of router-level specialists that have intimate familiarity with packet and state-machine formats for TCP, User Datagram Protocol (UDP), Real Time Protocol (RTP), Session Initiation Protocol (SIP), Hyper Text Transfer Protocol (HTTP), Simple Object Access Protocol (SOAP), IPsec, and so on, although this familiarity helps—they are part of teams that have a deep overall understanding of asset protection that encompasses a computer-, protocol-, financial-, organizational-, procedural-, probabilistic-, and game-theoretic view of the entire business of information security. Companies have known for many years (decades, in fact) how to assemble R&D teams, marketing teams, sales teams, engineering teams, operations teams, quality assurance (QA) teams, and HR teams, but IT risk management teams represent (by necessity) a new construct; unfortunately, there is limited established precedent for organizational dynamics in this arena. This is the issue under study in this book. While a search at an online bookseller with the keywords "computer security" identifies over 8000 items/books, a search with the keywords "information technology risk management" yields only a handful of relevant titles[8] (see Appendix 1.A for a compilation of some titles); finally, a press time search on keywords "security, HR, staffing, people, professionals" or variants yields even less relevant titles.

Punctuating the observations just made, to ultimately be successful, organizations have a requirement to develop "ready-to-go" technological and human resources to assess and address the universe of IT-related risk events, threats, and vulnerabilities; this is the case because IT liabilities cascade almost immediately into direct business liabilities. Studies show that automated system security vulnerability assessment tools by themselves are insufficient for complete risk analysis, not to say remediation: A team of effective practitioners is required to make customized use of the tools, correctly interpret findings, and apply appropriate, cost-effective remediation (also referred to as mitigation). This textbook takes a practical approach in its goal of describing how organizations can position themselves to properly handle the ever-increasing and perennially mutating risk exposures to their business-critical IT assets. There are many stakeholders involved in risk management, as shown in Table 1.3. Consequently, this book aims at assisting Chief Information Officers (CIOs), Chief Financial Officers (CFOs), Chief Technology Officers (CTOs), Chief Security Officers[9] (CSOs), and other technical officers, as well as *design, deploy, and run* an effective information security risk management program in their specific environments.

One useful perspective on security is the following [ENI200801]:

---

[8]A number of texts cover the concept of reducing project risk by proper Project Management techniques; this is not the topic of interest here.
[9]The term "Chief Information Security Office (CISO)" or "Information System Security Officers (ISSO)" is also used in the literature.

TABLE 1.3. Risk Management Stakeholders

Business and functional managers	Consumers (customers) of the IT development process
Chief Security Officer	Responsible for IT security (also known in some quarters as Chief Information Security Officer (CISO))
Commercial and federal Chief Information Officers	Senior managers that ensure the implementation of risk management for agency IT systems and the security provided for these IT systems
Corporate governance review board (a designated approving authority)	Responsible for the ultimate decision on whether to allow operation of an IT system (may also be known as a Steering Committee)
Information managers	Owners of data stored, processed, and transmitted by the IT systems
Information system auditors	Auditors of IT systems for financial, regulatory, and functional integrity
IT consultants	Professionals and contractors supporting clients in risk management
IT quality assurance personnel	Associates that test and ensure the integrity of the IT systems and data
IT security program managers	Managers that implement the security program
IT system and application developers (programmers)	Associates that develop and maintain software (e.g., applications, middleware, web services-based systems)
IT system managers	Owners of system software and/or hardware used to support IT functions
IT vendors	Develop (security) systems or packages that are used by organizations
Risk Management and Remediation Team	Responsible for comprehensive risk management (identification, assessment, containment) and security assurance
Senior management	Management individuals that make decisions about the IT security budget
Senior officers	Chief Information Officers (CIOs) and Chief Security Officers (CSOs) already mentioned above, along with Chief Financial Officers (CFOs), Chief Technology Officers (CTOs), and Chief Operating Officer (COO), all of whom make strategic decisions about the direction of the organization; the mission owners; the Chief Executive Officer (CEO) also bears responsibility
Technical security support personnel	Responsible for security architecture, security policies, security analysts
Technical support personnel	Manage and administer security for the IT systems (e.g., network, system, application, and database administrators)

- IT security administrators should expect to devote approximately one-third of their time addressing technical aspects; the remaining two-thirds should be spent developing policies and procedures, performing security reviews and analyzing risk exposures, addressing contingency planning, and promoting security awareness.
- Security depends on people more than on technology.
- Employees are a far greater threat to information security than outsiders.
- Security is like a chain: It is as strong as its weakest link.
- The degree of security depends on three factors: the risk that one is willing to tolerate, the functionality of the system, and the costs that one is prepared to pay.
- Security is not a status or a snapshot but an ongoing process.

The goal of this text is to help corporate stakeholders and officers to understand what it takes to deploy the array of requisite security line-functions, human assets, functional processes, decision-making methods, and support tools/mechanisms/controls in order to effectively address risk management and in order to establish reliable remediation programs. The text surveys industry approaches, best practices, and standards for how an organization can position itself to properly handle the ever-increasing and constantly mutating tsunami of risks exposures. Overall, the discussion places emphasis on designing, implementing, and "feeding and caring" for a risk assessment function and the supporting team that can properly engage to foresee, prevent, and/or rapidly remediate potential business-disrupting infractions. The book has two major sections.

Part 1 reviews industry practices in the area of risk assessment methodologies and mitigation. It provides an overview of available security risk analysis standards. In particular, the ISO/IEC 27000 series ("ISO27k") information security management standards are reviewed, along with numerous other standards such as AS/NZS 4360:2004, a risk management standard published jointly by Australia Standards and New Zealand Standards. This section also provides an overview of available security risk analysis methods. In particular, Control Objectives for Information and Related Technology (COBIT), which provides a comprehensive model guiding the implementation of IT governance processes/systems including information security controls, is reviewed, along with other methods such as OCTAVE, which, as noted, is a risk-based strategic assessment and planning technique for security published by CERT.

Part 2 focuses on developing "ready-to-go" technological and human resources within the organization, to effectively undertake the risk assessment and mitigation function. It looks at IT people issues, procedures, tools, and preparedness, and it places emphasis on implementing a risk assessment and management team that can properly foresee, prevent, and/or rapidly remediate potential infractions. It is then subdivided into two sections. The first section looks at the HR (organizational) factors related to the assembly, maintenance, expansion, and ongoing retraining of the staff that owns the information security program. It speaks to the IT/security "people issues," procedures, tools, and preparedness. Furthermore, because security is a "hot" industry, institutions need to establish the proper environment so that the staff's churning will be kept at a bare minimum and so that the security policy can be safeguarded. The second section then takes a more in-depth and real world approach as to the ongoing risk management process and builds off the material covered in the first section of the book.

There is a realization that effective leadership within the top levels of the organization and its related security functions are imperative: Organizational reputation, the uncompromised reliability of the technical infrastructure and normal business processes, protection of physical and financial assets, the safety of employees, and shareholder confidence all rely in various degrees upon the effectiveness of an accountable senior security executive [CSO200301]. What has generally been lacking, however, is a specific position at the senior governance level with the responsibility for developing, influencing, and directing an organization-wide protection strategy: In many organizations, accountability is diffused and is often shared among several managers in distinct departments, with ostensibly conflicting objectives. To address this issue, the establishment of a CSO function has proven useful. In turn, the risk assessment and remediation team discussed in this book would likely report into this focused organization. However, in some organizations a Chief Risk Officer (CRO) may oversee an entire organization that handles all risk management for the enterprise.

Security techniques have been around since the 1970s. Naturally, threats and vulnerabilities have evolved and mutated, and many new ones have emerged. Nonetheless, a sizeable number of the basic techniques remain the same; for example, sensitive data stored on removable media should be stored in an encrypted fashion (or at least the key data fields within that file), yet one continues to read stories of lost tapes, lost PCs, and lost memory sticks, all of which exposes critical data to a situation where there is a positive nonzero risk. According to the Open Security Foundation's DataLossDB, a project that documents known and reported data loss incidents worldwide, in 2008 alone there were approximately 246 incidents reported that could have most likely been avoided with a proper encryption solution deployed.

At this juncture, there is a broad understanding that the skills and competencies essential to achieving active protection and implementing mea-surably effective responses to the modern threat environment are far more critical than ever before [CSO200301]. Yet, few companies have a comprehensive, high-assurance company-wide mechanism in place. Furthermore, today more often than not, business continuity, security, and risk management are relegated to a handful of engineering-level individual(s). Surveys show that a majority of companies spend relatively little on security, even in the face of the avalanche of increased threats (caused by geopolitical events, higher penetration of Internet access to "rouge" countries, greater deployment of "weak" web-based software, etc.) Many Fortune 500 companies with thousands of IT professionals on staff may have no more than 6–12 security people on-board, and the majority of these people may only focus on implementing and maintaining perimeter defenses using packet-level firewalls. Some information-based companies have been in business for a decade or more and still do not have a security architecture in place. This is a mismatch between the potential risk and the resources allocated to counter the risk exposure.

The Information Security Forum's biennial information security status survey leads to the conclusion that because information risk is not well understood or managed, on average a business-critical information resource [CIT200701]

- Suffers an information incident almost every working day (average of 225 incidents a year)
- Has a 58% chance of experiencing a major incident over the course of a year

By implementing risk management, an organization not only will be able to reduce the information risk exposure it faces (reducing the chance of suffering major incidents), but also can save monetarily by reducing risk (which is, as defined here, the expected losses incurred from exposures). Controls cut the number of minor incidents suffered day-to-day, along with the inefficiencies that go with them. Unfortunately, according to the European Network and Information Security Agency (ENISA), some "open" problems in the area of risk management include [ENI200801] the following:

- Low awareness of risk management activities within public and private sector organizations
- Absence of a "common language" in the area of risk management to facilitate communication among stakeholders
- Lack of surveys on existing methods, tools and good practices
- Limited or nonexistent interoperability of methods and integration with corporate governance

At the same time, it is important that organizations have a balanced and proportionate response to the risk exposures affecting them. Risk management should thus help avoid an overreaction to risk exposures that can unnecessarily prevent legitimate activity and/or seriously distort resource allocation [ISO31000].

Finally, with the ongoing focus on cost reduction, security professionals are being asked to quantify the benefit that security brings to the business. Return on security investment (ROSI) is one such measure being used. A number of definitions and methodologies for calculating ROSI have been advanced of late. Some methods follow traditional financial return on investment (ROI) theory—for example, total cost of ownership—while others use concepts from fields such as insurance.

Current approaches to information security risk management are seen by industry observers as being incomplete in the sense that they fail to include all components of risk (assets, threats, and vulnerabilities). In addition, many organizations outsource information security risk evaluations, leading to generalizations rather than a company-specific determination. Self-directed assessments (as discussed in the chapters that follow) provide the context to understand the risks and to make informed decisions and tradeoffs [CAR200101]. To undertake effective self-directed assessments, a well-functioning risk management team is needed.

Risk management practitioners have identified components that must be in place prior to the implementation of a successful security risk management process and that must remain in place once it is underway; these practitioners list the following [MIC200601]:

- Executive sponsorship
- A well-defined list of risk management stakeholders
- Organizational maturity in terms of risk management
- An atmosphere of open communication
- A spirit of teamwork
- A holistic view of the organization
- Authority throughout the process

This book addresses these issues and walks a security manager through the process of developing and implementing an organizational machinery that will be able to identify and handle risks for their company. It takes a look at the current state of the software vulnerabilities from a general perspective and how they are handled. Then it walks the reader through an analysis of how risks relate to their organization. It is critical to create policies, standards, guidelines, and procedures that enable an organization to identify and mitigate information security risks. An effective team, perhaps less steeped in an avalanche of acronyms in their daily parlance, is potentially best-suited to address these issues.

ISO/IEC 27002 notes that: "Information can exist in many forms: it can be printed or written on paper, stored electronically, transmitted by post using electronic means, shown on films, or spoken in conversation. Whatever form information takes, or means by which it is shared or stored, it should always be appropriately protected." The IT organization typically manages the shared infrastructure of the enterprise, such as the servers, mainframes, data warehouses, networks, and intranets and, as such, operates as the custodian for a large portion of the corporate information content (including possibly information belonging to customers—e.g., credit card numbers, addresses, telephone numbers—and business partners.) However, with the trends to a mobile laptop/PDA-based workforce, not all an organization's information assets are managed by the IT organization. These information owners—including end users—need to strive to ensure that their information assets are protected; hence, in a microcosm, the techniques discussed here for IT are applicable to these users, as well.

REFERENCES

[BEA200801] J. Beachboard, A. Cole, et al. "Improving information security risk analysis practices for small- and medium-sized enterprises: A research agenda," *Issues in Informing Science and Information Technology*, Volume 5, 2008, Proceedings of Informing Science, Informing Science Institute.

[CAR200101] Carnegie Mellon, Software Engineering Institute, $OCTAVE^{SM}$ *Method Implementation Guide Version 2.0, Volume 1: Introduction*, C. J. Alberts, and A. J. Dorofee, June 2001.

[CIT200701] Driving information risk down to an acceptable level, using FIRM and Citicus ONE, Whitepaper, 2007. Ref. A020-R231. Citicus Limited, Holborn Gate, 330 High Holborn, London WC1V 7QT, United Kingdom.

[CSO200301] *Chief Security Officer (CSO) Guidelines*, ASIS Commission on Guidelines, ASIS International, November 24, 2003, 1625 Prince Street, Alexandria, VA 22314–2818, USA, www.asisonline.org

[ENI200801] European Network and Information security Agency (ENISA), 2008.

[HUB200701] D. Hubbard, *How to Measure Anything: Finding the Value of Intangibles in Business*, p. 46, John Wiley & Sons, Hoboken, NJ, 2007.

[ISO31000] ISO/TMB WG on Risk management, ISO/CD 31000, *Risk Management—Guidelines on Principles and Implementation of Risk Management*, ISO 2007.

[ITP200901] IT Policy Compliance Group, Managing Spend on Information Security and Audit for Better Results, February 2009, Managing Director, Jim Hurley.

[LOW200901] J. Lowy, "*FAA says Hackers broke into agency computers*," Associated Press, Feb. 10, 2009.

[MAR200601] *MAGERIT, Version 2: Methodology for Information Systems Risk Analysis and Management. Book I—The Method*, Published by Ministerio de Administraciones Públicas, Madrid, 20 June 2006 (v 1.1), NIPO: 326-06-044-8.

[MIC200601] Microsoft Solutions for Security and Compliance and Microsoft Security Center of Excellence, *The Security Risk Management Guide*, Microsoft Corporation, Redmond, WA, 2006.

[STO200201] G. Stoneburner, A. Goguen, and A. Feringa, "Risk Management Guide for Information Technology Systems—Recommendations of the National Institute of Standards and Technology", Special Publication 800–30, July 2002, Computer Security Division Information Technology Laboratory, National Institute of Standards and Technology Gaithersburg, MD 20899–8930. [This document may be used by nongovernmental organizations on a voluntary basis. It is not subject to copyright.]

APPENDIX 1A: BIBLIOGRAPHY OF RELATED LITERATURE

1A.1 Scantiness of Risk Management Teams References

An assessment of the literature shows that there is little on the market for senior corporate planners and decision-makers to review that takes the perspective of *holistic corporate business continuity and security*, including proven approaches to IT risk management. Many of the guides on the market utilize a piecemeal formulation of the integrity, reliability, and survivability challenges of an organization; for example, they typically look *discretely* at firewalls, intrusion detection systems, security on Unix, Linux security, virus management, e-mail security, and so on. Furthermore, there is little on the topic of how to develop ready-to-go teams within the organization to proactively address and rapidly dispose of risks to the IT/networking infrastructure that will impact the organization in the years to come, which is the topic of the present text.

Some of the titles are shown below.

- A. Shoniregun, *Impacts and Risk Assessment of Technology for Internet Security: Enabled Information Small Medium Enterprises*, ISBN-13 9780387243436, Springer, New York, 2005.
- B. Schneier, *Secrets & Lies: Digital Security in a Networked World*, John Wiley & Sons, Hoboken, NJ, 2004.
- B. Sterneckert, *Critical Incident Management*, ISBN 084930010X, CRC Press, Boca Raton, FL, 2003.
- C. Alberts and A. Dorofee, *Managing Information Security Risks: The OCTAVE(sm) Approach*; Addison-Wesley; Boston, MA; 2002.
- D. L. Anderson and G. V. Post, *Managing Information Systems: Using Cases within an Industry Context to Solve Business Problems with Information Technology*, ISBN 0201611767, Pearson Education, Upper Saddle River, NJ, 1999.
- E. Jordan and L. Silcock, *Beating IT Risks*, ISBN-13 9780470021903, John Wiley & Sons, Hoboken, NJ, 2005.
- G. E. Beroggi (editor) and W. A. Wallace (editor), *Computer Supported Risk Management*, ISBN-13 9780792333722, Springer, New York, 1995.
- G. E. Beroggi and W. A. Wallace, *Operational Risk Management: The Integration of Decision, Communications and Multimedia Technologies*, ISBN-13 9780792381785, Springer, New York, 1998.
- G. Hoffman, *Managing Operational Risk: 20 Firmwide Best Practice Strategies*, ISBN 0471412686, John Wiley & Sons, Hoboken, NJ, 2002.
- G. Stoneburner, A. Goguen, A. Feringa, *Risk Management Guide for Information Technology Systems and Underlying Technical Models for Information Technology Security*, ISBN 0756731909, Diane Publishing Company, Darby, PA, 2002.

- G. Stoneburner, *Risk Management Guide for Information Technology Systems: Recommendations of the National Institute of Standards and Technology*, ISBN 0160674492, United States Government Printing Office, Washington, DC, 2002.
- G. Westerman and R. Hunter, *IT Risk: Turning Business Threats into Competitive Advantage*, ISBN-13 9781422106662, Harvard Business School Press, Boston, MA, 2007.
- I. Lim, *Information Security Cost Management*, ISBN-13 9780849392757, CRC Press, Boca Raton, FL, 2006.
- J. Armstrong, D. Dresner, and M. Rhys-Jones, *Managing Risk: Technology and Communications*, ISBN-13 9780754524687. Butterworth-Heinemann, Oxford, UK, 2004.
- J. Bryson, *Managing Information Services: A Transformational Approach*, ISBN-13 9780754646310, Ashgate Publishing, Aldershot, Hampshire, UK, 2006.
- J. F. Kuong (Editor), *Threats and Risks Compendium for Enterprise Risk Management: A Model to Reduce Your Organization's Exposure from All Types of Vulnerabilities*, Volume. 1: *Physical Access Perimeter*, ISBN 0940706628, Management Advisory Publications, Wellesley Hills, M. 2003.
- J. McCumber, *Assessing and Managing Security Risk in IT Systems: A Structured Methodology*, Auerbach, Boca Raton, FL, 2005.
- A. Jaquith, *Security Metrics: Replacing Fear, Uncertainty, and Doubt*, ISBN-13 9780321349989, *Symantec Press Series*, Cupertino, CA, 2007.
- M. D. Lutchen, *Managing IT as a Business: A Survival Guide for CEO's*, ISBN 0471471046, John Wiley & Sons, Hoboken, NJ, 2003.
- M. E. Whitman and H. J. Mattord, *Principles of Information Security*, third edition, ISBN-13 9781423901778, Course Technology, Florence, KY, 2008.
- N. G. G. Carr, *Does IT Matter? Information Technology and the Corrosion of Competitive Advantage*, ISBN 1591394449, Harvard Business School Publishing, Boston, MA, 2004.
- R. Baskerville (Editor), J. Stageman, and J. I. DeGross (editor), *Organizational and Social Perspectives on Information Technology: IFIP TC8 WG8.2 International Working Conference on the Social and Organizational Perspective on Research and Practice in Information Technology*, June 9–11, 2000, Aalborg, Denmark, ISBN-13 9780792378365, Springer, New York, 2000.
- R. E. Susskind, *The Future of Law: Facing the Challenges of Information Technology*, ISBN-13 9780198764960, Oxford University Press, New York, 1998.
- T. R. Peltier, *Information Security Risk Analysis*, second edition, Auerbach, Boca Raton, FL, 2005.

1A.2 Scantiness of Host Security References

The literature on host security is rather scant. Below are the first 40 hits under a Google Book search with the exact expression "host security." Even 500-page books have just a few pages (if any) on the topic of host security. Most of the literature emphasis seems to be on the simpler issues of blocking TCP ports by a firewall, what people call "network security" (but should in fact be called fixed-network perimeter security, as contracted to mobile devices—such a employee PCs used at airports and coffee shops—simply entering the network and bypassing the firewall). With the increased penetration of mobile devices and the expected introduction of IPv6 in the next few years, the issue of host security needs to get renewed attention.

(*Note:* The title *Web Commerce Technology Handbook* in the Google list is by one of these authors.)

(*Note:* The term "endpoint security" is now also being used to refer to host-based security; however, a search on that term only yielded one text at press time: M. Kadrich, *Endpoint Security*, Addison Wesley Professional, Pub. Date: April 2007, ISBN-13: 9780321436955.)

Information Security Management Handbook, Page 267
by Harold F. Tipton, and Micki Krause, Business & Economics, 2005, 578 pages

CRM Host Security The security of the host and the network is often focused on by security professionals without a good understanding of the intricacies of . . . .

Web Security, Web Security, Privacy and Commerce, Page 396
by Simson Garfinkel, and Gene Spafford, Computers, 2001, 756 pages

CHAPTER 15 Host Security for Servers. In this chapter: • Current Host Security Problems Securing the Host Computer • Minimizing Risk by Minimizing Services . . . .

Firewalls and Internet Security: Repelling the Wily Hacker, Page 253
by William R. Cheswick, Steven M. Bellovin, and Aviel D. Rubin, 1996

In some small companies, the developers might have a small collection of UNIX-based hosts with strong host security, but the sales and management teams may . . . .

A Practical Guide to Red Hat Linux 8: Fedora Core and Red Hat Enterprise Linux, Page 1416
by Mark G. Sobell, Computers, 2003, 1616 pages

. . . Host Security. Your host must be secure. Simple security steps include preventing remote logins and leaving the /etc/hosts. equiv and individual users' . . . .

LPI Linux Certification in a Nutshell, Page 445
by Steven Pritchard, Bruno Pessanha, Linux Professional Institute, Linux Professional Institute, Nicolai Langfeldt, Jeff Dean, and James Stanger, Computers, 2006, 961 pages

Objective 2: Set Up Host Security Once a Linux system is installed and working, you may need to do nothing more to it. However, if you have specific . . . .

Surviving Security: How to Integrate People, Process, and Technology, Page 241
by Amanda Andress, Computers, 2003, 502 pages
ATA In general, host security addresses weaknesses in default operating . . . .
One of the biggest issues with host security is that it does not scale well. . . .

Linux and Windows: A Guide to Interoperability, Page 376
by Ed Bradford, and Lou Mauget, Computers, 2002, 430 pages
Host Security. Let us discuss physical access, local software system . . . . At the host security level, it would be as secure as the room, but quite useless. . . .

Building Internet Firewalls: Internet and Web Security, Page 19
by Elizabeth D. Zwicky, Simon Cooper, and D. Brent Chapman, Computers, 2000, 869 pages
A host security model may be highly appropriate for small sites, ... Indeed, all sites should include some level of host security in their overall security . . .

Web-to-Host Connectivity - Page 116
by Anura Gurugé, Lisa Lindgren, and Computers, 2000, 566 pages
WEB-TO-HOST SECURITY Security is one of the most pressing concerns confronting IT managers, but one that has received scant attention in the emerging . . . .

Network Security Hacks: 100 Industrial-Strength Tips & Tools, Page 1
by Andrew Lockhart, Computers, 2004, 298 pages
CHAPTER ONE Unix Host Security Hacks-20 Networking is all about connecting computers together, so it follows that a computer network is no more secure . . . .

Information Security and Cryptology: ICISC 2000, Third International . . . , Page 256
by Dongho Won, Computers, 2000, 260 pages
It may exchange the host security information with other agents to find out . . . . Agent Report Manager generates the host security evaluation result report . . . .

Handbook of Information Security: Threats, Vulnerabilities, Prevention . . . , Page 153
by Hossein Bidgoli, Technology & Engineering, 2006, 3366 pages
Figure 3: (a) interagent security, (b) agent–host security, ... In agent–host security, we can distinguish two aspects: (bl) host security and (b2) agent . . . .

Apache Security: The Complete Guide to Securing Your Apache Web Server, Page 224
by Ivan Ristic, Computers, 2005, 396 pages
. . . host security . . .

Security Technologies for the World Wide Web, Page 50
by Rolf Oppligcr, Computers, 2003, 416 pages
Host security is generally hard to achieve and does not scale well in the sense
that as the number of hosts increases, the ability to ensure that security . . . .

Linux All-in-One Desk Reference for Dummies, Page 552
by Naba Barkakati, Computers, 2006, 840 pages
. . . to many vulnerabilities, such as denial of service, execution of arbitrary
code, and root-level access to the system. Host security . . . .

Data Networks: Routing, Security, and Performance Optimization, Page 377
by Tony Kenyon, Computers, 2002, 807 pages
Example design l: simple end-to-end host security. As shown in Figure 5.20,
two hosts are connected through the Internet (or an intranet) without any
IPSec . . . .

Designing a Total Data Solution: Technology, Implementation and Deployment, Page 183
by Roxanne E. Burkey, and Charles V. Breakfield, Computers, 2000, 499
pages
GATEWAY-TO-HOST SECURITY Gateway security is often not considered until after the product is inhouse and already being used for
development. . . .

Designing and Building Enterprise Dmzs, Page 617
by Ido Dubrawsky, Hal Flynn, and C. Tate Baumrucker, Computers, 2006,
714 pages
Testing Bastion Host Security. Whether you are implementing a bastion
host from scratch or securing one that you inherited, the first step will be
to test . . . .

SUSE Linux 10 For Dummies, Page 290
by Nabajyoti Barkakati, Computers, 2005, 356 pages
Understanding Linux Security. To secure a Linux system, you have to tackle
two broad categories of security. issues: * < * Host security issues that
relate to. . . .

Security + Certification: Exam Guide, Page 9
by Gregory B. White, Computer Networks, 558 pages

Security Principles There are three ways an organization can choose to address the protection of its networks: Ignore security issues, provide host security.

Master Data Management and Customer Data Integration for a Global Enterprise, Page 160
by Alex Berson, Larry Dubov, and Lawrence Dubov, Computers, 2007, 432 pages
Platform (Host) Security Platform or host security deals with the security threats that affect the actual device and make it vulnerable to outside or . . . .

Network Security Hacks, Second Edition, Page 58
by Andrew Lockhart
. . . CHAPTER TWO: Windows Host Security Hacks 23–36. This chapter shows some ways to keep your Windows system up-to-date and secure, thereby making your. . . .

Securing Ajax Applications: Ensuring the Safety of the Dynamic Web, Page 103
by Christopher Wells, Computers, 2007, 233 pages
Host Security Image your web server as a gladiator about to go into battle. If it's going to have any chance of survival, it must be battle ready. . . .

Red Hat Enterprise Linux 4 For Dummies, Page 147
by Terry Collings, Computers, 2005, 408 pages
Implementing Host Security After you have a basic understanding of system security (as explained in the first part of this chapter), look at specific . . . .

How to Cheat at Designing a Windows Server 2003 Active Directory . . . , Page 382
by Brian Barber, Melissa Craft, Melissa M. Meyer, Michael Cross, and Hal Kurz, Computers, 2006, 505 pages
. . . Host security . . .

Network Security Architectures: Expert Guidance on Designing Secure Networks, Page 142
by Sean Convery, Computers, 2004, 739 pages
Unlike identity technologies for which you wouldn't implement both OTP and PKI for the same application, host security options can be stacked together to . . . .

LPI Linux Certification in a Nutshell: A Desktop Quick Reference, Page 458
by Jeffrey Dean, Linux Professional Institute, Computers, 2001, 551 pages
Objective 2: Set Up Host Security Once a Linux system is installed and working, you may need to do nothing more to it. However, if you have specific . . . .

Building DMZs for Enterprise Networks, Page 121
by Robert Shimonski, Thomas W. Shinder, and Will Schmied, Computers, 2003, 744 pages
Host Security Software. Ensuring the reliability and integrity of the DMZ system means using host integrity- monitoring software to report activity that . . . .

Building Internet Firewalls, Page 15
by D. Brent Chapman and Elizabeth D. Zwicky, Computers, 1995, 517 pages
Even with all that work done correctly, host security still often fails due to bugs in . . . . Host security also relies on the good intentions and the skill of . . . .

MAC OS X Internals: A Systems Approach, Page 1050
by Amit Singh, Computers, 2006, 1641 pages
The host special ports are host port, host privileged port, and host security port. These ports are used for exporting different interfaces to the host . . . .

Multi-operating System Networking: Living with Unix, Netware, and NT
by Raj Rajagopal, Computers, 2000, 1360 pages
GATEWAY-TO-HOST SECURITY. Gateway security is often not considered until after the product is in-house and already being used for development. . . .

Smart Card Security and Applications, Page 141
by Mike Hendry, Computers, 2001, 305 pages
These devices, which are known as host security modules (HSMs), come to form an important part of host system security (see Figure 10.10). . . .

Web Security, Page 142
by Amrit Tiwana, Computers, 1999, 425 pages
Host Security Problems—Where Disaster Begins Servers commonly were based on UNIX platforms until a few years ago. NT now is becoming a dominant platform . . . .

Managing IP Networks with Cisco Routers, Page 266
by Scott M. Ballew, TCP/IP (Computer network protocol), 1997, 334 pages
When you consider these potential internal security threats, the answer to the question, "Is host security still necessary when I have a firewall? . . .

Encyclopedia of Computer Science and Technology: Volume 40, Supplement 25, Page 171
by Jack Belzer, Allen Kent, Albert G. Holzman, and James G. Williams, Computers, 1999, 500 pages

Looking at agent–host security, we can distinguish two aspects: host security . . . . The approach for achieving host security is to authenticate agents and to . . . .

RHCE Red Hat Certified Engineer Linux Study Guide: Linux Study Guide (exam . . . , Page 584

by Michael Jang, Syngress Media, Inc., Computers, 2002, 703 pages

CERTIFICATION OBJECTIVE 10.02 Basic Host Security. A network is only as secure as the most open system in that network. Although no system can be 1 00 . . . .

Web Commerce Technology Handbook, Page 124

by Daniel Minoli, and Emma Minoli, Business & Economics, 1997, 621 pages

This must be accomplished using host security mechanisms; the firewall comes into play if the . . . Host security is a discipline that goes back to the 1960s. . . .

Core Security Patterns: Best Practices and Strategies for J2EE, Web Services . . . , Page 193

by Christopher Steel, Ramesh Nagappan, and Ray Lai, Computers, 2005, 1041 pages

. . . Host security . . .

Host Integrity Monitoring Using Osiris and Samhain: Using Osiris and Samhain, Page 103

by Brian Wotring, Bruce Potter, Marcus J. Ranum, and Rainer Wichmann, Computers, 2005, 421 pages

Table 4.1 Common Bank Security. Measures bank security, host security limited, entry/exit points (thick doors with locks), guards with guns, alarm system, . . .

Proceedings of the 1985 Symposium on Security and Privacy, April 22–24, 1985 . . . , Page 65

by IEEE Computer Society Technical Committee on Security and Privacy, Computers, 1985, 241 pages

Because host-security level information is very stable, updates of this host security table are easily accomplished by periodic manual table updates by the . . . .

INFORMATION SECURITY RISK MANAGEMENT DEFINED

Building on the observations of Chapter 1, this chapter further describes the information security environment, provides definitions, and motivates the need for risk management and risk management teams. In Chapter 1 we introduced working definitions of some key terms we use in the text; here we complement these definitions by looking briefly at some risk-related industry definitions, as well as providing a short mathematical formulation of the basic term "risk." A survey of some of the threats and vulnerabilities impacting organizations is also included; while threats evolve over time, a snapshot of some of the press-time concerns illustrates the breath of exposure that organizations face.

2.1 KEY RISK MANAGEMENT DEFINITIONS

2.1.1 Survey of Industry Definitions

ISO/IEC 27002:2005 defines "Information Security" as the "preservation of confidentiality, integrity, and availability of information" and ISO/IEC 27005:2008 defines risk as "a combination of the consequences that would follow from the occurrence of an unwanted event and the likelihood of the occurrence of the event" [ISO27005]. The standard describes a risk analysis process that requires one to identify (i) information assets at risk, (ii) the potential threats or threat sources, (iii) the potential vulnerabilities, and (iv) the potential consequences (impacts) if risks materialize.

More generally, the third draft of ISO/IEC27000 defines terms as follows (in the context of information security management systems) [ISO27000]:

- **Threat:** A potential source of an incident attack that may result in adverse changes to an asset or group of assets of an organization.
- **Vulnerability:** A weakness of an asset that can be exploited by a threat.

Information Technology Risk Management in Enterprise Environments: A Review of Industry Practices and a Practial Guide to Risk Management Teams, by Jake Kouns and Daniel Minoli
Copyright © 2010 John Wiley & Sons, Inc.

- **Impact:** A measure of the effect of an event.
- **Risk:** The (mathematical) combination of the likelihood of an event and its impact—that is, the expected value of the loss.
- **Information Security Risks:** The coincidence of threats acting on vulnerabilities to cause impacts.
- **Control:** Means of managing risk, including policies, procedures, guidelines, practices, or organizational structures, which can be administrative, technical, management, or legal in nature.
- **Certification:** ISO/IEC 27001 certification is the process by which an organization's Information Security Management System (ISMS) is examined against the ISO/IEC 27001 specification by an accredited certification body.
- **Certification Body** (also called a registration body, assessment and registration body, or registrar): A Third party that assesses and certifies that the ISMS of an organization meets the requirements of a standard (for example, ISO/IEC 27001).

Others use this definition [CIS200701]:

- **Threat:** A potential cause of an unwanted event that may result in harm to an organization.
- **Vulnerability:** A characteristic (including a weakness) of an information asset or group of information assets that can be exploited by a threat.

The Australia/New Zealand Standard for Risk Management (AS/NZS 4360:2004) defines risk as

". . . the possibility of something happening that impacts on your objectives. It is the chance to either make a gain or a loss. It is measured in terms of likelihood and consequence."

The National Institute of Standards and Technology (NIST) defines the terms as follows [NIS199801]:

- **Threats:** Actions or events (intentional or unintentional) which, if realized, will result in waste, fraud, abuse, or disruption of operations. Threats are always present, and the rate of threat occurrence cannot be controlled. Therefore, IT security safeguards, must be designed to prevent or minimize any impact on the affected IT system.
- **Vulnerabilities:** Weaknesses in an IT system's security environment. Threats may exploit or act through a vulnerability to adversely affect the IT system. Safeguards are used to mitigate or eliminate vulnerabilities.

- **Risk management:** The process whereby the threats, vulnerabilities, and potential impacts from security incidents are evaluated against the cost of safeguard implementation. It is the ongoing process of assessing the risk to IT resources and information, as part of a risk-based approach used to determine adequate security for a system, by analyzing the threats and vulnerabilities and selecting appropriate cost-effective controls to achieve and maintain an acceptable level of risk. The objective of risk management is to ensure that all IT assets are afforded reasonable protection against waste, fraud, abuse, and disruption of operations.

Risk management as described in NIST SP 800-16 includes the following subprocesses, among others:

- Risk assessment
- Risk analysis
- Risk mitigation
- Uncertainty analysis
- Threats assessment
- Vulnerabilities assessment
- Probability estimation
- Rate of occurrence estimation
- Asset valuation
- Adequate and appropriate protection of assets
- Cost–benefit analysis
- Application security reviews/audits
- System security reviews/audits
- Verification reviews
- Internal control reviews
- Audits

NIST SP 800-39 describes a process for risk management that includes the following steps: (i) categorizing information and information systems with regard to mission and business impacts; (ii) selecting and documenting security controls needed for risk mitigation; (iii) implementing security controls in organizational information systems and supporting infrastructure; (iv) assessing security controls to determine effectiveness; (v) authorizing information systems and supporting infrastructure and explicitly accepting mission/business risk; and (vi) monitoring of the security state of information systems and operational environments.

In broader terms, IT risk management can be seen as a subset of the discipline of enterprise risk management (ERM), although we do not emphasize this approach in this book; see Appendix 2B for a short discussion of ERM.

The European Network and Information security Agency (ENISA) uses the following definitions [ENI200801]:

- **Threat:** Any circumstance or event with the potential to adversely impact an asset through unauthorized access, destruction, disclosure, modification of data, and/or denial of service.
- **Vulnerability:** The existence of a weakness, design, or implementation error that can lead to an unexpected, undesirable event compromising the security of the computer system, network, application, or protocol involved.
- **Risk Management:** The process, distinct from risk assessment, of weighing policy alternatives in consultation with interested parties, considering risk assessment and other legitimate factors, and selecting appropriate prevention and control options.
- **Risk Assessment:** A scientific and technologically-based process consisting of three steps, risk identification, risk analysis and risk evaluation.
- **Risk Identification:** The process to find, list and characterize elements of risk.
- **Risk Analysis:** The systematic use of information to identify sources and to estimate the risk. Risk analysis provides a basis for risk evaluation, risk treatment and risk acceptance.
- **Risk Evaluation:** The process of comparing the estimated risk against given risk criteria to determine the significance of risk. Risk criteria are terms of reference by which the significance or risk is assessed. Risk criteria can include: associated cost and benefits; legal and statutory requirements; socioeconomic aspects; the concerns of stakeholders; priorities; and other inputs to the assessment.
- **Risk Treatment:** The process of selection and implementation of measures to modify risk. Risk treatment measures can include avoiding, optimizing, transferring, or retaining risk.
- **Risk Acceptance:** The potential that a given threat will exploit vulnerabilities of an asset or group of assets and thereby cause harm to the organization.

OCTAVE (CERT) takes the approach (advocated by some including ENISA as noted above) that risk assessment is *part* of the risk management process. In that view, after initialization, risk management is an ongoing activity that encompasses the analysis, planning, implementation, control, and monitoring of implemented measurements and the enforced security policy. Risk assessment, on the other hand, is executed at discrete time points—in this view, for example semiannually or on demand—and (until the performance of the next assessment) provides a temporary view of assessed risk exposures.

MAGERIT (a risk management method described in Chapter 4) defines key terms as follows [MAR200601]:

- **Risk:** An estimate of the degree of exposure or threat to one or more assets causing damage or prejudice to the organization. The risk shows what could happen to the assets if they are not suitably protected. It is important to know which features are of interest in each asset as well as the degree to which these features are in danger—that is, to analyze the system.
- **Risk Analysis:** A systematic process for estimating the size of the risks to which an organization is exposed.
- **Risk Management:** The selection and implementation of safeguards for knowing, preventing, reducing, or controlling the identified risks.

ISO/IEC CD Guide 73 on Risk Management (companion document to the ISO31000 standard) defines "risk" as "risk effect of uncertainty on objectives" and notes that risk management involves applying logical and systematic methods for [GUI200701]

- Communicating and consulting throughout this process;
- Establishing the organization's context for identifying, analyzing, evaluating, treating, and monitoring risk associated with any activity, product, function or process; and,
- Reporting the results appropriately.

Figure 2.1, based on ISO Guide 73, provides a taxonomy of risk-management-related terms.

2.1.2 Adopted Definitions

As introduced in Chapter 1 and taking the definitions identified above into consideration, the terminology utilized in this text is as follows:

- **Risk Exposure (also, liability):** A state of uncertainty where some of the possibilities (also colloquially called "risks") involve a loss, catastrophe, or other undesirable outcome. An environment exposed to risk events, threats, and/or vulnerabilities. Each new risk event, threat, and/or vulnerability gives rise to new risk exposure.
- **Measurement of Risk:** A set of possibilities each with quantified probabilities and quantified losses.
- **Risk (singular):** The expected loss—Namely, the aggregation (summation) of the possibilities, their probabilities, and the loss associated with each possibility.
- **Residual Risk:** The value of risk remaining after security measures have been applied—namely, the risk that remains after mitigation (countermeasures) has been applied.
- **Risks (plural) (colloquial):** Individual possibilities (risk events) that are encountered with risk exposures.

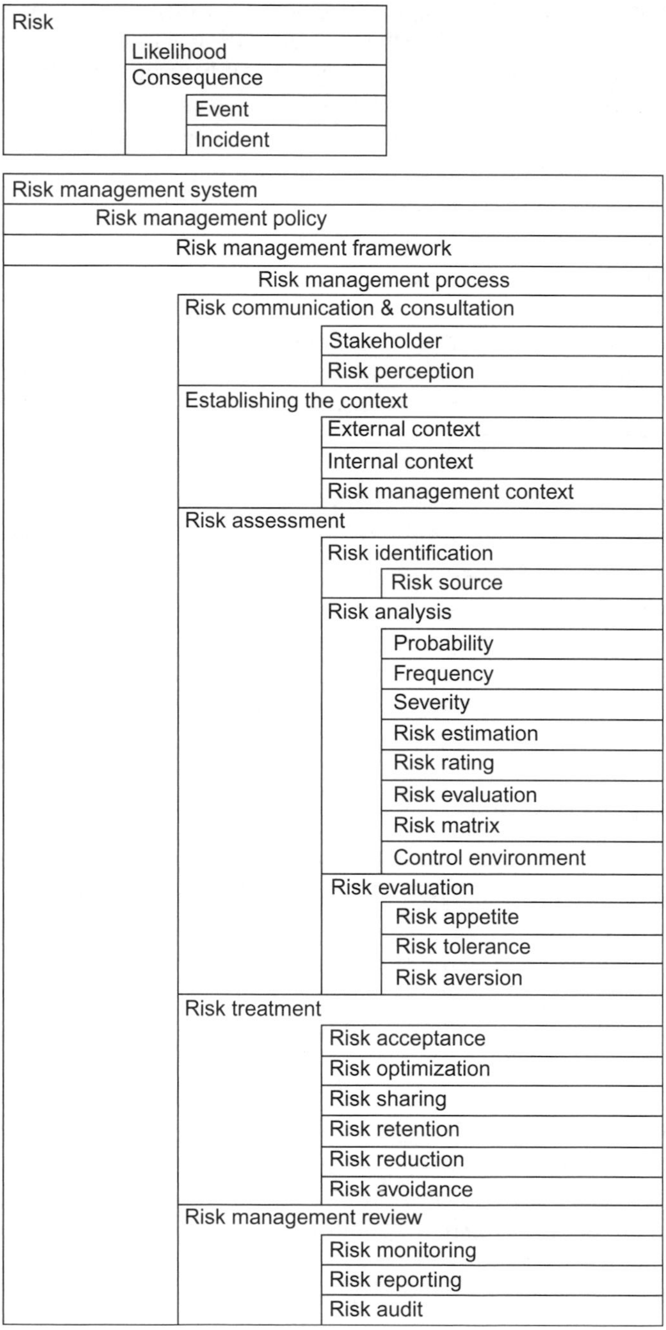

Risk			
	Likelihood		
	Consequence		
		Event	
		Incident	

Risk management system				
	Risk management policy			
		Risk management framework		
			Risk management process	
			Risk communication & consultation	
				Stakeholder
				Risk perception
			Establishing the context	
				External context
				Internal context
				Risk management context
			Risk assessment	
				Risk identification
					Risk source
				Risk analysis
					Probability
					Frequency
					Severity
					Risk estimation
					Risk rating
					Risk evaluation
					Risk matrix
					Control environment
				Risk evaluation
					Risk appetite
					Risk tolerance
					Risk aversion
			Risk treatment	
				Risk acceptance
				Risk optimization
				Risk sharing
				Risk retention
				Risk reduction
				Risk avoidance
			Risk management review	
				Risk monitoring
				Risk reporting
				Risk audit

FIGURE 2.1. Taxonomy of risk management-related Terms per ISO/IEC Guide 73 "Risk Management—Vocabulary."

- **Risk-Exposing Event (also called risk event):** Any changes in the state of the environment that have the potential of creating a new state where there is nonzero risk.
- **Risk Management:** The process of identifying risk, analyzing and assessing risk, and taking steps to reduce risk to an acceptable level. Entails
  - (Ongoing) identification of threats, vulnerabilities, or (risk) events impacting the set of IT assets owned by the organization,
  - Risk assessment,
  - Risk mitigation planning,
  - Risk mitigation implementation, and
  - Evaluation of the mitigation's effectiveness.
- **Risk Identification:** The process of identifying threats, vulnerabilities, or events (malicious or nonmalicious, deterministic/planned or random) impacting the set of IT assets owned by the organization.
- **Risk Assessment:** The process of calculating quantitatively the potential damage and/or monetary cost caused by a threat, by a vulnerability, or by an event impacting the set of IT assets owned by the organization. Identification of the potential damage to the IT assets and/or to the business processes based on previous internal and external events, input from subject matter experts, and audits. Specifically, this entails (a) quantifying the potential damage and (b) quantifying the probability that damage will occur
- **Risk Mitigation Planning:** Process for controlling and mitigating IT risks. It typically includes cost–benefit analysis and the selection, implementation, test, and security evaluation of safeguards.
- **Risk Mitigation Implementation:** Deploying and placing in service equipment and/or solutions identified during the risk mitigation planning phase, or actuating new corrective processes.
- **Evaluation of the Mitigation's Effectiveness:** Monitoring the environment for effectiveness against the previous set of threats, vulnerabilities, or events and determining if new/different threats, vulnerabilities, or events result from the modifications made to the environment.

Note: In the definition used in this text, risk management includes risk assessment.

The Glossary following Chapter 10 provides a basic glossary of other terms used throughout the text. There is value in using an agreed set of definitions to bring clarity to the field. The reader may wish to consult reference [MIN200601], which contains over 5500 security terms.

Controls can be used to mitigate risks. The control can be further classified as either preventive or detective:

- Preventive controls inhibit attempts to violate security policy and include such controls as access control enforcement, physical security and encryption.

- Detective controls warn of violations or attempted violations of security policy and include such controls as audit trails, intrusion detection methods, and checksums.

The following control may be employed, among others (see Table 2.1): management controls, acquisition/development/installation/implementation controls, operational controls, awareness, training, and education controls, and, technical controls.

Finally, there are some guiding principles that can and/or should be used for risk management activities, including adoption of a standard (for certification), a method, or a tool. Some security professionals advocate the following principles, which make a lot of sense [COL200701]:

- *Risk review must be a business-driven process.*
- *Risk assessment findings must use the language of the business.*
- *Risk assessment findings must be linked to the organization's business activities and risks.*
- *Risk assessment findings must present a picture that is comprehensible to the business from which decisions can be made.*
- *The risk assessment findings need to reflect the risks caused by the complexity of the information system, even if it does not reflect the complexity itself.*

These issues will be covered in more detail in the chapters that follow.

2.2   A MATHEMATICAL FORMULATION OF RISK

We begin with a brief discussion of possibility versus probability. **Possibility** is a binary statement of whether a particular event belongs to the sample space (of a probability distribution) or not. **Probability** is a measure of how likely it is that particular event will occur. There are two "views" of probability: a "*frequentist* view" and a "*subjective probability* view." Probability, in the *frequentist* view, which is the most common view (particularly in scientific environments), is the frequency of an experiment that is repeated infinitely many times.

Perform a certain well-defined experiment N times, and look at the times the outcome A fits a specified criterion; let this number be n. The observed frequency is freq(A) = n/N:

$$p(A) = \lim_{N \to \infty} (n/N) = \lim_{N \to \infty} freq(A)$$

Subjective probability view—Bayesian statistics—is where the probability is interpreted as the "*degree of belief*" in a stated proposition.

TABLE 2.1. Controls Used for Risk Management as Defined in NIST SP 800-16

Management Controls
Actions taken to manage the development, maintenance, and use of the system, including system-specific policies, procedures, and rules of behavior, individual roles and responsibilities, individual accountability, and personnel security decisions.

System/Application Responsibilities
    Program and functional managers
    Owners
    Custodians
    Contractors
    Related security program managers
    IT system security manager
    Users
System/Application-Specific Policies and Procedures
Standard Operating Procedures
Personnel Security
    Background investigations
    Position sensitivity
    Separation of duties/compartmentalization
System Rules of Behavior
    Assignment and limitation of system privileges
    Connection to other systems and networks
    Intellectual property/copyright issues
    Remote access/work at home issues
    Official vs. unofficial system use
    Individual accountability
Sanctions or Penalties for Violations

Acquisition/Development/ Installation/Implementation Controls
The process of ensuring that adequate controls are considered, evaluated, selected, designed, and built into the system during its early planning and development stages and that an ongoing process is established to ensure continued operation at an acceptable level of risk during the installation, implementation, and operation stages.

Life-Cycle Planning
Security Activities in Life-Cycle Stages
Security Plan Development and Maintenance
Security Specifications
Configuration Management
Change Control Procedures
Design Review and Testing
Authority to Operate
    Certification/Recertification
    Accreditation/Re-accreditation
Acquisition Specifications
Contracts, Agreements and Other Obligations
Acceptance Testing
Prototyping

Operational Controls
The day-to-day procedures and mechanisms used to protect operational systems and applications. Operational controls affect the system and application environment.

Physical and Environmental Protection
    Physical security program
    Environmental controls
    Natural threats
    Facility management
    Fire prevention and protection

TABLE 2.1. (Continued)

	Electrical/power
	Housekeeping
	Physical access controls
	Intrusion detection/alarms
	Maintenance
	Water/plumbing
	Mobile and portable, systems
	Production, Input/Output Controls
	Document labeling, handling, shipping, and storing
	Media labeling, handling, shipping, and storing
	Disposal of sensitive material
	Magnetic cleaning and clearing
	Contingency planning
	Backups
	Contingency/Disaster Recovery Plan Development
	Contingency/disaster recovery plan testing
	Contracting for contingency services
	Contracting for disaster recovery services
	Insurance/government self-insurance
	Audit and Variance Detection
	System logs and records
	Deviations from standard activity
	Hardware and System Software Maintenance Controls
	Application Software Maintenance Controls
	Documentation
Awareness, Training, and Education Controls	These controls include the following considerations: (1) *Awareness* programs set the stage for training by changing organizational attitudes to realize the importance of security and the adverse consequences of its failure. (2) The purpose of *training* is to teach people the skills that will enable them to perform their jobs more effectively. (3) *Education* is targeted for IT security professionals and focuses on developing the ability and vision to perform complex, multi-disciplinary activities.

Technical Controls
 Technical controls consist of hardware and software controls used to provide automated protection to the IT system or applications. Technical controls
	User Identification and Authentication
	   Passwords
	   Tokens
	   Biometrics
	   Single Log-in
	 Authorization/Access Controls

TABLE 2.1. (Continued)

operate within the technical system and applications.	Logical access controls
	Role-based access
	System/application privileges
	Integrity/Validation Controls
	Compliance with security specifications and requirements
	Malicious program/virus protection, detection, and removal
	Authentication messages
	Reconciliation routines
	Audit trail mechanisms
	Transaction monitoring
	Reconstruction of transactions
	Confidentiality controls
	Cryptography
	Incident Response
	Fraud, waste, or abuse
	Hackers and unauthorized user activities
	Incident reporting
	Incident investigation
	Prosecution
	Public Access Controls
	Access controls
	Need-to-know
	Privileges
	Control Objectives
	Protection requirements

External (or even internal) agents may give rise to threats. Threats can generate risk. There are various definitions of *risk* that are specific to the application and/or situation. Typically, the definition *risk* is

Risk = (Probability of event occuring) × (Impact of event occurring).

As can be seen, risk is proportional to both the expected losses that may be caused by an event (impact or damage of event occurring) and to the probability of this event. Greater loss and greater event likelihood result in a greater overall risk. Risk can be avoided or mitigated; the management of risk is therefore called risk management.

Uncertainty is described in terms of having an underlying probability distribution that describes the likelihood of certain outcomes from the sample space set that will occur (especially if the same exact/abstract experiment is tried for a large number of time.) One may have uncertainty without risk (say the damage was 0) but would not have risk without uncertainty.[10] The measure of uncertainty refers to the probabilities assigned to outcomes from the sample space; the measure of risk requires both probabilities for outcomes and losses quantified for outcomes.

In the next section, we will spend some time discussing risk from a mathematical perspective. Some readers without a background in this discipline may opt to skip this section.

2.2.1   What Is Risk? A Formal Definition

One can start from a more general perspective. A **loss function** is a function that maps an event (an element of a sample space) onto a real number representing the economic cost associated with the event.

The *expected loss* (also known as risk) is

$$\Lambda = \int_{-\infty}^{\infty} \lambda(x) f(x)\, dx,$$

where $\lambda(x)$ is the loss function and $f(x)$ is the probability density function for continuous random variable X (a comparable formula is available for discrete distributions.) Minimum expected loss (or minimum risk) is typically used as a criterion for choosing between alternative courses of action.

Note: The use of a quadratic loss function is common because it is more mathematically tractable than other loss functions. A quadratic loss function is symmetric: An error above the target causes the same loss as the same magnitude of error below the target. If the target is t, then a quadratic loss function is

$$\lambda(x) = C|t - x|^2$$

for some constant C.

2.2.2   Risk in IT Environments

Let the IT domain at a given firm be comprised of a set of assets $A = \{A_1, A_2, A_3, \dots\}$. A_i can be an actual asset (physical or logical), or it can be a company value-generation (including revenue-generating) process. That is, A_i is the

---

[10]We exclude here the trivial case when the probability is 1 ("no uncertainty" in this case), but when there is a sure damage that is understood to result if/as the event took place. For example, when dropping a ceramic cup from the 20th floor of a building and having it hit the ground–the probability of damage is 1 (or 0.999999999999) and the loss is the cost of the cup as well as other potential damage as a result.

physical or logical IT asset, or A_i is the value-generation (including revenue-generating) IT-supported process. A threat is an exogenous (inimical) action that has a probability > 0 of causing damage to an asset.

Let $\Theta_{1,i}$, $\Theta_{2,i}$, and $\Theta_{3,i}$ be threats (exogenous inimical actions, activities, attacks, random events, incident, and so on) that cause damage $D(\Theta_{1,i}, A_i)$, $D(\Theta_{2,i}, A_i)$, and $D(\Theta_{3,i}, A_i)$ to assets A_i within a given institution's IT domain, with probability $p(\Theta_{1,i}, A_i)$, $p(\Theta_{2,i}, A_i)$, $p(\Theta_{3,i}, A_i)$, and so on [we interpret here the concept of probability with the "frequentist model", that is, if a large number T of (identical) institutions were subjected to threat Θ_j, then $T \times p(\Theta_j, A_i)$ would experience damage with asset A_i].

Note: The A_i's, the values $D(\Theta_{1,i}, A_i)$, and the values $p(\Theta_{1,i}, A_i)$ are specific to a given firm (in fact, some of the $\Theta_{1,i}$'s are also specific to a given firm); another firm may have different A_i's, namely, $D(\Theta_{1,i}, A_i)$ and $p(\Theta_{1,i}, A_i)$.

Damage $D(\Theta_j, A_i)$ to asset A_i is defined as the total cost of restoral, including, if required, the deployment of a replacement asset doing the same function at the same level of performance and also any potential business revenue loss (or other losses) caused by an unmitigated threat Θ_j.

Note that for simplicity we assume a point probability (rather than a full probabilistic distribution) of damage resulting from a threat. See Figure 2.2. A threat is mitigated when an asset (per definition above) is protected by a protection measure R_x.

Let $A_i \oplus R_x = A_i \cup R_x$, that is, asset A_i remediated with remediation measure R_x. The symbol $\oplus$ is used to represent "convolution," the "addition of," and "the enhancement with." Assume that Θ_1, Θ_2, and Θ_3 cause damage $D(\Theta_1, A_i \oplus R_x)$, $D(\Theta_2, A_i \oplus R_x)$, and $D(\Theta_3, A_i \oplus R_x)$ to assets $A_i \oplus R_x$, with probability $q(\Theta_1, A_i \oplus R_x)$, $q(\Theta_2, A_i \oplus R_x)$, $q(\Theta_3, A_i \oplus R_x)$, and so on, with

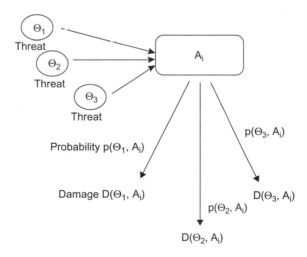

FIGURE 2.2. Threats, probability of damage, and damage.

$$q(\Theta_1, A_i \oplus R_x) < p(\Theta_1, A_i).$$

Note that usually in the case of a physical asset, the damage $D(\Theta_1, A_i)$ is less than or equal to $V(A_i)$, where $V(A_i)$ is the value of asset A_i; however, $D(\Theta_1, A_i)$ can be much larger than $V(A_i)$ for a logical asset (as, for example, for a database[11]). Also note that $V(A_i) = \beta \times K(A_i)$ for some unbounded β, $0 < \beta < \infty$, where $K(A_i)$ is the cost of asset A_i.

One can compute

Probability(damage to A_i)

$\quad = 1 - $ Probability(no damage to A_i)

$\quad = 1 - (1 - p(\Theta_1, A_i)) \times (1 - p(\Theta_2, A_i)) \times (1 - p(\Theta_3, A_i)) \dots.$

For two threats we obtain

Probability(damage to A_i)

$= $ Probability(damage to A_i by Θ_1) $\times$ Probability(no damage to A_i by Θ_2) $+$ Probability(no damage to A_i by Θ_1) $\times$ Probability(damage to A_i by Θ_2) $+$ Probability(damage to A_i by Θ_1) $\times$ Probability(damage to A_i by Θ_2)

$= 1 - (1 - $ Probability$(\Theta_1, A_i)) \times (1 - $ Probability$((\Theta_2, A_i)).$

As noted, risk is typically defined as the likelihood of damage or loss. Hence it is a function of two components, namely, the **likelihood** that an unwanted incident will occur and the **impact** that could result from the incident. We employ the definition *risk* as follows:

As above, the *expected loss* (risk) is

$$\Lambda = \int_{-\infty}^{\infty} \lambda(x) f(x) dx,$$

which for a distribution with a single probability is

Risk $= $ (Probability of event occurring) $\times$ (Imapct of event occurring).

More precisely,

---

[11]For example, a thief could steal the author's laptop, which could have a depreciated value of say $500, but if the author had no backup whatsoever for a manuscript (such as the one for this book) that might have taken him 250 hours to generate, say at an equivalent hourly rate of $50, then the damage would be much larger ($12,500 in this hypothetical example).

$$\text{Risk}(\Theta_j, A_i) = \text{Expected loss due to threat } \Theta_j = D(\Theta_j, A_i) \times p(\Theta_j, A_i)$$

and

$$\text{Risk}(\Theta_j, A_i \oplus R_x) = \text{Expected loss due to threat } \Theta_j$$
$$= D(\Theta_j, A_i \oplus R_x) \times q(\Theta_j, A_i \oplus R_x).$$

When multiple threats are at play, the expression becomes more complex. For two threats, one has

$$\text{Risk}(A_i) = [p(\Theta_1, A_i)] \times [1 - p(\Theta_2, A_i)] \times D(\Theta_1, A_i)$$
$$+ [p(\Theta_2, A_i)] \times [1 - p(\Theta_1, A_i)] \times D(\Theta_2, A_i)$$
$$+ [p(\Theta_1, A_i)] \times [p(\Theta_2, A_i)] \times [D(\Theta_1, A_i) + D(\Theta_2, A_i)].$$

Naturally, there will be a cost $C(\Theta_j, A_i \oplus R_x)$ to deal with remediation R_x to deploy asset $A_i \oplus R_x$ to reduce the risk of Θ_j.

Note: Risk can be quoted as being a positive number representing a loss. One might state that there is a risk (loss) of $10,000. However, in a typical *cash flow analysis* all three numbers Risk (Θ_j, A_i), $C(\Theta_j, A_i \oplus R_x)$, and Risk $(\Theta_j, A_i \oplus R_x)$ should formally be considered as negative. In fact, that is the underlying sense when one states that there is a loss of $10,000, namely, the financial position is $-$10,000.

We define the threat profile for asset A_i at level v to be the set

$$\Omega = \{\Theta_j \text{ for all } j \text{ where } p(\Theta_j, A_i) > v\}.$$

If $v = 0$, this set may be large; if v takes some value greater than 0, such as $v = 0.1$, the set may be more manageable.

The expenditure of $C(\Theta_j, A_i \oplus R_x)$ will result is a risk reduction of

$$\text{Risk}(\Theta_j, A_i) - \text{Risk}(\Theta_j, A_i \oplus R_x)$$

(Risk$(\Theta_j, A_i \oplus R_x)$ is the residual risk). Define the benefit $B(\Theta_j, A_i \oplus R_x)$ to be the cost difference between the expense needed for remediation and the reduction in risk due to the remediation R_x:

$$B(\Theta_j, A_i \oplus R_x) = \{\text{Risk}(\Theta_j, A_i) - \text{Risk}(\Theta_j, A_i \oplus R_x)\} - C(\Theta_j, A_i \oplus R_x).$$

Generally, one would like

$$C(\Theta_j, A_i \oplus R_x) < \text{Risk}(\Theta_j, A_i) - \text{Risk}(\Theta_j, A_i \oplus R_x),$$

namely,

$$B(\Theta_j, A_i \oplus R_x) > 0$$

(call this a "course of pragmatics"), but there may be instances where risk reduction is mandated by regulation or where the risk must be reduced regardless of cost (when nonfinancial consequences are high or undesirable). See Figure 2.3.

Figure 2.4 shows that there may be the opportunity to establish a theoretical optimal point.

If there are multiple possible remediations, say R_k, with $k = 1, \ldots, r$, typically one would want to find R_o, such that

$$\text{Max } B_{k=1,\ldots,r}(\Theta_j, A_i \oplus R_r) = B_o(\Theta_j, A_i \oplus R_o).$$

If a firm has a set of assets $A = \{A_1, A_2, A_3, \ldots, A_z\}$, then the total firm's risk is clearly

$$\text{Total firm risk} = \sum_{i=1,\ldots,z} \text{Risk}(\Theta_j, A_i).$$

The total firm benefit is clearly

$$\text{Total firm benefit from remediation} = \sum_{i=1,\ldots z} B_o(\Theta_j, A_i \oplus R_o).$$

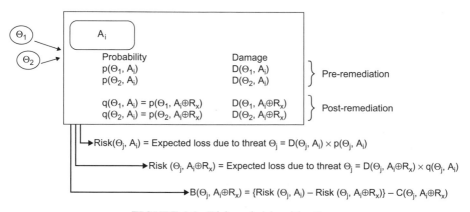

FIGURE 2.3. Risk and risk mitigation.

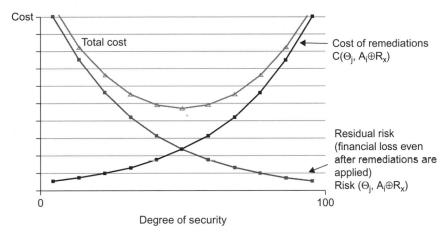

FIGURE 2.4. Optimization point.

If one ordered the asset list $A_1, A_2, A_3, \ldots, A_z$, such that

$$B_o\left(\Theta_j, A_1 \oplus R_o\right) < B_o(\Theta_j, A_2 \oplus R_o) < B_o(\Theta_j, A_3 \oplus R_o) < \cdots < B_o(\Theta_j, A_z \oplus R_o)$$

one can define the "pragmatic" set A_s^o :

$$A_s^o = \{A_1, A_2, A_3, \ldots, A_s\} \text{ with } s = 1, 2, \ldots, z$$

and

> Optimal benefit for partial remediation of assets 1 through $s =$
> Optimal benefit for partial remediation of assets A_s^o (a pragmatic set) $=$
> $\sum_{i=1,\ldots s}, B_o(\Theta_j, A_i \oplus R_o)$.

2.2.3 Risk Management Procedures

With the mechanisms described above, we now can define a few key terms.

> ***Risk Assessment:*** For each IT asset A_i, identify threats Θ_j, $p(\Theta_j, A_i)$, and $D(\Theta_j, A_i)$, for $j = 1, \ldots, s$. Then compute Risk$(\Theta_j, A_i) =$ Expected loss due to threat $\Theta_j = D(\Theta_j, A_i) \times p(\Theta_j, A_i)$.
>
> ***Risk Mediation:*** For each asset A_i of the set A of IT asset (or some subset B of A, or for a "pragmatic set" A_s^o) identify remediation improvements/ redesigns/asset augmentation R_i that maximizes the total firm benefit from remediation, that is, maximizes $\sum_{i=1,\ldots, z} B_o(\Theta_j, A_i \oplus R_o)$. To do this, one needs to

(i) Establish $q(\Theta_j, A_i \oplus R_i)$,

(ii) Compute the $\text{Risk}(\Theta_j, A_i \oplus R_i)$,

(iii) Establish the cost $C(\Theta_j, A_i \oplus R_i)$, and,

(iv) Find R_o for A_i, such that $\text{Max } B_{k=1,\dots,r}(\Theta_j, A_i \oplus R_r) = B_o(\Theta_j, A_i \oplus R_o)$

Note: Risk management methodologies, such as those discussed in Chapters 4 and 5, require (in principle) the comprehensive identification of threats. As just noted, for each IT asset A_i, one needs to identify threats Θ_j, $p(\Theta_j, A_i)$ and $D(\Theta_j, A_i)$ for $j = 1,\dots,s$. Developing comprehensive lists associated with natural and man-made disasters and the diverse and ever-expanding list of technical and behavioral exploits can prove to be a difficult if not insurmountable task and one highly dependent upon the knowledge and thoroughness of the analyst [BEA200801]. One pragmatic approach is to aggregate threats into threat classes (say, a dozen such classes), thereby reducing the workload without fully eliminating the granularity of information required for organizations to deploy controls [WHI200801].

An example follows.

Example. Let $\Theta_{1,i}$, = Virus A, which destroys Word files. Let $\Theta_{2,i}$, = Virus B, which destroys Excel files. Let A_i be Albert's computer (A_i = Albert's computer), where it will take $D(\Theta_{1,i}, A_i) = \$2000$ in labor (40 hours) to restore the Word files and it will take $D(\Theta_{2,i}, A_i) = \$500$ in labor (10 hours) to restore the Excel files. Assume that the probabilities of infections are $p(\Theta_{1,i}, A_i) = 0.1$ and $p(\Theta_{2,i}, A_i) = 0.3$.

$$\text{Probability(damage to } A_i)$$
$$= 1 - (1 - p(\Theta_1, A_i)) \times (1 - p(\Theta_2, A_i))$$
$$= 1 - 0.9 \times 0.7 = 0.37, \text{ which is also}$$
$$= 0.1 \times 0.7 + 0.9 \times 0.3 + 0.1 \times 0.3,$$

$$\text{Risk}(A_i) = [p(\Theta_1, A_i)] \times [1 - p(\Theta_2, A_i)] \times D(\Theta_1, A_i)$$
$$+ [p(\Theta_2, A_i)] \times [1 - p(\Theta_1, A_i)] \times D(\Theta_2, A_i)$$
$$+ [p(\Theta_1, A_i)] \times [p(\Theta_2, A_i)] \times [D(\Theta_1, A_i) + D(\Theta_2, A_i)]$$
$$= 0.1 \times 0.7 \times 2000 + 0.9 \times 0.3 \times 500 + 0.1 \times 0.3 \times 2500$$
$$= 140 + 135 + 75 = 350.$$

Assume that Albert can buy and install a firewall (to get a new asset $A_i \oplus \text{FW}$) such that

$$q(\Theta_1, A_i \oplus \text{FW}) = 0.01 \text{ and } q(\Theta_{2,i}, A_i) = 0.03.$$

Now

Probability(damage to $A_i \oplus \mathrm{FW}$)

$$= 1 - (1 - q(\Theta_1, A_i \oplus \mathrm{FW})) \times (1 - q(\Theta_2, A_i \oplus \mathrm{FW}))$$

$$= 1 - 0.99 \times 0.97 = 0.0397, \text{ which is also}$$

$$= 0.01 \times 0.97 + 0.99 \times 0.03 + 0.01 \times 0.03,$$

$$
\begin{aligned}
\mathrm{Risk}(A_i \oplus \mathrm{FW}) &= [q(\Theta_1, A_i \oplus \mathrm{FW})] \times [1 - q(\Theta_2, A_i \oplus \mathrm{FW})] \times D(\Theta_1, A_i \oplus \mathrm{FW}) \\
&\quad + [q(\Theta_2, A_i \oplus \mathrm{FW})] \times [1 - q(\Theta_1, A_i \oplus \mathrm{FW})] \times D(\Theta_2, A_i \oplus \mathrm{FW}) \\
&\quad + [q(\Theta_1, A_i \oplus \mathrm{FW})] \times [q(\Theta_2, A_i \oplus \mathrm{FW})] \times [D(\Theta_1, A_i \oplus \mathrm{FW}) \\
&\quad + D(\Theta_2, A_i \oplus \mathrm{FW})] \\
&= 0.01 \times 0.97 \times 2000 + 0.99 \times 0.03 \times 500 + 0.01 \times 0.03 \times 2500 \\
&= 35.
\end{aligned}
$$

Thus, the risk has been reduced by $315. If the cost of the firewall is less than this figure, one could consider this initiative to be viable. For example, Albert could buy a software firewall that costs $49. Assume that he used it for 5 years (with upgrades of course). That would equate to an equivalent expenditure of $204.32 (when considering a net present value with $i = 10\%$), for a $B(\Theta_j, A_i \oplus \mathrm{FW}) = \$110.67$. However, if Albert purchased a hardware-based firewall and spent $700, then $B(\Theta_j, A_i \oplus \mathrm{FW}) = -\$385$; that is, Albert spent more than the risk required and more than the advantage secured with the firewall. Note in closing that the risk $\mathrm{Risk}(\Theta_j, A_i)$ due to threat Θ_j to asset A_i typically can change over time; and new threats arise, as depicted graphically in Figure 2.5.

Observations. In real life it may be somewhat difficult to obtain and/or estimate probabilities; and even if the values can be defined, the level of effort to resource this may not be reasonable. One approach is to establish three or five

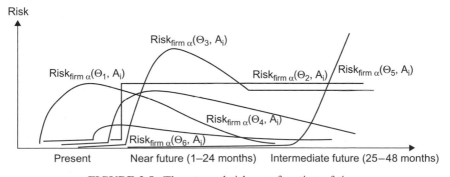

FIGURE 2.5. Threats and risk as a function of time

bands of values and then use a synthetic estimate for these. For example, one could use the following:

A subset of events has the characteristic that each such event in the subset will occur with low probability, another subset with medium probability, and another subset with high probability, where

- Low probability of outcome is, say, $p = 0.2$
- Medium probability of outcome is, say, $p = 0.6$
- High probability of outcome is, say, $p = 0.9$

Or, a subset of events has the characteristic that each such event in the subset will occur with very low probability, a subset of events will occur with low probability another subset with medium probability, another subset with high probability, and another subset with very high probability, where we have

- Extremely low probability of outcome is, say, $p = 0.01$
- Low probability of outcome is, say, $p = 0.2$
- Medium probability of outcome is, say, $p = 0.6$
- High probability of outcome is, say, $p = 0.9$
- Very high probability of outcome; say, $p = 0.99$

Another approach, is to move to a qualitative mode, effectively by stating that a subset of events has the characteristic that each such event in the subset will with low probability, and another subset with high probability, where we have

- Low probability of outcome is, say, $p = 0.2$
- High probability of outcome is, say, $p = 0.9$

In many cases an organization that will be addressing risks will not have an extensive mathematical background. It is possible to continue with the approach outlined previously while at the same time making it much easier to understand using nonmathematic terms. For example, using the very first example, the organization can still have the three different levels of probability of outcome, however, instead of only describing it as Low or $p = 0.2$, we can insert actual timeframes.

- Low probability of outcome; event occurs in 5–10 years
- Medium probability of outcome; event occurs in 1–5 years
- High probability of outcome; event occurs within 1 year

This type of a strategy can allow a practitioner to continue to define the outcome in a way that will allow for further analysis, while at the same time put some context that is not too vague (such as saying Low alone is not descriptive enough) or complicated.

Financial Metrics. A quantitative risk analysis requires the following data points:

- Monetary values for assets
- A list of significant threats
- The probability of each threat occurring
- The loss potential for the company on a per-threat basis over 12 months
- Recommended safeguards, controls (and control costs), and remediation/ implementation actions

In this section we look at some of the metrics that are typically evaluated during a quantitative risk assessment such as asset valuation; costing controls; determining return on security investment (ROSI); and calculating values for the exposure factor (EF), the single loss expectancy (SLE), the annual rate of occurrence (ARO), and the annual loss expectancy (ALE).[12]

Calculating the Damage. Determining the monetary value $V(A_i)$ of an asset is part of security risk management. The goal is ultimately to determine $D(\Theta_j, A_i)$, but obtaining $V(A_i)$ is a place to start. In some cases, the value is the depreciated cost $C(A_i)$; in other cases the value (greatly) exceed[13] the $C(A_i)$. Managers often rely on the value of an asset to guide them in determining how much money and time they should spend securing it. Organizations typically maintain a list of asset values as part of their business continuity plans and/or in an asset management system. The following factors come into play in determining $D(\Theta_j, A_i)$:

- The overall value of the asset to the organization.
- The immediate financial impact of losing the asset.
- The indirect business impact of losing the asset.

For the overall value, consider an example of the impact of temporary disruption of an e-commerce website that normally runs seven days a week, 24 hours a day, generating an average of $1000 per hour in revenue. Here the annual value of the website in terms of sales revenue is $8.7M.

---

[12]A discourse of security without reference to financial considerations is completely illusory. Security mechanisms, remediations, equipment, strategies, and decisions are all driven by financial realities and imperatives. One could argue that other books, articles, dictionaries would not address these areas because they are not directly related to security and risk management. Let us postulate herewith that a book on security or risk management that omits financial terms is certainly **not** worth purchasing or using as a reference (or a security assessment, plan, or strategy, for that matter, if these are devoid of financial considerations); saving paper helps greening of the environment.
[13]For example, consider the cost of an asset (such as a server or telecom equipment) in the context of an installation, where the installation cost (IC) is high, such that the total cost to have the asset in operation is $C(A_i) + IC(A_i)$.

For the immediate financial impact of losing the asset, consider that a six-hour outage would result in a loss of $6000 (in actuality the revenue typically depends upon the time of day, the day of the week, the season, and so on—but this may be a good-enough approximation because if one assumes that the disruptive event occurs on a random(ized) basis, then the "average" loss would indeed be $6000). In this example, the company may also have to spend $2000 in labor to repair the damage. The total damage is $8000.

For the indirect business impact, in this example, the company may find that it would spend $3000 on advertising to counteract the negative publicity from such an incident. There is also a potential of future business lost due to a lack of customer confidence.

Exposure Factor (EF). EF represents the percentage of loss that a realized threat could have on a certain asset. It is the percentage of damage (loss) that an organization would experience if a given asset A_i were in fact compromised by a threat/exposure. A compromised asset may not result in the total loss of its function/utility; hence, EF represents the expected asset value loss due to an actual compromise. EF can be interpreted as the loss potential. We introduced earlier $V(A_i)$; we can then define

$$\text{EF}(A_i) = V(A_i) \text{ before compromise}/V(A_i) \text{ after compromise.}$$

Both $V(A_i)$ and $\text{EF}(A_i)$ can be high. See Table 2.2 for a view.

Single Loss Expectancy (SLE). SLE is the total amount of revenue that is lost from a single occurrence of the risk. It is a monetary amount that is assigned to a single event that represents the company's potential loss amount if a specific threat exploits a vulnerability. One calculates the SLE by multiplying the asset value by EF.

Example. If a server room has an asset value of $350,000, and a fire results in damages worth an estimated 12.5% of its value, then the SLE in this case would be $37,500.

Annual Rate of Occurrence (ARO). ARO is the normalized rate at which the risk exposure resulting in actual damage occurs during one year. The ARO is similar to the probability of a qualitative risk analysis. Obtaining the ARO is typically difficult because there is little actuarial data available (some insurance firms may have some such data available, but the data is not published.) One can get a heuristic estimate the ARO based on past experience, but past performance is no guarantee of future results.

Annual Loss Expectancy (ALE). ALE is the total amount of money that an organization will lose in one year if nothing is done to mitigate the risk. ALE is obtained by multiplying the SLE by the ARO. ALE provides a budgeting

TABLE 2.2. Relationship of $V(A_i)$ and EF (A_i)

	$V(A_i)$	EF(A_i)
Hardware	Low (e.g., low-end router, PC), medium (e.g., Layer 2 switch, server), high (e.g., mainframe, storage system)	Generally low, except in cases of theft, sabotage, or physical penetration/casualty (e.g., fire by arson)
Software	Low (e.g., single application in PC), medium-high (business application)	Even for low-end software, EF can be high if there are a large number of instances (e.g., hundred of thousands of PCs, point-of-sale terminals, scanners, etc.)
Database	Generally medium-to-high	Can be high if the database is completely compromised and there is no backup; or if it is stolen and it included company secrets, customer data, etc.

number that can be used to establish controls or safeguards to prevent this type of damage. The information security community has widely adopted the approach of calculating annualized loss expectancy. Some observers cite limitations of ALE, such as [JAQ200701]

- The inherent difficulty in modeling outliers
- The lack of data for estimating probabilities of occurrence or loss expectancies
- Sensitivity of the ALE model to small changes in assumptions

Example. If a fire at the server room results in $37,500 in damages, and the probability of a fire taking place has an ARO value of 0.05 (indicating one fire in 20 years), then the ALE would be $1875.

Cost of Controls. To establish the cost of controls it requires estimating the cost of acquiring, testing, deploying, operating, and maintaining each control.

Example. To reduce the risk of fire damaging the server room, the organization might consider deploying an automated fire suppression system. Clearly, this system has an initial cost as well as a maintenance cost.

Return on Security Investment (ROSI). ROSI is used to estimate the cost of controls as follows:

$$ROSI = (ALE \text{ before control}) - (ALE \text{ after control})$$
$$- (\text{Annual cost of control}).$$

Example. Consider the case where the ALE of an attacker on an e-commerce server is $6000, and where after the safeguards are implemented, the ALE becomes $2000; assume that the annual cost of maintenance and operation of the safeguard is $1000. Then, the ROSI is

$$ROSI = \$6000 - \$2000 - \$1000 = \$3000.$$

Pragmatics. As discussed so far, the fundamental element of the risk management process is the undertaking of threat assessments and risk analyses that are specifically relevant to the organization in question. The basic approach for conducting such analyses is relatively straightforward: identify (and prioritize) assets to be protected; identify relevant threats and the probability of their occurrence; and, compare the expected losses with the costs of implementing relevant countermeasures. The difficulties in effectively conducting such analyses arise from the fact that identifying *all* relevant threats and *reliably* estimating the probability of occurrences have proven to be difficult and, in some cases, even impossible. Similarly, estimating costs associated with various types of system failures or compromises, even qualitatively, is a challenging process [BEA200801]. While the models for performing risk analyses are not difficult to understand, appropriately applying the models in specific organizational environments is not a formulaic task, such as would be an academic test for some certification. A fair degree of intellectual versatility is required to bridge the theory to the practice and to the heuristics.

2.3 TYPICAL THREATS/RISK EVENTS

According to ISO 31000, the following are desirable attributes of a risk management program:

- An emphasis on continual improvement in risk management through the setting of organizational performance goals, measurement, review, and the subsequent modification of processes, systems, resources, capability and skills.
- Comprehensive, fully defined and fully accepted accountability for risks, risk controls, and risk treatment tasks.
- All decision-making within the organization, whatever the level of importance and significance, involves the explicit consideration of risks and the application of risk management to some appropriate degree.

- Continual communications with—and highly visible, comprehensive, and frequent internal and external reporting of risk management performance to all—stakeholders, as part of a governance process.
- Risk management being viewed as central to the organization's management processes so that risks are considered in terms of the effect of uncertainty on objectives. The organization's governance structure and process are founded on the management of risk.

Unfortunately, today when people talk security, most people simply talk about writing a few lines of filtering code on a router or perimeter firewall pivoted on TCP ports to "prevent" a few kinds of transport-layer flows to be admitted into an intranet; or, at most, implementing a few well-known security products in a default configuration without the understanding of what they were sold. This clearly only gives a false sense of security and provides very little if anything for business continuity and disaster/infraction recovery. For example, an organization that implements a firewall without fully understanding the technology and information assets of an organization may exclude some flows, but the filter might allow an e-mail (SMTP) flow; in this case, a virus or other security-damaging code might "sneak in" under that flow. Or, other damaging code is admitted under a normally accepted mundane TCP flow. Malicious code giving rise to what are called "blended threats" is now very common. Blended threats combines the characteristics of viruses, worms, Trojan Horses, and malicious code with server and Internet vulnerabilities to initiate, transmit, and spread an attack (see Table 2.3). Since these threats utilize multiple methods and techniques, the damaging code often spreads rapidly and can cause widespread infractions to IT assets.

Organizations remain vulnerable to new blended threats arising on a continual basis that exploit known software/system vulnerabilities as a method of propagation. Technologies that are just being deployed also afford attractive opportunities for malicious code propagators. Market penetration and increasing unauthorized usage of instant messaging, peer-to-peer applications, and SIP (Session Initiation Protocol)-based Voice over IP (VoIP) gateways make these programs an attractive infection vector. All of this points to the need for cohesive, comprehensive security capabilities in the corporate environment. Table 2.4 lists just a few risk events in the universe of risk events (see Appendix 2A for another view.) Environments where there is "teleworking," including "working from home," "mobile/dispersed staff," "road warriors," and other forms of mobile working, require particular security considerations and risk management. According to some observers, despite the availability of numerous methods to conduct information security risk analyses, small and medium-sized enterprises (SMEs) (say, firms with less than 250 employees) face organizational challenges managing the deployment and use of these tools and methods [BEA200801]. However, these firms need to redouble their efforts to address the issue.

Table 2.5 identifies some of the tools that may be used for risk remediation. Teams of well-positioned people are needed to optimally use these protective

TABLE 2.3. Basic Infraction Mechanisms

Mechanism	Description
Hoax	Usually an e-mail that gets sent in chain-letter mode describing some devastating, but highly unlikely virus. Hoaxes are detectable as having no file attachment and having no reference to a third party who can validate the claim, as well as by the general tone of the message.
Joke	A harmless program that causes various benign activities to display on the computer (for example, an unexpected screen saver).
Physical access	Direct access to systems or networks, allowing passive or active intrusion
Trojan horse	A program that neither replicates nor copies itself, but causes damage or compromises the security of the computer. Typically, an individual e-mails a Trojan Horse to a recipient (it does not e-mail itself), and it may arrive in the form of a joke program or software of some sort.
Virus	A program or code that replicates itself. A virus infects another program, boot sector, partition sector, or document that supports macros, by inserting itself or attaching itself to that medium. Most viruses only replicate, though many do a large amount of damage as well.
Worm	A program that makes copies of itself—for example, from one disk drive to another or by using e-mail or another transport mechanism. The worm may do damage and compromise the security of the computer. It may arrive in the form of a joke program or software of some sort.

Source: Courtesy of Symantec.

measures. As a minimum, risk management should include the following [CIS200701] (also see Appendix 2A):

- Proactive and timely identification of software vulnerabilities, and patching/updating of systems.
- Deployment of data confidentiality controls to protect personal and proprietary data against unauthorized access or disclosure, including physical, legal, and logical access controls (for example, strong encryption of laptops' hard drives, of data backups, or CD ROM storage, particularly when being transported).
- Deployment of data integrity controls (including transmission controls) to improve the quality, completeness, and accuracy of data in the computer systems.
- Deployment of system integrity controls to avoid having computer and networking systems subjected to unauthorized and/or undesired changes such as malware infections and hacks.

TABLE 2.4. Example of Threats/Risk Events

IT Factors

1. Defective software
2. Virus/worm/Trojan horse/spyware propagation within intranet or extranet
3. Obsolence
4. PC failure (OS/hardware)
5. Server failure (OS/hardware)
6. Tape library failure
7. Tape backup software failure
8. Loss of software
9. Poor perimeter defenses/firewalls
10. Poor or non-existent host/endpoint defenses
11. Poor or non-existent risk management team

External Social Factors

1. Social chaos—riots, social breakdown
2. Strike—unlimited period

External Criminal Factors

1. Terrorism attack
2. Bomb explosion
3. Hacking

External Business Factors

1. Virus /malware
2. Interruption of power supply
3. Logistics failure of critical supplies for day-to-day operations (e.g., fuel for generators, spare parts)

External Environment Factors

1. Pandemic / epidemic
2. Snow storm / heavy snowfall
3. Lightening strike
4. Gale storm / tornado hurricane
5. Earthquake
6. Fire (forest, fields)
7. Flood (river, ground water)

External Accident Factors

1. Nuclear/biological/chemical hazards
2. Plane crash

Internal Social Factors

1. Strike—unknown period
2. Massive resignation

TABLE 2.4. (Continued)

Internal Criminal Factors

1. Sabotage act (disgruntled employees)
2. Stress burst

Internal Accident Factors

1. Gas / fuel explosion
2. Power failure for unacceptable period of time (internal cause)
3. Air conditioning / water supply interruption
4. Contaminated air conditioning (bacteria, airborne particles/dust)
5. Fire on premise
6. HVAC infrastructure
7. Flood / humidity (e.g., pipe bursting)
8. Food poisoning / food chain

External Social Factors

1. Social chaos—riots, social breakdown
2. Social chaos—riots, social breakdown—suppliers in other regions
3. Extreme social chaos - riots, social breakdown

External Criminal Factors

1. Intentional illegal interference
2. Intentional economic interference

Internal Accident Factors

1. Non-IT end user error/maintenance error (contractors, internal staff, and so on)
2. IT user error/maintenance error (contractors, internal staff, and so on)

LAN/WAN Factors

1. Switch failure
2. Cable failure
3. VPN device failure
4. Router failure
5. Firewall failure
6. Telco carrier failure

Voice Communication/PBX Factors

1. PBX CPU/card failure
2. CO Trunk failure
3. PBX CPU failure
4. VoIP system failure/penetration

TABLE 2.5. Basic Tools That Can be Utilized by Risk Assessment Teams (Partial List)

- Content encryption
- Digital signing of documents/files
- Digitally signing parts of documents
- Email security
- File encryption
- Firewalls/proxies
- Folder encryption
- Information security management systems (ISMSs)
- Instant messaging security
- Intrusion detection systems (IDSs)/intrusion protection systems (IPSs)
- Secure file deletion
- Secure private networks
- Text encryption
- Videoconferencing security (e.g., video encryption mechanisms)
- Virus screening/disinfectant software
- Voice security (e.g., voice encryption mechanisms)
- VPNs
- Wireless security (e.g., data encryption mechanisms)

- Hardening of IT assets such as utilizing secure operating systems; including the de-installation of unnecessary applications and services.
- Routine and intensive security testing.

A risk remediation (mitigation) activity might include internal technical controls (for example, network port closure, the upgrade of router passwords from the trivial "cisco," "ops," "admin" verbiage), system external technical controls (for example, having a firewall appropriately configured), or training of some key staff.

Of late there have been discussions related to information security management systems (ISMSs). An ISMS, a term is used in the ISO/IEC 27001 context, is a set of policies concerned with information security management (ISM). A real-life implementation of an ISMS might be a computerized system (tool) that can be used by the organization as one of several tools to protect its information assets (hardware, software, data, document, network, and so on) from threats, risk events, and vulnerabilities (such as incidents and accidents, internal crime, data loss, and so on.) Systems and tools are discussed in more detail in chapters that follow.

2.4 WHAT IS AN ENTERPRISE ARCHITECTURE?

In order to get a better perspective on which IT assets require consideration for risk management, we briefly define the concept of enterprise architecture

(EA). A number of large companies have deployed some sort of enterprise architecture framework (AF) that typically provides a layered organized view of the IT assets. Each of these layers needs to be protected. As described in American National Standards Institute/Institute of Electrical and Electronics Engineers (ANSI/IEEE) Std 1471-2000, *Recommended Practice for Architectural Description of Software-Intensive Systems*, an EA is "the fundamental organization of a system, embodied in its components, their relationships to each other and the environment, and the principles governing its design and evolution." (Reference [MIN200801] provides a more detailed treatment of the EA topic.)

A metaphor can be drawn by thinking of a corporate/IT blueprint for the planning of a city or a large development. Specifically, then, the blueprint provides the macro view of how elements (roads, lots, utilities—read: platforms, networks, applications, applications' logical components) fit, particularly in relation to one another. The purpose in life for an EA is to create a map for the IT assets and for the business processes, along with a set of governance principles that drive an ongoing discussion about business strategy and how it can be expressed through IT. The EA seeks to create a unified IT environment (standardized hardware and software systems) across the firm or all of the firm's business units, with tight symbiotic links to the business side of the organization and its strategy. More specifically, the goals are to promote alignment, standardization, reuse of existing IT assets, and the sharing of common methods for project management and software development across the organization. The end result, theoretically, is that the enterprise architecture will make the IT function less expensive, more strategic, and more responsive [KOC200502]. A byproduct of an EA/AF is a layered taxonomy of the organization's IT assets, which is of interest in the context of risk management.

There are a number of AFs to develop an EA (see Table 2.6). The most commonly used framework at press time, based on industry surveys, was the Zachman Framework, followed by organization's own locally developed frameworks, followed by The Open Group Architecture Framework (TOGAF), and commercial-level Department of Defense Technical Reference Model (DoD TRM) (this covers about two-thirds of all enterprises.)

Most frameworks contain a number basic domains or layers, as follows: (i) *Business architecture*: documentation that outlines the company's most important business processes; (ii) *Information architecture*: identifies where important blocks of information, such as a customer record, are kept and how one typically accesses them; (iii) *Application system architecture*: a map of the relationships of software applications to one another; and (iv) *Infrastructure Technology architecture*: a blueprint for the gamut of hardware, storage systems, and networks. IT assets at all four of these layers can suffer risk exposure and be impacted by threats, vulnerabilities, and risk events. Therefore, IT assets at all four of these layers require risk management.

There are a number of models/modeling techniques, as noted; however, there is at this time no complete industry-wide consensus of what an

TABLE 2.6. Enterprise Architecture (EA) Frameworks (Partial List)

 1. Zachman Enterprise Architecture Framework (ZIFA)
 2. The Open Group Architecture Framework (TOGAF)
 3. Extended Enterprise Architecture Framework (E2AF)
 4. Enterprise Architecture Planning (EAP)
 5. Federal Enterprise Architecture Framework (FEAF)
 6. Treasury Enterprise Architecture Framework (TEAF)
 7. Integrated Architecture Framework (IAF)
 8. Joint Technical Architecture (JTA)
 9. Command, Control, Communications, Computers, Intelligence, Surveillance, and Reconnaissance (C4ISR) and DoD Architecture Framework (DoDAF)
10. Department of Defense Technical Reference Model (DoD TRM)
11. Technical Architecture Framework for Information Management (TAFIM)
12. Computer Integrated Manufacturing Open System Architecture (CIMOSA)
13. Purdue Enterprise Reference Architecture (PERA)
14. Standards and Architecture for eGovernment Applications (SAGA)
15. European Union—IDABC & European Interoperability Framework
16. ISO/IEC 14252 (IEEE Std 1003.0)
17. IEEE Std 1471-2000 IEEE Recommended Practice for Architectural Description

architectural layered model should be; therefore various models exist and/or can be used. One case where standardization in the layered model has been accomplished is Open Systems Interconnection Reference Model (OSIRM) published in 1984 by the International Organization for Standardization (ISO) (this model, however, only applies to communications). In the context of architecture, an important recent development in IT architecture practice has been the emergence of standards for architecture description, principally through the adoption by ANSI and the IEEE of ANSI/IEEE Std 1471-2000. One of the aims of this standard is to promote a more consistent, more systematic approach to the creation of views (a view is a representation of a whole system from the perspective of a related set of concerns) [TOG200501]. However, the adoption of this model is still far from being universal.

Fundamentally, all AF models seek in *some way* to make use of the concept of a generic service/object-oriented architecture where sets of like-functions are grouped into re-usable service modules that can be described as objects; more complex capabilities are then built from appropriate assembly of these basic modules (just like, by analogy, matter is comprised of various combinations of atoms of the elements).

A firm may have developed a full suite of architectures for the various framework layers or may only have a partially developed architecture, as illustrated in Figure 2.6 Fortune 500 firms may have several dozens (if not hundreds) of applications with this type of complexity; trying to position

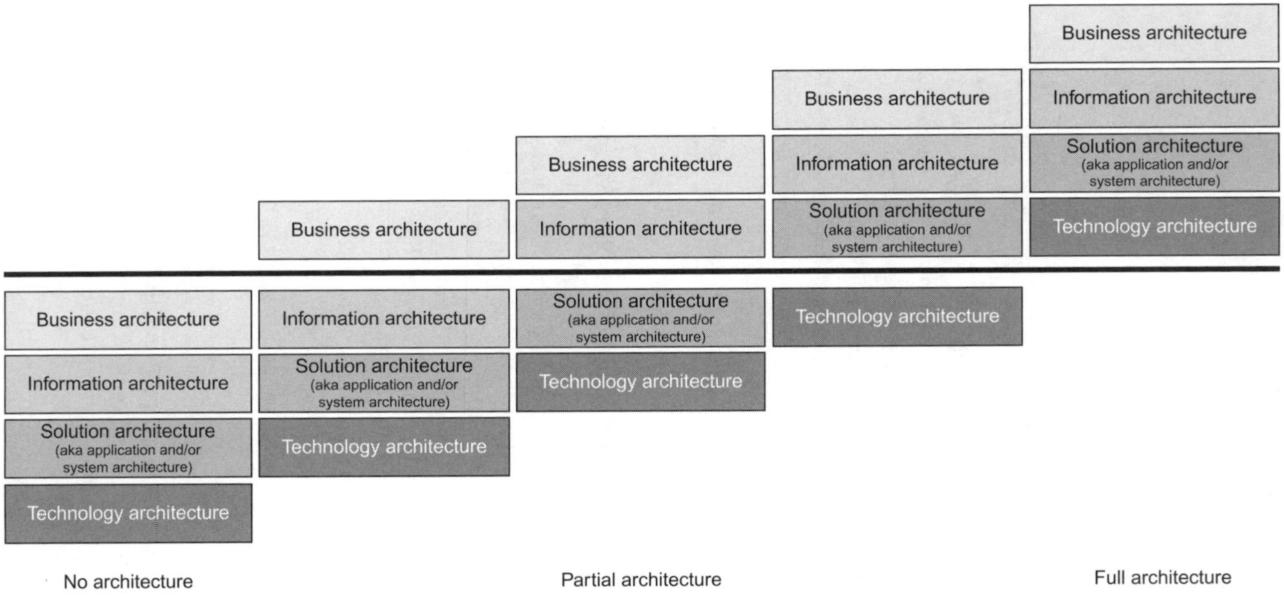
Business architecture
Business architecture
Information architecture
Business architecture
Information architecture
Solution architecture
(aka application and/or system architecture)
Business architecture
Information architecture
Solution architecture
(aka application and/or system architecture)
Technology architecture
Business architecture
Information architecture
Solution architecture
(aka application and/or system architecture)
Technology architecture
Information architecture
Solution architecture
(aka application and/or system architecture)
Technology architecture
Solution architecture
(aka application and/or system architecture)
Technology architecture
Technology architecture
No architecture
Partial architecture
Full architecture

FIGURE 2.6. Maturity of enterprise architecture development at a firm.

oneself strategically in this environment without an enterprise architecture plan is completely futile. At this juncture it is not just the large organizations that have adopted enterprise architecture: Smaller organizations are also adopting this approach (however, the architecture maturity is at a higher level in larger firms than in smaller firms) [IEA200501]. Every organization that seeks to manage its IT complexity in a cost-effective manner for rapid system deployment should consider making the appropriate and balanced investment in enterprise architecture.

This topic is revisited in Chapter 9.

REFERENCES

[BEA200801] J. Beachboard, A. Cole, et al., *"Improving information security risk analysis practices for small- and medium-sized enterprises: A Research Agenda,"* Issues in Informing Science and Information Technology, Volume 5, 2008, Proceedings of Informing Science, Informing Science Institute.

[CIS200701] CISSPforum and ISO27k Implementer's Forum, "Top Information Security Risks for 2008," White Paper, December 2007.

[COL200701] L. Coles-Kemp and R. E. Overill, *"On the role of the Facilitator in information security risk assessment,"* Journal of Computer Virology (2007), 3:143–148, DOI 10.1007/s11416-007-0040-6, EICAR 2007 Best Academic Papers, Springer-Verlag, France, 2007.

[COS200401] Enterprise Risk Management—Integrated Framework, Executive Summary, White Paper of the Committee of Sponsoring Organizations of the Treadway Commission (COSO), September 2004.

[ENI200801] European Network and Information Security Agency (ENISA), 2008.

[GUI200701] ISO TMB WG on Risk Management, Committee Draft ISO/IEC CD Guide 73, Risk management—Vocabulary, 2007.

[IEA200501] J. Schekkerman, Institute For Enterprise Architecture Developments (IFEAD), "Trends in enterprise architecture 2005," *Reports of the Third Measurement*, December 2005, Edition 1.0, Suikerpeergaarde 4, 3824BC Amersfoort, The Netherlands.

[ISO27000] ISO/IEC 27000, "Information technology—Security techniques—Information security management systems—fundamentals and Vocabulary" (draft).

[ISO27005] ISO/IEC 27005:2008, "Information technology—security Techniques—information security risk management."

[JAQ200701] A. Jaquith, A. *Security Metrics: Replacing Fear, Uncertainty, and Doubt,* Addison-Wesley Pearson Education, Upper Saddle River, NJ, 2007.

[KOC200502] C. Koch, "Enterprise architecture: A new blueprint for the enterprise," *CIO Magazine,* March 1, 2005.

[MAR200601] MAGERIT—Version 2: Methodology for Information Systems Risk Analysis and Management. Book I — The Method, Published by Ministerio De Administraciones Pu?blicas, Madrid, 20 June 2006 (v 1.1), NIPO: 326-06-044-8.

[MIN200601] D. Minoli and J. Cordovana, *Minoli-Cordovana Authoritative Computer and Network Security Dictionary,* John Wiley & Sons, Hoboken, NJ, 2006.

[MIN200801] D. Minoli, *Enterprise Architecture A to Z*, Taylor and Francis/CRC, New York, 2008.

[PEL200301] T. R. Peltier, J. Peltier, and J. A. Blackley, *Managing A Network Vulnerability Assessment*, CRC Press, New York, 2003.

[TOG200501] TOGAF, Preliminary Phase: Framework and Principles, http://www.opengroup.org/architecture/togaf8-doc/arch/p2/p2_prelim.htm

[WHI200801] M. E. Whitman, H. J. Mattord, *Principles of Information Security*, third edition, ISBN-13 9781423901778, Course Technology, Florence, KY, 2008.

APPENDIX 2A: THE CISSPFORUM/ISO27K IMPLEMENTERS FORUM INFORMATION SECURITY RISK LIST FOR 2008

This appendix, drawn directly from reference [CIS200701], provides an updated snapshot of information security treats, vulnerabilities, impacts, and risk events. While extensive, it is still only a partial list.

2A.1 Information Security Threats

- Imposition of legal and regulatory obligations, such as the need for adequate information security controls to protect personal data and enforced breach disclosures.
- Organized crime or terrorist groups using identity theft or other forms of compromise or extortion (e.g., DoS and Domain Name System (DNS) attacks) to finance or support criminal activities
- Cyber-criminals, either skilled Black Hats themselves or those able to direct or pay others to do their bidding
- Malware authors responsible for viruses, worms, Trojans (particularly key loggers)
- Phishers including spear phishers targeting individuals with carefully crafted attacks
- Spammers and other obnoxious, self-serving marketers wasting network bandwidth and filling inboxes with junk, using botnets and malware
- Negligent staff such as programmers, technical architects, testers and project managers who cause or fail to prevent vulnerabilities (such as those listed in Section 2A.2)
- Storms, tornados, floods—Acts of God or intentional acts such as arson that may disrupt, damage, or destroy information assets and services
- Fraudsters who simply use IT while exploiting control weaknesses in the IT-enabled business processes, or directly exploit control weaknesses within the IT systems themselves, or exploit other control weaknesses involving printed or other information rather than computer data and systems
- Hackers, ranging from evil Black Hats down to Gray or White Hats (who may be well-meaning but also cause security incidents)

- Unethical competitors (for example, using industrial espionage to steal trade secrets, customer lists, and so on) or foreign powers targeting commercial and national secrets through espionage, social engineering, physical/network penetration, phishing, and/or malware
- Disgruntled/untrained/ignorant employees who make genuine, if naive, human errors, misuse/misconfigure system security functions, or ignore security policies and good practices
- Saboteurs who destroy, or threaten to destroy, information assets or who [threaten to] deny access to same (extortion)
- Unauthorized access to, or modification or disclosure of, information assets (hardware, software, data, information)
- Nation states with advanced information warfare capabilities attacking critical information infrastructure to cause disruption or DoS
- Technical advances such as quantum computing (it is only a matter of time before all current encryption algorithms are rendered obsolete) [MIN200601].

2A.2 Information Security Vulnerabilities

- Software bugs and design flaws, particularly those in mass-market software such as Windows and TCP/IP stacks (usually exploited by hackers, fraudsters, and other criminals)
- Complexity in IT, including "bloatware" and "richness" in general (modern, general-purpose computers and IP networks are "bad" for security) (usually "exploited," inadvertently causing more errors or deliberately by hackers, fraudsters, and other criminals)
- Inadequate investment in appropriate information security controls, at least partly due to the apparent disconnect between solid information security and commercial success (potentially exploited by all threats if security controls are weak or missing)
- Insufficient attention to humans factors in system design and implementation, including cognitive biases and "laziness" (causes errors and is exploited by hackers, ID thieves, fraudsters, and other criminals)
- Unwarranted confidence in inherently flawed or missing security controls, including both a general lack of awareness of the items in these lists and dependence on compliance certificates resulting from incompetent or fraudulent audits (exploited by hackers and fraudsters)
- "Management" who, in the main "still just doesn't get information security" and "insists that it be buried deep out of sight, out of mind in the bowels of IT"(exploited by all threats, for the same reasons as lack of investment in security)
- Ignorance, carelessness, negligence, or idle curiosity by users (exploited by untrained or mis/uninformed people who accidentally cause damage or discover exploitable control weaknesses)

- Poor or missing governance of information assets such as lack of accountability for their protection, incomplete/inaccurate asset inventories, and lack of risk analysis and security controls design and implementation (exploited by all threats, for the same reasons as lack of investment in security)
- Frequent change in the business, IT, and security arena, leading to a degree of helplessness and consequent denial or abdication of responsibilities (exploited by all threats, for the same reasons as lack of investment in security)
- Inadequate contingency planning and preparedness for unpredictable/ unusual or extreme information security incidents (exploited by accident or perhaps deliberately by a competitor, criminal, saboteur, or terrorist creating a crisis to eventuate a disaster)
- Legacy systems (e.g., SCADA[14], safety-certified medical, space, aerospace, and other systems) running on legacy platforms, often unsupported and no longer security-patched, that form part of a critical business process/data chain (exploited by accident or by hackers targeting old well-known vulnerabilities)
- Bugs in microprocessor designs and microcode that create opportunities for hackers to subvert trusted kernel routines including encryption and virtualization (potentially exploitable by skilled hackers and script kiddies)
- Lack of will, concern, and/or ability to impress the need for information security on youngsters and young adults (exploited by all threats, for the same reasons as lack of investment in security)

2A.3 Information Security Impacts

- Disruption to organizational routines and processes with consequent interruption to trading capabilities, loss of income, and so on
- Direct financial losses through information theft and fraud, whether simply the "background noise" or exceptional and obvious in nature
- Decrease in shareholder value because of negative impact on customer relations, lost sales, and decline in public confidence (a very significant impact for those at the Board level)
- (Necessary) expenditure on information security controls at every stage of the systems and process development lifecycles
- Replacement costs for equipment and data damaged, stolen, corrupted, or lost in incidents
- Loss of competitive advantage (affects nations as well as corporations)

---

[14]SCADA (Supervisory Control and Data Acquisition) is a computer system monitoring and controlling a process, namely, an industrial control system.

- Loss of privacy, such as by Big Brother snooping on ordinary citizens by their governments and authorities, by generalized decay of personal privacy inherent in modern society, and as a result of criminal activities such as identity theft
- Reputational damage causing brand devaluation, lost customers, customer complaints and defection (affects individuals on Facebook, inter alia, as well as corporations)
- Loss of confidence in IT, seeding doubts and holding back valid commercial and noncommercial exploitation of IT
- Jail time, fines, suspension of licenses, and/or other sanctions for those held accountable for serious legal or regulatory noncompliance and other information security breaches (another key motivator for the Board of Directors)
- Reduced profitability, growth, and compensation caused by the background noise of security incidents, control costs, and unspecified doubts about the effectiveness of security
- Impaired growth due to inflexible and/or over-complex infrastructure/ system/application environments
- Injury or loss of life if safety-critical systems fail, misbehave, or are maliciously controlled (these are fairly rare events at this juncture)
- Cyber-terrorism. Nations are also developing information warfare capabilities.

2A.4 Information Security Risk Events

- Theft of personal data by criminals, or loss of laptops and computer media, leading to criminal prosecution of senior management, regulatory fines, loss of public confidence in trusted organizations, and significantly increasing the probability of identity theft for the data subject concerned (such incidents have occurred in recent years and more are expected in the future.) (Proving cause-and-effect linkages between data exposure and ID theft is challenging unless the criminals are rash enough to exploit compromised data sets in their entirety)
- Information leakage, extraction or loss of valuable and/or private information. Introduction of unauthorized/malicious software through widespread unauthorized and/or uncontrolled use of portable devices and transportable computer media (for example USB memory sticks, Bluetooth-enabled devices), with some potential for deliberate attacks propagated on such devices/media (Trojan-infected USB sticks, CD-ROMs, and so on.)
- Social engineering/pretexting or targeted phishing and malware attacks on call center staff to obtain unauthorized access to personal data that can be exploited by fraudsters for identity theft

- Environmental disasters due to Acts of God or intentional acts that severely affects the business survivability of organizations due to lack of business continuity and disaster recovery planning/management
- Poor information security studies, risk assessments, projects/assignments and/or staffing/organization, causing failed, wasteful, excessive, or otherwise inadequate controls and practices selection, implementations, performance measurement, monitoring, and/or auditing
- Deception, including frauds (such as identity theft through phishing, social engineering, spyware, and so on), repudiation (for example, someone denying that they made an online purchase and perhaps manipulating and falsifying transaction histories), and false allegations (for example, uploading compromising information on one's computer)
- Endangerment—accidentally or intentionally putting information or systems "in harm's way" (for example, someone accidentally publishing highly sensitive internal information to the Internet, leading to loss of personal privacy and/or commercial disadvantage and perhaps prosecution)
- Unauthorized exploitation of intellectual property including plagiarism and outright theft of text and/or audio/visual content by unethical members of the public or organizations, causing "opportunity costs" (lost sales) and investigation/prosecution costs for the rightful intellectual property owners if they choose to defend their rights.

2A.5 Information Security Controls

- Investment in a comprehensive and systematic Information Security Management System (ISMS) incorporating high-quality information assurance processes. The ISMS should ideally but not obligatorily be based on internationally accepted "good security practices" such as those embodied in the ISO/IEC 27000 series and NIST SP800 standards, or on the Information Security Forum's *Standard of Good Practices for Information Security*, among others
- Data confidentiality controls to protect personal and proprietary data against unauthorized access or disclosure, including physical, legal, and logical access controls, both technical and procedural in nature (for example, strong encryption of laptops' hard drives, of data backups, or of CD ROM storage, particularly when being transported)
- Data integrity controls to improve the quality, completeness, and accuracy of data in the computer systems through data entry, processing, output, and transmission controls
- System integrity controls to avoid computer and networking systems being undermined by unauthorized or otherwise undesired changes such as malware infections and hacks

- Proactive technical vulnerability management including timely identification of vulnerabilities, patching and updating of systems, and proactive hardening such as choice of secure operating systems, de-installation of unnecessary applications and services, and intensive security testing
- "Anti-everything" software to minimize the malware, spam, spyware, and intrusion incidents on systems, both client workstations and servers
- Proactive IT auditing, monitoring, and reporting processes to identify and respond to risk exposure before these cause incidents. This should be in addition to traditional reactive/after-the-fact auditing and post-incident analysis
- Enforcement of rights and compliance obligations in relation to Intellectual Property ownership, intellectual property governance, personal data protection, and so on, through moral, legal, regulatory, and other means
- Resilience engineering: designing, building, testing, operating, and maintaining both business processes and IT systems to provide reliable and secure services by reducing vulnerabilities and single points of failure (this will minimize unplanned down time and other disruptive incidents even if the threat materializes)
- Contingency arrangements including backups, redundant assts, IT disaster recovery plans, audits. Exercise (testing) of these contingency arrangements
- Information security awareness, training, and education. Helping employees understand and fulfill their security obligations (for example, recognizing and responding appropriately to potential social engineering attacks). Motivating the employees to "do the right thing" and avoid insecure activities (for example, using a laptop at an airport). Creating a security culture.

APPENDIX 2B: WHAT IS ENTERPRISE RISK MANAGEMENT (ERM)?

IT Risk Management can in theory be seen as a subset of the discipline of enterprise risk management (ERM), although we do not emphasize this approach here. ERM is defined in a number of ways, including the following from the Committee of Sponsoring Organizations of the Treadway Commission (COSO) [COS200401]:

> Enterprise risk management is a process, effected by an entity's board of directors, management and other personnel, applied in strategy setting and across the enterprise, designed to identify potential events that may affect the entity, and manage risk to be within its risk appetite, to provide reasonable assurance regarding the achievement of entity objectives.

Hence, ERM deals with how organizations manage risk, providing a basis for application across organizations, industries, and sectors. ERM focuses on achievement of objectives established by a particular entity and provides a basis for defining enterprise risk management effectiveness. ERM consists of eight interrelated components [COS200401]:

- *Internal Environment.* The internal environment encompasses the tone of an organization, and sets the basis for how risk is viewed and addressed by an entity's people, including risk management philosophy and risk appetite, integrity and ethical values, and the environment in which they operate.
- *Objective Setting.* Objectives must exist before management can identify potential events affecting their achievement. Enterprise risk management ensures that management has in place a process to set objectives and that the chosen objectives support and align with the entity's mission and are consistent with its risk appetite.
- *Event Identification.* Internal and external events affecting achievement of an entity's objectives must be identified, distinguishing between risks and opportunities. Opportunities are channeled back to management's strategy or objective-setting processes.
- *Risk Assessment.* Risks (risk events) are analyzed, considering likelihood and impact, as a basis for determining how they should be managed. Risks are assessed on an inherent and a residual basis.
- *Risk Response.* Management selects risk responses—avoiding, accepting, reducing, or sharing risk—developing a set of actions to align risks with the entity's risk tolerances and risk appetite.
- *Control Activities.* Policies and procedures are established and implemented to help ensure that the risk responses are effectively carried out.
- *Information and Communication.* Relevant information is identified, captured, and communicated in a form and timeframe that enable people to carry out their responsibilities. Effective communication also occurs in a broader sense, flowing down, across, and up the entity.
- *Monitoring.* The entirety of enterprise risk management is monitored, with modifications made as necessary. Monitoring is accomplished through ongoing management activities, separate evaluations, or both.

CHAPTER 3

INFORMATION SECURITY RISK MANAGEMENT STANDARDS

As we have seen in the previous chapters, information security and, hence, risk management are universally applicable to all types of organizations, including commercial enterprises of various sizes (from small businesses to multinational companies), government agencies, government departments, not-for-profit institutions, academic institutions, medical institutions, media companies, banks, brokerage companies, and insurance companies—in fact applicable to any organization that creates, receives, stores, or transmits information vital to its operation. The specific information security requirements, risk exposure, and ensuing risk will be unique in each situation, but often a common approach and methodology can be employed. Risk management is the endeavor of balancing potential adverse impacts against the costs of deploying safeguards. We have already noted that IT risk management encompasses five major processes:

1. (Ongoing) identification of threats, vulnerabilities, or (risk) events impacting the set of IT assets owned by the organization
2. Risk assessment
3. Risk mitigation planning
4. Risk mitigation implementation
5. Evaluation of the mitigation's effectiveness

Fortunately, the stakeholders and risk management teams do not have to start from scratch when contemplating and/or undertaking these processes because a body of knowledge has emerged to support the risk management process. As early as 1989, the U.K. Department of Trade and Industry (DTI) established a working group that produced the User Code of Practice that was essentially a list of security controls considered good practice at the time. Figure 3.1 presents the development timeline leading to the ISO Code of Practice, ISO/IEC

Information Technology Risk Management in Enterprise Environments: A Review of Industry Practices and a Practial Guide to Risk Management Teams, by Jake Kouns and Daniel Minoli
Copyright © 2010 John Wiley & Sons, Inc.

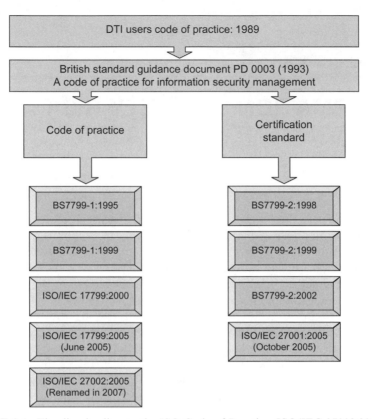

FIGURE 3.1. Timeline leading to the ISO Code of Practice, ISO/IEC 27002:2005, and the Information Security System Requirements standard ISO/IEC 27001:2005.

27002:2005 and the Information Security Systems Requirements standard, ISO/IEC 27001:2005. In addition, standards organizations in Canada, Australia/New Zealand, and Japan developed early versions of risk management standards in the mid-to-late 1990s. Beginning with the release of ISO/IEC 17799:2000, the International Organization for Standardization (ISO) got involved and has continued to expand the field of information security by producing a suite of standards.

This chapter provides a brief overview of the available information security, risk analysis standards. In particular, we will provide a general overview of ISO's[15] ISO/IEC 27000 series of information security management system standards. Table 3.1 provides a short list of the relevant information security and/or risk management standards.

---

[15]ISO cooperates with the International Electrotechnical Commission (IEC), hence the standards also have the IEC label

TABLE 3.1. Information Security Standards with Risk Management Relevance (Partial List)

British Standards Institute (BSI)	BS7799-1:1999, "Code of Practice for Information Security Management," was retired with the release of ISO/IEC 17799:2000.
	BS7799-2:2002 was the latest BSI specification for an information security management system certification. After the release of ISO/IEC 17799:2005, it was "fast tracked" by ISO to become ISO/IEC 27001:2005, the certification standard
	BS7799-3:2006, "Information security management systems guidelines for information security risk management," the standard provides guidance and support for the implementation of a risk management process and is generic enough to be of use to small, medium, and large organizations. Clauses include:

- Information security risks in the organizational context
- Risk assessment
- Risk treatment and management decision-making
- Ongoing risk management activities
- Examples of legal and regulatory compliance
- Information security risks and organizational risks
- Examples of assets, threats, vulnerabilities, and risk assessment methods
- Risk management tools
- Relationship between ISO/IEC 27001:2005 and BS7799-3:2006

International Organization for Standardization (ISO)	ISO/IEC 13335-1:2004, "Information technology—Security techniques—Management of information and communications technology security, Part 1: Concepts and models for information and communications technology security management." The standard contains generally accepted descriptions of concepts and models for information and communications technology security management. See text for other parts of the standard.
	The ISO/IEC 27000 family of information security management standards (also known as "ISO27k") ISO/IEC 27002:2005, "Code of Practice for Information Security Management." *Note*: ISO/IEC 27002:2005 was previously known as ISO/IEC 17799:2005 until renamed in 2007. The rename was initiated by the ISO, who wanted to align the information security standards under a common naming structure (the "ISO 27000 series").
	ISO/IEC 27001:2005, "Information Security Management Systems—Requirements," "fast tracked" by ISO to become the certification standard paired with ISO/IEC 27002/17799:2005.

TABLE 3.1. (Continued)

	ISO/IEC 18028:2006, "Information technology—Security techniques—IT network security"
	Five-part standard (ISO/IEC 18028-1 to 18028-5) containing generally accepted guidelines on the security aspects of the management, operation, and use of information technology networks. The standard is an extension of the guidelines provided in ISO/IEC 13335 and ISO/IEC 17799 focusing on network security risks.
	ISO/IEC TR 18044:2004, "Information technology—Security techniques—Information security incident management."
	It provides, in part, information on the benefits to be obtained from and the key issues associated with a good information security incident management approach (to convince corporate management and those personnel who will report to and receive feedback from a scheme that the scheme should be introduced and used). It also provides a description of the information security incident management process.
	ISO DIS (Draft International Standard) 31000, "Risk Management Principles and Guidelines on Implementation"
	This draft standard (targeted for 2009) is based on AS/NZS 4360 and COSO-ERM and provides guidelines on the principles and implementation of risk management in general (not IT or information security specific).
National Institute of Standards and Technology (NIST)	SP 800-12, -16, -18, -23, -24, -25, -26, -30, -31, -32, -33, -34, -36, -37, -39, -41, -42, -43, -44, -45, -48, -50, -53, -55, -61, -64, -68 Computer Security Standards
Australian Standard/ New Zealand Standard (AS/NZS)	AS/NZS 4360:2004
Information Security Forum (ISF)	"The ISF Standard of Good Practice"
	A high-level standard promulgating a series of good practice standards related to information security. Consists of a comprehensive set of information security-specific controls:

- Controls aimed at complying with legal and regulatory requirements, such as Sarbanes–Oxley Act 2002, the Payment Card Industry (PCI) Data Security Standard, Basel II 1998, and the EU Directive on Data Protection
- Coverage of the main security controls in other major information security-related standards, such as ISO/IEC 27002 (17799) and COBIT

The Standard of Good Practice is comprised of five parts:

- Security management (enterprise-wide)
- Critical business applications
- Computer installations
- Networks
- Systems development

3.1   ISO/IEC 13335

ISO 13335 (originally a set of technical reports) embodies a set of guidelines for the management of IT security, focusing on technical security control measures. ISO/IEC 13335 is an assessor-led approach. The standard is comprised of four different parts, where the first part identifies the overall process and shows the different components necessary to complete a risk assessment.

- ISO/IEC 13335-1:2004, Information technology—Security techniques—Management of information and communications technology security, Part 1: Concepts and models for information and communications technology security management. It presents the concepts and models fundamental to a basic understanding of information and communication technology (ICT) security, and it addresses the general management issues that are essential to the successful planning, implementation and operation of ICT security. In this part of the standard the fundamental security concepts are explained; next the policy and strategy principles are explained, followed by a description of the necessary organizational structure for implementing security; and, finally, the management function, and in particular the process of risk management, is explained. This section of the standard is useful because it defines the principles that underpin an information security framework and explains in more detail the structures that support the framework [COL200701].
- ISO/IEC 13335-2, Management of information and communications technology security, Part 2: Information security risk management. This standard was intended to replace ISO/IEC TR 13335-3:1998 and ISO/IEC TR 13335-4:2000. Part 2 of ISO/IEC 13335 (currently 2nd WD) provides operational guidance on ICT security.
- ISO TR 13335-3:1998 Information technologyy—Guidelines for the Management of IT Security, Part 3: Techniques for the management of IT Security. Covers techniques for the management of IT security. Has been included in ISO/IEC 27005:2008, Information security risk management (now an International Standard under publication). ISO TR 13335-3 provides guidance on implementing a risk assessment, together with a range of possible risk calculation models. It identifies four approaches to risk analysis, ranging from the baseline approach to a detailed risk assessment methodology. It identifies the process flow of risk assessment as follows [COL200701]:
  - Identification of assets to be included in the risk assessment
  - Valuation of assets and establishment of dependencies between assets
  - Threat and vulnerability assessment on the assets within the scope of the risk assessment
  - Identification of existing or planned safeguards
  - Assessment of risk exposures

- ISO TR 13335-4:2000 covers the selection of safeguards (countermeasures, meaning technical security controls). Has been included in ISO/IEC 27005:2008, Information security risk management (now a Published International Standard).

3.2 ISO/IEC 17799 (ISO/IEC 27002:2005)

ISO 17799 is used colloquially as a generic term to describe two distinct documents: ISO17799 (aka ISO 27002), which is a set of security controls (a code of practice), and ISO 27001 (formerly BS7799-2), which is a standard "specification" for an Information Security Management System (ISMS). The ISO 17799 standard has its genesis in the late 1980s in the Information Security "Code of Practice" from the UK's Department of Trade and Industry. The initial release of BS 7799 was based to a degree on an internal document by the Royal Dutch/Shell Group entitled Information Security Policy Manual. The manual's emphasis on mainframe security concepts and lack of explicit considerations related to the Internet suggests that it was based on material developed at an earlier point in time.

In 1995 the British Standards Institute (BSI) (now known as BSI British Standards[16]) released British Standard BS7799.[17] A second part, BS7799-2:1998, to be used for certification purposes, was added in February 1998. The first revision of the standard, BS7799:1999, followed a public consultation period and resulted in an extensive revision which was released with Part 1 and Part 2 in April 1999. BS7799-1:1999 was proposed as an ISO standard via the "Fast Track" mechanism in October 1999 and was published with minor amendments as ISO/IEC 17799:2000 in December 2000.

BS 7799-2:1999 was revised and officially launched in September 2002, as BS7799-2:2002 and was used for ISMS certification audits until the release of ISO/IEC 27001:2005 in October 2005. The latest revision of the ISO/IEC 17799 standard followed another consultation period and resulted in an extension that which was released in June 2005 as ISO/IEC 17799:2005. BS7799-2:2002 was revised and released in October 2005 as an ISO standard, ISO/IEC 27001:2005. The most recent change was in name only when ISO/IEC 17799:2005 was changed to ISO/IEC 27002:2005. More information on both standards is provided below.

The reader should focus on the 27000 series described next.

3.3 ISO/IEC 27000 SERIES

The ISO/IEC 27000 series of standards (also known as "ISO27k") provides a comprehensive introduction to information security, risk management,

---

[16]BSI British Standards is the National Standards Body of the UK.
[17]BS 7799:1995 is retired at this juncture, except for Part 3.

and management systems. The 27000 series is a family of information security management standards that provides, generally accepted best practices and guidance on establishing, operating, monitoring, reviewing, maintaining, and improving a documented ISMS. An ISMS aims at protecting the confidentiality, integrity, and availability of the information and information processing facilities within an organization. The ISMS is in effect the information security governance/management processes that is and/or can be used by an organization to handle information security and risk management. These standards are intended to be used as a group to establish, operate, monitor, review maintain, improve, and gain certification for a documented ISMS. See Table 3.2 for a listing of standards in this family. As of press time, only ISO/IEC 27001, 27002, 27005, and 27006 were actually issued.

Note: Some material in this section is sourced to the ISO27k Implementers Forum (http://www.iso27001security.com) [IMP200801], a global community of nearly 1500 information security professionals who are actively using the ISO/IEC 27000 series standards.

3.3.1 ISO/IEC 27000, Information Technology—Security Techniques—Information Security Management Systems— Fundamentals and Vocabulary (Draft at Press Time)

ISO/IEC 27000 specifies the fundamental principles, concepts, and vocabulary for the ISO/IEC 27000 series of recommendations. ISO/IEC 27000 (under development at press time) aims at describing the fundamentals and vocabulary. It is a recognized fact that several key terms in information security (such as "risk") have different meanings according to the context and the user or user community. In general, few people define terms precisely; this invariably creates confusion and impairs formal assessment—hence the value of a vocabulary (and this is also why we have defined the terms we use in Chapter 2). ISO/IEC 27000 was at Final Draft or Distribution International Standard (FDIS) stage at press time, with a 2009 publication target.

3.3.2 ISO/IEC 27001:2005, Information Technology—Security Techniques—Specification for an Information Security Management System

ISO/IEC 27001:2005 was published as an ISO standard in October 2005. The standard defines the requirements for an ISMS. An ISMS is a management system for dealing with information security risk exposures—namely, a framework of policies, procedures, physical, legal, and technical security controls forming part of the organization's overall risk management processes. The standard specifies a set of requirements for the establishment, implementation, monitoring and review, maintenance, and improvement of an ISMS. ISO/IEC 27001 incorporates Deming's Plan-Do-Check-Act

TABLE 3.2. ISO/IEC 27000 Series of Standards

ISO/IEC 27000	(under development) Standard will provide an overview/introduction to the ISO27k standards as a whole plus the specialist vocabulary used in ISO27k.
ISO/IEC 27001:2005	ISMS requirements specification used for the certification of an organization's ISMS.
ISO/IEC 27002:2005	Standard that encompasses the code of practice for information security management describing a set of information security control objectives and a set of generally accepted best practice security controls.
ISO/IEC 27003	(under development) Standard will provide implementation guidance for ISO/IEC 27001.
ISO/IEC 27004	(under development) Standard will be an information security management measurement standard recommending metrics to facilitate an improvement in the effectiveness of an ISMS.
ISO/IEC 27005:2008	A key information security risk management standard that provides advice on information security risk management.
ISO/IEC 27006:2007	A guide to the certification or registration process for accredited ISMS certification or registration bodies.
ISO/IEC 27007	(under development) Standard will be a guideline for auditing ISMSs.
ISO/IEC TR 27008	(under development) Standard will provide guidance on auditing information security controls.
ISO/IEC 27009	(under development) Standard will provide guidance on information security governance.
ISO/IEC 27010	(under development) Standard will provide guidance on information security management for sector-to-sector communications.
ISO/IEC 27011	(under development) Standard (also known as X.1051) will provide information security management guidelines for telecommunications.
ISO/IEC 27012	(under development) Standard will provide information security management systems guidance for e-government applications
ISO/IEC 27013	(under development) Standard will provide information security management systems guidance for financial services organizations.
ISO/IEC 27031	(under development) Standard will be an information and communication technology (ICT)-focused standard on business continuity.
ISO/IEC 27032	(under development) Standard will provide guidelines for cybersecurity.
ISO/IEC 27033	(under development) Standard will replace the multi-part ISO/IEC 18028 standard on IT network security.
ISO/IEC 27034	(under development) Standard will provide guidelines for application security.
ISO/IEC 27035	(under development) Standard will replace ISO TR 18044 on security incident management.
ISO 27799	Recommendation that provides health sector specific ISMS implementation guidance.

Note: The titles, scope, and/or content of as-yet unpublished standards may change prior to their publication.

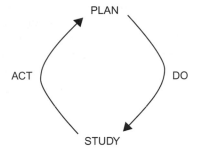

PLAN: Plan ahead for change. Analyze and predict the results.
DO: Execute the plan, taking small steps in controlled circumstances.
STUDY: CHECK, study the results.
ACT: Take action to standardize or improve the process.

FIGURE 3.2. The Deming (PDCA) cycle.

(PDCA) cycle.[18] ISO/IEC 27001 was being revised at press time; the revised standard is expected to be published by 2010. The ISMS is described in the standard using the PDCA process (see Figure 3.2), given that security controls have to be continually reviewed and adjusted to incorporate changes in the security threats, vulnerabilities and impacts of information security failures. In this case,

Plan = define requirements, assess risks, decide which controls are applicable;

Do = implement and operate the ISMS;

Check = monitor and review the ISMS;

Act = maintain and continuously improve the ISMS.

ISO/IEC 27001 is principally a *management system* standard, therefore, compliance requires the organization to have a defined set of management controls in place. Annex A of ISO/IEC 27001:2005 outlines 133 best practice security controls that should be considered by organizations to mitigate identified risks to their information assets. ISO/IEC 27002:2005 provides a more detailed description of each of the security controls along with implementation advice. ISO/IEC 27001:2005 does not mandate the implementation of specific information security controls. Organizations seeking compliance

---

[18]The Deming cycle, or PDCA cycle (also known as the Deming Wheel or the Continuous Improvement Spiral), is a continuous quality improvement model consisting of a logical sequence of four repetitive steps for continuous improvement and learning: "Plan, Do, Study (Check) and Act." The concept originated in the 1920s with Walter A. Shewhart, who introduced the "Plan, Do, and See" method. W. Edwards Deming, the Total Quality Management (TQM) practitioner, modified the Shewart cycle to become the PDSA. Deming was Japan as part of the occupation forces of the allies after World War II and taught Quality Improvement methods to the Japanese, including the use of statistics and the PDSA cycle.

and/or certification to ISO/IEC 27001:2005 are allowed to choose the information security controls from Annex A that are applicable to their environment along with other controls that are appropriate. ISO/IEC 27001:2005 is the formal standard against which organizations may seek certification of their ISMSs. ISO/IEC 27001:2005 describes the process for assessing risks and selecting, implementing and managing specific security controls. According to ISO/IEC, the standard allows the following:

- Use within organizations to formulate security requirements and objectives
- Use within organizations as a way to ensure that security risks are cost-effectively managed
- Use within organizations to ensure compliance with laws and regulations
- Use within an organization as a process framework for the implementation and management of controls to ensure that the specific security objectives of an organization are met
- The definition of new information security management processes
- Identification and clarification of existing information security management processes
- Use by the management of organizations to determine the status of information security management activities
- Use by the internal and external auditors of organizations to demonstrate the information security policies, directives, and standards adopted by an organization and determine the degree of compliance with those policies, directives and standards
- Use by organizations to provide relevant information about information security policies, directives, standards, and procedures to trading partners and other organizations that they interact with for operational or commercial reasons
- Implementation of business enabling information security
- Use by organizations to provide relevant information about information security to customers

ISO/IEC 27001 has the following sections:

0. Introduction. Description of the process approach, which is based on the PDCA cycle.
1. Scope. Description of generic ISMS requirements suitable for various types of organizations.
2. Normative References. ISO/IEC 27002:2005 in particular.
3. Terms and Definitions
4. Information Security Management System. This section of the standard contains the "core" of the standard, based on the PDCA cycle. Also,

this section specifies documents that are required and must be controlled. The material explains that records must be generated and controlled to prove the operation of the ISMS (for example, certification audit purposes.)

5. **Management Responsibility.** This section of the standard advocates that management must demonstrate their commitment to the ISMS. Commitment is to be demonstrated by allocating adequate resources to implement and operate the ISMS.

6. **Internal ISMS Audits.** This section of the standard emphasizes the fact that the organization must conduct periodic internal audits to ensure that the ISMS incorporates adequate controls that operate effectively.

7. **Management Review of the ISMS.** This section of the standard makes the case that management must review the suitability, adequacy and effectiveness of the ISMS on a regular basis (for example, at least once a year), assessing opportunities for improvements.

8. **ISMS Improvements.** This section of the standard makes the case that the organization must continually improve the ISMS by assessing and implementing changes to ensure the ISMS' suitability and effectiveness, addressing nonconformance (noncompliance) and, where possible, preventing recurrent issues.

The appendices to the standard are as follows:

Annex A—Control Objectives and Controls. The annex contains a list of titles of the control sections in ISO/IEC 27002.

Annex B—OECD (Organization for Economic Co-operation and Development) Principles and the ISO/IEC 27002 International Standard. The annex contains a table showing which parts of the standard satisfy key principles laid out in the OECD Guidelines for the Security of Information Systems and Networks.

Annex C—Correspondence Between ISO 9001:2000, ISO 14001:2004 and the ISO/IEC 27002 International Standard. ISO/IEC 27001 shares the same basic structure of other management systems standards; as a consequence, an organization that implements any one of these management standards should already be familiar with concepts such as PDCA, records, and audits.

Certification against an accepted standard (e.g., ISO/IEC 27001:2005) is increasingly being demanded business partners, suppliers, and other entities that are concerned about information security. Independent assessment engenders rigor and formality to the implementation process; in turn, this typically implies improvements to information security and reduced risk. There are number of certification bodies worldwide that have been accredited by various national standards organizations that can perform certification audits in accordance with ISO/IEC 27001:2005 and issue certificates. The United Kingdom Accreditation Service or UKAS is the accreditation body in the United Kingdom and has accredited BSI along with about 18 other organizations as Certification Bodies (CBs). The ANSI-ASQ National Accreditation Board (ANAB) is the U.S. accreditation body for management system registrars or Certification Bodies.

The ANSI-ASQ National Accreditation Board and UKAS are members of the International Accreditation Forum (IAF) and are signatories of the IAF multilateral recognition arrangements. Through these arrangements, the ANSI-ASQ National Accreditation Board and UKAS cooperate with other accreditation bodies around the world to provide value to the organization it has accredited and their clients, ensuring that accredited certificates are recognized internationally. The global conformity assessment system ensures confidence and reduces risk for customers engaging in trade worldwide.

There are around 5000 ISO/IEC 27001:2005 certified organizations at press time. Considering an estimated 50 million corporations/institutions in the world, one can see that universal acceptance is far from complete. In addition, certifications are issued based on a specifically defined scope that may not cover the entire organization. One thing that certification to ISO/IEC 27001:2005 does ensure is that the organization has formally documented and implemented the mandatory management system elements of the standard as defined in clauses 4.0 through 8.0. In addition, organizations can seek certification based on a scope that they define, such as a portion of their critical business and not their entire organization.

3.3.3   ISO/IEC 27002:2005, Information Technology—Security Techniques—Code of Practice for Information Security Management

ISO/IEC 27002:2005 is concerned with the security of information assets; in its view, this is well beyond just the IT systems. The standard takes the implicit view that the IT group is the custodian of a proportion of the organization's information assets and is charged with securing them; however, there is also a vast quantity of written information (embodying the knowledge and experience of employees) that resides outside IT.

ISO/IEC 27002 identifies a set of controls (133 to be exact, under 39 security objectives) to address information security risk exposures in the area of confidentiality, integrity, and availability. ISO/IEC 27002 is a code of practice, advisory document, not a formal specification: It provides a listing of best-practice information security control measures that organizations should consider to secure information assets. Information assets include (as covered in Chapters 1 and 2) IT equipment, networking equipment, storage equipment, data content, and so forth, at all layers of the architecture framework (for example, TOGAF) model. The control objectives listed in ISO/IEC 27002 can be interpreted as a generic functional specification for an organization's information security management controls architecture. ISO/IEC 27002 is widely used and is referenced by the ISMS certification standard ISO/IEC 27001. ISO/IEC JTC1/SC27 has started the process of revising ISO/IEC 27002, with possible re-publication in 2011.

As noted earlier, ISO/IEC 17799:2005 was renumbered ISO/IEC 27002:2005 in 2007 to bring it into the ISO/IEC 27000 family (the text remains word-for-word identical to ISO/IEC 17799:2005.) ₅

Organizations that adopt ISO/IEC 27002 and seek to be certified compliant to ISO/IEC 27001 should assess their information security risks and apply appropriate controls, using the standard for guidance. As noted, ISO/IEC 27002 specifics 39 control objectives along with 133 security controls, but the standard does not make specific controls mandatory; the organization is free to select and implement controls that are appropriate to them and their environment. Some of the controls in the standard are not necessarily applicable in every instance; furthermore, the generic wording of the standard may not reflect an organization's exact requirements. Not making specific controls mandatory enables the standard to be broadly applicable and affords organizations implementation flexibility. There are no formal compliance certificates based on ISO/IEC 27002 itself (as stated above, organizations can get their information security governance/management processes—the information security management system—certified against ISO/IEC 27001).

The content of ISO/IEC 27002 is covered next.

0. **Introduction.** Describes how to make use of the standard.
1. **Scope.** Describes the scope that encompasses information security management recommendations for individuals responsible for initiating, implementing, or maintaining security.
2. **Terms and Definitions**
3. **Structure of this Standard.** This section of the standard explains that the crux of the standard consists of control objectives, suggested controls, and implementation guidance.
4. **Risk Assessment and Treatment.** This section of the standard provides a short discussion of risk management (a reference to ISO/IEC 27005 may be added in the 2011 revision, which provides guidance on selecting and using appropriate methods to analyze information security risk).

The following sections align with the security controls defined in Annex A of ISO/IEC 27001:2005:

5. **Security Policy.** This section of the standard contains one security objective and two security controls and advocates that (appropriate) management within organizations needs to define a policy to document their direction of, and support for, information security. There should be a high-level information security policy statement defining the key information security directives and mandates for the organization. The guiding policy naturally

needs to be supported by a comprehensive apparatus of specific corporate information security policies (an information security policy manual often describes the policies.) The apparatus of specific corporate information security policies is supported, in turn, by a set of institutional information security standards, procedures and guidelines.

Note: The ISMS policy required by ISO/IEC 27001:2005 is considered a superset of the information security policy described above.

6. **Organization of Information Security.** This section of the standard contains two security objectives and eleven security controls and makes the case that appropriate information security governance structure should be designed and implemented. Security considerations need to cover the internal organization and external parties. The (internal) organization is best served by a management framework for information security where senior management provides direction and commits support. Clearly, roles and responsibilities need to be defined for the information security function. Other guidance in this section includes, but is not limited to the following: Confidentiality agreements should reflect the organization's needs; contacts should be established with relevant authorities (e.g., law enforcement) and appropriate special interest groups; and, information security should be independently reviewed. In reference to external parties, it is axiomatic that information security should not be compromised by the introduction of third party products or services, and risk exposures should be assessed and mitigated when dealing with customers and other third parties.

7. **Asset Management.** This section of the standard contains two security objectives and five security controls and makes (the obvious) case that organizations need to be in a position to understand what information assets they hold, and to manage their security appropriately. All IT assets should be accounted for and have a defined owner. A comprehensive inventory of information assets should be maintained; as noted, IT assets include but are not limited to IT hardware, software, data, system documentation, storage media, supporting assets such as computer room air conditioners and UPSs, and ICT services. The inventory should record ownership and location of the assets, and owners should identify acceptable uses. The section of the standard also recommends that information assets (data) should be classified according to its need for security protection and labeled in such a manner.

8. **Human Resources Security.** This section of the standard contains three security objectives and nine security controls and punctuates that the organization should manage system access rights and IT assets for "joiners, movers, and leavers" and should undertake suitable security awareness, training, and educational activities. Section 8.1 of the standard focuses on "Prior to Employment" and notes that security responsibilities need to be taken into account when recruiting permanent employees,

contractors, and temporary staff (for example, by utilizing adequate job descriptions, preemployment screening, etc.) and included in contracts (for example, terms and conditions of employment and other signed agreements on security roles and responsibilities). Section 8.2 focuses on "During Employment" and calls attention to management responsibilities regarding information security. Specifically, employees and third-party IT users need to be educated and trained in security procedures. A formal disciplinary process is needs to be in place to handle security breaches. Section 8.3 focuses on "Termination or Change of Employment" and discusses security aspects of an employee's exit from the organization (including the return of corporate assets and removal of access rights). Applicable procedures also need to be codified for change of responsibilities within an organization—for example, a lateral move to a different group within the organization which has different (data access) privileges/responsibilities.

9. **Physical and Environmental Security.** This section of the standard contains two security objectives and 13 security controls and discusses how hardware assets should be physically protected against malicious or accidental damage or loss and also should be protected from over-heating, radio-frequency interference, loss of electrical power, and so on. The need for concentric layers of physical controls to protect sensitive IT facilities from unauthorized access is discussed. IT equipment, communications equipment, and on-site/on-campus cabling should be protected against physical damage, fire, flood, damaging storms, sabotage, and other risk exposures.

10. **Communications and Operations Management.** This section of the standard contains 10 security objectives and 32 security controls that describe the security controls for systems and network management; it covers issues listed in Table 3.3.

11. **Access Control.** This section of the standard contains seven security objectives and 25 security controls and discusses logical access to IT systems, networks, and data and reinforces clearly that access must be suitably controlled to prevent unauthorized use. A number of issues are addressed in the section: (i) Business requirement for access control (requirements to control access to information assets should be clearly documented in an access control policy); (ii) user access management (allocation of access rights should be formally controlled through (a) user registration and administration procedures including special restrictions over the allocation of privileges and management of passwords and (b) periodic access rights reviews; (iii) user responsibilities (maintaining effective access controls such as choosing strong passwords and keeping them confidential); (iv) network access control (access to network services should be controlled and policy should be defined and remote users must be authenticated—also remote diagnostic ports should be securely controlled); (v) operating system access control (advocates use of operating

TABLE 3.3. Communications and Operations Management, ISO 27002

Topic	Description/Recommendation
Operational procedures and responsibilities	This subsection of the standard makes the case that IT operating responsibilities and procedures should be documented. Changes to IT facilities and systems should be controlled. Duties should be segregated between different people where relevant (for example, access to development and operational systems should be segregated).
Third-party service delivery management	This subsection of the standard makes the case that security requirements should be taken into account in third-party service delivery (for example, IT facilities management or outsourcing), from contractual terms to ongoing monitoring and change management.
System planning and acceptance	This subsection of the standard covers IT capacity planning and production acceptance processes.
Protection against malicious and mobile code	This subsection of the standard describes the need for anti-malware controls, including user awareness. Security controls for mobile code associated with a number of middleware services are also covered. Mobile code is code that can be transmitted across the network and executed on the far end; Java is one example of a language that supports such mode of operation.
Backup	This subsection of the standard covers routine data backups and rehearsed restoration.
Network security management	This subsection of the standard covers secure network management, network security monitoring and other controls. Additionally, it covers security of commercial network services such as private networks and managed firewalls and so on.
Media handling	This subsection of the standard makes the case that operating procedures should be defined to protect documents and computer media containing data, system information, and so on. Procedures should be defined for securely handling, transporting and storing backup media and system documentation. Also disposal of backup media, documents, and so on should be logged and controlled.
Exchange of information	This subsection of the standard makes the case that information exchanges between organizations should be controlled by using appropriate policies and procedures, and legal agreements. Security procedures and standards need to be in place to protect information and physical media in transit, including electronic messaging (for example, e-mail, EDI, and IM) and business information systems. Information exchanges must also comply with applicable legislation.
Electronic commerce services	This subsection of the standard makes the case that the security implications of e-commerce (online transaction systems)

(Continued)

TABLE 3.3. (Continued)

Topic	Description/Recommendation
	should be evaluated and suitable controls implemented. The integrity and availability of information published online (for example, on websites) should also be protected.
Monitoring	This subsection of the standard covers security event/audit/ fault logging and system alarm/alert monitoring to detect unauthorized use. It also discusses the need to secure systems/network element logs.

system access control facilities and utilities, such as user authentication with unique user IDs and managed passwords, recording use of privileges and system security alarms); (vi) application and information access control (access to and within application systems should be controlled in accordance with a defined access control policy); and (vii) mobile computing and teleworking (formal policies covering the secure use of laptops, PDAs, cellphones, etc., and secure teleworking must be defined.)

12. **Information Systems Acquisition, Development, and Maintenance.** This section of the standard contains six security objectives and 16 security controls and emphasizes that information security must be taken into account during the process of specifying, building/acquiring, testing, implementing, and maintaining IT systems. Some of the issues discussed include: (i) security requirements of IT systems (automated and manual security control requirements must be identified during the requirements stage of the systems development or procurement process, and incorporated into business cases); (ii) correct processing in application systems (data entry, processing and dissemination validation controls and message authentication must be provided); (iii) cryptographic controls (policies should be defined, covering digital signatures, nonrepudiation, management of keys, and digital certificates); (iv) security of system files (access to system files—executable programs and source code—must be controlled; (v) security in development and support processes (application system managers must assume the responsibility for controlling access to the project environment and support environments—for example, formal change control processes should be applied, including technical reviews; checks should be made for information leakage via covert channels and Trojans); and (vi) technical vulnerability management (systems/applications vulnerabilities must be controlled by monitoring for the release of security alerts by observers including the vendor of the system/application, risk-assessing the situation, and then promptly applying relevant security patches.)

13. **Information Security Incident Management.** This section of the standard contains two security objectives and five security controls and highlights that information security events, incidents and weaknesses should be

promptly reported and properly managed by organizations. An incident reporting/alarm procedure must be put in place, along with the associated response and escalation procedures. Definition of responsibilities and procedures are required to manage incidents consistently and effectively, to implement continuous improvement (learning the lessons), and to collect forensic evidence. Every employees, contractors, and business partner should be informed of their incident reporting responsibilities.

14. **Business Continuity Management.** This section of the standard contains one security objective and five security controls and describes the relationship between IT disaster recovery planning, business continuity management and contingency planning. At one end of the spectrum is the requisite analysis and creation of relevant documentation; at the other end of the spectrum is a process for periodic testing of the plans.

15. **Compliance.** This section of the standard contains two security objectives and ten security controls and addresses some of the compliance issues, including (i) compliance with legal requirements (for example applicable legislation such as copyright, data protection, protection of financial data); (ii) compliance with security policies and standards, and technical compliance (designated managers in the organization, along with system owners, must ensure compliance with security policies and standards); and (iii) Information systems audit considerations (even audit tools/ facilities must also be protected against unauthorized use).

Note: There are a number of "27001 Toolkits" on the market that provide a collection of ISMS implementation guidelines and sample documents that may help during the implementation process.

3.3.4 ISO/IEC 27003 Information Technology—Security Techniques—Information Security Management System Implementation Guidance (Draft)

ISO/IEC 27003 (at Final Committee Draft stage at press time) seeks to provide implementation guidance for organizations implementing the ISO/IEC 27001 standard. Publication was expected in 2010. According to the ISO committee developing the standard, the scope of ISO/IEC 27003 is to provide practical guidance for establishing and implementing an information security management system in accordance with ISO/IEC 27001. It describes the implementation of an ISMS focusing on the part from the first approval for the ISMS implementation in an organization to the beginning of the ISMS operations that correspond to the plan and do phases of an ISMS PDCA cycle. The standard includes the explanations of the design activities related to operating, monitoring, reviewing, and improving an ISMS. The key sections of the Committee Draft are shown in Table 3.4.

TABLE 3.4. Key Sections of ISO/IEC 27003

Section	Subsection
Obtain management approval for implementation of ISMS	Overview on management approval for implementation
	Define objectives, information security needs, business requirements for ISMS
	Define initial ISMS scope
	Create the business case & project setup
	Obtain management approval and commitment to Implement an ISMS
Defining ISMS scope and ISMS policy	Overview on defining ISMS scope and ISMS policy
	Define organizational boundaries
	Define information communication technology boundaries
	Define physical boundaries
	Complete boundaries for ISMS scope
	Develop the ISMS policy
Conducting business analysis	Overview on conducting a business analysis
	Defining information security requirements supporting the ISMS
	Creating information assets inventory
	Generating an information security assessment
Conducting risk assessment	Overview on conducting a risk assessment
	Risk assessment description
	Conduct risk assessment
	Plan risk treatment and select controls
Designing the ISMS	Overview on designing an ISMS
	Designing organizational security
	Designing ICT and physical security
	Designing the Monitoring and Measuring Requirements for ISMS recording
	Produce the ISMS Implementation Plan
Implementing the ISMS	Overview on ISMS Implementation
	Carry out ISMS Implementation Projects
	Implementation of monitoring
	ISMS Procedures and Control Documentation
	ISMS Measurement Procedure Documentation

3.3.5   ISO/IEC 27004 Information Technology—Security Techniques—Information Security Management—Measurement (Second Final Committee Draft)

ISO/IEC 27004 aims at covering information security management measurements. Work on the standard started in the middle of the decade, and publication was expected by early 2010. The standard provides input on how organizations can measure and report the effectiveness of their ISMSs. It covers both the security management processes defined in ISO/IEC 27001 and the security controls defined in ISO/IEC 27002.

According to the ISO committee developing the standard, it provides guidance and advice on the development and use of measures and measurement in order to assess the effectiveness of an ISMS, including the ISMS policy and objectives and security controls as specified in ISO/IEC 27001. ISO/IEC 27004 also aims at providing guidance on the specification and use of measurement techniques for providing assurance as regards the effectiveness of information security management systems. The standard is intended to be applicable to a wide range of organizations with a correspondingly wide range of information security management systems. It can be used to create a base for each organization to collect, analyze, and communicate data related to ISMS processes.

3.3.6   ISO/IEC 27005:2008 Information Technology—Security Techniques—Information Security Risk Management

ISO/IEC 27005:2008 provides guidelines for information security risk management. It supports the concepts specified in ISO/IEC 27001 and is designed to assist the implementation of information security based on a risk management approach. ISO/IEC 27005 offers general advice on choosing and using risk analysis or assessment methods without specifying any specific risk analysis method.

3.4   ISO/IEC 31000

There are a number of risk-related standards published by ISO and other standards bodies, as well as other standards that refer to risk management, as noted above, but until recently there was no central ISO document that provides a consistent approach to risk management. In 2005, ISO initiated a New Work Item Proposal (NWIP) to look at developing a guidance standard on risk management. Work started on the standard in 2006, and the document had progressed to a Draft International Standard by press time [NSA200701]. ISO 31000 Draft International Standard (DIS), "Risk management—Guidelines on principles and implementation of risk management," is intended to become the first international standard on risk management, upon approval. ISO 31000 provides generic guidelines for the principles involved in effective implementation of risk management. The standard also harmonizes risk management processes and definitions in existing and future standards. The standard can be applied to a wide range of activities, decisions, and operations of any public, private, or community enterprise, association, group, or individual. ISO 31000 provides guidelines on the principles and implementation of risk management in general (not IT or information security specific), namely it provides a general framework for managing risk exposures. It is not intended to be used for the purposes of certification.

In conjunction with developing ISO 31000, the ISO Risk Management Working Group is also looking at updating ISO/IEC Guide 73, "Risk Management—Vocabulary." This guide provides a basic vocabulary of the definitions of risk management generic terms. The guide aims to encourage a mutual and consistent understanding and a coherent approach to the description of activities relating to the management of risk [NSA200701]. The release of ISO/IEC Guide 73 CD2, which is a revision of the existing Guide 73 and provides a risk management vocabulary, is also expected in 2009 (ISO 31000 DIS refers to the definitions in Guide 73.)

ISO 31000 observes that to be most effective, an organization's risk management should adhere to the principles such as these [ISO31000]:

(a) Risk management should create value. Risk management should contribute to the demonstrable achievement of objectives and improvement of, for example, efficiency in operations, environmental protection, financial performance, corporate governance, human health and safety, product quality, legal and regulatory compliance, public acceptance, and reputation.

(b) Risk management should be an integral part of organizational processes. Risk management should be part of the responsibilities of management and an integral part of the normal organizational processes as well as of all project and change management processes. Risk management should not be a standalone activity or be separate from the main activities and processes of the organization.

(c) Risk management should be part of decision-making. Risk management can help prioritize actions and distinguish among alternative courses of action. Risk management helps decision makers make informed choices. Ultimately, risk management can help with decisions on whether a risk is unacceptable and whether risk controls will be adequate and effective.

(d) Risk management should explicitly address uncertainty. Risk management deals with those aspects of decision making that are uncertain, the nature of that uncertainty, and how it may be treated.

(e) Risk management should be systematic and structured. Risk management approaches should ensure where practicable that the results are consistent, comparable and reliable.

(f) Risk management should be based on the best available information. The inputs to the process of managing risk should be based on information sources such as experience, feedback, observation, forecasts, and expert judgment. However, decision makers should be informed of and may need to take into account any limitations of the data or modeling used or the possibility of divergence among experts.

(g) Risk management should be tailored. Risk management should be aligned with the organization's external and internal context and risk profile.

(h) Risk management should take into account human factors. The organization's risk management should recognize the capabilities, perceptions, and intentions of external and internal people that may facilitate or hinder attainment of the organization's objectives.

(i) Risk management should be transparent and inclusive. Appropriate and timely involvement and inclusion of stakeholders and, in particular, decision makers at all levels of the organization should ensure that risk management remains relevant and up to date. Involvement also allows stakeholders to be properly represented and to have their views taken into account in determining risk criteria, stakeholders' perceptions and levels of tolerable risk.

(j) Risk management should be dynamic, iterative, and responsive to change. As internal and external events occur, context and knowledge change, monitoring and review take place, new risks emerge, and others decrease. An organization should ensure that risk management continually senses and responds to change.

(k) Risk management should be capable of continual improvement and enhancement. Organizations should develop strategies to improve their risk management maturity alongside all other aspects of their organization.

Publication of the ISO 31000 Standard was underway at press time; by 2009 it had reached Final Draft International Standard (FDIS) status. AS/NZS 4360:2004 (see below) has been used as a point-of-departure in the formation of the ISO document. Figure 1.4 depicted the ISO 31000 process.

3.5 NIST STANDARDS

Table 3.5 identifies some of the applicable NIST standards; this is a comprehensive set of standards. In particular, NIST SP 800-16, NIST SP 800-24, NIST SP 800-30, and NIST SP 800-39 cover risk management. Subjects covered in the NIST standards include the following:

- Managing risk
  - Threats
  - Vulnerabilities
  - Risk
  - Relationships between threats, vulnerabilities, risks
- Threats from "authorized system users"
- Increased threats and vulnerabilities from connection to external systems and networks
  - "Hacker" threats
  - Malicious software programs and virus threats

TABLE 3.5. NIST Computer Security Standards (Partial List)

NIST	**SP (Special Publication) 800-12** An Introduction to Computer Security: The NIST Handbook

NIST **SP (Special Publication) 800-12** An Introduction to Computer Security: The NIST Handbook
SP 800-16 Information Technology Security Training Requirements: A Role- and Performance-Based Model
SP 800-18 Guide for Developing Security Plans for Information Technology Systems
SP 800-23 Guideline to Federal Organizations on Security Assurance and Acquisition/Use of Tested/Evaluated Products
SP 800-24 PBX Vulnerability Assessment - Finding Holes in Your PBX Before Someone Else Does
SP 800-25 Federal Agency Use of Public Key Technology for Digital Signatures and Authentication
SP 800-26 Security Self-Assessment Guide for Information Technology Systems
SP 800-30 Risk Management Guide for Information Technology Systems
SP 800-31 Intrusion Detection Systems (IDS)
SP 800-32 Introduction to Public Key Technology and the Federal PKI Infrastructure
SP 800-33 Underlying Technical Models for Information Technology Security
SP 800-34 Contingency Planning Guide for Information Technology Systems
SP 800-36 Guide to Selecting Information Technology Security Products
SP 800-37 Guide for the Security Certification and Accreditation of Federal Information Systems
SP 800-39 Managing Risk from Information Systems—An Organizational Perspective" (draft published April 2008)
SP 800-41 Guidelines on Firewalls and Firewall Policy
SP 800-42 Guideline on Network Security Testing
SP 800-43 Systems Administration Guidance for Windows 2000 Professional
SP 800-44 Guidelines on Securing Public Web Servers
DRAFT SP 800-53 Recommended Security Controls for Federal Information Systems
SP 800-55 Security Metrics Guide for Information Technology Systems
SP 800-61 Computer Security Incident Handling Guide
SP 800-64 Security Considerations in the Information System Development Life Cycle
SP 800-68 Guidance for Securing Microsoft Windows XP Systems for IT Professionals: A NIST Security Configuration Checklist

- Types of security controls (safeguards, countermeasures)
  - Management controls
  - Acquisition/development/installation/implementation controls
  - Operational controls

- Security awareness and training controls
- Technical controls
- How different categories of controls work together
- Examples of security controls for:
  - Confidentiality protection
  - Availability protection
  - Integrity protection
- Added security controls for connecting external systems and networks
- Protecting assets through IT security awareness and training programs
- Contingency-disaster recovery planning
  - Importance of plan to deal with unexpected problems
  - Importance of testing plan and applying lessons learned
- "Acceptable levels of risk" versus "absolute protection from risk"
- "Adequate" and "appropriate" controls
  - Unique protection requirements of IT systems and information
  - Severity, probability, and extent of potential harm
  - Cost effective/cost benefits
  - Reduction of risk versus elimination of risk
- Working together with other security disciplines
- Importance of internal and external audits, reviews, and evaluations in security decisions

Note: The material that follows in this subsection is based directly on NIST documentation.

3.5.1   NIST SP 800-16

NIST SP 800-16, "Information Technology Security Training Requirements: A Role- and Performance-Based Model," covers (among other topics) controls. Specifically, it covers Management Controls; Acquisition/Development/Installation/Implementation Controls; Operational Controls; and Technical Controls. Management Controls highlighted in NIST SP 800-16 include the following:

1. System/application-specific policies and procedures
2. Standard operating procedures
3. Personnel security
   a. Background investigations/security clearances
   b. Roles and responsibilities
   c. Separation of duties
   d. Role-based access controls

4. System rules of behavior contribute to an effective security environment
   a. Organization-specific user rules
   b. System-specific user rules
      i. Assignment and limitation of system privileges
      ii. Intellectual property/copyright issues
      iii. Remote access and work at home issues
      iv. Official versus unofficial system use
      v. Individual accountability
      vi. Sanctions or penalties for violations
5. Individual accountability contributes to system and information quality
   a. Individual acceptance of responsibilities
   b. Signed individual accountability agreements
6. IT security awareness and training
   a. Determining IT security training requirements for individuals
   b. Effect of IT security awareness and training programs on personal responsibility and positive behavioral changes
   c. "Computer ethics"
   d. System-specific user IT security training
7. User responsibilities for inappropriate actions of others

Acquisition/Development/Installation/Implementation Controls highlighted in NIST SP 800-16 include the following:

1. System life-cycle stages and functions
2. IT security requirements in system life-cycle stages
   a. Initiation stage
   b. Development stage
   c. Test and evaluation stage
   d. Implementation stage
   e. Operations stage
   f. Termination stage
3. Formal system security plan for management of a system
   a. Identification of system mission, purpose, and assets
   b. Definition of system protection needs
   c. Identification of responsible people
   d. Identification of system security controls in-place or planned and milestone dates for implementation of planned controls
4. Relationship of configuration and change management programs to IT security goals
5. Testing system security controls synergistically and certification
6. Senior manager approval (accredit) an IT system for operation

Operational Controls highlighted in NIST SP 800-16 include the following:

1. Physical and environmental protection
   a. Physical access controls
   b. Intrusion detection
   c. Fire/water/moisture/heat/electrical maintenance
   d. Mobile and portable systems
2. Marking, handling, shipping, storing, cleaning, and clearing
3. Contingency planning
   a. Importance of developing and testing contingency/disaster recovery plans
   b. Importance of users providing accurate information about processing needs, allowable downtime and applications that can wait
   c. Responsibility for backup copies of data files and software programs
   d. Simple user contingency planning steps

Technical Controls highlighted in NIST SP 800-16 include the following:

1. How technical (role-based access) controls support management (security rules) controls
   a. User identification and passwords/tokens
   b. User role-based access privileges
   c. Public access controls
2. How system controls can allow positive association of actions to individuals
   a. Audit trails
   b. System monitoring
3. Recognizing attacks by hackers, authorized or unauthorized users
   a. Effects of hacker attack on authorized users
   b. Unauthorized use or actions by authorized users
   c. Reporting incidents
4. User actions to prevent damage from malicious software or computer virus attacks
   a. Organization-specific procedures for reporting virus incidents
   b. Technical support and help from security incident response teams
   c. Software products to scan, detect, and remove computer viruses
5. Role of cryptography in protecting information

The standard also identifies some typical (but not necessarily all-inclusive) responsibilities of risk management personnel, based on practitioner's tier (junior, intermediate, and senior staff), as follows:

Junior Staff. Expected to

- Understand categories of risk and participate in the design and development of operational IT security program procedures
- Apply organization-specific IT security program elements to the implementation of the program and identify areas of weakness
- Participate in the review of an organization's IT security program and evaluate the extent to which the program is being managed effectively
- Identify general and system-specific IT security specifications that pertain to a particular system acquisition being planned.

Intermediate Staff. Expected to

- Establish acceptable levels of risk and translate the IT security program elements into operational procedures for providing adequate and appropriate protection of the organization's IT resources
- Analyze patterns of noncompliance and take appropriate administrative or programmatic actions to minimize security risks
- Develop compliance findings and recommendations, as well as security-related portions of acquisition documents

Advanced Staff. Expected to

- Design, develop, and direct the activities necessary to marshal the organizational structures, processes, and people for an effective IT security program implementation
- Direct the implementation of appropriate operational structures and processes to ensure an effective IT security program
- Direct the review of the management of an organization's IT security program, validate findings and recommendations, and establish follow-up monitoring for corrective actions
- Ensure that security-related portions of the system acquisition documents meet all identified security needs

3.5.2 NIST SP 800-30

NIST SP 800-30, "Risk Management Guide for Information Technology Systems," provides an overview of risk management, how it fits into the system development life cycle (SDLC), and the roles of individuals who support and use this process. It also describes the risk assessment methodology and nine primary steps in conducting a risk assessment of an IT system. The document also describes the risk mitigation process, including risk mitigation options and strategy, approach for control implementation, control categories, cost–benefit analysis, and residual risk. Finally, the document also discusses the good practice and need for an ongoing risk evaluation and assessment and the factors that will lead to a successful risk management program. NIST SP 800-30 is targeted to

- Senior management, the mission owners, who make decisions about the IT security budget
- (Federal) chief information officers, who ensure the implementation of risk management for (agency) IT systems and the security provided for these IT systems
- The Designated Approving Authority (DAA), who is responsible for the final decision on whether to allow operation of an IT system
- The IT security program manager, who implements the security program
- Information system security officers (ISSO), who are responsible for IT security
- IT system owners of system software and/or hardware used to support IT functions
- Information owners of data stored, processed, and transmitted by the IT systems
- Business or functional managers, who are responsible for the IT procurement process
- Technical support personnel (e.g., network, system, application, and database administrators; computer specialists; data security analysts), who manage and administer security for the IT systems
- IT system and application programmers, who develop and maintain code that could affect system and data integrity
- IT quality assurance personnel, who test and ensure the integrity of the IT systems and data
- Information system auditors, who audit IT systems
- IT consultants, who support clients in risk management

Risk assessment is the first process in the risk management methodology. Organizations use risk assessment to determine the extent of the potential threat and the risk associated with an IT system throughout its SDLC. The output of this process helps to identify appropriate controls for reducing or eliminating risk during the risk mitigation process.

As we have noted in Chapter 2, risk is a function of (a) the likelihood that a given threat source will exercise a particular potential vulnerability and (b) the resulting impact of that adverse event on the organization.

To determine the likelihood of a future adverse event, threats to an IT system must be analyzed in conjunction with the potential vulnerabilities and the controls in place for the IT system. Impact refers to the magnitude of harm that could be caused by a threat's exercise of a vulnerability. The level of impact is governed by the potential mission impacts and in turn produces a relative value for the IT assets and resources affected (e.g., the criticality and sensitivity of the IT system components and data). The risk assessment methodology encompasses nine primary steps, which are described in detail in the document:

- Step 1: System Characterization
- Step 2: Threat Identification
- Step 3: Vulnerability Identification
- Step 4: Control Analysis
- Step 5: Likelihood Determination
- Step 6: Impact Analysis
- Step 7: Risk Determination
- Step 8: Control Recommendations
- Step 9: Results Documentation.

Steps 2, 3, 4, and 6 can be conducted in parallel after Step 1 has been completed. Figure 1.2 in Chapter 1 depicts these steps and the inputs to and outputs from each step.

3.5.3 NIST SP 800-39

NIST SP 800-39, "Managing Risk from Information Systems—An Organizational Perspective" (draft published April 2008), describes a *Risk Management Framework (RMF)*. RMF provides organizations with a structured, yet flexible, process for managing risk related to the operation and use of information systems. The RMF can be used by organizations to determine the appropriate risk mitigation needed to protect the information systems and infrastructure supporting organizational mission/business processes. Figure 3.3 provides a graphical overview of the RMF along with the organization-wide inputs necessary for organizations to effectively apply the framework to the information systems supporting the organization's missions and business processes. There is a good degree of similarity between the NIST SP 800-39 approach and ISO/IEC 27001.

The RMF process includes (i) categorizing information and information systems with regard to mission and business impacts (FIPS 199 and Special Publication 800-60), (ii) selecting and documenting security controls needed for risk mitigation (FIPS 200 and Special Publication 800-53), (iii) implementing security controls in organizational information systems and supporting infrastructure (Special Publication 800-70), (iv) assessing security controls to determine effectiveness (Special Publication 800-53A), (v) authorizing information systems and supporting infrastructure and explicitly accepting mission/business risk (Special Publication 800-37), and (vi) monitoring of the security state of information systems and operational environments (Special Publications 800-53A and 800-37).

Stakeholders, as defined in NIST SP 800-39, include the following:

- Individuals with mission/business/information ownership responsibilities (e.g., agency heads, authorizing officials, information owners)

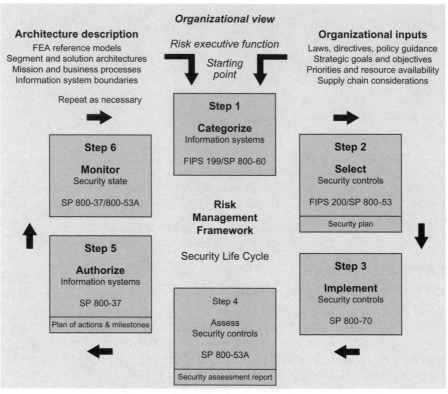

- FIPS Publication 199, *Standards for Security Categorization of Federal Information and Information Systems;*
- FIPS Publication 200, *Minimum Security Requirements for Federal Information and Information Systems;*
- NIST Special Publication 800-18, *Guide for Developing Security Plans for Federal Information Systems;*
- NIST Special Publication 800-30, *Revision 1, Guide for Conducting Risk Assessments;*
- NIST Special Publication 800-37, *Guide for the Security Certification and Accreditation of Federal Information Systems;*
- NIST Special Publication 800-53, *Recommended Security Controls for Federal Information Systems;*
- NIST Special Publication 800-53A, *Guide for Assessing the Security Controls in Federal Information Systems;*
- NIST Special Publication 800-59, *Guideline for Identifying an Information System as a National Security System;*
- NIST Special Publication 800-60, *Guide for Mapping Types of Information and Information Systems to Security Categories;*
- NIST Special Publication 800-70, *Security Configuration Checklists Program for IT Products: Guidance for Checklists Users and Developers;*
- NIST Special Publication 800-100, *Information Security Handbook, A Guide for Managers.*

FIGURE 3.3. NIST SP 800-39 Risk Management Framework (RMF).

- Individuals with information system/security management responsibilities (e.g., chief information officers, senior agency information security officers, security managers)
- Individuals with information system design and development responsibilities (e.g., program managers, enterprise architects, information technology product vendors, system integrators)
- Individuals with information system/security implementation and operational responsibilities (e.g., information system owners, system security officers)
- Individuals with information system/security assessment and monitoring responsibilities (e.g., auditors, assessors, Inspectors General, evaluators, validators, and certification agents)

Note: Authorizing officials are officials within an organization that have the authority to formally assume responsibility for operating an information system at an acceptable level of risk to organizational operations, organizational assets, individuals, other organizations, and the Nation. Authorizing officials are accountable for their authorization decisions.

NIST SP 800-39 makes the case that to help protect organizations from the adverse effects of ongoing, serious, and increasingly sophisticated *threats* to information systems, organizations should employ a risk-based protection strategy. Risk-based protection strategies are characterized by identifying, understanding, mitigating as appropriate, and explicitly accepting the residual risks associated with the operation and use of information systems. Risk-based protection strategies require authorizing officials to

- Determine, with input from the risk executive function and senior agency information security officer, the appropriate balance between the risks from and the benefits of using information systems to carry out organizational mission/business processes
- Approve the selection of security controls for information systems and the supporting infrastructure necessary to achieve this balance
- Take responsibility for the information security solutions agreed upon and implemented within the information systems supporting the organization's mission/business processes
- Acknowledge, understand, and explicitly accept the risks to organizational operations and assets, individuals, other organizations, and the Nation that result from the operation and use of information systems
- Be accountable for the results of information security-related decisions
- Monitor the continued acceptability of organizational risk from information systems over time

Risk-based protection strategies, as described in NIST SP 800-39, focus on managing risks from information systems based on real-world conditions and making the management decisions explicit—an essential requirement for establishing and maintaining trust among organizations. A primary consideration of any risk-based protection strategy is to effectively integrate risks from the operation and use of information systems into existing organizational processes dealing with other types of organizational risks (e.g., program and investment risks). This integrated approach moves the management of information system-related risks from an isolated process to an integral part of an overall process for managing the totality of risks organization-wide. Risk-based protection strategies are necessary to help ensure that organizations are adequately protected against the growing sophistication of threats to information systems. The serious nature of the threats, along with the dynamic environment in which modern organizations operate, demand flexible, scalable, and mobile defenses that can be tailored to rapidly changing conditions including the emergence of new threats, vulnerabilities, and technologies. Risk-based protection strategies support the overall goals and objectives of organizations, can be tightly coupled to enterprise architectures, and can operate effectively within system development life cycles. By empowering senior leaders to make explicit risk management decisions, these strategies also provide the flexibility necessary for the selection and employment of appropriate security controls for organizational information systems to achieve common-sense, cost-effective information security solutions.

NIST SP 800-39 notes that organizations are becoming increasingly reliant on information system services and information provided by external providers as well as partnerships established to carry out important mission and business processes. The need for *trust relationships* among organizations arises both from the partnerships established to share information and conduct business and from an organization's use of external providers of information and information system services. In many cases, while external providers bring greater productivity and cost efficiencies to the organization, they may also bring greater risk. This risk must be appropriately managed given the mission and business goals and objectives. Relationships among cooperating organizations are established and maintained in a variety of ways, for example, through joint ventures, business partnerships, outsourcing arrangements (i.e., through contracts, interagency and intra-agency agreements, lines of business arrangements), licensing agreements, and/or supply chain exchanges (i.e., supply chain collaborations or partnerships). The growing dependence on external service providers and partnerships with domestic and international public and private sector participants presents new challenges for organizations, especially in the area of information security. These challenges include

- Defining the types of services/information to be provided to the organization or the types of information to be shared/exchanged in partnering arrangements

- Describing how the services/information are to be protected in accordance with the security requirements of the organization
- Obtaining the relevant information from external providers and from business partners needed to support and maintain trust (including visibility into risk decisions to understand the participating/cooperating organization's risk management strategies and risk tolerance)
- Determining if the risk to organizational operations and assets, individuals, other organizations, or the nation resulting from the use of the services or information or the participation in the partnership is at an acceptable level

NIST SP 800-39 also notes that organizations need to manage risk exposures from supply chains. A supply chain is a system of organizations, people, activities, information, and resources, possibly international in scope, that provides products or services to consumers. Domestic and international supply chains are becoming increasingly important to the national and economic security interests of the United States because of the growing dependence on products and services produced or maintained in worldwide markets. Uncertainty in the supply chain and the growing sophistication and diversity of international cyber threats increase the potential for a range of adverse effects on organizational operations and assets, individuals, other organizations, and the nation. Global commercial supply chains provide adversaries with opportunities to manipulate information technology products that are routinely used by public and private sector organizations (e.g., federal agencies, contractors) in the information systems that support U.S. critical infrastructure applications. Malicious activity at any point in the supply chain poses downstream risks to the mission/business processes that are supported by those information systems. These risk exposures include

- The introduction of exploitable vulnerabilities into information systems when products containing malicious code and other malware are integrated into the systems
- Inability/difficulty in determining the trustworthiness of information systems that depend upon commercial information technology products to provide many of the security controls necessary to ensure adequate security
- Inability/difficulty in determining the trustworthiness of information systems service providers (e.g., installation, operations, and maintenance) that provide many of the security controls necessary to ensure adequate security

3.6 AS/NZS 4360

AS/NZS 4360:2004 is a risk management standard published jointly by Australia Standards and New Zealand Standards; the companion document

HB 436:2004, Risk Management Guidelines, expands on AS/NZS 4360 and is also a relevant reference. AS/NZS 4360 (originally published as AS/NZS 4360:1995, with second edition 1999 and third edition 2004) describes an approach to risk management process, but it is not a goal of the standard to create uniformity in risk management systems; the design and specific implementation of the risk management system is influenced by the detailed needs of an organization, its objectives, products and services. The standard provides a generic guide for establishing and implementing the risk management process involving identification, analysis, assessment, treatment, and continuous risk monitoring. The standard has broad applicability including commercial organizations, enterprises, and government entities.

In AS/NZS 4360:2004, "risk" is defined as "the chance of something happening that will have an impact on objectives" (recall that in this text, this chance is known as the probability of the risk exposure event.) Risk is "measured in terms of a combination of the consequences of an event and their likelihood" (in this text, risk is the measure of the expected loss). "Risk management" is defined as "the culture, processes, and structures that are directed toward realizing potential opportunities whilst managing adverse effects." "Risk sharing" is defined as "sharing with another party the burden of loss, or benefit of gain from a particular risk." "Stakeholders" are persons and organizations "who may affect, be affected by, or *perceive* themselves to be affected by a decision, activity or risk" [STA200401]. Controls aim at minimizing negative risk *and* enhancing positive opportunities.

The AS/NZS 4360 process has a first step that calls for the need to "communicate and consult." It proposes a "dialogue with stakeholders . . . focused on consultation rather than a one-way flow of information from the decision maker to other stakeholders." The standard acknowledges that stakeholder perceptions are as important as the estimates of experts and insiders. Other steps (seven in all) include "establish the context, identify risks, analyze risks, evaluate risks, treat risks, and monitor and review" [KLO200401]. Risk management involves managing to achieve an appropriate balance between realizing opportunities for gains while minimizing losses. It is an integral part of good management practice and an essential element of good corporate governance.

Figure 1.5 in Chapter 1 depicted pictorially the risk management steps embodied in the standard.

REFERENCES

[COL200701] L. Coles-Kemp, R. E. Overill, "On the role of the facilitator in information security, risk assessment," Journal of Computer Virology (2007) 3:143–148, DOI 10.1007/s11416-007-0040-6, *EICAR 2007 Best Academic Papers*, Springer-Verlag, France, 2007.

[IMP200801] ISO27k Implementers Forum (http://www.iso27001security.com), 2008.

[KLO200401] H. F. Kloman, *Risk Management Reports*, November 2004, Volume 31, No. 11.

[NIS199801] NIST SP 800-16, *Information Technology Security Training Requirements: A Role- and Performance-Based Model*, M. Wilson, D. E. de Zafra, S. I. Pitcher, J. D. Tressler, and J. B. Ippolito, editors, NIST, April 1998.

[NSA200701] L. Hendy, ISO 31000 Risk Management Guidance Standard, NSAI, 1 Swift Square, Northwood, Santry Dublin 9, Ireland, July 2007.

[STA200401] Standards Australia, GPO Box 5420, Sydney, NSW 2001, Australia. Also, Standards New Zealand, Private Bag 2439, Wellington 6020, New Zealand. www.standards.com.au.

APPENDIX 3A: ORGANIZATION FOR ECONOMIC COOPERATION AND DEVELOPMENT (OECD) GUIDELINES FOR THE SECURITY OF INFORMATION SYSTEMS AND NETWORKS: TOWARD A CULTURE OF SECURITY

This appendix includes the OECD guidelines referenced in the ISO27k standards. The appendix is based directly on OECD documentation.

Pursuant to Article 1 of the Convention signed in Paris on 14th December 1960, and which came into force on 30th September 1961, the Organization for Economic Cooperation and Development (OECD) shall promote policies designed to

- Achieve the highest sustainable economic growth and employment and a rising standard of living in member countries, while maintaining financial stability, and thus to contribute to the development of the world economy
- Contribute to sound economic expansion in member as well as nonmember countries in the process of economic development
- Contribute to the expansion of world trade on a multilateral, nondiscriminatory basis in accordance with international obligations

The original member countries of the OECD are Austria, Belgium, Canada, Denmark, France, Germany, Greece, Iceland, Ireland, Italy, Luxembourg, the Netherlands, Norway, Portugal, Spain, Sweden, Switzerland, Turkey, the United Kingdom, and the United States. The following countries became Members subsequently through accession at the dates indicated: Japan (28th April 1964), Finland (28th January 1969), Australia (7th June 1971), New Zealand (29th May 1973), Mexico (18th May 1994), the Czech Republic (21st December 1995), Hungary (7th May 1996), Poland (22nd November 1996), Korea (12th December 1996), and the Slovak Republic (14th December 2000). The Commission of the European Communities takes part in the work of the OECD (Article 13 of the OECD Convention).

The Security Guidelines were first completed in 1992 and were reviewed in 1997. The current review was undertaken in 2001 by the Working Party on Information Security and Privacy (WPISP), pursuant to a mandate from the Committee for Information, Computer, and Communications Policy (ICCP), and accelerated in the aftermath of the September 11, 2001 tragedy. Drafting was undertaken by an Expert Group of the WPISP which met in Washington, DC, on 10–11 December 2001, Sydney on 12–13 February 2002, and Paris on 4 and 6 March 2002. The WPISP met in Paris on 5–6 March 2002, 22–23 April 2002 and 25–26 June 2002. The present *OECD Guidelines for the Security of Information Systems and Networks: Towards a Culture of Security* were adopted as a Recommendation of the OECD Council at its 1037th Session on 25 July 2002.

1. **Awareness: Participants should be aware of the need for security of information systems and networks and what they can do to enhance security.** Awareness of the risks and available safeguards is the first line of defense for the security of information systems and networks. Information systems and networks can be affected by both internal and external risks. Participants should understand that security failures may significantly harm systems and networks under their control. They should also be aware of the potential harm to others arising from interconnectivity and interdependency. Participants should be aware of the configuration of, and available updates for, their system, its place within networks, good practices that they can implement to enhance security, and the needs of other participants.

2. **Responsibility: All participants are responsible for the security of information systems and networks.** Participants depend upon interconnected local and global information systems and networks and should understand their responsibility for the security of those information systems and networks. They should be accountable in a manner appropriate to their individual roles. Participants should review their own policies, practices, measures, and procedures regularly and assess whether these are appropriate to their environment. Those who develop, design, and supply products and services should address system and network security and distribute appropriate information including updates in a timely manner so that users are better able to understand the security functionality of products and services and their responsibilities related to security.

3. **Response: Participants should act in a timely and cooperative manner to prevent, detect and respond to security incidents.** Recognizing the interconnectivity of information systems and networks and the potential for rapid and widespread damage, participants should act in a timely and cooperative manner to address security incidents. They should share information about threats and vulnerabilities, as appropriate, and implement procedures for rapid and effective cooperation to prevent, detect and respond to security incidents. Where permissible, this may involve cross-border information sharing and cooperation.

4. **Ethics: Participants should respect the legitimate interests of others.** Given the pervasiveness of information systems and networks in our

societies, participants need to recognize that their action or inaction may harm others. Ethical conduct is therefore crucial, and participants should strive to develop and adopt best practices and to promote conduct that recognizes security needs and respects the legitimate interests of others.

5. **Democracy: The security of information systems and networks should be compatible with essential values of a democratic society.** Security should be implemented in a manner consistent with the values recognized by democratic societies including the freedom to exchange thoughts and ideas, the free flow of information, the confidentiality of information and communication, the appropriate protection of personal information, openness and transparency.

6. **Risk assessment: Participants should conduct risk assessments.** Risk assessment identifies threats and vulnerabilities and should be sufficiently broad-based to encompass key internal and external factors, such as technology, physical and human factors, policies, and third-party services with security implications. Risk assessment will allow determination of the acceptable level of risk and assist the selection of appropriate controls to manage the risk of potential harm to information systems and networks in light of the nature and importance of the information to be protected. Because of the growing interconnectivity of information systems, risk assessment should include consideration of the potential harm that may originate from others or be caused to others.

7. **Security design and implementation: Participants should incorporate security as an essential element of information systems and networks.** Systems, networks, and policies need to be properly designed, implemented, and coordinated to optimize security. A major, but not exclusive, focus of this effort is the design and adoption of appropriate safeguards and solutions to avoid or limit potential harm from identified threats and vulnerabilities. Both technical and nontechnical safeguards and solutions are required and should be proportionate to the value of the information on the organization's systems and networks. Security should be a fundamental element of all products, services, systems, and networks, as well as an integral part of system design and architecture. For end users, security design and implementation consists largely of selecting and configuring products and services for their system.

8. **Security management: Participants should adopt a comprehensive approach to security management.** Security management should be based on risk assessment and should be dynamic, encompassing all levels of participants' activities and all aspects of their operations. It should include forward-looking responses to emerging threats and address prevention, detection, and response to incidents, systems recovery, ongoing maintenance, review, and audit. Information system and network security policies, practices, measures, and procedures should be coordinated and

integrated to create a coherent system of security. The requirements of security management depend upon the level of involvement, the role of the participant, the risk involved, and system requirements.

9. **Reassessment: Participants should review and reassess the security of information systems and networks, and should make appropriate modifications to security policies, practices, measures, and procedures.** New and changing threats and vulnerabilities are continuously discovered. Participants should continually review, reassess, and modify all aspects of security to deal with these evolving risks.

CHAPTER 4

A SURVEY OF AVAILABLE INFORMATION SECURITY RISK MANAGEMENT METHODS AND TOOLS

As we have noted, the ability to manage risk is one of the key business requirements of any organization. Risk management methods and tools enable the organization to plan and implement programs to maximize their opportunities and to control the impact of potential threats. This chapter provides an overview of available security risk analysis methods; tools are identified but not described.[19] This chapter is abstracted from information made available by the respective owners of the various systems.

4.1 OVERVIEW

A risk management method is a well-defined process (a sequences of activities) typically, but not always, based on a published standard—that systematizes the five phases or macro-tasks that comprise risk management, namely,

- (Ongoing) identification of threats, vulnerabilities, or (risk) events impacting the organization's IT assets
- Risk assessment
- Risk mitigation planning
- Risk mitigation implementation
- Evaluation of the mitigation's effectiveness

A method or framework for managing risks aims at assisting an organization manage its risk exposures effectively through the application of the risk management process at various levels within of the organization. The method

[19]The reader should be able to easily find online information for these tools.

Information Technology Risk Management in Enterprise Environments: A Review of Industry Practices and a Practial Guide to Risk Management Teams, by Jake Kouns and Daniel Minoli
Copyright © 2010 John Wiley & Sons, Inc.

or framework should ensure that risk information derived from these processes is adequately reported and used as a basis for decision-making at all relevant organizational levels [ISO31000].

Security risk management/risk analysis methods include (but are not limited to) the ones shown on the left column of Table 4.1. A number of these (but not all) are discussed in this chapter. One of the better-known methods is *Control Objectives for Information and Related Technology* (COBIT®) which provides a comprehensive model guiding the implementation of IT governance processes/systems, including information security controls. Another well-known method is *Operationally Critical Threat, Asset, and Vulnerability Evaluation* (OCTAVE®), which is a risk-based strategic assessment and planning technique for security, published by CERT [CER200901]. COBIT and OCTAVE are discussed in more detail in Chapter 5.

As seen in Table 4.1, there is no dearth of guides, methodical approaches, and support tools, all of which aim at an objective analysis intended to determine the amount of risk that various IT assets and systems are subject to. The challenge of all these approaches is the complexity of the problem they face, a complexity in the sense that there are many elements to be considered and that, if they are not rigorous, the conclusions will be unreliable [MAR200601]. Since most methods and approaches entail some levels of complexity, this situation may in principle create impedance to their effective adoption and application, especially for smaller firms. However, the downside of not implementing risk management should be self-evident. Fortunately, various standards and good practices exist for the creation these methods. Some examples include (also see Chapter 3) [ENI200801]

- A method based on a national standard
- A method based on an international standard (e.g., [ISO27000])
- A method based on a de facto standard (e.g., [OCTAVE])
- A method based on a sector standard
- A method based on an individual basic protection profile for the IT-systems of an organization
- Adoption of an already existing risk analysis of similar systems (e.g., based on an existing protection profiles according to common criteria [CC][20]).

---

[20]During the 1990s, evaluation criteria to assess the security of an information system proliferated worldwide. This proliferation had the potential to hinder international trade. Eventually, this situation brought about an agreement for convergence, called "Common Criteria for Information Technology Security Evaluation," known for short as "Common Criteria (CC). In Baltimore (Maryland, USA) on 23 May 2000, Germany, Australia, Canada, Spain, the United States, Finland, France, Greece, Italy, Norway, New Zealand, the Netherlands, and the United Kingdom ratified their adherence to the Arrangement on the Recognition of the Common Criteria Certificates in the field of Information Technology Security (hereinafter, the Arrangement). Later, they were joined by Israel, Sweden, Austria, Turkey, Hungary, Japan, the Czech Republic, Korea, Singapore, and India. The CC allow (i) the definition of security functions in products and systems and (ii) the determination of the criteria for evaluating (the quality) of these functions.

TABLE 4.1. Risk Management/Risk Analysis Methods and Tools

Risk Management Methods	Risk Management Tools
• Austrian IT Security Handbook	• Acuity Stream
• Control Objectives for Information and Related Technology (COBIT)	• Archer
• CCTA Risk Assessment and Management Methodology (CRAMM)	• Axur
	• Callio
	• Casis
• Dutch A&K Analysis	• Citicus ONE
• EBIOS	• Cobra
• ETSI	• CRAMM
• Factor Analysis of Information Risk (FAIR)	• EAR / PILAR
• Fundamental Information Risk Management (FIRM)	• EBIOS
	• GSTool
• Failure Modes and Effects Analysis (FMEA)	• GxSGSI
• Facilitated Risk Assessment Process (FRAP)	• ISAMM
• Information Risk Assessment Methodologies (IRAM)	• MIGRA
	• Modulo Risk Manager
• ISAMM	• OCTAVE
• Information Security Forum (ISF) Methods	• Proteus Enterprise
• ISO TR 13335 (a Technical Report which is a precursor to ISO/IEC 27005);	• RA2 Art of Risk
• ISO/IEC 27001	• Resolver Ballot
• ISO/IEC 31000	• Resolver Risk
• IT Grundschutz	• Risicare
• Metodologia de Analisis y Gestion de Riesgos de los Sistemas de Informacion (MAGERIT)	• Riskwatch
	• RM Studio
• MEHARI	• Risk Manager
• MIGRA	• RiskOptix
• NIST SP 800-30	• RSAM
• NIST SP 800-39	• vsRisk
• NSA IAM / IEM / IA-CMM	
• OCTAVE	
• Open Source Security Testing Methodology Manual (OSSTMM)	
• Practical Threat Analysis (PTA)	
• Simple to Apply Risk Assessment (SARA)	
• Security Officers Management and Analysis Project (SOMAP)	
• Simplified Process for Risk Identification (SPRINT)	

In this context, here is a noteworthy observation from Microsoft [MIC200601]:

> The definition of acceptable risk, and the approach to manage risk, varies for every organization. There is no right or wrong answer; there are many risk management models in use today. Each model has tradeoffs that balance accuracy, resources, time, complexity, and subjectivity. Investing in a risk management process—with a solid framework and clearly defined roles and responsibilities—prepares the organization to articulate priorities, plan to mitigate threats, and address the next threat or vulnerability to the business.

Products (tools) are computer-based systems that provide instantiations of the risk management methods. Some organizations may opt to generate their own specific instantiations of a method, with the goal of arriving at a tool that is most suitable for them. With this approach, national or international standards (or a combination) are taken as a foundation while existing organization-specific security mechanisms, policies, and/or infrastructure can be adapted to work within the framework of the selected method and be the basis of the DIY (do-it-yourself) tool. However, given the plethora of available risk management methods, perhaps the organization is best served by an existing method developed by industry consensus, or at least by industry input. One advantage of this industry-based approach is that once the (basic setup) work is done and the effort is expended, the added benefit is that certification against the methodology (e.g., ISO27000) can also be secured, giving stakeholders and potential business partners a comfort level about the integrity of information management.

The information included in this chapter is based in large measure on material published by various owner/proponents of these methods and tools; references are noted.

4.2   RISK MANAGEMENT/RISK ANALYSIS METHODS

4.2.1   Austrian IT Security Handbook

This 1998 document from the Bundeskanzleramt (Austrian Federal Chancellery) is comprised of two parts. Part 1 provides a description of the IT security management process, including the need for development of security policies, risk analysis, design of security concepts, implementation of the security plan, and follow-up activities. Part 2 is a collection of 230 baseline security measures. A tool supporting the implementation is available as a prototype. The Austrian IT Security Handbook was originally developed for government organizations and is now available for all types of business. The handbook is compliant with ISO/IEC IS 13335, the German IT-Grundschutzhandbuch and partly with ISO/IEC IS 17799 [ENI200801, AUS200901]. The handbook contains a generic description of risk assessment, but does not specify a special method. The document covers the following risk management-related topics:

- Risk identification
- Risk analysis
- Risk evaluation
- Risk assessment
- Risk treatment
- Risk acceptance
- Risk communication

4.2.2 CCTA Risk Assessment and Management Methodology (CRAMM)

CRAMM is a risk analysis method originally developed by the British government organization CCTA (Central Communication and Telecommunication Agency), now renamed the Office of Government Commerce (OGC). A tool having the same name supports the method: CRAMM. The CRAMM method is rather difficult to use without the CRAMM tool [ENI200801]. Based on the UK Government's preferred risk assessment methodology, CRAMM has been completely redeveloped by Siemens Enterprise Communications Limited to become a total information security toolkit that includes [SIE200901]

- A comprehensive risk assessment tool that is fully compliant with ISO 27001
- A range of help tools to support information security managers to plan and manage security
- Wizards to rapidly create pro-forma information security policies and other related documentation
- Tools that support the key processes in business continuity management
- A database of over 3000 security controls referenced to relevant risks and ranked by effectiveness and cost
- Companion tools to help achieve certification or compliance to ISO 27001

CRAMM is the UK government's preferred risk analysis method, but it is also used in many other countries by large organizations, such as government bodies and industry. CRAMM includes a comprehensive range of risk assessment tools that are fully compliant with ISO 27001 and which address tasks such as

- Asset dependency modeling
- Business impact assessment

- Identifying and assessing threats and vulnerabilities
- Assessing levels of risk
- Identifying required and justified controls on the basis of the risk assessment

CRAMM's risk assessment tools can be used to answer single questions, to look at organizations, processes, applications and systems or to investigate complete infrastructures or organizations. Users have the option of a rapid risk assessment tool or a full, more rigorous, analysis.

The risk assessment tools allow the user to explore different issues and answer many different questions. Examples include [SIE200901]

- Determining if there is a requirement for specific controls, for example, strong authentication, encryption, power protection, or hardware redundancy
- Identify the security functionality required for a new application
- Developing the security requirements for an outsourcing or managed service agreement
- Reviewing the requirements for physical and environmental security at a new site
- Examining the implications of allowing users to connect to the Internet
- Demonstrating compliance with legislation such as the Data Protection Act
- Developing a security policy for a new system
- Auditing the suitability and status of security controls on an existing system
- Demonstrating to an ISO 27001 auditor that a "ISO 27001-compliant" risk assessment has been undertaken and that appropriate security controls have been identified

CRAMM contains a variety of tools to help evaluate the findings of a risk assessment, including

- Determining the relative priority of controls
- Recording the estimated costs of implementing the controls
- Modeling changes to the risk assessment, using "what-if?" calculations
- Backtracking through the risk assessment to show the justification for specific controls

CRAMM provides a staged and disciplined approach embracing both technical (e.g., IT hardware and software) and nontechnical (e.g., physical and human) aspects of security. In order to assess these components, a CRAMM-based process is divided into three stages:

- Asset identification and valuation
- Threat and vulnerability assessment
- Countermeasure selection and recommendation

CRAMM enables the reviewer to identify the physical (e.g., IT hardware), software (e.g., application packages), data (e.g., the information held on the IT system), and location assets that make up the information system. Each of these assets can be valued. Physical assets are valued in terms of the replacement cost. Data and software assets are valued in terms of the impact that would result if the information were to be unavailable, destroyed, disclosed, or modified. Having understood the extent of potential problems, the next stage is to identify just how likely such problems are to occur. CRAMM covers the full range of deliberate and accidental threats that may affect information systems, including:

- Hacking
- Viruses
- Failures of equipment or software
- Willful damage or terrorism
- Errors by people

This stage concludes by calculating the level of the underlying or actual risk.

CRAMM contains a countermeasure library consisting of over 3000 detailed countermeasures organized into over 70 logical groupings. The CRAMM software uses the measures of risks determined during the previous stage and compares them against the security level (a threshold level associated with each countermeasure) in order to identify if the risks are sufficiently great to justify the installation of a particular countermeasure. CRAMM provides a series of help facilities, including backtracking, "what if?", prioritization functions, and reporting tools to assist with the implementation of countermeasures and the active management of the identified risks.

4.2.3 Dutch A&K Analysis

The Afhankelijkheids- en Kwetsbaarheidsanalyse (A&K analysis) method was developed by the Rijks Computer Centrum (RCC). The Dutch Ministry of Internal Affairs completed the development in 1996 and published a handbook describing the method (the method has not been updated since that time.) The A&K analysis is the preferred method for risk analysis by Dutch government bodies; Dutch companies also often use A&K analysis.

4.2.4 EBIOS

EBIOS® (Expression des Besoins et Identification des Objectifs de Sécurité) (Expression of Needs and Identification of Security Objectives) is a method published by the Central Information Systems Security Division of France (Direction Centrale de la Sécurité des Systémes d'Information, Premier Ministre). There is also a freeware tool supporting the method. It was created in 1995 and was based on tested experience in information systems security (ISS) consulting and support for contracting authorities. The EBIOS method can be used to assess and treat risks relating to ISS. It can also be used to communicate this information within the organization and to partners, and therefore it assists in the ISS risk management process. EBIOS is also a negotiation and decision-making tool: It provides information to support decision-making (detailed descriptions, strategic stakes, detailed risks with their impact on the organization, and explicit security objectives and requirements) [EBI200301].

EBIOS facilitates increased awareness by stakeholders involved in a project (top management, financial, legal or human resources departments, contracting authorities, prime contractors, users), increases the involvement of information system actors, and standardizes the vocabulary. EBIOS is compatible with international standards such as ISO/IEC 13335, ISO/IEC 15408, and ISO/IEC 17799. EBIOS is used in the public sector (all ministries and bodies under their administration) and in the private sector (consulting firms, small and large companies) in France and abroad (European Union, Quebec, Belgium, Tunisia, Luxembourg, among others.) EBIOS can be used during the design phase or on an existing system. At the design stage, it can be integrated into project management to determine security specifications as the project progresses. For an existing system, it takes into account the existing security measures and integrates security into the operating systems.

The EBIOS best practices describe the use of the results for the various security approaches:

- Preparing ISS master plans
- Preparing ISS policies
- Preparing certification policies
- Writing protection profiles
- Writing security target descriptions
- Writing System-Specific Security Requirement Statements (SSRS) for NATO
- Comparison between the study prior to design and the study of existing systems, etc.

Unlike scenario-based risk analysis approaches, the structured approach of the EBIOS method allows the component elements of risks to be identified (entities and vulnerabilities, attack methods and threat agents, essential elements and sensitivities, and so on). This methodical construction supports an exhaustive risk analysis. EBIOS is designed to provide ongoing risk analysis and global ISS consistency. The specific study of a system can be based on a global study of the organization; a study can be updated at regular intervals to provide continuous risk management; the study of a comparable system can also be used as a reference [EBI200301].

The EBIOS method can be adapted to any specific context and adjusted to existing methodological tools and habits without compromising the general philosophy of the approach. Its scope covers everything from a global study of an organization's complete information system to a detailed study of a specific system (website, electronic messaging, recruitment management, etc.). Selected parts of the approach can be used separately to conduct, for example, a vulnerability analysis (just the threat study) or to identify the strategic elements (context study, nondetailed expression of needs, non-detailed study of threats).

The EBIOS approach consists of a cycle of five phases [ENI200801]:

- Phase 1 deals with context analysis in terms of global business process dependency on the information system (contribution to global stakes, accurate perimeter definition, relevant decomposition into information flows and functions).
- Both the security needs analysis and threat analysis are conducted in phases 2 and 3 in a strong dichotomy, yielding an objective vision of their conflicting nature.
- In phases 4 and 5, this conflict, once arbitrated through traceable reasoning, yields an objective diagnostic on risks. The necessary and sufficient security objectives (and further security requirements) are then stated, proof of coverage is furnished, and residual risks is made explicit.

4.2.5 ETSI Threat Vulnerability and Risk Analysis (TVRA) Method

The European Telecommunications Standards Institute (ETSI) has developed a methodology that is particularly well suited to networking applications [ETSI200301]. The method is depicted in Figure 4.1.

The core of the ETSI model starts with the identification of the inventory of IT assets. Each asset in a system has a certain importance such that an attack on the asset would have a great or lesser impact. A value between 1 and 3 can be assigned to this impact as follows:

1. Low: The concerned party is not harmed very strongly, and the possible damage is slight.
2. Medium: The threat addresses the interests of providers and/or subscribers and cannot be neglected.
3. High: A basis of business is threatened, and severe damage might occur in this context.

The next step is to classify the vulnerabilities and threats. A systematic scrutiny of an environment (or even a networking standard) allows one to

FIGURE 4.1. ETSI TS102 165-1 Method.

identify a range of possible security weaknesses. Such weaknesses are only be categorized as vulnerabilities if a plausible threat would exploit that weakness. For each potential weakness, it is necessary to consider the following aspects in order to identify it as a vulnerability:

- Availability of knowledge necessary to understand and manipulate the asset
- The existence of a possible agent that could exploit the weakness and its capability to do so in terms of
  - The time need to mount an attack
  - The expertise required to mount an attack
  - The availability of an opportunity to mount an attack
  - The complexity of any equipment required for an attack

Mapping tables can be used to formulate a vulnerability rating for each attack type by considering the attack characteristics above.

The next step in the method is to quantify the likelihood and the impact of threats. The Vulnerability Rating defined in the previous step is used to determine the likelihood of a particular type of attack being made on an asset. See Table 4.2.

The step that follows deals with the determination of the risk. The intensity of an attack may of itself be a factor in determining risk to the system or asset under attack. The TVRA method assigns values to the various levels of intensity as follows:

TABLE 4.2. Quantification of the Likelihood and the Impact of Threats

Vulnerability Rating	Likelihood of Attack	Value
Beyond high	Unlikely	1
High	Unlikely	1
Moderate	Possible	2
Basic	Likely	3
No rating	Likely	3

TABLE 4.3. Determining the Impact of an Attack

Asset Impact	Threat Intensity		
	0	1	2
1	1	2	3
2	2	3	3
3	3	3	3

1. A single instance of the attack is expected
2. Moderate intensity of attack is expected
3. High intensity of attack is expected

Using these intensity values and the asset impact indicators developed in the earlier step, a numerical value representing the impact of an attack is determined as shown in Table 4.3.

The product of these impact values and the likelihood of occurrence serves as a measurement of the risk that the concerned asset might be compromised, as shown in Table 4.4.

The final step is to specify countermeasures. Security countermeasures are assets that are added to a system in order to reduce the risk of one or more aspect of security being compromised. The purpose of countermeasures is:

• To reduce the likelihood of an attack or
• To reduce the impact of an attack

Countermeasures are normally specified as internal changes to a standardized system. Although the TVRA method will identify the security risks that need to be countered, it will not automatically define the necessary countermeasures. These can only be determined by inspection and experience. Once countermeasures have been specified, it is essential that a further analysis of the risks is carried out as it is possible that the countermeasures themselves will introduce new weaknesses to the system specification. Countermeasures can be specified in a number of different places depending on the nature of measures themselves.

TABLE 4.4. Qualitative Measure of Risk

Value	Classification	Explanation
1, 2, 3	Minor	No essential assets are concerned, or the attack is unlikely. Threats causing minor risks have no primary need for countermeasures.
4	Major	Threats on relevant assets are likely to occur, although their impact is unlikely to be fatal. Major risks should be handled seriously and should be minimized by the appropriate use of countermeasures.
6, 9	Critical	The primary interests of the providers and/or subscribers are threatened and the effort required from a potential attacker to implement the threat(s) is not high. Critical risks should be minimized with highest priority.

ETSI then applies the analysis to the case of a communication protocol, offering guidance as follows:

- Countermeasures that require extensions to the protocol or service that they protect can be included in the appropriate base standard
- Countermeasures that depend upon previously specified security functions can be included by reference to the appropriate standards from within the base standard or a separate security standard
- Countermeasures that depend on security functions which have not previously been standardized can be specified in a separate security standard

Whichever method (or combination of methods) is chosen, an overview of the implementation of countermeasures should either be included as part of the TVRA report or be specified in a separate security document.

4.2.6   FAIR (Factor Analysis of Information Risk)

FAIR (Factor Analysis of Information Risk) is a framework for understanding, analyzing, and measuring information risk; it is a proprietary information security risk analysis method from Risk Management Insight LLC. FAIR provides a reasoned and logical framework for answering these questions [JON200501]:

- **A taxonomy** of the factors that make up information risk. This taxonomy provides a foundational understanding of information risk, without which one could not reasonably do the rest. It also provides a set of standard definitions for terminology.
- **A method for measuring** the factors that drive information risk, including threat event frequency, vulnerability, and loss.

- **A computational engine** that derives risk by mathematically simulating the relationships between the measured factors.
- **A simulation model** that allows one to apply the taxonomy, measurement method, and computational engine to build and analyze risk scenarios of virtually any size or complexity.

For example, FAIR points out that the notion of defining threat communities is a tool for understanding who and what organizations are up against as they try to manage risk. Issues cover:

- Motive
- Primary intent
- Sponsorship
- Preferred general target characteristics
- Preferred specific target characteristics
- Preferred targets
- Capability
- Personal risk tolerance
- Concern for collateral damage

For example, the following threat community profile may fit a "Terrorist threat community" [JON200501]:

- Motive: ideology
- Primary intent: damage/destroy
- Sponsorship: unofficial
- Preferred general target characteristics: entities or people who clearly represent a conflicting ideology
- Preferred specific target characteristics: high profile, high visibility
- Preferred targets: human, infrastructure (buildings, communications, power, etc.)
- Capability: varies by attack vector (technological: moderate)
- Personal risk tolerance: high
- Concern for collateral damage: low

The following threat communities are examples of the human malicious threat landscape many organizations face, which FAIR addresses:

Internal
- Employees
- Contractors (and vendors)
- Partners

External

- Cyber-criminals (professional hackers)
- Spies
- Nonprofessional hackers
- Activists
- Nation-state intelligence services (e.g., counterparts to the CIA, etc.)
- Malware (virus/worm/etc.) authors

4.2.7 FIRM (Fundamental Information Risk Management)

FIRM is a method published by the Information Security Forum (ISF). The FIRM methodology is the product of a major research program conducted by the ISF involving 50 Member organizations. It distils examples of successful practice from members and insights gained from analysis of massive amounts of data from the ISF's biannual Information Security Status Survey. It is a methodology for the monitoring and control of information risk at the enterprise level. The ISF is responsible for the development and improvement of this methodology. Software products supporting the implementation of FIRM in a corporate environment are available from Citicus Limited. FIRM enables information risk to be systematically managed by enterprises of all sizes.

The "FIRM Implementation Guide and FIRM Supporting Material" provides [CIT200701]:

- A practical approach for managing information risk systematically across enterprises of all sizes
- Comprehensive implementation guidelines, which explain how to gain support for the approach and how to get it up and running.

ISF, in fact, has a suite of Risk Management products/modules which refer to each other and can be used complementarily. These products are:

1. The Standard of Good Practice for Information Security
2. FIRM and the revised FIRM Scorecard
3. ISF's Information Security Status Survey
4. Information Risk Analysis Methodologies (IRAM) project
5. SARA (Simple to Apply Risk Analysis)
6. SPRINT (Simplified Process for Risk Identification)

This suite can be used as follows:

- Risk identification: (IRAM, SARA, SPRINT)
- Risk analysis: (IRAM, SARA, SPRINT)
- Risk evaluation: (IRAM, SARA, FIRM Scorecard)

The Information Risk Scorecard is a form used to collect a range of important details about a particular information resource such as criticality, level of threat, business impact, and vulnerability. The Information Security Status Survey is a comprehensive Risk Management tool that evaluates a range of security controls used by organizations to control the business risks associated with their IT-based information systems. SARA is a methodology for analyzing information risk in critical information systems, including Planning; Identification of Business Requirements for Security; Assessment of Vulnerability and Control Requirements; and Reporting. SPRINT is an easy-to-use methodology for assessing business impact and for analyzing information risk in important but not critical information systems (it complements the Forum's SARA methodology, which is better suited to analyzing the risks associated with critical business systems.) SPRINT first helps decide the level of risk associated with a system. After the risks are understood, SPRINT helps determine how to proceed and, if the SPRINT process continues, culminates in the production of an agreed plan of action for keeping risks within acceptable limits. SPRINT can help [ENI200801]

- Identify the vulnerabilities of existing systems and the safeguards needed to protect against them
- Define the security requirements for systems under development and define the controls needed to satisfy them

4.2.8 FMEA (Failure Modes and Effects Analysis)

FMEA is a method commonly used in engineering design. It aims at examining potential ways in which a system (or process) might fail and thereby cause adverse effects [IEC200001, SAE200201, MIL198001]. In FMEA the *actual* causes of failures are given less focus compared to other risk analysis methods; the focus is more on the methodology. Organizations can use FMEA, for example, to [CRO200201]

- Develop product or process requirements that minimize the likelihood of those failures
- Evaluate the requirements obtained from the customer or other participants in the design process to ensure that those requirements do not introduce potential failures
- Identify design characteristics that contribute to failures and design them out of the system or at least minimize the resulting effects
- Develop methods and procedures to develop and test the product/process to ensure that the failures have been successfully eliminated
- Track and manage potential risks in the design; tracking the risks contributes to the development of corporate memory and the success of future products as well

- Ensure that any failures that could occur will not injure or seriously impact the customer of the product/process

The process of IT Security Risk Management as conceived in FMEA includes steps such as these [MIT200701]:

1. Listing the assets under consideration and understanding their intended use
2. Collecting security-related requirements for the assets
3. Elaboration of threats and applying them to systems to determine vulnerabilities including actors, threat paths, and possible outcomes
4. Scoring of risks
5. Proposing and implementing mitigations for vulnerabilities appropriate to the firm's domain

A brief description of how FMEA can be used follows, based on the description provided in reference [MIT200701]. In FMEA, likelihood is the probability that a vulnerability may be exploited within the construct of the associated threat environment. The following factors should be considered:

- Length of time vulnerability has been exposed
- Threat source: motivation and capability of the actor

Even when some of the threats may be amenable to more precise probability estimation, in general it is useful to stick to the three likelihood levels High, Medium, and Low, as described in Table 4.5 (also as discussed in Chapter 2).

Almost invariably a rough categorization (High, Medium, Low) will be sufficient to evaluate the potential severity of most adverse security events (see Table 4.6). The number of severity levels used may depend on the specific needs of the system involved.

In FMEA the scoring of a risk is determined by combining likelihood and severity of an attack. It determines the ranking of the risk mitigation measures.

TABLE 4.5. Likelihood Levels

Threat Likelihood	Threat Source	Effect of Controls
High	Highly motivated and Sufficiently capable	Are infective toward the vulnerability
Medium	Motivated and capable	Are in place and may impede exploitation of the vulnerability
Low	Minor Motivation or capability (e.g., incidental attack)	Are in place and prevent, or at least significantly impede, the vulnerability from being exploited

TABLE 4.6. Severity Levels

Severity	Definition
High	Exercise of the vulnerability may (1) result in the very costly loss of major tangible assets or resources, (2) significantly violate, compromise, or impede an organization's mission, reputation, or interest, or (3) result in human death or serious injury.
Medium	Exercise of the vulnerability may (1) result in the costly loss of tangible assets or resources, (2) violate, compromise, or impede an organization's mission, reputation, or interest, or (3) result in human injury.
Low	Exercise of the vulnerability may (1) result in the loss of some tangible assets or resources; (2) noticeably affect an organization's mission, reputation, or interest.

TABLE 4.7. Sample Risk Scores as Derived from Likelihood and Severity Levels

	Severity		
Threat Likelihood	Low	Medium	High
High	Low	High	High
Medium	Low	Medium	High
Low	Low	Low	Medium

TABLE 4.8. Risk Scores and Urgency of Mitigation Activities

Risk Score	Necessary Actions
High	Strong need for corrective measures. An existing system may continue to operate, but a corrective action plan or other risk mitigation measure must be put in place as soon as possible.
Medium	Corrective actions are needed and a plan must be developed to incorporate these actions within a reasonable period of time.
Low	The system's owner must determine whether corrective actions are still required or decide to accept the risk.

There is no simple universal agreement that determines what risk score is acceptable, and what score needs the implementation of risk mitigation measures. The actual priority for risk mitigation depends on the particular firm/application/environment. It is assumed that the risk management team and management will define the acceptable risk level for each system. By combining the likelihood and severity levels into a table such as Table 4.7, the team can assign risk scores of High, Medium, and Low.

The risk management team should agree on the correlation of risk scores that require the definition of follow-up actions before discussing specific risks. A sample description of risk scores is shown in Table 4.8; it represents (a) the score of a risk to which an asset might be exposed if a given vulnerability were exploited and (b) the corresponding need for corrective measures.

After having performed the above-described steps, the organization has the relevant data available to define necessary risk mitigation measures. The goal is to develop measures that will best reduce the risk to an acceptable score. Once a mitigation plan is developed, a Risk Management Matrix offers a post-mitigation risk estimation to explicitly determine the final risk. If new risks appear or risk scores are not low enough, then the process should be repeated.

A risk mitigation effort might include internal technical controls, system external technical controls, or the training of some key staff. In general, mitigations span technology, processes, and people. If a risk cannot sufficiently be mitigated in design control, the risk must be properly documented and assigned to the operational environment. At the conclusion of the process, the risk management team must approve the implemented risk mitigation measures and the summary of the residual risks.

4.2.9 FRAP (Facilitated Risk Assessment Process)

FRAP (Facilitated Risk Assessment Process[21]) is a qualitative method for assessing information security risks defined in T. R. Peltier's book, *Information Security Risk Analysis*, second edition, CRC Press, New York, 2005. It is a method for qualitative risk analysis and assessment that identifies potential risk exposure events. FRAP utilizes concepts defined in BS7799-3:2006 and ISO/IEC TR 13335-3:1998. The distinguishing feature of FRAP is that it is a facilitator-led approach: the business side of the organization drives the risk assessment process, and the security analyst acts as a facilitator. The method provides an easy-to-apply information security risk analysis spanning the enterprise. With FRAP

- Threats can be identified
- Probability that a threat will occur can be assessed
- The impact if the threat does occur can be assessed
- The risk levels can be established
- Mitigating controls and safeguards are identified
- Implementation action plan can be developed

While FRAP does not provide a detailed risk assessment methodology per se, it does provide a framework for showing how a facilitator-led process can produce findings that are easily comprehensible by a business not used to information security. The process is composed of a pre-FRAP session, a FRAP session, and a post-FRAP report generation [COL200701]:

[21]Some also call this method the Facilitated Risk Analysis and Assessment Process (FRAP).

- The purpose of the pre-FRAP meeting is to conduct the analysis necessary to prepare the assessment scope, the assessment definitions, and the process for prioritizing threats and to agree on logistics. The pre-FRAP session identifies FRAP team members and the assets that need to be formally assessed. The asset identification process is derived pre-screening, which takes place ahead of the pre-FRAP meeting.
- During the FRAP session itself, the threats are identified and the risk level identified by assessing the likelihood of the threat occurring.

By introducing the role of the facilitator, this risk assessment process automatically enssures that risk review is a business-driven process because the stakeholders are required to own and drive the process, all the assessment activities require the involvement of the stakeholders, and the output is the result of the assessment of the stakeholders. The facilitator guides the organization by helping the organization to select the most appropriate methodology at each stage in the assessment and then by supporting the organization in using the methodology to articulate the different aspects of risk [COL200701].

4.2.10 ISAMM (Information Security Assessment and Monitoring Method)

ISAMM is an Information Security Management Systems (ISMS)-supporting risk management method designed by the Telindus Group. It is a quantitative risk management methodology where the assessed risks are expressed in monetary units, through annual loss expectancy (ALE). This risk-based approach helps the firm define the ISMS, the major milestone for obtaining ISO 27001 certification. As we saw in Chapter 2, with ALE being the annual expected loss or cost should a threat or a group of threats materialize, we obtain

$$\text{Annual loss expectancy (ALE)} = [\text{Probability}] \times [\text{Average impact}]$$

This analysis forms the basis for the ROI-based approach and the economic justification capabilities of ISAMM with respect to the risk treatment plan. ISAMM allows a planner to show and simulate the reducing effect on the risk ALE for each improvement measure and enables the planner to compare this with its cost of implementation. Experience showed that this visualization of security is highly welcomed by business management, CIO, financial and budget controllers, and corporate risk managers. When required, ISAMM can also be used as a pure qualitative methodology [TEL200901]. Telindus has also developed a related software tool.

The methodology helps a firm with

- An identification of the relevant assets and threats

- An assessment, given the actual vulnerability level, of these threats' probability and impact
- A representation of the actual risks, using the probabilities and impact A decision support for acceptability or nonacceptability of risks
- A decision support for selection of appropriate safeguards for the treatment of the nonacceptable risks
- Graphic representations and reports to support the risk communication process

An ISAMM risk assessment contains four main parts: (i) scoping (ii) assessment of compliance (vulnerability) and threats (iii) validation of compliance and threats and (iv) result—calculation and reporting.

4.2.11   ISO/IEC Baselines

We implicitly discussed the ISO-based approaches in Chapter 3 when we surveyed the various ISO standards.

ISO/IEC 13335-2 (ISO/IEC 27005) is an ISO standard describing the complete process of information security risk management. The appendices contain examples of information security risk assessment approaches along with lists of possible threats, vulnerabilities, and security controls. ISO/IEC IS 13335-2 can be seen as the basic information risk management standard at an international level, setting a framework for the definition of the risk management process.

ISO/IEC 17799:2005 is considered to be a good practice for initial threat identification. It is not per se a method for evaluation or for the management of risks. The document identifies various issues that have to be taken into account to properly manage an information system. Tools such as Callio Secura, Cobra, Ebios, ISAMM, Proteus, Ra2, and RiskWatch (among several others) make reference to this standard.

ISO/IEC 27001 (BS7799-2:2002) focuses on the process of certification. It facilitates the comparison of an information security management system through a series of controls. This standard does not cover risk analysis or certification of the risk management per se, but a certificate granted according to this standard confirms the compliance of an organization with defined requirements arising from information security management principles and with a set of security controls [ENI200801].

The reader is referred to Chapter 3 for additional details.

4.2.12   ISO 31000 Methodology

As we noted in Chapter 3, ISO 31000 is a draft ISO standard expected to be released by press time. The ISO 31000 framework/method is not intended to describe a management system per se; but rather, it is intended to assist the organization to integrate risk management within its overall management system. The simplified summary that follows is based directly on the ISO 31000 DIS [ISO31000], but the reader is strongly urged to refer directly to the standard. Figure 1.4 in Chapter 1 depicted this framework in graphical form.

Step 1: Understanding the Organization and Its Environment. It is important to understand both external and internal environment of the organization since these environments can contribute importantly to the design of the framework. Aspects of the organization's external environment that may be considered include (i) the cultural, political, legal, regulatory, financial, economic, and competitive environment, (ii) the key drivers and trends having impact on the objectives of the organization, and (iii) the perceptions and values of external stakeholders. It is also necessary to understand the organization in terms of

- Capabilities, understood in terms of resources and knowledge (e.g., capital, people, competencies, processes, systems, and technologies)
- Information flows and decisio-making processes
- Internal stakeholders
- Objectives and the strategies that are in place to achieve them
- Perceptions, values, and culture
- Policies and processes
- Standards and reference models adopted by the organization Structures (e.g., governance, roles, and accountabilities)

Step 2: Define the Risk Management Policy. The risk management policy of the firm must be clearly defined. The policy should describe the organization's objectives for and commitment to risk management. The policy may specify the following aspects, among others:

- Accountabilities and responsibilities for managing risk
- Commitment to the periodic review and verification of the risk management policy and framework and its continual improvement
- Links between this policy and the organization's objectives
- Organization's risk acceptance level
- Organization's rationale for managing risk
- Processes and methods to be used for managing risk
- Resources available to assist those accountable or responsible for managing risk

Step 3: Achieve Integration into Organizational Processes. Risk management should be embedded in all the organization's practices and business processes so that it is relevant, effective, efficient, and sustained. In particular, risk management should be embedded into the policy development, business, and strategic planning and change management processes.

Step 4: Define Accountability. The organization should ensure that there is accountability and authority for managing risks, the adequacy and effectiveness of risk controls, and the implementation as well as sustaining of the risk management process.

Step 5: Identify Resources. The organization should develop the practical means by which it implements risk management including allocating appropriate resources for the risk management function. Consideration should be given to the following:

- Documented processes and procedures
- Information systems
- People and skills
- Resources needed for each step of the risk management process

Step 6: Establishing Internal Communication and Reporting Mechanisms. The organization should establish internal communication and reporting mechanisms to ensure that relevant information derived from the application of risk management is available at appropriate levels in the organization as a basis for decision making in support of the achievement of the organization's objectives.

Step 7: Establishing External Communication and Reporting Mechanisms. The organization should develop and implement a plan as to how it will communicate with external stakeholders. This typically involves

- Communicating with stakeholders in the event of a crisis or contingency
- Engaging appropriate external stakeholders and ensuring an effective exchange of information
- Internal and external reporting due to legal, regulatory, and corporate governance requirements
- Internal reporting on the framework and its effectiveness and the outcomes
- Making disclosures as required by legalization
- Receiving feedback on communications
- Using communication to provide transparency and build confidence in the organization

Step 8: Developing a Plan for Implementation. There should be an organization-wide plan for ensuring that the management of risk is embedded throughout the organization, integrated with normal business practice, and maintained through monitoring and reviewing of risks, controls, and changes in the internal and external environments.

Step 9: Implementing the Framework for Managing Risk. In implementing the organizations framework for managing risk, the organization should consider:

- Applying the risk management policy and process to the organizational processes according to its plan
- Communicating with stakeholders to ensure that its risk management framework remains appropriate
- Decision making, including the development and setting of objectives, aligned with the application of the risk management process
- Designating a person accountable for implementation of the framework
- Holding information and training sessions

Step 10: Implementing the Process Itself. See details below.

Step 11: Monitoring and Review of the Framework. To ensure that risk management is sustained, an organization should:

- Periodically measure progress against the risk management plan
- Periodically review whether the risk management framework, policy, and plan are still appropriate given the organizations' internal and external context
- Report on risks, progress with the risk management plan and how well the risk management policy is being followed
- Review the effectiveness of the risk management process including the adequacy of controls

Step 12: Continual Improvement of the Framework. Based on the review, decisions should be made on how the risk management framework, policy, and plan can be improved.

Details on Step 10: Process for Managing Risk.

Step 10.1: Communication and Consultation. Communication and consultation with internal and external stakeholders should take place at each stage of the risk management process. Therefore, a plan to communicate and consult with both internal and external stakeholders should be developed at an early stage. This plan should address issues relating to the risk itself, its consequences (if known), and the measures being taken to manage it.

Step 10.2: Establishing the Context. The risk management process should be aligned with the organization's culture, processes, and structure. Establishing the context defines the basic parameters for managing risk and sets the scope and criteria for the rest of the process. The context may include both internal and external parameters relevant for the organization. While many of these parameters are similar to those considered in the design of the risk management framework, when applying the risk management process, they need to be considered in greater detail and particularly how they relate to the scope of the particular risk management process.

- **Establishing the External Context**. External context is anything outside the organization that may influence objectives. Understanding the external context is important to ensure that external stakeholders, their objectives and concerns are considered when developing risk criteria. It is based on the organization wide context but with specific details of legal and regulatory requirements, stakeholder perceptions, and other aspects of risks specific to the scope of the risks management process.
- **Establishing the Internal Context**. Internal context is anything within the organization that may influence the way in which an organization will manage risk.
- **Establishing the Risk Management Process Context**. The objectives, strategies, scope and parameters of the activities of the organization or those parts of the organization where the risk management process is being applied should be established. The management of risk should be undertaken with full consideration of the need to justify the resources used in carrying out risk management. The resources required, responsibilities and authorities, and the records to be kept should also be specified.

Step 10.3: Developing Risk Criteria. The organization should develop the criteria against which risk is to be evaluated based on the context. Risk criteria express the organization's values, objectives, and resources. Risk criteria should be consistent with the organization's risk management policy. When defining risk criteria, factors to be considered should include the following:

- How likelihood will be defined
- How the level of risk is to be determined
- Nature and types of consequences that may occur and how they will be measured
- The level at which risk becomes acceptable
- The time frame of the likelihood and/or consequence
- What level of risk may require treatment

- Whether combinations of multiple risks should be taken into account

Step 10.4: Risk Assessment. Risk assessment is the overall process of risk identification, risk analysis, and risk evaluation.

- **Risk Identification**. Risk identification seeks to identify the risks that are relevant to the objectives. The organization should identify sources of risk exposures, events or sets of circumstances, and their potential consequences. The aim of this step is to generate a comprehensive list of risk events based on those events and circumstances that might enhance, prevent, degrade, or delay the achievement of the objectives.
- **Risk Analysis**. Risk analysis deals with developing an understanding of the risk. Risk analysis provides an input to risk evaluation and to decisions on whether risks need to be treated and the most appropriate risk treatment strategies. Risk analysis involves consideration of the causes and sources of risk exposures, their positive and negative consequences, and the likelihood that those consequences may occur.
- **Risk Evaluation**. The purpose of risk evaluation is to assist in making decisions, based on the outcomes of risk analysis, about which risks need treatment and treatment priorities. Risk evaluation involves comparing the level of risk found during the analysis process with risk criteria established when the context was considered.
- **Risk Treatment**. Risk treatment involves (a) selecting one or more options for addressing risks and (b) implementing those options. Selecting the most appropriate risk treatment option involves balancing the costs and effort of implementation against the benefits derived. Risk treatment options should consider the values and perceptions of stakeholders and the most appropriate ways to communicate with them.

Step 10.5: Preparing and Implementing Risk Treatment Plans. The purpose of risk treatment plans is to record how the chosen treatment options will be implemented. The information provided in treatment plans may include

- Expected benefit to be gained
- Performance measures and constraints
- Persons who are accountable for approving the plan and those responsible for implementing the plan
- Proposed actions
- Reporting and monitoring requirements
- Resource requirements
- Timing

Step 10.6: Recording the Risk Management Process. Risk management activities should be traceable. In the risk management process, records provide the foundation for improvement in methods, in tools, and in the overall process. Decisions concerning the creation of records should take into account

- Benefits of re-using information for management purposes
- Costs and effort involved in creating and maintaining records
- Legal, regulatory, and operational needs for records
- Method of access, retrievability and storage media
- Retention period
- Sensitivity of information

Step 10.7: Monitoring and Review. Monitoring and review is concerned with

- Analyzing and learning lessons from events, changes and trends
- Detecting changes in the external and internal context, including changes to the risk itself which may require revision of risk treatments and priorities
- Ensuring that the risk control and treatment measures are effective in both design and operation

4.2.13   IT-Grundschutz (IT Baseline Protection Manual)

IT-Grundschutz provides a method for an organization to establish an Information Security Management System (ISMS). It is published by the Federal Office for Information Security (BSI) which is the central IT security service provider for the German government. The key approach in IT-Grundschutz is to provide a framework for IT security management, offering information for commonly used IT components (modules). See Figure 4.2.

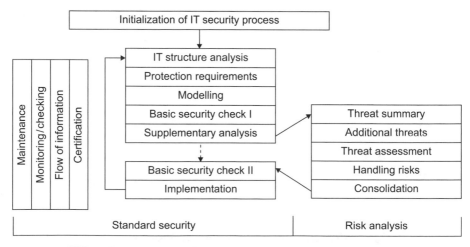

FIGURE 4.2. IT-Grundschutz (IT Baseline Protection Manual).

The method includes both generic IT security recommendations for establishing an applicable IT security process and detailed technical recommendations to achieve the necessary IT security level for a specific domain.

The IT security process advocated by IT-Grundschutz consists of the following steps:

- Initialization of the Process: Definition of IT security goals and business environment; establishment of an organizational structure for IT security; provision of necessary resources
- Creation of the IT Security Concept: IT-structure analysis; assessment of protection requirements; modeling; IT security check; implementation planning and fulfillment; maintenance, monitoring, and improvement of the process
- IT-Grundschutz Certification (optional)

IT-Grundschutz modules include lists of relevant threats and required countermeasures in a relatively technical level. These elements can be expanded, complemented, or adapted to the needs of an organization. The model is implemented in a companion tool, namely the BSI IT-Grundschutz tool (GSTOOL).

4.2.14 MAGERIT (Metodologia de Analisis y Gestion de Riesgos de los Sistemas de Informacion) (Methodology for Information Systems Risk Analysis and Management)

The CSAE (Consejo Superior de Administración Electrónica]—Higher Council for Electronic Government) prepared and promulgated MAGERIT v2[22] in response to the fact that the government (and, in general, the whole society) is increasingly dependent on information technologies for achieving its service objectives; use of IT-based mechanisms exposes users to risk, which must be minimized with security countermeasures. With MAGERIT v2, risk analysis has been punctuated as a necessary step for security management, as recognized in the Organization for Economic Cooperation and Development (OECD) guidelines (OECD Guidelines for the Security of Information Systems and Networks, 2002), which state in principle 6: "*Risk evaluation. The participants must carry out risk evaluations.*" (See Chapter 3.)

Related software (EAR/ PILAR) produces a wide variety of deliverables in standardized and customizable formats, textual and graphical.

MAGERIT seeks to achieve the following objectives [MAR200601]:

1. To make those responsible for information systems aware of the existence of risks and of the need to treat them in time.
2. To offer a systematic method for analyzing these risks.

[22]MAGERIT v1 was published in 1997. MAGERIT v2 was published in 2005.

3. To help in describing and planning the appropriate measures for keeping the risks under control.

4. To prepare the organization for the processes of evaluating, auditing, certifying or accrediting, as relevant in each case.

5. To achieve uniformity in the reports containing the findings and conclusions from a risk analysis and management project, recommending the following format:

   - *Value model*. Description of the value of the assets for the organization as well as the dependencies between the various assets.
   - *Risk map*. The account of the threats to which the assets are exposed.
   - *Safeguard evaluation*. Evaluation of the effectiveness of the existing safeguards in relation to the risk facing them.
   - *Risk status*. Classification of the assets by their residual risk; that is, by what could happen, taking the safeguards used into consideration.
   - *Deficiencies report*. Absence or weakness of the safeguards that appear appropriate to reduce the risks to the system.
   - *Security plan*. Group of security programs that put the risk management decisions into action.

The risk analysis and management tasks are not an end in themselves but form part of the continuous activity of security management. Risk analysis provides a model of the system in terms of assets, threats, and safeguards and is the foundation for controlling all activities on a well founded base. Risk management is the structuring of the security actions to meet the needs detected through analysis. Figure 4.3 depicts the MAGERIT approach [MAR200601].

MAGERIT places emphasis on awareness and training. The best security plan will be seriously compromised without the active collaboration of the persons involved in the information system, especially if the attitude is negative, and contrary or one of "fighting against the security measures." This requires the creation of a "security culture" which, coming from top management, encourages the awareness of all those involved of its need and relevance.

There are two basic elements of this culture:

- A corporate security policy that is understood (written so as to be understood by those who are not experts in the matter), published, and kept updated.
- Continuous training at all levels, with reminders of routine precautions and specialized activities, depending on the responsibility of each work post.

MAGERIT also gives emphasis to incidents and recovery. Persons involved must be aware of their role and continued relevance to prevent problems and to react when they do occur. It is important to create a culture of responsibility in

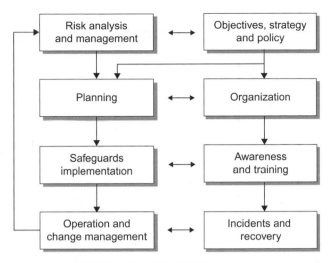

FIGURE 4.3. MAGERIT approach.

which potential problems, discovered by those close to the affected assets, can be channeled toward the decision points. Thus, the safeguards system will respond to the situation. When an incident occurs, time starts to act against the system: Its survival depends on the speed and correctness of the reporting and reaction activities. Any error, lack of precision, or ambiguity in these critical moments is amplified, turning what could be a mere incident into a disaster. MAGERIT states that is necessary to learn continuously from both successes and failures and then to incorporate them into the risk analysis and management process. The maturity of an organization is reflected in the orderliness and realism of its value model and, as a result, in the suitability of all types of safeguards, from tactical measures to an optimal organization.

MAGERIT's method is captured graphically in Figure 4.4. It assumes that safeguards will be deployed to reduce the risk to an acceptable residual risk. The safeguards discussed include:

- **Technical Safeguards:** in applications, equipment, and communications.
- **Physical Safeguards:** protecting the working environment for persons and equipment.
- **Organizational Measures:** for preventing and managing incidents.
- **Personnel Policy:** which in the final analysis is the essential and most delicate step: a policy for hiring, permanent training, incident reporting organization, reaction plans and disciplinary measures.

MAGERIT v2 has been structured into three books: *The Method*, the *Elements Catalogue* and a *Guide to Techniques* [ENI200801, MAR200601]:

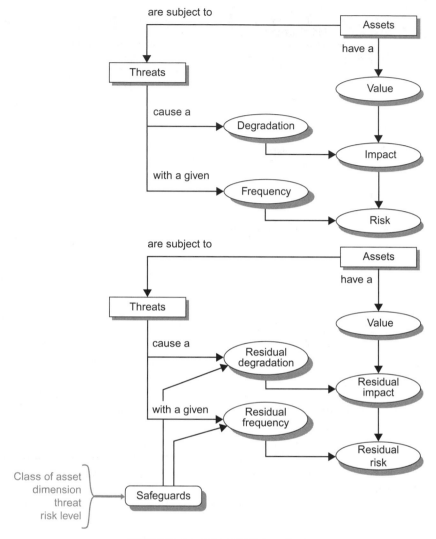

FIGURE 4.4. MAGERIT method.

- **Book I:** Methodology. It describes the core steps and basic tasks to carry out a project for risk analysis and management; the formal description of the project; the application to the development of information systems and it provides a large number of practical clues, as well as the theoretical foundations, together with some other complementary information.
  - After an introduction in Chapter 1, the guide describes the method from three perspectives.
  - Chapter 2 describes the steps for carrying out an analysis of the risk status and for managing its mitigation. This is an entirely conceptual

presentation. The risk assessment phases supported by this method are:

- *Risk identification*: Assets: identification, classification, dependencies between assets, and value.
- *Threats*: identification relationship with assets and evaluation of vulnerability.
- *Safeguards*: identification and evaluation. Tool support.
- *Risk analysis*: Accumulated impact and risk. Deflected impact and risk. Tool support.
- *Risk evaluation*: From technical risks into business risks.
  The risk management phases supported by this method are:
- *Risk assessment*: See above
- *Risk treatment*: Support of scenarios: phases, what if, security projects, long-term objectives.
- *Risk acceptance*: Security indicators
- *Risk communication*: Definition of reports containing the findings and conclusions from a risk analysis and management project: value model, risk map, safeguard evaluation, risk status, deficiencies report and security plan.

- Chapter 3 describes the basic tasks to be carried out in a risk analysis and management project, on the understanding that it is not sufficient to have a clear idea of concepts, but it is necessary to guide roles, activities, milestones, and documentation so that the risk analysis and management project is constantly under control.

- Chapter 4 applies the methodology to the development of information systems on the understanding that system development projects must include risks from the start, both the risks to which they are exposed and those that the applications themselves introduce into the system.

- As a complement, Chapter 5 discusses a series of practical aspects arising from the accumulated experience over time for carrying out a really effective analysis and management.

- **Book II:** Catalogue of elements. It provides standard elements and criteria for information systems and risk modeling: asset classes, valuation dimensions, valuation criteria, typical threats, and safeguards to be considered; it also describes the reports containing the findings and conclusions (value model, risk map, safeguard evaluation, risk status, deficiencies report, and security plan), thus contributing to achieve uniformity.

- **Book III:** Practical techniques. It describes techniques frequently used to carry out risk analysis and management projects such as: tabular and algorithmic analysis; threat trees, cost–benefit analysis, dataflow diagrams, process charts, graphical techniques, project planning, working sessions (interviews, meetings, presentations), and Delphi analysis.

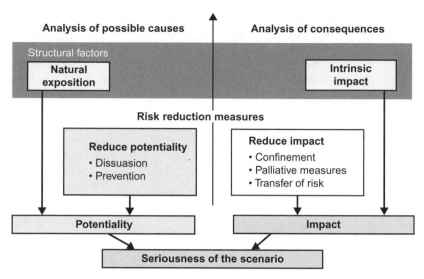

FIGURE 4.5. MEHARI risk model.

4.2.15   MEHARI (Méthode Harmonisée d'Analyse de Risques — Harmonised Risk Analysis Method)

MEHARI is a risk analysis and management method developed by CLUSIF (Club de la Sécurité de l'Information Français) and supported by software managed by the company Risicare (http://www.risicare.fr). MEHARI, originally developed in 1996, aims at assisting the executives (operating managers, CISO, CIO, risk manager, auditor) in their efforts to manage the security of Information and IT resources and to reduce the associated risks. MEHARI is compliant to ISO 13335 risk management standard and is suitable for the ISMS process described by ISO 27001. It allows the stakeholder to develop security plans, based on a list of vulnerability control points and an accurate monitoring process to achieve a continual improvement cycle. MEHARI provides:

- A risk model and associated assessment tools to evaluate (see Figure 4.5)
  - The intrinsic potentiality of predefined risk situations (i.e., while no security measure is in place)
  - The intrinsic level of consequences of the risk situation (i.e., if no measure is in place)
  - Each opportunity to reduce the risk thanks to additional security measures depending on their efficiency
- Automated calculations of the seriousness level of the risks
- A structured process with associated guidelines
- Knowledge bases of risk situations

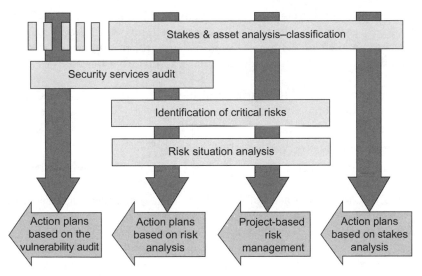

FIGURE 4.6. Methodology embodied in MEHARI.

- Rules for the consolidation of the risk analysis resulting in an optimal setting of action plans

MEHARI provides a modular framework (method), along with tools and knowledge bases to enable the stakeholder to [CLU200801]

- Analyze the major stakes
- Analyze the vulnerabilities
- Decrease and manage the risks
- Monitor the security of information

Figure 4.6 depicts the methodology embodied in MEHARI.

Analyzing the Major Stakes. This[23] module analyzes the security stakes and the dependencies of the business processes on information; specifically, it allows for the

- Identification of consequences of threats, which may be caused or facilitated by security weaknesses or deficiencies
- Evaluation of the level of these consequences for the organization

---

[23]This material is based on material from CLUSIF [CLU200801].

The focus of this analysis is set on the objectives and expectations of the business units of the organization, thus they will not change. It involves the top management and decision makers of the organization or entity (from business process to the information system) under consideration. The results from this analysis are

- A scale of value of the harm resulting from security incidents centered upon business impacts
- A formal classification of
  - primary assets (processes, information)
  - supporting assets (including premises, offices, IT and networks, etc.)

This analysis does not consist of an audit of incidents already observed, but is an assessment of the major likely risk situations and of the level of seriousness of their consequences. This analysis of the stakes aims generally at

- Implementing selective efforts for information security and avoiding to spend on lower stakes
- Avoiding to create useless constraints to users
- Defining priorities
- Answering to the obvious question of a decision maker about security budgets "is it really necessary?"

In this analysis, MEHARI provides

- A strict concern of the business requirements and a solid binding of managers and executives
- A guide for its implementation and standard outputs
- Direct inputs and links towards a detailed risk analysis

Analyzing the Vulnerabilities. This is the identification of weaknesses and defects in the security measures in place. It aims at arriving at a measurement of the quality of the existing security measures. CLUSIF has established and maintains, within MEHARI, a knowledge base of more than 1000 control points, sorted by "security services," which are analyzed during this phase. The vulnerability analysis may aim at

- Verifying that there is no unacceptable weak point otherwise; immediate action plans must be established
- Evaluating the efficiency and reality of the security measures; it is then necessary to use a complete checklist
- Comparing the organization to current standards or state of the art or best practices (the conformance to a standard being more important than the level of expertise of the audit base used)

For this vulnerability analysis, MEHARI provides

- A complete consideration of the effective context of the organization:
  - Include all types of information and the information system in its broad sense.
  - Consider any relevant workflow and the work environment.
- An implementation guide plus knowledge bases, including questionnaires and reference manual of the security services
- Processes appropriate to the interlocutor in charge and to the context of the vulnerability analysis
- Direct links toward the risk analysis due to the weaknesses brought to the fore

The vulnerability analysis provides a measured evaluation of the security measures. The MEHARI knowledge base is structured by security domains and services, each having definite objectives for the reduction of probability or consequences for tangible risk situations. As such, MEHARI vulnerability analysis allows one to

- Correct unacceptable weaknesses with immediate action plans
- Measure the effectiveness of the security measures in place and guarantee their efficiency
- Prepare the risk analysis itself, including the discovered weaknesses
- Measure the organization's compliance to current best practices and security standards

Managing and Decreasing and the Risks. The risk analysis module of MEHARI covers

- The identification of situations that may hamper the expected results of the organization or any part of it.
- The evaluation of
  - The probability level of such situations
  - The possible consequences
  - Decision criteria to reduce, transfer, or retain, the risk
- The bringing upfront of security measures able to reduce the risk to an acceptable level

This risk analysis aims at

- Defining the measures which will better fit to the context and the stakes: this being a classical process based on a risk analysis driven security policy
- Organizing a risk management process and guarantee that all the critical risk situations have been identified and considered: this being a risk driven policy of security management

- Analyzing and manage the risks for a new project (IT application, business process, site, etc.)

Monitoring the Security of Information. Security monitoring requires

- A structured framework for the definition of annual objectives and steps of the action plans
- Indicators allowing us to compare the results to the objectives
  - Quantitatively and qualitatively
  - Relatively to assigned delays
- Inputs from external sources allowing the planner to benchmark the organization

What MEHARI provides in this domain:

- A flexible framework, consistent with different processes and management styles for security, because
  - Organizations may decide to change their way to monitor security
  - The requirements of management may follow the maturity level reached by the organization
- Several synthetic reports and measurements
  - Risk and vulnerability levels
  - Security themes (16 criteria such as access control, continuity planning, ...)
  - Compliance measurement to all ISO 17799:2005 controls
  - Dashboard of critical risks

4.2.16 Microsoft's Security Risk Management Guide

Microsoft's approach, as defined in its _Microsoft Solutions for Security and Compliance and Microsoft Security Center of Excellence, Security Risk Management Guide,_ is focused on how to plan, establish, and maintain a successful security risk management process in organizations of all sizes and types [MIC200601]. Figure 4.7 depicts the Microsoft security risk management process; also see Figure 1.6 in Chapter 1 of this book. The Security Risk Management Guide comprises six chapters and several appendices and tools to help organize firms' security risk management projects. This is a well-thought-out document.[24] The process combines quantitative and qualitative analysis, return on security investment (ROSI), and other best practices. Chapter 1 is an overview.

Chapter 2: Survey of Security Risk Management Practices. Chapter 2 lays a foundation for the Microsoft security risk management process by reviewing the different ways that organizations have approached security risk management in

---

[24]This summary is based on the Microsoft guide.

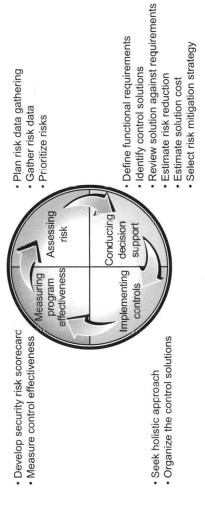

- Develop security risk scorecard
- Measure control effectiveness

- Plan risk data gathering
- Gather risk data
- Prioritize risks

- Seek holistic approach
- Organize the control solutions

- Define functional requirements
- Identify control solutions
- Review solution against requirements
- Estimate risk reduction
- Estimate solution cost
- Select risk mitigation strategy

Measuring program effectiveness

Assessing risk

Conducting decision support

Implementing controls

FIGURE 4.7. The Microsoft security risk management process.

the past. Readers who are already well versed in security risk management may want to skim through the chapter quickly; others who are relatively new to security or risk management are encouraged to read it thoroughly. The chapter starts with a review of the strengths and weaknesses of the proactive and reactive approaches to risk management. It then revisits in detail the concept of organizational risk management maturity. Finally, the chapter assesses and compares qualitative risk management and quantitative risk management, the two traditional methods. Then a process is presented as an alternative method, one that provides a balance between these methodologies, resulting in a process that has proven to be effective within Microsoft. Topics are:

Comparing Approaches to Risk Management
The Reactive Approach
The Proactive Approach
Approaches to Risk Prioritization
Quantitative Risk Assessment
Details of the Quantitative Approach
Qualitative Risk Assessment
Comparing the Two Approaches
The Microsoft Security Risk Management Process

Chapter 3: Security Risk Management Overview. This chapter provides a more detailed look at the Microsoft security risk management process and introduces some of the important concepts and keys to success. It also provides advice on how to prepare for the process by using effective planning and building a strong Security Risk Management Team with well-defined roles and responsibilities. Topics are

The Four Phases of the Microsoft Security Risk Management Process
Level of Effort
Laying the Foundation for the Microsoft Security Risk Management Process
Risk Management vs. Risk Assessment
Communicating Risk
Determining Your Organization's Risk Management Maturity Level
Organizational Risk Management Maturity Level Self-Assessment
Defining Roles and Responsibilities
Building the Security Risk Management Team

Chapter 4: Assessing Risk. This chapter explains the assessing risk phase of the Microsoft security risk management process in detail. Steps in this phase include planning, facilitated data gathering, and risk prioritization. The risk assessment process consists of multiple tasks, some of which can be quite demanding for a large organization. For example, identifying and determining values of business assets may take a lot of time. Other tasks such as identifying threats and vulnerabilities require a lot of technical expertise. The challenges related to these tasks illustrate the importance of proper planning and building a solid Security Risk Management Team, as Chapter 3, "Security Risk Management Overview," emphasizes.

In the summary risk prioritization, the security risk management team uses a qualitative approach to triage the full list of security risks so that it can quickly identify the most significant ones for further analysis. The top risks are then subjected to a detailed analysis using quantitative techniques. This results in a short list of the most significant risks with detailed metrics that the team can use to make sensible decisions during the next phase of the process. Topics are

Required Inputs for the Assessing Risk Phase
Participants in the Assessing Risk Phase
Tools Provided for the Assessing Risk Phase
Required Output for the Assessing Risk Phase
Planning
Alignment
Scoping
Stakeholder Acceptance
Preparing for Success: Setting Expectations
Embracing Subjectivity
Facilitated Data Gathering
Data Gathering Keys to Success
Building Support
Discussing versus Interrogating
Building Goodwill
Risk Discussion Preparation
Identifying Risk Assessment Inputs
Identifying and Classifying Assets
Assets
Asset Classes
Organizing Risk Information
Organizing by Defense-in-Depth Layers
Defining Threats and Vulnerabilities
Estimating Asset Exposure
Estimating Probability of Threats
Facilitating Risk Discussions
Meeting Preparations

Facilitating Discussions
    Task One: Determining Organizational Assets and Scenarios
    Task Two: Identifying Threats
    Task Three: Identifying Vulnerabilities
    Task Four: Estimating Asset Exposure
    Task Five: Identifying Existing Controls and Probability of Exploit
Summarizing the Risk Discussion
Defining Impact Statements
Data Gathering Summary
Risk Prioritization
Primary Tasks and Deliverables
Preparing for Success
Prioritizing Security Risks
Conducting Summary Level Risk Prioritization
Conducting Detailed Level Risk Prioritization
Quantifying Risk
    Task One: Assign Monetary Values to Asset Classes
    Task Two: Identify the Asset Value
    Task Three: Produce the Single Loss Expectancy Value (SLE)
    Task Four: Determine the Annual Rate of Occurrence (ARO)
    Task Five: Determine the Annual Loss Expectancy (ALE)
Facilitating Success in the Conducting Decision Support Phase

Chapter 5: Conducting Decision Support. During the decision support phase of the process, the security risk management team determines how to address the key risks in the most effective and cost efficient manner. The team identifies controls; determines costs associated with acquiring, implementing, and supporting each control; assesses the degree of risk reduction that each control achieves; and, finally, works with the Security Steering Committee to determine which controls to implement. The end result is a clear and actionable plan to control or accept each of the top risks identified in the assessing risk phase. Topics are

Required Input for the Conducting Decision Support Phase
Participants in the Conducting Decision Support Phase
Tools Provided for the Conducting Decision Support Phase
Required Outputs for the Decision Support Phase
Considering the Decision Support Options
Accepting the Current Risk
Implementing Controls to Reduce Risk

Keys to Success
Building Consensus
Avoiding Filibusters
Identifying and Comparing Controls
   Step One: Defining Functional Requirements
   Step Two: Identifying Control Solutions
Organizational Controls
Operational Controls
Technological Controls
Step Three: Reviewing the Solution Against Requirements
Step Four: Estimating Risk Reduction
Step Five: Estimating Solution Cost
   Acquisition Costs
   Implementation Costs
   Ongoing Costs
   Communication Costs
   Training Costs for IT Staff
   Training Costs for Users
   Costs to Productivity and Convenience
   Costs for Auditing and Verifying Effectiveness

Step Six: Selecting the Risk Mitigation Solution.
Chapter 6: Implementing Controls and Measuring Program Effectiveness.
This chapter covers the last two phases of the Microsoft security risk management process: Implementing Controls and Measuring Program Effectiveness. The Implementing Controls phase is self-explanatory: The mitigation owners create and execute plans based on the list of control solutions that emerged during the decision support process to mitigate the risks identified in the assessing risk phase. The chapter provides links to prescriptive guidance that an organization's mitigation owners may find helpful for addressing a variety of risks. The Measuring Program Effectiveness phase is an ongoing one in which the security risk management team periodically verifies that the controls implemented during the preceding phase are actually providing the expected degree of protection.

Another step of this phase is estimating the overall progress that the organization is making with regard to security risk management as a whole. The chapter introduces the concept of a "Security Risk Scorecard" that one can use to track how the organization is performing. Finally, the chapter explains the importance of watching for changes in the computing environment such as the addition or removal of systems and applications or the appearance of new threats and vulnerabilities. These types of changes may require prompt action by the organization to protect itself from new or changing risks. Topics are

Implementing Controls
Required Input for the Implementing Controls Phase
Participants in the Implementing Controls Phase
Tools Provided for the Implementing Controls Phase
Required Outputs for the Implementing Controls Phase
Organizing the Control Solutions
Network Defenses
Host Defenses
Application Defenses
Data Defenses
Measuring Program Effectiveness
Required Inputs for the Measuring Program Effectiveness Phase
Participants in the Measuring Program Effectiveness Phase
Tools Provided for the Measuring Program Effectiveness Phase
Required Outputs for the Measuring Program Effectiveness Phase
Developing Your Organization's Security Risk Scorecard
Measuring Control Effectiveness
Reassessing New and Changed Assets and Security Risks

The Microsoft guide offers a lot of good concepts, and it is worth reading.

4.2.17   MIGRA (Metodologia Integrata per la Gestione del Rischio Aziendale)

MIGRA now in Version 2.1 is a qualitative risk assessment and management methodology applicable to both IT and other tangible assets. MIGRA forces the analyst to consider threats, attacks, security measures, and components of the security perimeter. MIGRA defines

- A security and risk taxonomy for the two considered domains (information and tangible assets)
- A logical framework for generating a model of the security perimeter to be analyzed
- An algorithm (based on questionnaires) for assessing, on a four-level qualitative scale (High, Medium, Low, Negligible/Not applicable), the value of both information and tangible assets relevant to the above perimeter
- A scheme for performing threat and vulnerability analysis
- A procedure for calculating (on a qualitative scale) risk
- A mechanism to identify in every scenario a set of appropriate security measures

- A procedure to perform gap and compliance analysis with reference to corporate security policies, norms, standards, guidelines, and best practices

The structure of MIGRA is as follows [ELS200901]:

- **The Knowledge Base**. Contains the possible threats, attacks, vulnerabilities, and agents, as well as the countermeasures at varying levels of effectiveness, applicable in a specific context.
- **The Analysis Scenario Representation Tool**. Allows the user to define the boundaries and security features of the analysis perimeter, using the paradigms contained in the knowledge base.
- **The Risk Analysis and Conformity Engine**. Automatically analyses risk and compliance inside the perimeter in question, drawing attention to failings (gap analysis), improvements to introduce and risk indicators.
- **Presentation of Results and What-If Analysis**. Displays or prints the results of security analyses in various forms, enabling users to observe how the risk profile changes when proposed actions are put into effect.

MIGRA provides an alignment with and support for the requirements of ISO 27001:2005, in case certification is required.

4.2.18   NIST

The NIST methodologies are described in the standards that we discussed in the previous chapter. Refer to Chapter 3 for a description of

- **NIST SP 800-30:** "Risk Management Guide for Information Technology Systems"
- **NIST SP 800-39:** "Managing Risk from Information Systems—An Organizational Perspective," available as a draft at press time.

4.2.19   National Security Agency (NSA) IAM / IEM / IA-CMM

The National Security Agency (NSA) provides various services to identify and analyze vulnerabilities in operational system/networks.[25] Since NSA has limited resources to meet the ever-growing demand for INFOSEC Assurance services, the INFOSEC Assurance Training and Rating Program (IATRP) was developed as a partnership between NSA and private INFOSEC Assurance providers. NSA's IATRP Program sets the standards for INFOSEC Assurance

---

[25]Under the authority from National Security Directive (NSD) 42, the National Security Agency (NSA) is tasked with raising the Information Security (INFOSEC) Assurance (IA) posture of National Security Systems of U.S. Government agencies and departments. The Memorandum of Understanding (MOU) in place between NSA and the National Institutes of Technology (NIST) also allows NSA to examine non-national security systems as well.

services through the INFOSEC assurance methodologies (INFOSEC Assessment Methodology, INFOSEC Evaluation Methodology), trains and certifies individuals in the methodologies, and rates INFOSEC Assurance organizations through the use of a standard metric INFOSEC Assurance—Capability Maturity Model (IA-CMM). NSA then provides this information to consumers so they are better informed when negotiating with INFOSEC Assurance Providers. The following capabilities are supported [IAT200901]:

- **INFOSEC Assessment Methodology (IAM).** The IAM consists of a standard set of activities required to perform an INFOSEC assessment. In other words, the methodology explains the depth and breadth of the assessment activities that must be performed to be acceptable within the IATRP. The IAM "sets the bar" for what needs to be done for an activity to be considered a complete INFOSEC Assessment. Providers who advertise an INFOSEC assessment capability and consumers seeking assistance in performing INFOSEC Assessments should use the IAM as the baseline for their discussions. Because the IAM is a baseline, providers can expand upon it to further meet the needs of the customers. However, any "expansion" must not reduce or interfere with the original intent of any IAM activity.

- **INFOSEC Evaluation Methodology (IEM).** The IEM consists of a standard set of activities required to perform an INFOSEC evaluation. In other words, the methodology explains the depth and breadth of the evaluation activities that must be performed to be acceptable within the IATRP. The IEM "sets the bar" for what needs to be done for an activity to be considered a complete INFOSEC Evaluation. Providers who advertise an INFOSEC evaluation capability and consumers seeking assistance in performing INFOSEC Evaluations should use the IEM as the baseline for their discussions. Because the IEM is a baseline, providers can expand upon it to further meet the needs of the customers. However, any "expansion" must not reduce or interfere with the original intent of any IEM activity.

- **INFOSEC Assurance—Capability Maturity Model (IA-CMM).** IA-CMM) is based on the System Security Engineering Capability Maturity Model (SSE-CMM) and modified to address the INFOSEC assurance processes. Whereas IATRP methodology training focuses on an individual's ability to conduct an INFOSEC assurance service, the IA-CMM appraisal focuses on a provider organization's capability to support INFOSEC analyst in conducting their mission objectives (i.e., to provide quality INFOSEC Assurance or Evaluation). The IA-CMM is used to measure two things: the maturity of processes (specific functions) that produce products (e.g., identified vulnerabilities, countermeasures, and threats) and the level of compliance a process has with respect to an IATRP methodology. Capability maturity is a measurement of the level of assurance that an organization can perform a process consistently (i.e., providing a consistent product from the process). The IA-CMM identifies nine process areas related to performing INFOSEC assurance services. For each of the nine process areas, the IA-CMM defines six levels of process maturity from Level 0 to Level 5. The higher the maturity levels, the more likely the process will be performed consistently. From this consistency, quality can be implied but not guaranteed. In CMM processes, it is conceivable that a well-defined process that consistently produces a poor product can receive a fairly high maturity rating. The IA-CMM counters this by focusing on the process areas as they relate to the IATRP methodologies. The use of standardized IATRP methodology products adds additional assurance of quality (i.e., the right products are being produced).

At the conclusion of an IA-CMM appraisal, the organization will be assigned an IA-CMM Ratings Profile. This is a list of nine numbers (one for each process area) from 0 to 5. The organization will also receive check marks for each of 9 process areas that is compliant with the IATRP methodology. For example, an organization has an "identify impact" process area rating of 2 and a check for IAM. This means that the process area is not only at a capability maturity level of 2, but is also compliant for the IAM (i.e., proven all IAM related products are produced). Each IATRP methodology (e.g., IAM, IEM) will have separate compliance requirements. Thus, each methodology will have a separate check box for the organization's rating.

When a customer is deciding on an INFOSEC assurance provider organization, they can use the IA-CMM rating profile along with the experience of the INFOSEC analysts to determine what is best to meet their needs. The lower the process area maturity rating, the more dependence the consumer should put on the experience of the individual analyst.

In order to maintain a corporate IA-CMM rating, the following guidelines must be met:

- If the organization has received a rating of 1 in any process area, an appraisal must be completed within 18 months from the date of the current rating.
- If the organization has received a rating of 2 in any process area, an appraisal must be completed within 30 months from the date of the current rating.
- If the organization has received a rating of 3 or better across all process area, an appraisal must be completed within 42 months from the date of the current rating.

4.2.20   Open Source Approach

Some have advocated an "open source" approach for the following [BEA200801]:

- A multilevel risk assessment methodology and set of decision heuristics designed to minimize the intellectual effort required to conduct infrastructure level risk assessments, especially for small and medium enterprises
- A set of decision heuristics to assist in the quantification of organizational costs, financial as well as nonfinancial
- A knowledge base of probability estimates associated with specified classes of threats for use in the application of the aforementioned methodology
- Automated tool(s) capable of supporting the execution of the aforementioned methodology and heuristics

The assumption is that the adoption of an open development approach can result in improved methodologies by fostering broad participation in the development of simplified risk models and the collection of risk data that can be used to populate those models. Furthermore, proponents are of the opinion that an open content approach can result in the production and dissemination of higher quality risk management data by exposing the methods and assumptions under which such data have been produced.

There are some open source code risk management projects, as follows:

- CORAS is a European Union (EU) funded effort to develop software supporting model based risk assessment for use in improving security during the systems design process.
- Open source management of risk (OSMR) is a model-based risk analysis tool based on the ISO 17799.
- Automated security self-evaluation tool (ASSET) is a tool used by the Computer Security Resource Center (CRSC) of the National Institute of Standards and Technology (NIST) aimed at federal agencies.
- OGRCM3 project of the Security Officers Management and Analysis Project (SOMAP.org) develops and documents a methodology on how toÂmeasure and manage risk. One of the main goals of SOMAP.org is to develop and maintain open source information security risk management documents, tools, and utilities. It is their stated belief that risk management processes and best practices need to be developed and published in an open and free kind of way. They see information security as not being a competitive issue and only freely available and cooperatively developed risk management utilities, and tools can potentially lead to a better security management and to further development of the whole IT risk management field.
- OCTAVE-S by the Carnegie Mellon Software Engineering Institute is specifically designed to meet the risk analysis needs of smaller organizations.

An open source security testing methodology deserving mention is the Open Source Security Testing Methodology Manual (OSSTMM). OSSTMM provides a methodology for a security test, also referred to as an OSSTMM audit in this context. The goal is to obtain an accurate measurement of security at an operational level that is clear of assumptions and anecdotal evidence. As a methodology, it is designed to be consistent and repeatable and, being an open source, it allows for free dissemination of information and intellectual property. The OSSTMM was first developed in 2000.

In recent years the OSSTMM has encompassed many security channels, being enhanced with the applied experience of thousands of reviewers. By 2005, the OSSTMM was no longer just considered an ethical hacking framework, but it had become an accepted methodology to determine if security defenses within organization are being applied at the optimal operational level. As audits became a common requirement, the need for a solid methodology manifested itself and practitioners realized that they need more than compliance reports for a specific regulation or legislation. Hence, in 2006 the OSSTMM changed from defining tests based on solutions, such as firewall tests and router tests, to a framework for a reliable security test. With Version 3 planned to be released in the later part of 2009, the OSSTMM encompasses tests from all channels: human, physical, wireless, telecommunications, and data networks. A set of security metrics, called risk assessment values (RAVs), provide a tool that generates a graphical representation of state; the tool also shows changes in state over time. These capabilities integrate well with a "dashboard" for management.

OSSTMM is beneficial for both internal and external testing, allowing a comparison/combination of the two. Quantitative risk management can be done from report findings of the OSSTMM Audit. The OSSTMM includes information for project planning, quantifying results, and the rules of engagement for performing security audits. The methodology can be integrated with existing laws and policies to ensure a thorough security audit through all channels.

Other open source methods are also being discussed. Utilizing the logic of structured decomposition associated with top-down systems analysis, a top-level model could be populated with information gained from a short questionnaire, as exemplified below. Such a model could provide estimates of ALEs [BEA200801].

1. What is your organization's estimated annual revenue or budget?
2. Rate your organization's dependence upon IT to accomplish its mission.
3. Rate your organization's dependence on internet access to its mission.
4. Rate your organization's staff and management knowledge or expertise with respect to information security awareness/training.
5. Rate the effectiveness of your organization's technical security countermeasures.
6. Rate the effectiveness of your organization's management controls, information security policy, and procedures.

7. Does your organization have verified data backup procedures?
8. Does your organization have a verified business or disaster recovery plan?
9. Does your organization have verified incident response capability?

The goal is to be able to input the answers to such questions into an open source model capable of making a rough calculation of information assurance risks associated with its current practices. The key to producing a useful estimate is the availability of reasonably good risk estimates and means for calculating the financial costs associated with various types of system failure. Such an open source model did not exist at press time, but it was being advocated. Refer to [BEA200801] for further discussion of these concepts.

4.2.21   PTA (Practical Threat Analysis)

PTA is a quantitative threat modeling methodology and a risk assessment tool promulgated by the company PTA Technologies. PTA provides a mechanism to maintain dynamic threat models capable of reacting to changes in the system's assets and vulnerabilities. With PTA an analyst can maintain a growing database of threats, create documentation for security reviews, and produce reports showing the importance of various threats and the priorities of the corresponding countermeasures [PTA200901].

PTA automatically recalculates threats and countermeasures implementation priorities and provides decision makers with an updated mitigation plan that reflects changes in threat realities. Countermeasure's priorities are a function of the system's assets values, level of potential damage, threats probabilities, and degrees of mitigation provided by countermeasures. The system-recommended mitigation plan is composed of the countermeasures that are the most cost-effective against the identified threats. Figure 4.8 depicts the environment as seen by PTA. The PTA threat modeling and risk assessment steps are as follows [PTA200901]:

1. **Identifying Assets**. Mapping of system asset's financial values and potential losses due to damages. Asset's values are the basis for calculating threats, risks and countermeasures priorities.
2. **Identifying Vulnerabilities**. Identifying potential system vulnerabilities requires knowledge of the system's functionality, architecture, business and operational procedures, and types of users. This is a continuous iterative task coupled with the step of identifying threats (step 4).
3. **Defining Countermeasures**. Defining the countermeasures relevant to system vulnerabilities. The countermeasure's cost-effectiveness is calculated according to its estimated implementation cost.
4. **Building Threat Scenarios and Mitigation Plan**. Composing the potential threats scenarios and identifying the various threat's elements and parameters as follows:

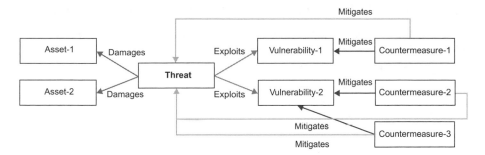

Threats exploit **vulnerabilities** and damage **assets.**
Countermeasures mitigate **vulnerabilities** and therefore might mitigate **threats**.

FIGURE 4.8. The PTA threat model.

- Entering a short description of the threat scenario.
- Identifying the threatened assets and the level of potential damage.
- Setting the threat's probability. The threat's risk level is automatically calculated based on the total damage that may be caused by the threat and the threat's probability.
- Identifying system's vulnerabilities exploited by the threat. Identification of system's vulnerabilities automatically populates a list of proposed countermeasures.
- Deciding on the actual mitigation plan by selecting the most effective combination of countermeasures.

Starting with Predefined Vulnerabilities and Threats: The threat analysis process can start with predefined entities of assets, vulnerabilities, and countermeasures typical of the system being analyzed.

Reviewing the Threat Analysis Results: Reviewing the threat analysis results can help improve the threat model and refine the model entities parameters. The basic analysis outcomes are described below.

- List of threats, their risk, and potential damage to assets when threats materialize.
- List of assets and the financial risk that threatens them.
- List of countermeasures, their overall mitigation effect, and cost-effectiveness relative to their contribution to system risk reduction.
- The maximal financial risk to the system, the final risk to the system (after all mitigation plans were implemented), and the current level of system risk according to the status of countermeasure's implementation.
- The optimized mitigation plan, which is composed of the countermeasures that are the most cost-effective against the identified threats

4.2.22 SOMAP (Security Officers Management and Analysis Project)

The Security Officers Management and Analysis Project (SOMAP.org) was mentioned above in the context of Open Source. Their activities are concentrated on four subprojects (see Figure 4.9) [SOM200901]:

- The Open Governance, Risk, and Compliance Maturity Management Methodology (OGRCM3) project develops and documents a methodology on how to measure and manage risk.
- The Open Risk Model Repository (ORIMOR) contains a database model that is used as the basis for our own risk management framework and tool.
- The Open Risk and Compliance Framework and Tool (ORICO) Framework and ORICO Tool are the (reference) implementation of our own maturity management methodology.

OGRCM3 contains an overview of the risk and compliance management process and an description on why and how to manage risk. Figure 4.9 depicts the model graphically.

Compliance Scoping. In this step, one defines what authority documents one will need and for which one will try to achieve compliance with.

Asset Management and Categorization. During this step, one manages one's assets, defines the responsibilities, and manages the changes since the last assessment.

Compliance Measurement and Documenting. This step is about measuring the compliance of the implemented controls with the requirements as

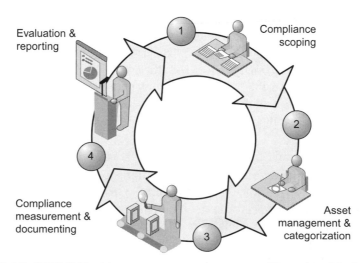

FIGURE 4.9. OGRCM3 risk management process as a life cycle with four steps, starting at the compliance scoping.

described in the authority documents chosen during the compliance scoping step. Different assessment measuring strategies can be used to measure the compliance level. Findings are documented for later evaluation and reporting.

Evaluation and Reporting. The last step contains the evaluation of the findings and the reporting of the facts to the upper management and other interested parties.

The ORMOR is actually three things in one:

- A central repository containing best practice details
- A model showing how to store risk management data
- An architecture to use a meta layer to store common type information

The ORICO is two projects in one.

- The Framework builds the foundation for a risk management tool. It implements all the building blocks like data abstraction and RAD tools which can be used when developing a risk management tool.
- The Tool is the reference implementation of the OGRCM3. It makes use of the ORICO Framework and is developed as a desktop as well as a web application.

4.2.23   Summary

Quite a number of methods were described in the subsections above. The question "How should I choose a risk analysis tool or method?" easily surfaces. The following are some of the issues worth considering, possibly in the order that a selection tree might be applied [IMP200801]:

- **Standard-based or not:** If an organization wishes to follow a standard and also (eventually) aspire to achieve certification, then clearly the methods that are based on standards are preferred. Few, if any, of the methods are based on ISO 27000 or ISO 31000, but this is expected to change over time.
- **Quantitative or Qualitative:** There is an industry debate as value of quantitative *versus* qualitative methods. Issues related to the ability to obtain true numerical values were discussed in Chapter 2. As a consequence, the goal of using pure quantitative methods in all circumstances is impractical due to the shortage of reliable data on incidents (probabilities and impacts), although they are potentially useful in some more narrowly defined situations. One solution is to use quick/simple qualitative risk assessments followed by risk analyses on selected high-risk areas using more detailed qualitative or quantitative methods.
- **Cost and Value:** Firms must assess the benefits to the organization from the tool, offset by the costs of acquiring, using and maintaining the tool.

- **Maintainability and Support:** Some methods use decision support software to support those undertaking the analysis, whereas others are procedural or can be supported by generic tools such as spreadsheets. It follows that they vary in the amount of technical expertise required to install, configure, and maintain them. Home-grown tools can be more easily and cheaply modified.
- **Usability:** Some methods and tools lead the user through the risk analysis process a step at a time, whereas others are more free-form but assume more knowledge and expertise of the users.
- **Scaleability:** The decision depends on questions such as these: Is the firm looking to support a relatively simple analysis of risks for a single process or IT system, an organization-wide analysis, or all of the above? Will the firm be completing the analysis just once or repeatedly? If so, how often?

The topic on selecting the most appropriate tool and methodology for a specific organization will be revisited in detail in Part 2 of this book.

REFERENCES

[AUS200901] The Federal Chancellery of the Austrian Government, Federal Chancellery, Bundeskanzleramt, Ballhausplatz 2, 1014 Vienna, Austria.

[BEA200801] J. Beachboard, A. Cole, et al, "Improving information security risk analysis practices for small- and medium-sized enterprises: A Research Agenda," *Issues in Informing Science and Information Technology*, Volume 5, 2008, Proceedings of Informing Science, Informing Science Institute.

[CER200901] CERT, Carnegie Mellon University's Software Engineering Institute, 4500 Fifth Avenue, Pittsburgh, PA 15213–2612, USA.

[CIT200701] Driving information risk down to an acceptable level, using FIRM and Citicus ONE, Whitepaper, 2007. Ref A020-R231. Citicus Limited, Holborn Gate, 330 High Holborn, London WC1V 7QT, United Kingdom.

[CLU200801] Club de la Sécurité de l'Information Français, Association loi de 1901, 30, rue Pierre Sémard 75009 Paris.

[COL200701] L. Coles-Kemp, R. E. Overill, "On the role of the facilitator in information security risk assessment," *J Comput Virol* (2007) *3*:143–148, DOI 10.1007/s11416-007-0040-6, *EICAR 2007 Best Academic Papers*, Springer-Verlag, France, 2007.

[CRO200201] K. Crow, "Failure Modes and Effects Analysis (FMEA)," DRM Associates Whitepaper, 2002. DRM Associates, 2613 Via Olivera, Palos Verdes, CA 90274, USA.

[EBI200301] Secrétariat Général de la Défense Nationale, Direction Centrale de la Sécurité des Systèmes d'Information, 51 Boulevard de LaTour-Maubourg-75700 Paris, France.

[ELS200901] Elsag Datamat S.p.A, Via Puccini 2, 16154 Genova, Italy.

[ENI200801] European Network and Information Security Agency (ENISA), 2008.

[ETSI200301] ETSI, "ETSI Threat Vulnerability and Risk Analysis (TVRA) Method," TS102 165-1, V4.1.1, 2003, http://portal.etsi.org/mbs/Security/Writing/TVRA.htm

[IAT200901] INFOSEC Assurance Training and Rating Program (IATRP), official website, 2009, *http://www.iatrp.com/*

[IEC200001] IEC 60812 Ed. 1.0: Analysis Techniques for System Reliability—Procedure for Failure Mode and Effects Analysis (FMEA).

[ISA200801] ISACA, 3701 Algonquin Road, Suite 1010, Rolling Meadows, IL 60008, USA.

[IMP200801] ISO27k Implementers Forum (http://www.iso27001security.com), 2008.

[ISO31000] ISO/TMB WG on Risk Management, ISO/CD 31000, Risk management— Guidelines on principles and implementation of risk management, ISO 2007.

[JON200501] J. A. Jones, *An Introduction to Factor Analysis of Information Risk (FAIR)*, 2005, http://www.riskmanagementinsight.com.

[MAR200601] MAGERIT, Version 2: Methodology for *Information Systems Risk Analysis and Management*. Book 1—The Method, Published by Ministerio de Asministraciones Publicas, Madrid, 20 June 2006 (v 1.1), NIPO: 326-06-044-8.

[MIC200601] Microsoft Solutions for Security and Compliance and Microsoft Security Center of Excellence, *The Security Risk Management Guide*, 2006, Microsoft Corporation, Redmond, WA.

[MIL198001] MIL-STD-1629A, Procedures for Performing a Failure Mode Effects and Criticality Analysis, November 24, 1980.

[MIT200701] MITA-NEMA/COCIR/JIRA SPC, Information Security Risk Management for Healthcare Systems, October 17, 2007, Whitepaper NEMA/COCIR/JIRA Security and Privacy Committee (SPC), Secretariat: MITA (Medical Imaging & Technology Alliance), 1300 North 17th Street, Suite 1752, Rosslyn, VA 22209 USA, www.medicalimaging.org

[PTA200901] PTA Technologies, 20 David Yelin St., Tel-Aviv 62964, Israel.

[SAE200201] SAE J-1739, Potential Failure Mode and Effects Analysis in Design and Potential Failure Mode and Effects Analysis in Manufacturing and Assembly Processes Reference Manual, August 1, 2002.

[SIE200901] Siemens Enterprise Communications Ltd., Brickhill Street, Willen Lake, Milton Keynes, MK15 0DJ, England.

[SOM200901] Security Officers Management and Analysis Project (SOMAP.org).

[TEL200901] Telindus Group nv (Headquarters), Geldenaaksebaan 335, B-3001 Heverlee, Belgium.

CHAPTER 5

METHODOLOGIES EXAMPLES: COBIT AND OCTAVE

Chapter 4 surveyed a number of risk management methods. One of the better-known methods, *Control Objectives for Information and related Technology* (COBIT®), which provides a comprehensive model guiding the implementation of IT governance processes/systems, including information security controls, is reviewed here, along with *Operationally Critical Threat, Asset, and Vulnerability Evaluation* (OCTAVE®), which is a risk-based strategic assessment and planning technique for security. This chapter provides some details on these two methods.

5.1   OVERVIEW

COBIT is published by ISACA®. COBIT is an IT governance framework and supporting toolset that allows managers to bridge the gap between control requirements, technical issues, and business risks. COBIT enables policy development and good practice for IT control throughout organizations. COBIT emphasizes regulatory compliance, helps organizations to increase the value attained from IT, enables alignment, and simplifies implementation of the COBIT framework. For an IT organization to be successful in delivering against business requirements, management should put an internal control system or framework in place. The COBIT control framework contributes to these needs by [ISA200801]:

- Making a link to the business requirements
- Organizing IT activities into a generally accepted process model
- Identifying the major IT resources to be leveraged
- Defining the management control objectives to be considered

---

Information Technology Risk Management in Enterprise Environments: A Review of Industry Practices and a Practial Guide to Risk Management Teams, by Jake Kouns and Daniel Minoli
Copyright © 2010 John Wiley & Sons, Inc.

ISACA is a worldwide organization focused on IT governance, control, security, and assurance; it was founded in 1969 and has more than 86,000 constituents in more than 160 countries, ISACA has become a pace-setting global organization for information governance, control, security and audit professionals. ISACA's IS auditing and IS control standards are used by practitioners worldwide. It sponsors the Certified Information Systems Auditor (CISA) certification, the Certified Information Security Manager (CISM) certification, and the Certified in the Governance of Enterprise IT (CGEIT) certification.

OCTAVE® published by Carnegie Mellon University's Computer Emergency Response Team (CERT®). It is a suite of tools, techniques, and methods for risk-based information security strategic assessment and planning. There are three OCTAVE methods:

- The original OCTAVE method, which forms the basis for the OCTAVE body of knowledge
- OCTAVE-S, for smaller organizations
- OCTAVE-Allegro, a streamlined approach for information security assessment and assurance

OCTAVE methods are founded on the OCTAVE criteria—a standard approach for a risk-driven and practice-based information security evaluation. The OCTAVE criteria establish the fundamental principles and attributes of risk management that are used by the OCTAVE methods. The OCTAVE methods are [CER200901] as follows:

- **Self-Directed.** Small teams of organizational personnel across business units and IT work together to address the security needs of the organization.
- **Flexible.** Each method can be tailored to the organization's unique risk environment, security and resiliency objectives, and skill level.
- **Evolved.** OCTAVE has helped to move the organization toward an operational risk-based view of security and addresses technology in a business context.

CERT is an organization devoted to (a) ensuring that appropriate technology and systems management practices are used to resist attacks on networked systems and (b) limiting damage and ensure continuity of critical services in spite of successful attacks, accidents, or failures. In 1988, the Morris worm crippled the Internet, inspiring the formation of a center to coordinate communication among experts during security emergencies and to help prevent future incidents. CERT has grown over the last two decades, adapting to the changes in technology and adding more areas of work to address new needs and threats. CERT is the home of the well-known CERT Coordination Center (CERT/CC) and is located at the Carnegie Mellon University's Software

Engineering Institute. CERT studies Internet security vulnerabilities, researches long-term changes in networked systems, and develops information and training related to security [CER200901].

The information included in this chapter is based in large measure on material published by various owner/proponents of these methods and tools; references are noted.

5.2   COBIT[26]

For many enterprises, information and the technology that supports it represent their most valuable, but often least understood, assets. Successful enterprises recognize the benefits of information technology and use it to drive their stakeholders' value. These enterprises also understand and manage the associated risks, such as increasing regulatory compliance and critical dependence of many business processes on IT. The need for assurance about the value of IT, the management of IT-related risks, and increased requirements for control over information are now understood as key elements of enterprise governance. Value, risk, and control constitute the core of IT governance.

IT governance is the responsibility of executives and the board of directors, and it consists of the leadership, organizational structures, and processes that ensure that the enterprise's IT sustains and extends the organization's strategies and objectives. Furthermore, IT governance integrates and institutionalizes good practices to ensure that the enterprise's IT supports the business objectives. IT governance enables the enterprise to take full advantage of its information, thereby maximizing benefits, capitalizing on opportunities, and gaining competitive advantage. These outcomes require (a) a framework for control over IT that fits with and supports the Committee of Sponsoring Organizations of the Treadway Commission's (COSO's) *Internal Control—Integrated Framework*, the widely accepted control framework for enterprise governance and risk management, and (b) similar compliant frameworks. Organizations should satisfy the quality, fiduciary, and security requirements for their information, as for all assets. Management should also optimize the use of available IT resources, including applications, information, infrastructure, and people. To discharge these responsibilities, as well as to achieve its objectives, management should understand the status of its enterprise architecture for IT and decide what governance and control it should provide.

Control Objectives for Information and Related Technology (COBIT®) provides good practices across a domain and process framework and presents

---

[26]This COBIT material is based on the IT Governance Institute's COBIT 4.1 Executive Summary of Framework paper and is used with permission.

activities in a manageable and logical structure. COBIT's good practices represent the consensus of experts. They are strongly focused more on control, less on execution. These practices will help optimize IT-enabled investments, ensure service delivery, and provide a measure against which to judge when things do go wrong. For IT to be successful in delivering against business requirements, management should put an internal control system or framework in place. The COBIT control framework contributes to these needs by

- Making a link to the business requirements
- Organizing IT activities into a generally accepted process model
- Identifying the major IT resources to be leveraged
- Defining the management control objectives to be considered

The business orientation of COBIT consists of linking business goals to IT goals, providing metrics and maturity models to measure their achievement, and identifying the associated responsibilities of business and IT process owners.

The process focus of COBIT is illustrated by a process model that subdivides IT into four domains and 34 processes in line with the responsibility areas of plan, build, run and monitor, providing an end-to-end view of IT. Enterprise architecture concepts help identify the resources essential for process success— that is, applications, information, infrastructure, and people. In summary, to provide the information that the enterprise needs to achieve its objectives, IT resources need to be managed by a set of naturally grouped processes. But how does the enterprise get IT under control such that it delivers the information the enterprise needs? How does it manage the risks and secure the IT resources on which it is so dependent? How does the enterprise ensure that IT achieves its objectives and supports the business?

First, management needs control objectives that define the ultimate goal of implementing policies, plans and procedures, and organizational structures designed to provide reasonable assurance that

- Business objectives are achieved
- Undesired events are prevented or detected and corrected

Second, in today's complex environments, management is continuously searching for condensed and timely information to make difficult decisions on value, risk, and control quickly and successfully. What should be measured, and how? Enterprises need an objective measure of where they are and where improvement is required, and they need to implement a management toolkit to monitor this improvement.

Figure 5.1 shows some traditional questions and the management information tools used to find the responses, but these dashboards need indicators, scorecards need measures and benchmarking needs a scale for comparison.

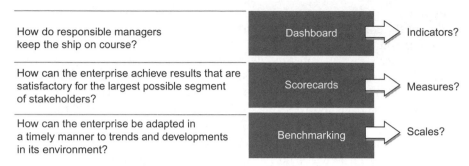

FIGURE 5.1. Management Information.

An answer to these requirements of determining and monitoring the appropriate IT control and performance level is COBIT's definition of

- **Benchmarking** of IT process performance and capability, expressed as maturity models, derived from the Software Engineering Institute's Capability Maturity Model (CMM)
- **Goals and metrics** of the IT processes to define and measure their outcome and performance based on the principles of Robert Kaplan and David Norton's balanced business scorecard
- **Activity goals** for getting these processes under control, based on COBIT's control objectives

The assessment of process capability based on the COBIT maturity models is a key part of IT governance implementation. After identifying critical IT processes and controls, maturity modeling enables gaps in capability to be identified and demonstrated to management. Action plans can then be developed to bring these processes up to the desired capability target level.

Thus, COBIT supports IT governance (Figure 5.2) by providing a framework to ensure that

- IT is aligned with the business
- IT enables the business and maximizes benefits
- IT resources are used responsibly
- IT risks are managed appropriately

Performance measurement is essential for IT governance. It is supported by COBIT and includes setting and monitoring measurable objectives of what the IT processes need to deliver (process outcome) and how to deliver it (process capability and performance). Many surveys have identified that the lack of transparency of IT's cost, value, and risks is one of the most important drivers for IT governance. While the other focus areas contribute, transparency is primarily achieved through performance measurement.

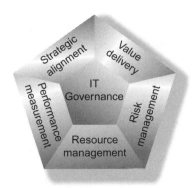

- **Strategic alignment** focuses on ensuring the linkage of business and IT plans; defining, maintaining and validating the IT value proposition; and aligning IT operations with enterprise operations.
- **Value delivery** is about executing the value proposition throughout the delivery cycle, ensuring that IT delivers the promised benefits against the strategy, concentrating on optimizing costs and proving the intrinsic value of IT.
- **Resource management** is about the optimal investment in, and the proper management of, critical IT resources: applications, information, infrastructure and people. Key issues relate to the optimization of knowledge and infrastructure.
- **Risk management** requires risk awareness by senior corporate officers, a clear understanding of the enterprise's appetite for risk, understanding of compliance requirments, transparency about the significant risks to the enterprise and embedding of risk management responsibilities into the organization.
- **Performance measurement** tracks and monitors strategy implementation, project completion, resource usage, process performance and service delivery, using, for example, balanced scorecards that translate strategy into action to achieve goals measurable beyond conventional accounting.

FIGURE 5.2. IT governance focus areas.

These IT governance focus areas describe the topics that executive management needs to address to govern IT within their enterprises. Operational management uses processes to organize and manage ongoing IT activities. COBIT provides a generic process model that represents all the processes normally found in IT functions, providing a common reference model understandable to operational IT and business managers. The COBIT process model has been mapped to the IT governance focus areas (see Appendix II, Mapping IT Processes to IT Governance Focus Areas, COSO, COBIT IT Resources and COBIT Information Criteria), providing a bridge between what operational managers need to execute and what executives wish to govern.

To achieve effective governance, executives require that controls be implemented by operational managers within a defined control framework for all IT processes. COBIT's IT control objectives are organized by IT process; therefore, the framework provides a clear link among IT governance requirements, IT processes and IT controls. COBIT is focused on what is required to achieve adequate management and control of IT, and is positioned at a high level. COBIT has been aligned and harmonized with other, more detailed IT standards and good practices (see Appendix IV, COBIT 4.1 Primary Reference Material). COBIT acts as an integrator of these different guidance materials, summarizing key objectives under one umbrella framework that also links to governance and business requirements.

COSO (and similar compliant frameworks) is generally accepted as the internal control framework for enterprises. COBIT is the generally accepted internal control framework for IT.

The COBIT products have been organized into three levels (Figure 5.3) designed to support

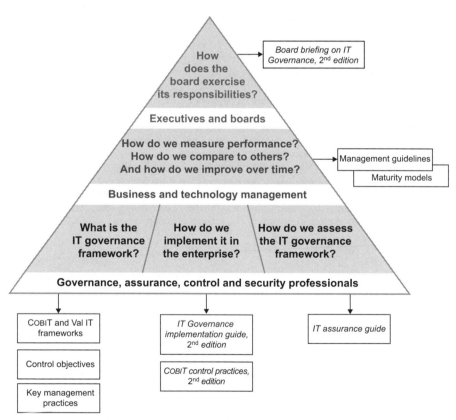

This COBIT-based product diagram presents the generally applicable products and their primary audience. There are also derived products for specific purposes (*IT Control objectives for Sarbanes-Oxley, 2nd Edition*), for domains such as security (COBIT *Security baseline and information security governance: Guidance for boards of directors and executive management*), or for specific enterprises (COBIT *Quickstart* for small and medium-sized enterprises or for large enterprises wishing to ramp up to a more extensive IT Governance implementation).

FIGURE 5.3. COBIT content diagram.

- Executive management and boards
- Business and IT management
- Governance, assurance, control, and security professionals

Briefly, the COBIT products include

- *Board Briefing on IT Governance, 2nd edition*—Helps executives under-stand why IT governance is important, what its issues are, and what their responsibility is for managing it
- Management guidelines/maturity models—Help assign responsibility, measure performance, and benchmark and address gaps in capability
- Frameworks—Organize IT governance objectives and good practices by IT domains and processes, and link them to business requirements
- Control objectives—Provide a complete set of high-level requirements to be considered by management for effective control of each IT process
- *IT Governance Implementation Guide: Using COBIT® and Val IT*^{TM}, *second edition*   Provides a generic road map for implementing IT govern-ance using the COBIT and Val IT^{TM} resources
- *COBIT® Control Practices: Guidance to Achieve Control Objectives for Successful IT Governance, second edition*—Provides guidance on why controls are worth implementing and how to implement them
- *IT Assurance Guide: Using COBIT®*—Provides guidance on how COBIT can be used to support a variety of assurance activities together with suggested testing steps for all the IT processes and control objectives

The COBIT content diagram depicted in Figure 5.3 presents the primary audiences, their questions on IT governance, and the generally applicable products that provide responses. There are also derived products for specific purposes, for domains such as security, or for specific enterprises.

All of these COBIT components interrelate, providing support for the governance, management, control and assurance needs of the different audi-ences, as shown in Figure 5.4.

COBIT is a framework and supporting tool set that allow managers to bridge the gap with respect to control requirements, technical issues, and business risks and communicate that level of control to stakeholders. COBIT enables the development of clear policies and good practice for IT control throughout enterprises. COBIT is continuously kept up to date and harmo-nized with other standards and guidance. Hence, COBIT has become the integrator for IT good practices and the umbrella framework for IT governance that helps in understanding and managing the risks and benefits associated with IT. The process structure of COBIT and its high-level, business-oriented approach provide an end-to-end view of IT and the decisions to be made about IT.

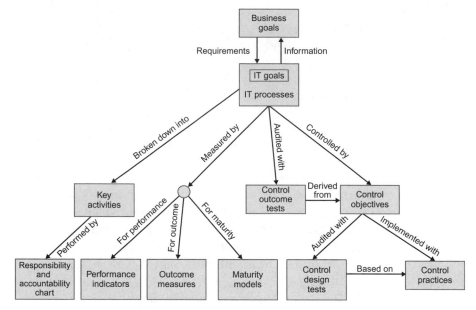

FIGURE 5.4. Interrelationships of COBIT components.

The benefits of implementing COBIT as a governance framework over IT include

- Better alignment, based on a business focus
- A view, understandable to management, of what IT does
- Clear ownership and responsibilities, based on process orientation
- General acceptability with third parties and regulators
- Shared understanding amongst all stakeholders, based on a common language
- Fulfillment of the COSO requirements for the IT control environment

The rest of this chapter provides a description of the COBIT framework and all of the core COBIT components, organized by COBIT's four IT domains and 34 IT processes. This provides a handy reference for all of the main COBIT guidance.

The most complete and up-to-date information on COBIT and related products, including online tools, implementation guides, case studies, newsletters, and educational materials, can be found at *www.isaca.org/cobit*.

5.2.1   COBIT Framework

COBIT Mission: To research, develop, publicize, and promote an authoritative, up-to-date, internationally accepted IT governance control framework for adoption by enterprises and day-to-day use by business managers, IT professionals, and assurance professionals.

5.2.2 The Need for a Control Framework for IT Governance

A control framework for IT governance defines the reasons IT governance is needed, the stakeholders, and what it needs to accomplish.

Why. Increasingly, top management is realizing the significant impact that information can have on the success of the enterprise. Management expects heightened understanding of the way IT is operated and the likelihood of its being leveraged successfully for competitive advantage. In particular, top management needs to know if information is being managed by the enterprise so that it is

- Likely to achieve its objectives
- Resilient enough to learn and adapt
- Judiciously managing the risks it faces
- Appropriately recognizing opportunities and acting upon them

Successful enterprises understand the risks and exploit the benefits of IT and find ways to deal with

- Aligning IT strategy with the business strategy
- Assuring investors and shareholders that a "standard of due care" around mitigating IT risks is being met by the organization
- Cascading IT strategy and goals down into the enterprise
- Obtaining value from IT investments
- Providing organizational structures that facilitate the implementation of strategy and goals
- Creating constructive relationships and effective communication between the business and IT, and with external partners
- Measuring IT's performance

Enterprises cannot deliver effectively against these business and governance requirements without adopting and implementing a governance and control framework for IT to

- Make a link to the business requirements
- Make performance against these requirements transparent
- Organize its activities into a generally accepted process model
- Identify the major resources to be leveraged
- Define the management control objectives to be considered

Furthermore, governance and control frameworks are becoming a part of IT management good practice and are an enabler for establishing IT governance and complying with continually increasing regulatory requirements.

IT good practices have become significant due to a number of factors:

- Business managers and boards demanding a better return from IT investments—that is, that IT delivers what the business needs to enhance stakeholder value
- Concern over the generally increasing level of IT expenditure
- The need to meet regulatory requirements for IT controls in areas such as privacy and financial reporting (e.g., the U.S. Sarbanes–Oxley Act, Basel II) and in specific sectors such as finance, pharmaceutical, and health care
- The selection of service providers and the management of service out-sourcing and acquisition
- Increasingly complex IT-related risks, such as network (perimeter) security
- IT governance initiatives that include adoption of control frameworks and good practices to help monitor and improve critical IT activities to increase business value and reduce business risk
- The need to optimize costs by following, where possible, standardized, rather than specially developed, approaches
- The growing maturity and consequent acceptance of well-regarded frameworks, such as COBIT, IT Infrastructure Library (ITIL), ISO 27000 series on information security-related standards, ISO 9001:2000 *Quality Management Systems—Requirements*, Capability Maturity Model® Integration (CMMI), Projects in Controlled Environments 2 (PRINCE2), and *A Guide to the Project Management Body of Knowledge* (PMBOK)
- The need for enterprises to assess how they are performing against generally accepted standards and their peers (benchmarking)

Who. A governance and control framework needs to serve a variety of internal and external stakeholders, each of whom has specific needs:

- Stakeholders within the enterprise who have an interest in generating value from IT investments:
  - Those who make investment decisions
  - Those who decide about requirements
  - Those who use IT services
- Internal and external stakeholders who provide IT services:
  - Those who manage the IT organization and processes
  - Those who develop capabilities
  - Those who operate the services

- Internal and external stakeholders who have a control/risk responsibility:
  - Those with security, privacy and/or risk responsibilities
  - Those performing compliance functions
  - Those requiring or providing assurance services

What. To meet the requirements listed in the previous section, a framework for IT governance and control should

- Provide a business focus to enable alignment between business and IT objectives
- Establish a process orientation to define the scope and extent of coverage, with a defined structure enabling easy navigation of content
- Be generally acceptable by being consistent with accepted IT good practices and standards and independent of specific technologies
- Supply a common language with a set of terms and definitions that are generally understandable by all stakeholders
- Help meet regulatory requirements by being consistent with generally accepted corporate governance standards (e.g., COSO) and IT controls expected by regulators and external auditors

5.2.3 How COBIT Meets the Need

In response to the needs described in the previous section, the COBIT framework was created with the main characteristics of being business-focused, process-oriented, controls-based, and measurement-driven.

Business-Focused. Business orientation is the main theme of COBIT. It is designed not only to be employed by IT service providers, users, and auditors, but also, and more important, to provide comprehensive guidance for management and business process owners.

The COBIT framework is based on the following principle (Figure 5.5):

To provide the information that the enterprise requires to achieve its objectives, the enterprise needs to invest in and manage and control IT resources using a structured set of processes to provide the services that deliver the required enterprise information.

Managing and controlling information are at the heart of the COBIT framework and help ensure alignment to business requirements.

5.2.4 COBIT's Information Criteria

To satisfy business objectives, information needs to conform to certain control criteria, which COBIT refers to as business requirements for information. Based on the broader-quality fiduciary and security requirements, seven distinct, certainly overlapping, information criteria are defined as follows:

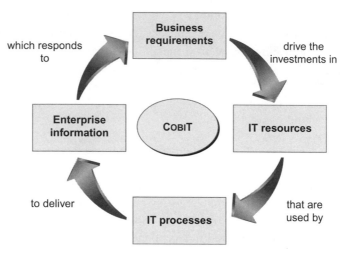

FIGURE 5.5. Basic COBIT principle.

- **Effectiveness** deals with information being relevant and pertinent to the business process as well as being delivered in a timely, correct, consistent and usable manner.
- **Efficiency** concerns the provision of information through the optimal (most productive and economical) use of resources.
- **Confidentiality** concerns the protection of sensitive information from unauthorized disclosure.
- **Integrity** relates to the accuracy and completeness of information as well as to its validity in accordance with business values and expectations.
- **Availability** relates to information being available when required by the business process now and in the future. It also concerns the safeguarding of necessary resources and associated capabilities.
- **Compliance** deals with complying with the laws, regulations and, contractual arrangements to which the business process is subject—that is, externally imposed business criteria as well as internal policies.
- **Reliability** relates to the provision of appropriate information for management to operate the entity and exercise its fiduciary and governance responsibilities.

5.2.5 Business Goals and IT Goals

While information criteria provide a generic method for defining the business requirements, defining a set of generic business and IT goals provides a business-related and more refined basis for establishing business requirements and developing the metrics that allow measurement against these goals. Every enterprise uses IT to enable business initiatives, and these can be represented as

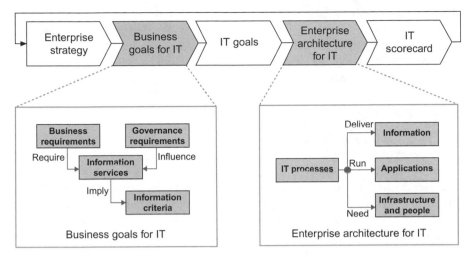

FIGURE 5.6. Defining IT goals and enterprise architecture for IT.

business goals for IT. COBIT Appendix I provides a matrix of generic business goals and IT goals and shows how they map to the information criteria. These generic examples can be used as a guide to determine the specific business requirements, goals, and metrics for the enterprise. (COBIT Appendix I is not included in this text.)

If IT is to successfully deliver services to support the enterprise's strategy, there should be a clear ownership and direction of the requirements by the business (the customer) and a clear understanding of what needs to be delivered, and how, by IT (the provider).

Figure 5.6 illustrates how the enterprise strategy should be translated by the business into objectives related to IT-enabled initiatives (the business goals for IT). These objectives should lead to a clear definition of IT's own objectives (the IT goals), which in turn define the IT resources and capabilities (the enterprise architecture for IT) required to successfully execute IT's part of the enterprise's strategy. Once the aligned goals have been defined, they need to be monitored to ensure that actual delivery matches expectations. This is achieved by metrics that are derived from the goals and captured in an IT scorecard. For the customer to understand the IT goals and IT scorecard, all of these objectives and associated metrics should be expressed in business terms meaningful to the customer. This, combined with an effective alignment of the hierarchy of objectives, will ensure that the business can confirm that IT is likely to support the enterprise's goals.

5.2.6 COBIT Framework

COBIT'S Appendix I, Tables Linking Goals and Processes, provides a global view of how generic business goals relate to IT goals, IT processes, and information criteria. The tables help demonstrate the scope of COBIT and the overall business relationship between COBIT and enterprise drivers. As Figure 5.6 illustrates, these drivers come from the business and from the governance layer of the enterprise, the former focusing more on functionality and speed of delivery, the latter more on cost efficiency, return on investment (ROI), and compliance.

5.2.7 IT Resources

The IT organization delivers against these goals by a clearly defined set of processes that use people skills and technology infrastructure to run automated business applications while leveraging business information. These resources, together with the processes, constitute an enterprise architecture for IT, as shown in Figure 5.6. To respond to the business requirements for IT, the enterprise needs to invest in the resources required to create an adequate technical capability (e.g., an enterprise resource planning [ERP] system) to support a business capability (e.g., implementing a supply chain) resulting in the desired outcome (e.g., increased sales and financial benefits).

The IT resources identified in COBIT can be defined as follows:

- **Applications** are the automated user systems and manual procedures that process the information.
- **Information** is the data, in all their forms, input, processed, and output by the information systems in whatever form is used by the business.
- **Infrastructure** is the technology and facilities (i.e., hardware, operating systems, database management systems, networking, multimedia, and the environment that houses and supports them) that enable the processing of the applications.
- **People** are the personnel required to plan, organize, acquire, implement, deliver, support, monitor, and evaluate the information systems and services. They may be internal, outsourced, or contracted as required.

Figure 5.7 summarizes how the business goals for IT influence how the IT resources need to be managed by the IT processes to deliver IT's goals.

Process-Oriented. COBIT defines IT activities in a generic process model within four domains. These domains are Plan and Organize, Acquire and Implement, Deliver and Support, and Monitor and Evaluate. The domains map to IT's traditional responsibility areas of plan, build, run, and monitor.

The COBIT framework provides a reference process model and common language for everyone in an enterprise to view and manage IT activities. Incorporating an operational model and a common language for all parts of the business involved in IT is one of the most important and initial steps toward good governance. It also provides a framework for measuring and monitoring IT performance, communicating with service providers, and integrating best management practices. A process model encourages process ownership,

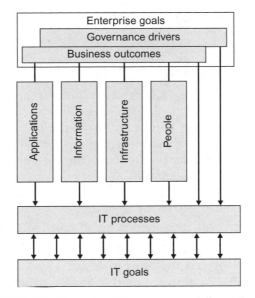

FIGURE 5.7. Managing IT resources to deliver IT goals.

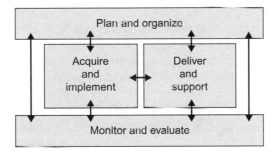

FIGURE 5.8. The four interrelated domains of COBIT.

enabling responsibilities and accountability to be defined. To govern IT effectively, it is important to appreciate the activities and risks within IT that need to be managed. They are usually ordered into the responsibility domains of plan, build, run, and monitor. Within the COBIT framework, these domains, as shown in Figure 5.8, are called

- **Plan and Organize (PO)**—Provides direction to solution delivery (AI) and service delivery (DS)
- **Acquire and Implement (AI)**—Provides the solutions and passes them to be turned into services
- **Deliver and Support (DS)**—Receives the solutions and makes them usable for end users

- **Monitor and Evaluate (ME)**—Monitors all processes to ensure that the direction provided is followed

5.2.8   Plan and Organize (PO)

This domain covers strategy and tactics, and it concerns the identification of the way IT can best contribute to the achievement of the business objectives. The realization of the strategic vision needs to be planned, communicated, and managed for different perspectives. A proper organization as well as technological infrastructure should be put in place. This domain typically addresses the following management questions:

- Are IT and the business strategy aligned?
- Is the enterprise achieving optimum use of its resources?
- Does everyone in the organization understand the IT objectives?
- Are IT risks understood and being managed?
- Is the quality of IT systems appropriate for business needs?

5.2.9   Acquire and Implement (AI)

To realize the IT strategy, IT solutions need to be identified, developed or acquired, as well as implemented and integrated into the business process. In addition, changes in and maintenance of existing systems are covered by this domain to make sure the solutions continue to meet business objectives. This domain typically addresses the following management questions:

- Are new projects likely to deliver solutions that meet business needs?
- Are new projects likely to be delivered on time and within budget?
- Will the new systems work properly when implemented?
- Will changes be made without upsetting current business operations?

5.2.10   Deliver and Support (DS)

This domain is concerned with the actual delivery of required services, which includes service delivery, management of security and continuity, service support for users, and management of data and operational facilities. It typically addresses the following management questions:

- Are IT services being delivered in line with business priorities?
- Are IT costs optimized?
- Is the workforce able to use the IT systems productively and safely?
- Are adequate confidentiality, integrity and availability in place for information security?

5.2.11 Monitor and Evaluate (ME)

All IT processes need to be regularly assessed over time for their quality and compliance with control requirements. This domain addresses performance management, monitoring of internal control, regulatory compliance and governance. It typically addresses the following management questions:

- Is IT's performance measured to detect problems before it is too late?
- Does management ensure that internal controls are effective and efficient?
- Can IT performance be linked back to business goals?
- Are adequate confidentiality, integrity and availability controls in place for information security?

Across these four domains, COBIT has identified 34 IT processes that are generally used (refer to Figure 5.22 for the complete list). While most enterprises have defined plan, build, run and monitor responsibilities for IT, and most have the same key processes, few will have the same process structure or apply all 34 COBIT processes. COBIT provides a complete list of processes that can be used to verify the completeness of activities and responsibilities; however, they need not all apply, and, even more, they can be combined as required by each enterprise.

For each of these 34 processes, a link is made to the business and IT goals that are supported. Information on how the goals can be measured, what the key activities and major deliverables are, and who is responsible for them is also provided.

Controls-Based. COBIT defines control objectives for all 34 processes, as well as overarching process and application controls.

5.2.12 Processes Need Controls

Control is defined as the policies, procedures, practices and organizational structures designed to provide reasonable assurance that business objectives will be achieved and undesired events will be prevented or detected and corrected.

5.2.13 Cobit Framework

IT control objectives provide a complete set of high-level requirements to be considered by management for effective control of each IT process. They

- Are statements of managerial actions to increase value or reduce risk
- Consist of policies, procedures, practices, and organizational structures
- Are designed to provide reasonable assurance that business objectives will be achieved and undesired events will be prevented or detected and corrected

Enterprise management needs to make choices relative to these control objectives by

- Selecting those that are applicable
- Deciding upon those that will be implemented
- Choosing how to implement them (frequency, span, automation, etc.)
- Accepting the risk of not implementing those that may apply

Guidance can be obtained from the standard control model shown in Figure 5.9. It follows the principles evident in this analogy: When the room temperature (standard) for the heating system (process) is set, the system will constantly check (compare) ambient room temperature (control information) and will signal (act) the heating system to provide more or less heat.

Operational management uses processes to organize and manage ongoing IT activities. COBIT provides a generic process model that represents all the processes normally found in IT functions, providing a common reference model understandable to operational IT and business managers. To achieve effective governance, controls need to be implemented by operational managers within a defined control framework for all IT processes. Since COBIT's IT control objectives are organized by IT process, the framework provides clear links amongst IT governance requirements, IT processes, and IT controls.

Each of COBIT's IT processes has a process description and a number of control objectives. As a whole, they are the characteristics of a well-managed process. The control objectives are identified by a two-character domain reference (PO, AI, DS, and ME) plus a process number and a control objective number. In addition to the control objectives, each COBIT process has generic control requirements that are identified by PCn, for process control number.

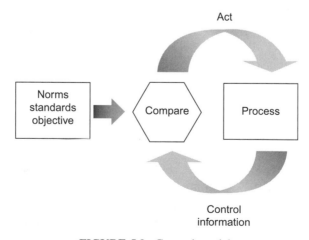

FIGURE 5.9. Control model.

They should be considered together with the process control objectives to have a complete view of control requirements.

PC1 Process Goals and Objectives. Define and communicate specific, measurable, actionable, realistic, results-oriented, and timely (SMARRT) process goals and objectives for the effective execution of each IT process. Ensure that they are linked to the business goals and supported by suitable metrics.

PC2 Process Ownership. Assign an owner for each IT process, and clearly define the roles and responsibilities of the process owner. Include, for example, responsibility for process design, interaction with other processes, accountability for the end results, measurement of process performance, and the identification of improvement opportunities.

PC3 Process Repeatability. Design and establish each key IT process such that it is repeatable and consistently produces the expected results. Provide for a logical but flexible and scaleable sequence of activities that will lead to the desired results and is agile enough to deal with exceptions and emergencies. Use consistent processes, where possible, and tailor only when unavoidable.

PC4 Roles and Responsibilities. Define the key activities and end deliverables of the process. Assign and communicate unambiguous roles and responsibilities for effective and efficient execution of the key activities and their documentation as well as accountability for the process end deliverables.

PC5 Policy, Plans, and Procedures. Define and communicate how all policies, plans, and procedures that drive an IT process are documented, reviewed, maintained, approved, stored, communicated and used for training. Assign responsibilities for each of these activities and, at appropriate times, review whether they are executed correctly. Ensure that the policies, plans, and procedures are accessible, correct, understood, and up to date.

PC6 Process Performance Improvement. Identify a set of metrics that provides insight into the outcomes and performance of the process. Establish targets that reflect on the process goals and performance indicators that enable the achievement of process goals. Define how the data are to be obtained. Compare actual measurements to targets and take action upon deviations, where necessary. Align metrics, targets, and methods with IT's overall performance monitoring approach.

Effective controls reduce risk, increase the likelihood of value delivery, and improve efficiency because there will be fewer errors and a more consistent management approach. In addition, COBIT provides examples for each process that are illustrative, but not prescriptive or exhaustive, of

- Generic inputs and outputs
- Activities and guidance on roles and responsibilities in a responsible, accountable, consulted, and informed (RACI) chart
- Key activity goals (the most important things to do)
- Metrics

In addition to appreciating what controls are required, process owners need to understand what inputs they require from others and what others require from their process. COBIT provides generic examples of the key inputs and outputs for each process, including external IT requirements. There are some outputs that are input to all other processes, marked as "ALL" in the output tables, but they are not mentioned as inputs in all processes and they typically include quality standards and metrics requirements, the IT process framework, documented roles and responsibilities, the enterprise IT control framework, IT policies, and personnel roles and responsibilities.

Understanding the roles and responsibilities for each process is key to effective governance. COBIT provides a RACI chart for each process. Accountable means "the buck stops here"—this is the person who provides direction and authorizes an activity. Responsibility is attributed to the person who gets the task done. The other two roles (consulted and informed) ensure that everyone who needs to be is involved and supports the process.

5.2.14   Business and IT Controls

The enterprise's system of internal controls impacts IT at three levels:

- At the executive management level, business objectives are set, policies are established, and decisions are made on how to deploy and manage the resources of the enterprise to execute the enterprise strategy. The overall approach to governance and control is established by the board and communicated throughout the enterprise. The IT control environment is directed by this top-level set of objectives and policies.
- At the business process level, controls are applied to specific business activities. Most business processes are automated and integrated with IT application systems, resulting in many of the controls at this level being automated as well. These controls are known as application controls. However, some controls within the business process remain as manual procedures, such as authorization for transactions, separation of duties, and manual reconciliations. Therefore, controls at the business process level are a combination of manual controls operated by the business and automated business and application controls. Both are the responsibility of the business to define and manage, although the application controls require the IT function to support their design and development.
- To support the business processes, IT provides IT services, usually in a shared service to many business processes, as many of the development and

operational IT processes are provided to the whole enterprise, and much of the IT infrastructure is provided as a common service (e.g., networks, databases, operating systems and storage). The controls applied to all IT service activities are known as IT general controls. The reliable operation of these general controls is necessary for reliance to be placed on application controls. For example, poor change management could jeopardize (accidentally or deliberately) the reliability of automated integrity checks.

5.2.15 IT General Controls and Application Controls

General controls are controls embedded in IT processes and services. Examples include

- Systems development
- Change management
- Security
- Computer operations

Controls embedded in business process applications are commonly referred to as application controls. Examples include

- Completeness
- Accuracy
- Validity
- Authorization
- Segregation of duties

COBIT assumes the design and implementation of automated application controls to be the responsibility of IT, covered in the Acquire and Implement domain, based on business requirements defined using COBIT's information criteria, as shown in Figure 5.10. The operational management and control responsibility for application controls is not with IT, but with the business process owner.

Hence, the responsibility for application controls is an end-to-end joint responsibility between business and IT, but the nature of the responsibilities changes as follows:

- The business is responsible to properly
  - Define functional and control requirements
  - Use automated services
- IT is responsible to
  - Automate and implement business functional and control requirements
  - Establish controls to maintain the integrity of applications controls

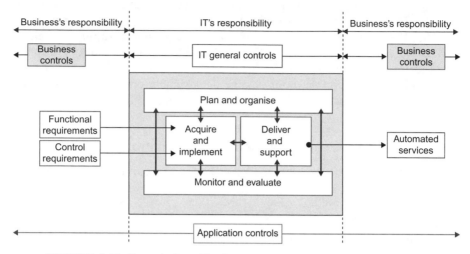

FIGURE 5.10. Boundaries of business, general and application controls.

Therefore, the COBIT IT processes cover general IT controls, but only the development aspects of application controls; responsibility for definition and operational usage is with the business. The following list provides a recommended set of application control objectives. They are identified by ACn, for application control number.

AC1 Source Data Preparation and Authorization. Ensure that source documents are prepared by authorized and qualified personnel following established procedures, taking into account adequate segregation of duties regarding the origination and approval of these documents. Errors and omissions can be minimized through good input form design. Detect errors and irregularities so they can be reported and corrected.

AC2 Source Data Collection and Entry. Establish that data input is performed in a timely manner by authorized and qualified staff. Correction and resubmission of data that were erroneously input should be performed without compromising original transaction authorization levels. Where appropriate for reconstruction, retain original source documents for the appropriate amount of time.

AC3 Accuracy, Completeness and Authenticity Checks. Ensure that transactions are accurate, complete, and valid. Validate data that were input, and edit or send back for correction as close to the point of origination as possible.

AC4 Processing Integrity and Validity. Maintain the integrity and validity of data throughout the processing cycle. Detection of erroneous transactions does not disrupt the processing of valid transactions.

AC5 Output Review, Reconciliation, and Error Handling. Establish procedures and associated responsibilities to ensure that output is handled in an authorized manner, delivered to the appropriate recipient, and protected during transmission; that verification, detection and correction of the accuracy of output occurs; and that information provided in the output is used.

AC6 Transaction Authentication, and Integrity. Before passing transaction data between internal applications and business/operational functions (in or outside the enterprise), check it for proper addressing, authenticity of origin and integrity of content. Maintain authenticity and integrity during transmission or transport.

Measurement-Driven. A basic need for every enterprise is to understand the status of its own IT systems and to decide what level of management and control the enterprise should provide. To decide on the right level, management should ask itself: How far should we go, and is the cost justified by the benefit?

Obtaining an objective view of an enterprise's own performance level is not easy. What should be measured and how? Enterprises need to (a) measure where they are and where improvement is required and (b) implement a management toolkit to monitor this improvement.

COBIT deals with these issues by providing

- Maturity models to enable benchmarking and identification of necessary capability improvements
- Performance goals and metrics for the IT processes, demonstrating how processes meet business and IT goals and are used for measuring internal process performance based on balanced scorecard principles
- Activity goals for enabling effective process performance

5.2.16 Maturity Models

Senior managers in corporate and public enterprises are increasingly asked to consider how well IT is being managed. In response to this, business cases require development for improvement and reaching the appropriate level of management and control over the information infrastructure. While few would argue that this is not a good thing, they need to consider the cost–benefit balance and these related questions:

- What are our industry peers doing, and how are we placed in relation to them?
- What is acceptable industry good practice, and how are we placed with regard to these practices?

- Based upon these comparisons, can we be said to be doing enough?
- How do we identify what is required to be done to reach an adequate level of management and control over our IT processes?

It can be difficult to supply meaningful answers to these questions. IT management is constantly on the lookout for benchmarking and self-assessment tools in response to the need to know what to do in an efficient manner. Starting from COBIT's processes, the process owner should be able to incrementally benchmark against that control objective. This responds to three needs:

1. A relative measure of where the enterprise is
2. A manner to efficiently decide where to go
3. A tool for measuring progress against the goal

Maturity modeling for management and control over IT processes is based on a method of evaluating the organization, so it can be rated from a maturity level of nonexistent (0) to optimized (5). This approach is derived from the maturity model that the Software Engineering Institute (SEI) defined for the maturity of software development capability. Although concepts of the SEI approach were followed, the COBIT implementation differs considerably from the original SEI, which was oriented toward software product engineering principles, organizations striving for excellence in these areas, and formal appraisal of maturity levels so that software developers could be "certified." In COBIT, a generic definition is provided for the COBIT maturity scale, which is similar to CMM but interpreted for the nature of COBIT's IT management processes. A specific model is provided from this generic scale for each of COBIT's 34 processes. Whatever the model, the scales should not be too granular, because that would render the system difficult to use and suggest a precision that is not justifiable because, in general, the purpose is to identify where issues are and how to set priorities for improvements. The purpose is not to assess the level of adherence to the control objectives.

The maturity levels are designed as profiles of IT processes that an enterprise would recognize as descriptions of possible current and future states. They are not designed for use as a threshold model, where one cannot move to the next higher level without having fulfilled all conditions of the lower level. With COBIT's maturity models, unlike the original SEI CMM approach, there is no intention to measure levels precisely or try to certify that a level has exactly been met. A COBIT maturity assessment is likely to result in a profile where conditions relevant to several maturity levels will be met, as shown in the example graph in Figure 5.11.

This is because when assessing maturity using COBIT's models, it will often be the case that some implementation will be in place at different levels even if it is not complete or sufficient. These strengths can be built on to further improve maturity. For example, some parts of the process can be

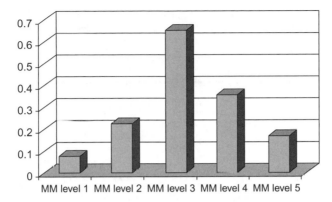

Possible maturity level of an IT process: The example illustrates a
process that is largely at level 3 but still has some compliance issues
with lower level requirements whilst already investing in performance
measurement (level 4) and optimization (level 5)

FIGURE 5.11. Possible maturity level of an IT process.

well-defined, and, even if it is incomplete, it would be misleading to say the
process is not defined at all.

Using the maturity models developed for each of COBIT's 34 IT processes,
management can identify

- The actual performance of the enterprise—Where the enterprise is today
- The current status of the industry—The comparison
- The enterprise's target for improvement—Where the enterprise wants to be
- The required growth path between "as is" and "to be"

To make the results easily usable in management briefings, where they will be
presented as a means to support the business case for future plans, a graphical
presentation method needs to be provided (Figure 5.12).

Possible Maturity Level of an IT Process. The example illustrates a process
that is largely at level 3 but still has some compliance issues with lower level
requirements while already investing in performance measurement (level 4) and
optimization (level 5).

The development of the graphical representation is based on the generic
maturity model descriptions shown in Figure 5.13.

COBIT is a framework developed for IT process management with a strong
focus on control. These scales need to be practical to apply and reasonably easy
to understand. The topic of IT process management is inherently complex and
subjective and, therefore, is best approached through facilitated assessments
that raise awareness, capture broad consensus, and motivate improvement.
These assessments can be performed either against the maturity level descriptions as a whole or with more rigor against each of the individual statements of

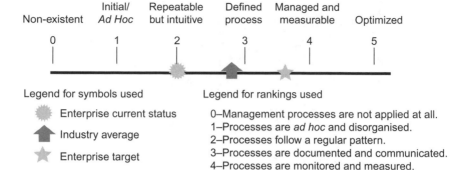

FIGURE 5.12. Graphic representation of maturity models.

---

0 Non-existent—Complete lack of any recognizable processes. The enterprise has not even recognized that there is an issue to be addressed.

1 Initial/Ad Hoc—There is evidence that the enterprise has recognized that the issues exist and need to be addressed. There are, however, no standardized processes; instead, there are *ad hoc* approaches that tend to be applied on an individual or case-by-case basis. The overall approach to management is disorganized.

2 Repeatable but Intuitive—Processes have developed to the stage where similar procedures are followed by different people undertaking the same task. There is no formal training or communication of standard procedures, and responsibility is left to the individual. There is a high degree of reliance on the knowledge of individuals and, therefore, errors are likely.

3 Defined process—Procedures have been standardized and documented, and communicated through training. It is mandated that these processes should be followed; however, it is unlikely that deviations will be detected. The procedures themselves are not sophisticated but are the formalization of existing practices.

4 Managed and measurable—Management monitors and measures compliance with procedures and takes action where processes appear not to be working effectively. Processes are under constant improvement and provide good practice. Automation and tools are used in a limited or fragmented way.

5 Optimized—Processes have been refined to a level of good practice, based on the results of continuous improvement and maturity modeling with other enterprises. IT is used in an integrated way to automate the workflow, providing tools to improve quality and effectiveness, making the enterprise quick to adapt.

FIGURE 5.13. Generic maturity model.

the descriptions. Either way, expertise in the enterprise's process under review is required.

The advantage of a maturity model approach is that it is relatively easy for management to place itself on the scale and appreciate what is involved if improved performance is needed. The scale includes 0 because it is quite possible that no process exists at all. The 0–5 scale is based on a simple maturity scale showing how a process evolves from a nonexistent capability to an optimized capability.

However, process management capability is not the same as process performance. The required capability, as determined by business and IT goals, may not need to be applied to the same level across the entire IT environment—for example, not consistently or to only a limited number of systems or units. Performance measurement, as covered in the next paragraphs, is essential in determining what the enterprise's actual performance is for its IT processes.

Although a properly applied capability already reduces risks, an enterprise still needs to analyze the controls necessary to ensure that risk is mitigated and value is obtained in line with the risk appetite and business objectives. These controls are guided by COBIT's control objectives. Appendix III in COBIT provides a maturity model on internal control that illustrates the maturity of an enterprise relative to establishment and performance of internal control. Often this analysis is initiated in response to external drivers, but ideally it should be instituted as documented by COBIT processes PO6 *Communicate management aims and directions* and ME2 *Monitor and evaluate internal control.*

Capability, coverage, and control are all dimensions of process maturity, as illustrated in Figure 5.14.

The maturity model is a way of measuring how well-developed management processes are—that is, how capable they actually are. How well-developed or capable they should be primarily depends on the IT goals and the underlying business needs they support. How much of that capability is actually deployed largely depends on the return an enterprise wants from the investment. For example, there will be critical processes and systems that need more and tighter security management than others that are less critical. On the other hand, the degree and sophistication of controls that need to be applied in a process are more driven by the enterprise's risk appetite and applicable compliance requirements.

The maturity model scales will help professionals explain to managers where IT process management shortcomings exist and set targets for where they need to be. The right maturity level will be influenced by the enterprise's business objectives, the operating environment, and industry practices. Specifically, the level of management maturity will depend on the enterprise's dependence on IT, its technology sophistication, and, most important, the value of its information. A strategic reference point for an enterprise to improve management and control of IT processes can be found by looking at emerging international standards and best-in-class practices. The emerging practices of today may become the expected level of performance of

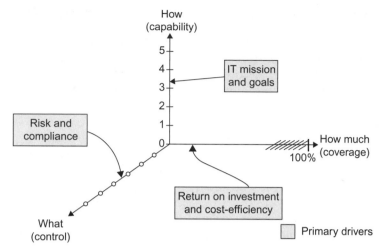

FIGURE 5.14. The three dimensions of maturity.

tomorrow and, therefore, are useful for planning where an enterprise wants to be over time.

The maturity models are built up starting from the generic qualitative model (see Figure 5.13), to which principles from the following attributes are added in an increasing manner through the levels:

- Awareness and communication
- Policies, plans and procedures
- Tools and automation
- Skills and expertise
- Responsibility and accountability
- Goal setting and measurement

The maturity attribute table shown in Figure 5.15 lists the characteristics of how IT processes are managed and describes how they evolve from a nonexistent to an optimized process. These attributes can be used for more comprehensive assessment, gap analysis and improvement planning. In summary, maturity models provide a generic profile of the stages through which enterprises evolve for management and control of IT processes. They are

- A set of requirements and the enabling aspects at the different maturity levels
- A scale where the difference can be made measurable in an easy manner
- A scale that lends itself to pragmatic comparison
- The basis for setting as-is and to-be positions

	Awareness and communication	Policies, plans and procedures	Tools and automation	Skills and expertise	Responsibility and accountability	Goal setting and measurement
1	Recognition of the need for the process is emerging. There is sporadic communication of the overall issues.	There are ad hoc approaches to processes and practices. The process and policies are undefined.	Some tools may exist; usage is based on standard desktop tools. There is no planned approach to the tool usage.	Skills required for the process are not identified. A training plan does not exist and no formal training occurs.	There is no definition of accountability and responsibility. People take ownership of issues based on their own initiative on a reactive basis.	Goals are not clear and no measurement takes place.
2	There is awareness of the need to act. Management communicates the overall issues.	Similar and common processes emerge, but are largely intuitive because of individual expertise. Some aspects of the process are repeatable because of individual expertise, and some documentation and informal understanding of policy and procedures may exist.	Common approaches to use of tools exist but are based or solutions developed by key individuals. Vendor tools may have been acquired, but are probably not applied correctly, and may even be shelfware.	Minimum skill requirements are identified for critical areas. Training is provided in response to needs, rather than on the basis of an agreed plan and informal training on the job occurs.	An individual assumes his/her responsibility and is usually held accountable, even if this is not formally agreed. There is confusion about responsibility when problems occur, and a culture of blame tends to exist.	Some goal setting occurs; some financial measures are established but are known only by senior management. There is inconsistent monitoring in isolated areas.
3	There is understanding of the need to act. Management is more formal and structured in its communication.	Usage of good practices emerges. The process, policies and procedures are defined and documented for all key activities.	A plan has been defined for use and standardization of tools to automate the process. Tools are being used for their basic purposes, but may not all be in accordance with the agreed plan, and may not be integrated with one another.	Skill requirements are defined and documented for all areas. A formal training plan has been developed, but formal training is still based on individual initiatives.	Process responsibility and accountability are defined and process owners have been identified. The process owner is unlikely to have the full authority to exercise the responsibilities.	Some effectiveness goals and measures are set, but are not communicated, and there is a clear link to business goals. Measurement processes emerge, but are not consistently applied. IT balanced scorecard ideas are being adopted, as is occasional intuitive application of root cause analysis.
4	There is understanding of the full requirements. Mature communication techniques are applied and standard communication tools are in use.	The process is sound and complete; internal best practices are applied. All aspects of the process are documented and repeatable. Policies have been approved and signed off on by management. Standards for developing and maintaining the processes and procedures are adopted and followed.	Tools are implemented according to a standardized plan, and some have been integrated with other related tools. Tools are being used in main areas to automate management of the process and monitor critical activities and controls.	Skill requirements are routinely updated for all areas, proficiency is ensured for all critical areas, and certification is encouraged. Mature training techniques are applied according to the training plan, and knowledge sharing is encouraged. All internal domain experts are involved, and the effectiveness of the training plan is assessed.	Process responsibility and accountability are accepted and working in a way that enables a process owner to fully discharge his/her responsibilities. A reward culture is in place that motivates positive action.	Efficiency and effectiveness are measured and communicated and linked to business goals and the IT strategic plan. The IT balanced scorecard is implemented in some areas with exceptions noted by management and root cause analysis is being standardised. Continuous improvement is emerging.
5	There is advanced, forward-looking understanding of requirements. Proactive communication of issues based on trends exists, mature communication techniques are applied, and integrated communication tools are in use.	External best practices and standards are applied. Process documentation is evolved to automated workflows. Processes, policies and procedures are standardised and integrated to enable end-to-end management and improvement.	Standardized tool sets are used across the enterprise. Tools are fully integrated with other related tools to enable end-to-end support of the processes. Tools are being used to support improvement of the process and automatically detect control exceptions.	The organization formally encourages continuous improvement of skills, based or clearly defined personal and organisational goals. Training and education support external best practices and use of leading-edge concepts and techniques. Knowledge sharing is an enterprise culture, and knowledge-based systems are being deployed. External experts and industry leaders are used for guidance.	Process owners are empowered to make decisions and take action. The acceptance of responsibility has been cascaded down throughout the organization in a consistent fashion.	There is an integrated performance measurement system linking IT performance to business goals by global application of the IT balanced scorecard. Exceptions are globally and consistently noted by management and root cause analysis is applied. Continuous improvement is a way of life.

FIGURE 5.15. Maturity attribute table.

- Support for gap analysis to determine what needs to be done to achieve a chosen level
- Taken together, a view of how IT is managed in the enterprise

The COBIT maturity models focus on maturity, but not necessarily on coverage and depth of control. They are not a number for which to strive, nor are they designed to be a formal basis for certification with discrete levels that create thresholds that are difficult to cross. However, they are designed to be always applicable, with levels that provide a description an enterprise can recognize as best fitting its processes. The right level is determined by the enterprise type, environment, and strategy. Coverage, depth of control, and how the capability is used and deployed are cost–benefit decisions. For example, a high level of security management may have to be focused only on the most critical enterprise systems. Another example would be the choice between a weekly manual review and a continuous automated control.

Finally, while higher levels of maturity increase control over the process, the enterprise still needs to determine, based on risk and value drivers, which control mechanisms it should apply. The generic business and IT goals defined in this framework will help with this analysis. The control mechanisms are guided by COBIT's control objectives and focus on what is done in the process; the maturity models primarily focus on how well a process is managed. Appendix III in COBIT provides a generic maturity model showing the status of the internal control environment and the establishment of internal controls in an enterprise.

A properly implemented control environment is attained when all three aspects of maturity (capability, coverage, and control) have been addressed. Improving maturity reduces risk and improves efficiency, leading to fewer errors, more predictable processes, and a cost-efficient use of resources.

5.2.17 Performance Measurement

Goals and metrics are defined in COBIT at three levels:

- IT goals and metrics that define what the business expects from IT and how to measure it
- Process goals and metrics that define what the IT process must deliver to support IT's objectives and how to measure it
- Activity goals and metrics that establish what needs to happen inside the process to achieve the required performance and how to measure it

Goals are defined top-down in that a business goal will determine a number of IT goals to support it. An IT goal is achieved by one process or the interaction of a number of processes. Therefore, IT goals help define the different process goals. In turn, each process goal requires a number of activities, thereby establishing the activity goals. Figure 5.16 provides examples of the business, IT, process, and activity goal relationship.

The terms KGI and KPI, used in previous versions of COBIT, have been replaced with two types of metrics:

- Outcome measures, previously key goal indicators (KGIs), indicate whether the goals have been met. These can be measured only after the fact and, therefore, are called "lag indicators."
- Performance indicators, previously key performance indicators (KPIs), indicate whether goals are likely to be met. They can be measured before the outcome is clear and, therefore, are called "lead indicators."

Figure 5.17 provides possible goal or outcome measures for the example used.

The outcome measure indicating that detection and resolution of unauthorized access are on target will also indicate that it will be more likely that IT services can resist and recover from attacks. That is, the outcome measure has become a performance indicator for the higher-level goal. Figure 5.18 illustrates how outcome measures for the example become performance metrics.

Outcome measures define measures that inform management—after the fact—whether an IT function, process, or activity has achieved its goals. The outcome measures of the IT functions are often expressed in terms of information criteria:

- Availability of information needed to support the business needs
- Absence of integrity and confidentiality risks
- Cost-efficiency of processes and operations
- Confirmation of reliability, effectiveness and compliance

Performance indicators define measures that determine how well the business, IT function, or IT process is performing in enabling the goals to be reached. They are lead indicators of whether goals will likely be reached, thereby driving the higher-level goals. They often measure the availability of appropriate capabilities, practices and skills, and the outcome of underlying activities. For example, a service delivered by IT is a goal for IT but a performance indicator and a capability for the business. This is why performance indicators are sometimes referred to as performance drivers, particularly in balanced scorecards.

Therefore, the metrics provided are an outcome measure of the IT function, IT process, or activity goal they measure, as well as a performance indicator driving the higher-level business, IT function, or IT process goal.

Figure 5.19 illustrates the relationship between the business, IT, process and activity goals, and the different metrics. From top left to top right, the goals cascade is illustrated. Below the goal is the outcome measure for the goal. The small arrow indicates that the same metric is a performance indicator for the higher-level goal.

196

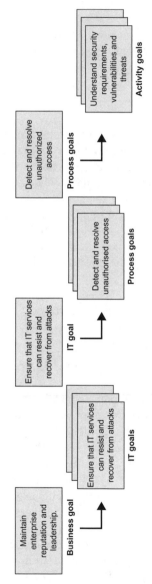

FIGURE 5.16. Example of goal relationships.

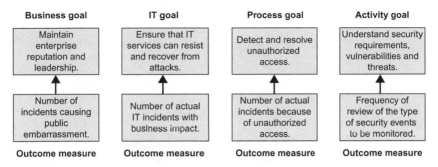

FIGURE 5.17. Possible outcome measures for the example in Figure 5.16.

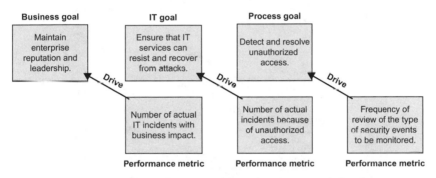

FIGURE 5.18. Possible performance drivers for the example in Figure 5.16.

The example provided is from DS5 *Ensure systems security*. COBIT provides metrics only up to the IT goals outcome as delineated by the dotted line. While they are also performance indicators for the business goals for IT, COBIT does not provide business goal outcome measures.

The business and IT goals used in the goals and metrics section of COBIT, including their relationship, are provided in Appendix I in COBIT. For each IT process in COBIT, the goals and metrics are presented, as noted in Figure 5.20.

The metrics have been developed with the following characteristics in mind:

- A high insight-to-effort ratio (i.e., insight into performance and the achievement of goals as compared to the effort to capture them)
- Comparable internally (e.g., percent against a base or numbers over time)
- Comparable externally irrespective of enterprise size or industry
- Better to have a few good metrics (may even be one very good one that could be influenced by different means) than a longer list of lower-quality metrics
- Easy to measure, not to be confused with targets

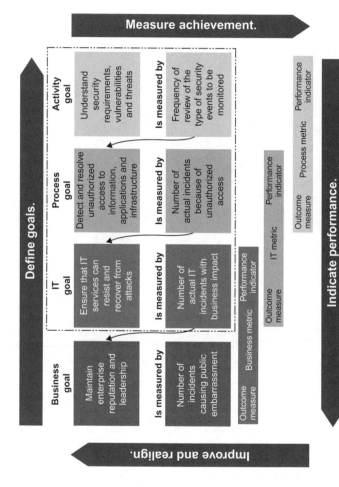

FIGURE 5.19. Relationship amongst process, goals, and metrics (DS5).

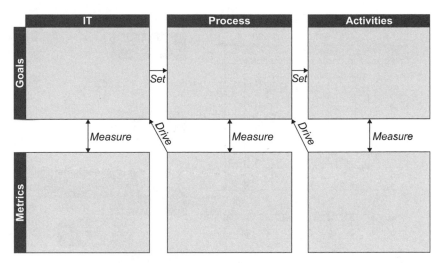

FIGURE 5.20. Presentation of goals and metrics.

The COBIT Framework Model. The COBIT framework, therefore, ties the businesses requirements for information and governance to the objectives of the IT services function. The COBIT process model enables IT activities and the resources that support them to be properly managed and controlled based on COBIT's control objectives, and aligned and monitored using COBIT's goals and metrics, as illustrated in Figure 5.21.

To summarize, IT resources are managed by IT processes to achieve IT goals that respond to the business requirements. This is the basic principle of the COBIT framework, as illustrated by the COBIT cube (Figure 5.22).

In more detail, the overall COBIT framework can be shown graphically, as depicted in Figure 5.23, with COBIT's process model of four domains containing 34 generic processes, managing the IT resources to deliver information to the business according to business and governance requirements.

COBIT's General Acceptability. COBIT is based on the analysis and harmonization of existing IT standards and good practices and conforms to generally accepted governance principles. It is positioned at a high level, is driven by business requirements, covers the full range of IT activities, and concentrates on *what* should be achieved rather than *how* to achieve effective governance, management, and control. Therefore, it acts as an integrator of IT governance practices and appeals to executive management; business and IT management; governance, assurance, and security professionals; and IT audit and control professionals. It is designed to be complementary to, and used together with, other standards and good practices.

Implementation of good practices should be consistent with the enterprise's governance and control framework, appropriate for the organization, and integrated with other methods and practices that are being used. Standards

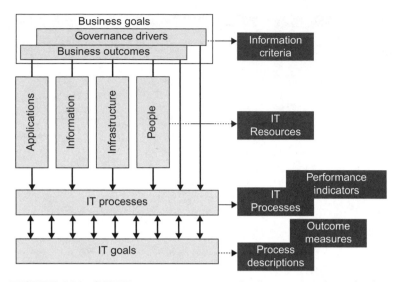

FIGURE 5.21. COBIT management, control, alignment, and monitoring.

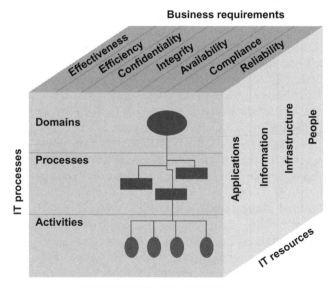

FIGURE 5.22. The COBIT cube.

and good practices are not a panacea. Their effectiveness depends on how they have been implemented and kept up to date. They are most useful when applied as a set of principles and as a starting point for tailoring specific procedures. To avoid practices becoming shelfware, management and staff should understand what to do, how to do it, and why it is important.

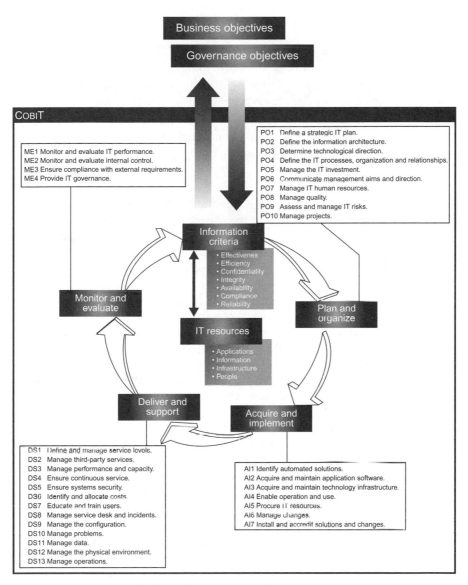

FIGURE 5.23. Overall COBIT framework.

To achieve alignment of good practice to business requirements, it is recommended that COBIT be used at the highest level, providing an overall control framework based on an IT process model that should generically suit every enterprise. Specific practices and standards covering discrete areas can be mapped up to the COBIT framework, thus providing a hierarchy of guidance materials.

COBIT appeals to different users:

- **Executive management**—To obtain value from IT investments and balance risk and control investment in an often unpredictable IT environment
- **Business management**—To obtain assurance on the management and control of IT services provided by internal or third parties
- **IT management**—To provide the IT services that the business requires to support the business strategy in a controlled and managed way
- **Auditors**—To substantiate their opinions and/or provide advice to management on internal controls

COBIT has been developed and is maintained by an independent, not-for-profit research institute, drawing on the expertise of its affiliated association's members, industry experts, and control and security professionals. Its content is based on ongoing research into IT good practice and is continuously maintained, providing an objective and practical resource for all types of users.

COBIT is oriented toward the objectives and scope of IT governance, ensuring that its control framework is comprehensive, in alignment with enterprise governance principles and, therefore, acceptable to boards, executive management, auditors, and regulators. In Appendix II of COBIT, a mapping is provided showing how COBIT's control objectives map onto the five focus areas of IT governance and the COSO control activities.

Figure 5.24 summarizes how the various elements of the COBIT framework map onto the IT governance focus areas.

COBIT Framework Navigation. For each of the COBIT IT processes, a description is provided, together with key goals and metrics in the form of a waterfall (Figure 5.25).

	Goals	Metrics	Practices	Maturity models
Strategic alignment	P	P		
Value delivery		P	S	P
Risk management		S	P	S
Resource management		S	P	P
Performance measurement	P	P		S

P = Primary enabler   S = Secondary enabler

FIGURE 5.24. COBIT framework and it governance focus areas.

Within each IT process, control objectives are provided as generic action statements of the minimum management good practices to ensure that the process is kept under control.

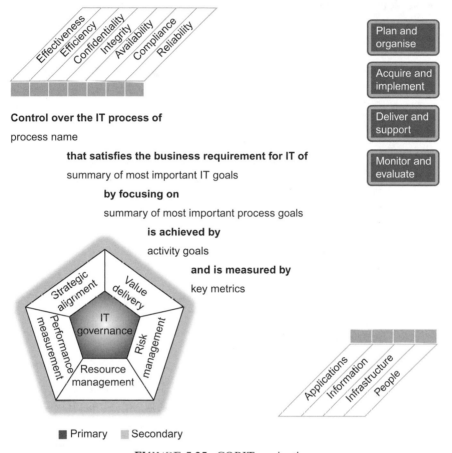

FIGURE 5.25. COBIT navigation.

Overview of Core COBIT Components. The COBIT framework is populated with the following core components, provided in the rest of this publication and organized by the 34 IT processes, giving a complete picture of how to control, manage, and measure each process. Each process is covered in four sections, and each section constitutes roughly one page, as follows:

- Section 1 (Figure 5.25) contains a process description summarizing the process objectives, with the process description represented in a waterfall. This page also shows the mapping of the process to the information criteria, IT resources, and IT governance focus areas by way of P to indicate primary relationship and S to indicate secondary.
- Section 2 contains the control objectives for this process.

- Section 3 contains the process inputs and outputs, RACI chart, goals, and metrics.
- Section 4 contains the maturity model for the process.

Another way of viewing the process performance content is as follows:

- Process inputs are what the process owner needs from others.
- The process description control objectives describe what the process owner needs to do.
- The process outputs are what the process owner has to deliver.
- The goals and metrics show how the process should be measured.
- The RACI chart defines what has to be delegated and to whom.
- The maturity model shows what has to be done to improve.

The roles in the RACI chart are categorized for all processes as

- Chief executive officer (CEO)
- Chief financial officer (CFO)
- Business executives
- Chief information officer (CIO)
- Business process owner
- Head operations
- Chief architect
- Head development
- Head IT administration (for large enterprises, the head of functions such as human resources, budgeting and internal control)
- The project management officer (PMO) or function
- Compliance, audit, risk, and security (groups with control responsibilities but not operational IT responsibilities)

Certain specific processes have an additional specialized role specific to the process—for example, service desk/incident manager for DS8.

It should be noted that while the material is collected from hundreds of experts, following rigorous research and review, the inputs, outputs, responsibilities, metrics, and goals are illustrative but not prescriptive or exhaustive. They provide a basis of expert knowledge from which each enterprise should select what efficiently and effectively applies to it based on enterprise strategy, goals, and policies.

Users of the COBIT Components. Management can use the COBIT material to evaluate IT processes using the business goals and IT goals detailed in Appendix I of COBIT to clarify the objectives of the IT processes and the process maturity models to assess actual performance. Implementors and auditors can identify applicable control requirements from the control objectives and responsibilities from the activities and associated RACI charts.

All potential users can benefit from using the COBIT content as an overall approach to managing and governing IT, together with more detailed standards such as

- ITIL for service delivery
- CMM for solution delivery
- ISO 17799 for information security
- PMBOK or PRINCE2 for project management

5.3 OCTAVE

As we now know, the first step in managing information security risk is to understand what the risk exposures are; once the firm has identified what the risk exposures are, one can build mitigation plans to address those risks. The OCTAVE[27] Method uses a three-phased approach to examine organizational and technology issues, assembling a comprehensive picture of the organization's information security needs. While the OCTAVE Method was developed with relatively large organizations in mind (300 employees or more), it can be tailored to suit a smaller organization.

5.3.1 The OCTAVE Approach

The OCTAVE Method is comprised of a series of workshops, either facilitated or conducted by an interdisciplinary analysis team of three to five of the organization's own personnel. The method takes advantage of knowledge from multiple levels of the organization, focusing on

- Identifying critical assets and the threats to those assets
- Identifying the vulnerabilities, both organizational and technological, that expose those threats, creating risk to the organization
- Developing a practice-based protection strategy and risk mitigation plans to support the organization's mission and priorities

OCTAVE requires that an evaluation be led and performed by a small, interdisciplinary analysis team of the organization's business and IT personnel.

---

[27]This material is summarized from Carnegie Mellon, Software Engineering Institute, *OCTAVE^{SM} Method Implementation Guide Version 2.0, Volume 1: Introduction*, C. J. Alberts and A. J. Dorofee, June 2001 [CAR200101]. The reader should consult this reference for a comprehensive treatment of this topic. This summary is intended to stimulate interest on the part of the reader to further research the topic directly with its source.

Team members work together to make decisions based on risks to critical information assets. These activities are supported by a catalog of good or known practices, as well as by surveys and worksheets that can be used to elicit and capture information during focused discussions and problem-solving sessions.

OCTAVE is an approach to information security risk evaluations that is systematic, context-driven, and self-directed. The method is based on a set of criteria that define the essential elements of an asset-driven, self-directed security risk evaluation for an organization. The approach is embodied in a set of criteria that define the essential elements of an asset-driven information security risk evaluation. The OCTAVE criteria require catalogs of information to measure organizational practices, analyze threats, and build protection strategies. These catalogs are

- Catalog of practices—a collection of good strategic and operational security practices
- Generic threat profile—a collection of major sources of threats
- Catalog of vulnerabilities—a collection of vulnerabilities based on platform and application

The OCTAVE Method is a complex activity requiring a team with a diverse set of skills and experiences. It is led and performed by an interdisciplinary analysis team made up of people from the business units and the IT department. The method is a self-directed security evaluation, but it also lends itself to using outside experts for specific activities, if necessary.

The *OCTAVE Method Implementation Guide* [CAR200101] provides everything that an analysis team needs to use the OCTAVE Method to conduct an evaluation in their organization. OCTAVE is meant to be tailored to specific organization and the specific domain. The Method Implementation Guide includes a complete set of detailed processes, worksheets, and instructions for each step in the method, as well as support material and guidance for tailoring. Figure 1.6 in Chapter 1 depicted a graphical view of the method. The Method Implementation Guide consists of multiple "volumes and appendices." The Method Implementation Guide contains everything one needs to perform an OCTAVE Risk Management implementation. While there are many ways that the OCTAVE Method can be implemented, this guide reflects the most probable scenario. There are 18 volumes in the OCTAVE guide. In general, the Method Implementation Guide includes

- Overview material
- Feedback form to return your experiences, critiques, and suggestions
- Guidance for preparing to do an OCTAVE
- Tailoring guidance

- Process descriptions and guidance
- Worksheets and instructions
- Slides and notes for presentations
- Surveys
- Catalogs
- References
- A complete example of all results, based on pilot tests and experience

Some of the details are as follows:

- **Volume 1: Introduction:** This volume includes a description of OCTAVE, guidance on how to use this guide, some suggestions relative to analysis team training, and a feedback form.
- **Volume 2: Preliminary Activities:** This contains guidelines for preparing to do an OCTAVE, including selecting the analysis team and participants, scheduling, and logistics. Also in this volume, one finds high-level tailoring guidance, along with briefings for senior managers and participants.
- **Volumes 3–12: The OCTAVE Process:** These volumes provide a complete set of information for the three phases and eight processes of the OCTAVE Method. Each process is documented in its own volume and generally includes an introduction, a summary of the process, example results, detailed process guidelines, worksheets, and a set of slides and notes. Process 8, which has two different types of workshops, is broken into two volumes, for convenience. In addition, an Asset Profile Workbook is in a separate volume and provides a complete set of all of the worksheets and results associated with a single critical asset. Volumes 3–12 define the OCTAVE Method and are the largest part of the guide.
  - Volume 3: Phase 1, Process 1: Identify Senior Management Knowledge
  - Volume 4: Phase 1, Process 2: Identify Operational Area Management Knowledge
  - Volume 5: Phase 1, Process 3: Identify Staff Knowledge
  - Volume 6: Phase 1, Process 4: Create Threat Profiles
  - Volume 7: Phase 2, Process 5: Identify Key Components
  - Volume 8: Phase 2, Process 6: Evaluate Selected Components
  - Volume 9: Phase 3, Process 7: Conduct Risk Analysis
  - Volume 10: Phase 3, Process 8, Workshop A: Develop Protection Strategy
  - Volume 11: Phase 3, Process 8, Workshop B: Select Protection Strategy
  - Volume 12: Asset Profile Workbook
- **Volume 13: After the Evaluation:** This is a short section providing guidance and an example of what to do after the evaluation is over.

- **Volume 14: Bibliography and Glossary:** This provides a long, but not exhaustive, list of references, websites, and other sources of information relative to information security, practices, and standards. A glossary provides the definitions for the key terms used throughout this guide.
- **Volume 15: Appendix A: OCTAVE Catalog of Practices:** This volume provides a set of good information security practices against which an organization measures itself for current practices and organizational vulnerabilities.
- **Volume 16: Appendix B: OCTAVE Data Flow:** This volume contains a data flow diagram showing, in concise format, all of the activities, inputs, outputs, and worksheets in the OCTAVE Method.
- **Volume 17: Appendix C: Complete Example Results:** This provides the complete set of example results (which are also found in smaller pieces throughout the guide).
- **Volume 18: Appendices D and E: White Papers:** Two papers, *Overview of the OCTAVE Method* and *OCTAVE Threat Profiles*, are provided in this volume.

The guide makes reference to

- Curious or casual readers
- Champions
- Sponsors and other managers
- Analysis team

A "champion" is a manager, someone who may be getting ready to implement OCTAVE (an analysis team member). Champions are those who see something they think will help their organization and then proceed to do whatever is needed to get it started. A champion could be a manager, a senior staff member, or a recognized expert within the organization. Managers reading this are likely looking to see what this is going to cost in terms of people and time while also trying to determine what role they might have to play. Analysis team members could be from the IT department or other business units within the organization.

5.3.2   The OCTAVE Method

The OCTAVE Method uses a three-phase approach to examine organizational and technology issues, assembling a comprehensive picture of the organization's information security needs. The method uses workshops to encourage open discussion and exchange of information about assets, security practices, and strategies.

Each phase consists of several processes, and each process has one or more workshops led or conducted by the analysis team. Some preparation activities are also necessary to establish a good foundation for successfully completing the evaluation.

Preparing for OCTAVE creates the foundation for a successful evaluation. Some keys to a successful evaluation are as follows:

- **Get Senior Management Sponsorship.** This is the most critical success factor. If senior managers support the process, people in the organization will actively participate.
- **Select the Analysis Team.** Team members need to have sufficient skills to lead the evaluation. They also need to know how to go outside the team to augment their knowledge and skills.
- **Scope OCTAVE.** The evaluation should include important operational areas. If the scope is too big, it will be hard to analyze all of the data. If it is too small, the results may not be as meaningful.
- **Select Participants.** Staff members from multiple organizational levels will contribute their knowledge. It is important for these people to understand their operational areas.

These three phases and their processes are described below.

Phase 1: Build Asset-Based Threat Profiles. This is an organizational evaluation. The analysis team determines which assets are most important to the organization (critical assets) and identifies what is currently being done to protect those assets. The processes of Phase 1 are:

- **Process 1: Identify Senior Management Knowledge.** Selected senior managers identify important assets, perceived threats, security requirements, current security practices, and organizational vulnerabilities.
- **Process 2: Identify Operational Area Management Knowledge.** Selected operational area managers identify important assets, perceived threats, security requirements, current security practices, and organizational vulnerabilities.
- **Process 3: Identify Staff Knowledge.** Selected general and IT staff members identify important assets, perceived threats, security requirements, current security practices, and organizational vulnerabilities.
- **Process 4: Create Threat Profiles.** The analysis team analyzes the information from Processes 1 to 3, selects critical assets, refines the associated security requirements, and identifies threats to those assets, creating threat profiles.

Phase 2: Identify Infrastructure Vulnerabilities. This is an evaluation of the information infrastructure. The analysis team examines key operational components for weaknesses (technology vulnerabilities) that can lead to unauthorized action against critical assets. The processes of Phase 2 are:

- **Process 5: Identify Key Components.** The analysis team identifies key information technology systems and components for each critical asset. Specific instances are then selected for evaluation.
- **Process 6: Evaluate Selected Components.** The analysis team examines the key systems and components for technology weaknesses. Vulnerability tools (software, checklists, scripts) are used. The results are examined and summarized, looking for the relevance to the critical assets and their threat profiles.

Phase 3: Develop Security Strategy and Plans. During this part of the evaluation, the analysis team identifies risks to the organization's critical assets and decides what to do about them. The processes of Phase 3 are:

- **Process 7: Conduct Risk Analysis.** The analysis team identifies the impact of threats to critical assets, creates criteria to evaluate those risks, and evaluates the impacts based on those criteria. This produces a risk profile for each critical asset.
- **Process 8: Develop Protection Strategy.** The analysis team creates a protection strategy for the organization and mitigation plans for critical assets, based upon an analysis of the information gathered. Senior managers then review, refine, and approve the strategy and plans.

After OCTAVE. Finally, at the end of the evaluation, implementation details will need to be added to the protection strategy and risk mitigation plans. Managers should also define steps for continuously reviewing and improving their security posture.

REFERENCES

[CAR200101] Carnegie Mellon, Software Engineering Institute, $OCTAVE^{SM}$ *Method Implementation Guide Version 2.0, Volume 1: Introduction*, C. J. Alberts and A. J. Dorofee, June 2001.

[CER200901] CERT, Carnegie Mellon University's Software Engineering Institute, 4500 Fifth Avenue, Pittsburgh, PA 15213-2612, USA.

[C41200901] IT Governance Institute, COBIT 4.1 Excerpt: Executive Summary, Framework. 3701 Algonquin Road, Suite 1010, Rolling Meadows, IL, 60008 USA.

[ISA200801] ISACA, 3701 Algonquin Road, Suite 1010, Rolling Meadows, Illinois 60008, USA.

PART II

DEVELOPING RISK MANAGEMENT TEAMS

CHAPTER 6

RISK MANAGEMENT ISSUES AND ORGANIZATION SPECIFICS

6.1 PURPOSE AND SCOPE

Part 1 of this text surveyed industry standards and methods to undertake risk management, focusing on the formal mechanisms that an existing risk management team ought to follow, or use portions of as a basis to handle risk mitigation in a predictable, effective, reliable, and cost-effective manner; it also focused on what certifications may be of interest to the organization. Part 2 of this text has two main objectives:

1. Assist organizations define, implement, assemble, and maintain a risk management/assessment team that is, thereby, optimally positioned to properly foresee and/or prevent and/or mitigate and/or rapidly remediate potential business-disrupting infractions (applying the methods and principles covered in Part 1).

2. Provide pragmatic guidance from a practitioner's perspective as to the risk management process itself, effectively picking the best from each of the methods described in Part 1 and making observations on "what works and what doesn't really work." This will assist organizations implement a "real world" program to support reliable risk management in general and risk assessment in particular. The reality is that if risk management becomes too complicated, it loses its core value to the organization.

The chapters that follow build off the material covered in the Part 1 of the book and punctuate key risk management issues as they relate to the specifics of an organization. Today's business world imperatives and the ever-changing IT solutions utilized to support these business imperatives require a repeatable and flexible process for risk management. Naturally, risk management policies and controls add some "limits" to what a business stakeholder in an organization

Information Technology Risk Management in Enterprise Environments: A Review of Industry Practices and a Practial Guide to Risk Management Teams, by Jake Kouns and Daniel Minoli
Copyright © 2010 John Wiley & Sons, Inc.

can or should do. As a simple example, a business stakeholder cannot just simply accept any e-mail attachment (e.g., zip files, executables, pornographic material, etc.) that is routed to the inbox; there will be policies as well as standards and, thus, mechanisms for parsing attachments and quarantining questionable ones. Yet, an organization must be able to quickly make and execute business decisions. Hence, risk management processes cannot be structured, and consequently perceived, as inflexible bureaucratic constructs slowing down the business' goal to market a product or a service.

Figure 6.1 depicts an ecosystem of risk management as a discipline. It depicts policies, (voluntary) standards, industry-developed methods, industry best practices, processes, procedures, tools, training, and certification.[28] We have already discussed standards, industry-developed methods, and industry best practices in Part 1 of this text. Additional terms can be defined as follows:

- **Policies:** Rules and practices that specify or regulate how a system or organization provides security services to protect sensitive and critical system resources.
- **Process:** A well-defined sequence of actions directed to some end. A process defines "what" needs to be done and which roles are involved. A process typically consists of the following [BAN200701]:
  - Roles and responsibilities of the people (roles) assigned to do the work
  - Appropriate tools and equipment to support individuals in doing their jobs
  - Procedures and methods defining "how" to do the tasks and relationships between the task
- **Procedure:** Documentation that defines "how" to do the task; usually only applies to a single role.

Additional concepts that have relevance to the risk management efforts include:

- **Company-Specific Technical Standards:** Specific technical configuration items that define settings for applications, operating systems, databases, networks and other software/hardware assets for the firm in question. Also, refered to as hardening standards.
- **Program:** In this context, an initiative that sets out to define policies, develop process(es) to support an activity (such as risk management/ assessment) that is consistent with the policies, and develop and implement supporting procedures.

---

[28]Actually, this ecosystem can be applied to more general environments, by replacing the RM label in the diagram with labels representing other disciplines.

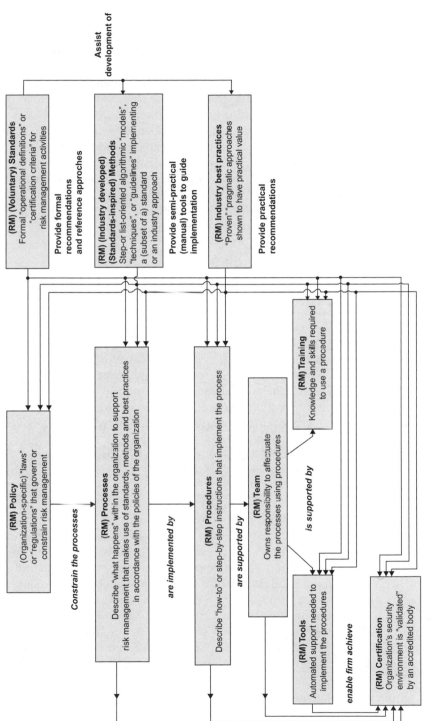

FIGURE 6.1. Ecosystem of the risk management as a discipline.

215

Figure 6.2 depicts graphically the scope of the approach to risk management discussed in Part 2. Part 2 looks at risk management-related policies, processes, procedure, teams, training, and basic level tools. In addition to focusing on the organization-specific issues of risk management as seen on the left-hand side of Figure 6.2, this section of the text, as noted, also deals with practitioner-level approaches to deal with issues and concerns related to actually implementing a risk management strategy at a firm or organization.

Note: In Figures 6.1 and 6.2 the policies are depicted as relating specifically to risk management. These policies are usually included in the overall set of corporate security policies (in other words, they are a subset of the larger set); hence, for the rest of this chapter when we refer to "Policies" we mean the entire set of corporate information security policies. In effect, the overall set of corporate information security policies are ultimately intended to reduce the risk of the firm to an acceptable and targeted level.

6.2 RISK MANAGEMENT POLICIES

Information security policies are the basic and critical building blocks of information security. They are unambiguous statements defining the key information security directives and mandates for the organization. An information security manual often describes the policies. For example, policies should be defined covering access management, encryption controls, logging and data collection, network perimeter security, and so on. As we noted in earlier chapters, risk management can be seen as the process of weighing policy alternatives in consultation with interested parties, considering risk assessment and other legitimate factors, and selecting appropriate prevention and control options [ENI200801].

"Policies," "standards," and "guidelines" are various documents that fall within the policy infrastructure. The following definitions are helpful [SAN200901]:

- (amplifying the definition given above) A policy is a document that outlines specific requirements or rules that must be met. In the information/network security realm, policies are usually point-specific, covering a single area. Furthermore, as just implied in passing, policies should be written down in a document and also be readily available to stakeholders and employees. For example, an "Application Service Provider (ASP) Policy" defines minimum security criteria that an ASP must execute in order to be considered for use on a project by the organization. Security policies may (but do not have to) make references to standards and guidelines that may exist within an organization.
- A standard is typically collections of system-specific or procedural-specific requirements that must be met by everyone. For example, a company might have a standard that describes how to harden a new server, network device or database that has been deployed on a corporate network and

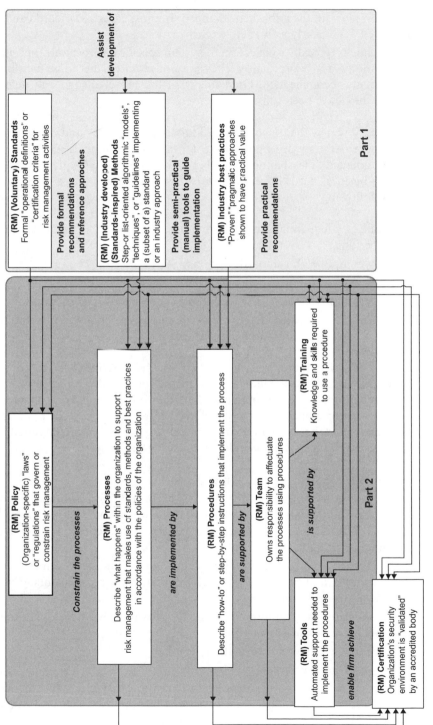

(RM) (Voluntary) Standards
Formal "operational definitions" or "certification criteria" for risk management activities

Provide formal recommendations and reference approches

(RM) (Industry developed) (Standards-inspired) Methods
Step-or list-oriented algorithmic "models", "techniques", or "guidelines" implementing a (subset of a) standard or an industry approach

Provide semi-practical (manual) tools to guide implementation

(RM) Industry best practices
"Proven" "pragmatic approaches shown to have practical value

Provide practical recommendations

Assist development of

Part 1

(RM) Policy
(Organization-specific) "laws" or "regulations" that govern or constrain risk management

Constrain the processes

(RM) Processes
Describe "what happens" within the organization to support risk management that makes use of standards, methods and best practices in accordance with the policies of the organization

are implemented by

(RM) Procedures
Describe "how-to" or step-by-step instructions that implement the process

are supported by

(RM) Team
Owns responsibility to affectuate the processes using procedures

is supported by

(RM) Training
Knowledge and skills required to use a procedure

(RM) Tools
Automated support needed to implement the procedures

enable firm achieve

(RM) Certification
Organization's security environment is "validated" by an accredited body

Part 2

FIGURE 6.2. Ecosystem discussed in Part 2 of the text.

217

must comply with the published standard. In most cases a standard can be measured very clearly as it is either met or not.

- A guideline is typically a collection of system specific or procedural specific "suggestions" for best practice. They are not requirements to be met, but are strongly recommended. Guidelines can be very challenging to determine if they have been fully implemented.

Firms should review their own policies, standards, practices, and procedures and assess whether they are appropriate to their environment. This review should be conducted at least annually and in many cases more frequently based on changing business needs or requirements. Some questions that are relevant include the following:

- Are policies adequate and cover the entire spectrum of IT-related assets and functions?
- Do they comply with standards such as ISO 17799/27002?
- Are they current to the evolving needs of the organization?
- Are they complete? Has a new technology been introduced or upcoming?
- Are these communicated effectively to all employees, including IT practitioners as well as the end-user population?

A corporate information security policy must be written so as to be understood by those who are not experts in the matter; the policy must be published and promulgated throughout the organization and kept updated. Information security policies typically include a large number of clear concise operative statements that span a wide range of corporate issues, often related to carious IT assets. Policies may include many of the following:

- Controlling access to information and systems
- Processing information and documents—for example, networks; system operations and administration; e-mail and the worldwide web; telephones and fax; data management; backup, recovery, and archiving; document handling; securing data
- Securing hardware, peripherals and other equipment; for example, cabling, printers and modems; working off premises or using outsourced processing; using secure storage
- Purchasing and maintaining commercial software; also developing and maintaining in-house software
- Controlling e-commerce information security
- Dealing with physical security
- Addressing personnel issues relating to security: contractual documentation; confidential personnel data; personnel information security responsibilities; HR management; staff leaving employment

- Complying with legal and policy requirements
- Detecting and responding to incidents: reporting information security incidents; investigating information security incidents; corrective activity
- Business continuity management

For example, in the area of access control a policy may state that *"The password standard must be fully implemented."* The password standard (one of the possible company-specific technical standards alluded to above) may state that

- Password shall be at least 10 characters long and shall contain at least one numeric and one special character
- Passwords shall be refreshed every 30 days
- Passwords shall not be shared among users
- Passwords shall not be written down on unprotected (paper) media, etc.

Figure 6.3 depicts an illustrative case of a fictitious company's corporate goals which include advancing the business goals (business facilitation), improving productivity, achieving service levels, meeting regulatory obligations, and operating securely. The last goal can be achieved through the effective institutionalization of security policies.

Table 6.1 compiled from SANS Institute documentation provides a listing of typical information security policy topics [SAN200901]. Appendix 6.A provides an illustrative example of an information security policy.

6.3   A SNAPSHOT OF RISK MANAGEMENT IN THE CORPORATE WORLD

We now return to risk management itself and make some motivational observations related to its implementation in the corporate and/or institutional world.

Risk management as a general concept has been well documented in a number of industries for many years; for example, insurance companies have always had risk managers in place (in spite of more recent doubts about the Insurance industry's ability to manage risk at the macroeconomic level). Starting in the 1980s (maybe even in the 1970s), IT has played a critical part in many aspects of the business operations; it follows naturally that risk management needs to become part of the "fabric" of IT. As already discussed, IT-related risk exposures originating from any number of known and unknown sources are becoming a daily fact of life in virtually every IT shop around the world. It follows that corporate management, typically delegated to the IT organization, must establish an information security program that enables the

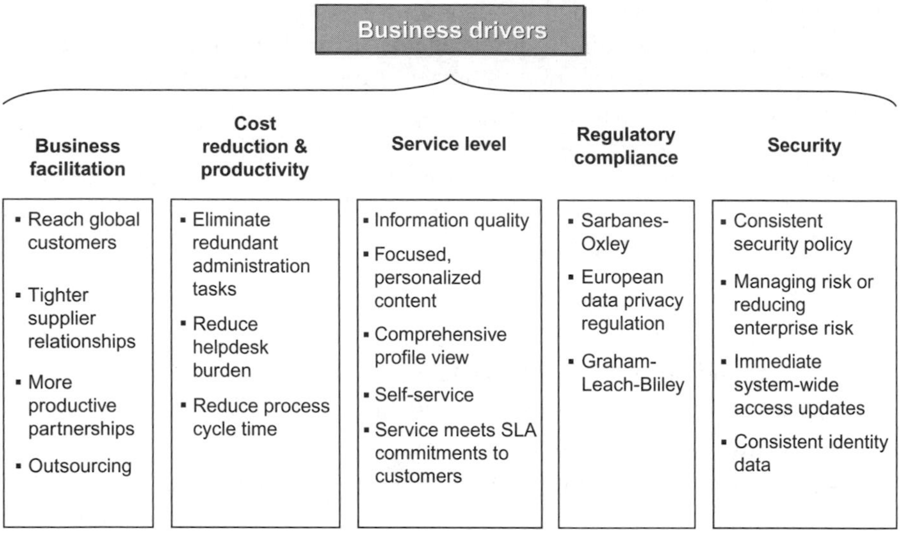

Business drivers				
Business facilitation	**Cost reduction & productivity**	**Service level**	**Regulatory compliance**	**Security**
• Reach global customers • Tighter supplier relationships • More productive partnerships • Outsourcing	• Eliminate redundant administration tasks • Reduce helpdesk burden • Reduce process cycle time	• Information quality • Focused, personalized content • Comprehensive profile view • Self-service • Service meets SLA commitments to customers	• Sarbanes-Oxley • European data privacy regulation • Graham-Leach-Bliley	• Consistent security policy • Managing risk or reducing enterprise risk • Immediate system-wide access updates • Consistent identity data

FIGURE 6.3. Example of corporate goals.

organization to seamlessly undertake routine risk management and to deploy reliable remediation initiatives.

Executive and/or senior-level management within an organization are typically expected to have the overall accountability for protecting information assets. However, in practice, senior-level management often takes a relatively small role in the application of risk assessment and information security in the organization. Usually, senior management delegates the function of information security, even though they may ultimately be accountable. This is why it is important to establish a well-structured risk management/assessment team in the organization. The establishment of a Chief Security Officer (CSO) or Chief Risk Officer (CRO) function is the best mechanism to highlight and punctuate the critical security functions and anchor the risk management team.

Information Security departments have been, or are in the process of being, created in organizations throughout the world. These departments have a plethora of responsibilities that run the gamut from policy setting, security architecture development, security services definition, security apparatus rollout (including product acquisition and configuration), and daily operation of the security apparatus. Functionally, information security is comprised of a number of subareas such as risk management, including mitigation planning; security policy generation; security architecture development; information security administration/operations (host, application, perimeter, operations, and network security; encryption identity management; etc.); business continuity planning; disaster recovery testing and auditing; fraud discovery and interdiction; and regulatory compliance, to name just a few. While there has been a

TABLE 6.1. Listing of Typical Security Policy Topics

Acceptable Encryption Policy	Defines requirements for encryption algorithms used within the organization.
Acceptable Use Policy	Defines acceptable use of equipment and computing services, and the appropriate employee security measures to protect the organization's corporate resources and proprietary information.
Analog/ISDN Line Policy	Defines standards for use of analog/ISDN lines for Fax sending and receiving, and for connection to computers.
Anti-Virus Process	Defines guidelines for effectively reducing the threat of computer viruses on the organization's network.
Application Service Provider Policy	Defines minimum security criteria that an ASP must execute in order to be considered for use on a project by the organization.
Application Service Provider Standards	Outlines the minimum security standards for the ASP. This policy is referenced in the ASP Policy above.
Acquisition Assessment Policy	Defines responsibilities regarding corporate acquisitions, and defines the minimum requirements of an acquisition assessment to be completed by the information security group.
Audit Vulnerability Scanning Policy	Defines the requirements and provides the authority for the information security team to conduct audits and risk assessments to ensure integrity of information/ resources, to investigate incidents, to ensure conformance to security policies, or to monitor user/ system activity where appropriate.
Automatically Forwarded Email Policy	Documents the requirement that no email will be automatically forwarded to an external destination without prior approval from the appropriate manager or director.
Bluetooth Device Security Policy	This policy provides for more secure Bluetooth Device operations. It protects the company from loss of Personally Identifiable Information (PII) and proprietary company data.
Database Credentials Coding Policy	Defines requirements for securely storing and retrieving database usernames and passwords.
Dial-in Access Policy	Defines appropriate dial-in access and its use by authorized personnel.
DMZ Lab Security Policy	Defines standards for all networks and equipment deployed in labs located in the "Demilitarized Zone" or external network segments.
E-mail Policy	Defines standards to prevent tarnishing the public image of the organization.
E-mail Retention	The Email Retention Policy is intended to help employees determine what information sent or received by email should be retained and for how long.

TABLE 6.1. (Continued)

Ethics Policy	Defines the means to establish a culture of openness, trust and integrity in business practices.
Extranet Policy	Defines the requirement that third party organizations requiring access to the organization's networks must sign a third-party connection agreement.
Information Sensitivity Policy	Defines the requirements for classifying and securing the organization's information in a manner appropriate to its sensitivity level.
Information System Audit Logging Requirements	Identifies specific requirements information systems must meet in order to generate appropriate audit logs and integrate with an enterprise's log management function.
Internal Lab Security Policy	Defines requirements for internal labs to ensure that confidential information and technologies are not compromised, and that production services and interests of the organization are protected from lab activities.
Internet DMZ Equipment Policy	Defines the standards to be met by all equipment owned and/or operated by the organization that is located outside the organization's Internet firewalls (the demilitarized zone).
Lab Anti-Virus Policy	Defines requirements which must be met by all computers connected to the organization's lab networks to ensure effective virus detection and prevention.
Password Protection Policy	Defines standards for creating, protecting, and changing strong passwords.
Personal Communication Device	Describes Information Security's requirements for Personal Communication Devices and Voicemail.
Remote Access Policy	Defines standards for connecting to the organization's network from any host or network external to the organization.
Removable Media Policy	Defines coverage of all computers and servers operating in an organization.
Remote Access - Mobile Computing and Storage Devices	To establish an authorized method for controlling mobile computing and storage devices that contain or access information resources.
Risk Assessment Policy	Defines the requirements and provides the authority for the information security team to identify, assess, and remediate risks to the organization's information infrastructure associated with conducting business.
Router Security Policy	Defines standards for minimal security configuration for routers and switches inside a production network, or used in a production capacity.
Server Security Policy	Defines standards for minimal security configuration for servers inside the organization's production network, or used in a production capacity.

TABLE 6.1. (Continued)

Server Malware Protection Policy	Outlines which server systems are required to have anti-virus and/or anti-spyware applications.
The Third Party Network Connection Agreement	Defines the standards and requirements, including legal requirements, needed in order to interconnect a third party organization's network to the production network. This agreement must be signed by both parties.
VPN Security Policy	Defines the requirements for Remote Access IPSec or L2TP Virtual Private Network (VPN) connections to the organization's network.
Wireless Communication Policy	Defines standards for wireless systems used to connect to the organization's networks.
Wireless Communication Standard	Defines standards for wireless systems used to connect to the organization's networks.

trend in favor of combining these functions under one corporate executive function, it is not clear how to best establish the subarea-to-subarea relationships to make the entire function operate in a demonstrably optimal manner. Naturally, there is not a one-size-fits-all solution either for the overall functions composition or for ways to deal with information risks. As one might suspect, there is not a canonical model that can give a definitive formula of how the organization should be created; in fact, there is relatively little usable information for a technology manager to even turn to for aid in the decision-making process.

The Information Security department of a firm or organization needs to be able to determine what constitutes a risk exposure and then determine if the risk exposure can be accepted and/or needs to be mitigated to protect business critical assets. Risk management is a fundamental function that spans across multiple IT departments. Different organizations are at a different state of maturity when it comes to risk management in general and risk assessment in particular. As noted elsewhere in this text, while some organizations have detailed and mature processes, a majority of organizations do not have any formal risk management mechanisms in place. Some organizations have taken small steps in managing risk exposures; however, risk management is often done as a "one-off" task and is not implemented as a sustainable program. In general, organizations need to improve their understanding of risk management and its implementation. Data on vulnerabilities and incidents clearly show that risk management is a long-term requirement and is not just a short-term issue and can be much larger than just a requirement for IT. It is critical for an organization to create and disseminate repeatable processes that allow an information security program to properly uncover, assess, analyze, and directly mitigate information security risk exposures. In the past, however, even when utilized, risk management has often been handled as a "parochial" rather than global issue; for example, risk exposures may be documented by vulnerability assessments teams after performing assessments on particular servers or applications, but, often, not across the enterprise.

Some organizations have programs based on internally developed processes, while other organizations have approaches that are based on recognized industry standards. In fact, the goal of some organizations is to have fully implemented every aspect of a particular standard. There are many risk assessment standards as seen in the first part of this book. Each of these standards has its supporters and detractors; various factions suggest that one standard is better than the other. The reality is that a particular standard may be better suited for a particular organization and another standard may be a better fit for another organization. In many instances, it may be better for an organization to take specific portions of each of the standards and implement them in a way that fits or better supports the particular organization in question.

6.3.1   Motivations for Risk Management

This section provides some additional background and motivation for the establishment of the risk assessment and mitigation apparatus that is advocated in the context of this book; some related motivation was provided in Chapter 1. The specific details related to the formation, management, and job responsibilities of the team are covered in the chapters that follow.

The situation related to IT security has become more challenging of late because the interval of time from when a vulnerability is disclosed until the instance an "exploit" is released that has the possibility of causing damage has decreased significantly in recent years ("exploit" is a technique or code that uses a vulnerability to provide system access to the attacker). What used to be months from the disclosure date until the time when an organization had to worry about being exploited has in the recent past shrunk to just about a month or even less (in some cases in a matter of a few days). This reduced time for exploit development forces organization to assess and react to risk exposures even faster than required previously. Annual vulnerability announcements now number in the thousands. There are many services that an organization can purchase to help manage this issue, and there are also public resources that provide the necessary structure, technology, and content to support that community requirement for vulnerability management. Well-organized databases, with verified contents and flexible search abilities, are helpful if these vulnerabilities are to be controlled by the security community.

The challenge to corporate planners just continues to get more onerous. It has been forecasted that in 2010 around 10,000 new vulnerabilities per year will be discovered in software applications. Considering that each vulnerability discovered has the ability to disrupt or bring a company's business to a complete halt, organizations must take risk management seriously and methodically determine how each risk exposure will be handled. The increased number of vulnerabilities being discovered also drives up the number of security incidents at organizations that have not properly addressed and mitigated their risks.

Information security professionals have endeavored over the years to rationalize to management the level of risk their particular organization faces by showing statistics such as number of vulnerability released. While these statistics are accurate and help to explain the shear volume of the issue, all too often the correlation between the number of vulnerabilities and the support from management has not been as direct as might be expected. The challenge is that general corporate management does not often see the number of vulnerabilities released as a direct potential of business impact. However, these vulnerabilities do result in actual infractions. It can be helpful to use a resource from the Open Security Foundation, a nonprofit organization that maintains the DataLossDB project whose mission is aimed at documenting known and reported data loss incidents world-wide. Figure 6.4 depicts data from Data-LossDB.org that indicate 1700 major data loss incidents have been recorded since January 2000. Clearly, there are costs associated with a data loss and/or breach. A data loss event or security breach are real world events that a business person can clearly understand. Risk management teams can ensure that an organization has the proper controls in place.

Planning for risk management can be proactive or reactive. Clearly, a proactive approach is ideal, but not always practical. A company's risk management department should work in conjunction with IT on projects as early as possible to identify potential issues along the way, which includes the architectural, engineering, implementation, operation, and change or decommissioning phases [BOL200701].

6.3.2   Justifying Risk Management Financially

No matter how concerned an organization is about information security issues, decision-makers and financial planners require some level of justification for resources being spent on security initiatives. If a justification comes from multiple places within the information security department, then there is not a clearly defined repeatable process that ensures that the information is presented accurately. The risk management function and subtending team that we advocate can provide a central clearinghouse within an organization that is able to communicate the qualitative and quantitative reasons as well as what must be accomplished to improve or fully mitigate a security risk.

As is the case for most other corporate functions, a financial underpinning is needed. Organizations need to be aware of the cost of improving security and estimate the benefits. This can be viewed as a return on investment (ROI calculation); in fact during the past decade, organizations have been forced to justify a financial ROI before implementing information security improvements/controls. One needs to go further to address the term return on security investment (ROSI) and describe in detail how the investment actually can be

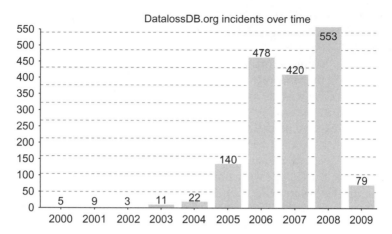

FIGURE 6.4. DatalossDB counts about 1700 incidents since January 2000.

viewed as preventing additional investments or damage in the future. In the simplest case, ROSI can be calculated from a risk assessment to simultaneously justify the investment into additional security infrastructure (tools and people) for an organization. For example, if an internal risk assessment is conducted and the results show that over 70% of the servers have not been patched for critical security vulnerabilities, it is relatively easy to use this information to justify the need to purchase a patch management product or additional resources to install and reduce the risk of exposure. The cost of a technology solution can be cross-referenced to the amount of time it takes an engineer to manually patch each server to determine the appropriate investment. In addition, the analysis must include the potential downtime and loss of revenues the organization sustained during the last incident of this nature. A risk assessment team, by its very nature, engages the executives in the organization in the process of understanding and rationalizing the reasoning behind the information security action plans. ROI and ROSI typically apply in the context of capital expenses (capex) needed to remediate a security gap—say, for example, the upgrade of firewalls, the purchase of an Intrusion Detection System, and so on.

Proving a positive net present value (NPV) against an event that may happen with low probability, but has a debilitating effect if it does happen, is generally difficult. For example, because of regulation that appeared in the 1980s and 1990s, financial firms now have disaster recovery and business continuity plans, even though these plans may be relatively expensive and the disruptive events (hopefully) rare. The same is now becoming the case for more routine information security initiatives. It turns out that a number of state-of-the-art technologies such as Voice over IP, Voice over Wi-Fi, Corporate Video on Demand, MultiProtocols Label Switching backbones, and so on, have been introduced of late in the corporate landscape without proving a positive NPV. In consideration of security incidents of late and with increased legislation, organizations have become more keenly aware of the need for a reliable information security program and for effective and dynamic corporate departments that keep the security apparatus up with evolving events. Executives are being held accountable for potential information security deficiencies by legislation as well as by auditors and shareholders. This shift has been a catalyst for a number of organizations to undertake information security improvements.

Risk is a measurement of expected loss by definition, as covered in Chapter 2. Hence, a well-defined process can demonstrate its financial soundness in clear terms. In addition to capex considerations, there is also the need for operational expenses (opex) to support and sustain (staff) the risk management team.

The following steps are needed as part of a risk management process: Assign a value to information assets; obtain timely information about relevant vulnerabilities; assess threats given the target environment and the potential for exploit code; determine the likelihood (probability) that an event/exposure will cause damage; and be able to respond appropriately should an attack occur. By utilizing the proper quantitative and qualitative risk assessment models, issues can be assessed in a prioritized fashion by the team and a determination can be made on the mitigation strategy. In some cases it may not make business sense to invest the resources to fully correct particular risks that an organization is faced with. As an example, a risk that costs twice as much to mitigate than the business asset itself is worth most likely does not deserve immediate attention in all scenarios.

While some risk exposures have a low probability, the sum of the expected values across the entire organization over the year may be a good indication of what the budget for the department should be. Another approach could be to allocate a fraction (say, 0.1%) of the top line of the firm to IT risk management.

Studies have shown that firms with the worst security/risk management practices experience more frequent and higher financial consequences from the loss of IT assets such as customer records than companies with more well-developed practices. A press time study by the IT Policy Compliance Group Practices found that practices implemented by organizations impact both the magnitude of financial loss (in this study, the findings related to outcomes being experienced in IT, spending on regulatory compliance, and industry performance profiles are compilations of benchmarks across 2648 organizations; the financial loss and return findings are from benchmarks conducted with 1260 organizations; the most recent findings focusing on the primary business and financial risks along with actions that organizations are taking to manage these risks are from benchmarks conducted with 481 organizations in late 2008; findings from benchmarks on the organizational structure for IT security, conducted with 253 organizations completed in late 2008, are also included; 90% of the organizations participating in the benchmarks were located in North America, and the remaining 10% of the participants come from countries located in Africa, Asia Pacific, Europe, the Middle East, and South America). Table 6.2 shows the data loss, business downtime, and financial loss of companies. Note that while for companies using best practices (13% of sample) the percentage loss is low and constant across the revenue domain, that case is quite different for typical (68% of sample) and/or "don't care" (19% of sample) companies. For example, some organizations are experiencing much more loss and theft of customer data while others have few, if any, such losses or thefts to report. Among those with the best track records, roughly 1 in 10 organizations consistently have the lowest rates of data loss or theft, the fewest number of regulatory deficiencies in IT to pass audit, and the least amount of business downtime due to failures and disruptions in IT. In contrast, almost 2 in 10 organizations consistently have the highest rates of data loss and theft, the most problems with regulatory compliance in IT, and the most business downtime due to failures and disruptions in IT. A majority of organizations are operating somewhere between these two extremes, with between 4 and 15 losses or thefts of sensitive information each year, 4–15 compliance deficiencies in IT that must be corrected to pass audit, and between 7 and 59 hours of business downtime due to failures and disruptions occurring in IT [ITP200901].

It should be noted that the losses identified in this empirical study are significantly higher than the losses we cited and postulated above, say at 0.1% of the top line.

One can also look at the empirical data rate as a function of the organization's revenue. Figure 6.5 depicts the financial exposure and occurrence rate as a function of the organization's revenue; as can be seen, smaller firms seem to be less able to cope with security issues (more occurrence of data loss and theft events) than a larger firm, perhaps due to the fact that they cannot reach critical mass in assembling a high-quality security/risk management team. Note, however, that the impact as measured in percent revenue loss is the same for both types of firms.

If one were to use the losses identified in this study for sizing the risk management/assessment team, such a team would actually be fairly large. At a more conservative level, in Chapter 8 we show that some empirical/heuristic observations that can be made (without great loss of generality) in reference to team sizing are as follows:

- For low probability of risk exposure the company revenue must be at around $4B/year before one FTE dedicated to risk management is justified. For revenue of $16B/year, 2–3 FTEs are justified.
- For medium probability of risk exposure the company revenue must be at around $2B/year before one FTE dedicated to risk management is justified. For revenue of $16B/year, a team of 4–5 FTEs is justified.
- For a relatively high probability of risk exposure the company revenue must be at around $1B/year before one FTE dedicated to risk management is justified. For revenue of $16B/year, a team of 8–11 FTEs is justified.
- For high probability of risk exposure the company revenue must be at around $500M/year before one FTE dedicated to risk management is justified. For revenue of $16B/year, a team of 20–30 FTEs is justified.

TABLE 6.2. Data Loss, Business Downtime, and Financial Loss of Companies

		Yearly Data Loss/Theft	Yearly Compliance Deficiencies	Yearly Business Downtime from IT Failures
Worst Firm (Practices)	19%	16 or more	16 or more	60 hours or more
Normative	68%	4 to 15	4 to 15	7 to 59 hours
Best	13%	3 or less	3 or less	6 or less
	N: 2,648			

Business Risks from the Use of IT	Worst (Percentage of Revenue)	Normative (Percentage of Revenue)	Best (Percentage of Revenue)
Data loss and theft	9.6%	6.4%	0.4%
Business downtime	2.8%	0.28%	0.028%

Average Annualized Financial Loss Rates — Data Loss-Theft and Downtime (as a percentage of time)

Annual Revenue of Budget	Worst Practices	Normative Practices	Best Practices
$50 million	$1.5 million	$240,000	$20,500
$500 million	$19 million	$3.3 million	$211,000
$5 billion	$329 million	$60 million	$2.25 million
$50 billion	$5 billion	$1.2 billion	$25 million
$50 million	3.00%	0.48%	0.04%
$500 million	3.80%	0.66%	0.04%
$5 billion	6.58%	1.20%	0.05%
$50 billion	10.00%	2.40%	0.05%

Source: IT Policy Compliance Group, 2009.

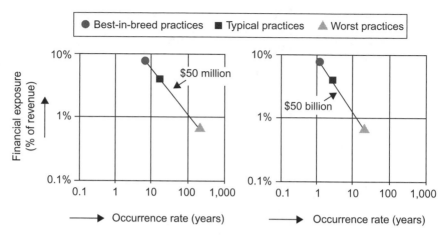

Source: IT Policy Compliance Group, 2009

FIGURE 6.5. Financial exposure and occurrence rate as a function of the organization's revenue.

6.3.3   The Human Factors

While the majority of Information Security departments have a reasonably trained workforce that handles information security issues (and they may have a decent set of security tools), process gaps exist when the information security department is unable to properly identify and assess risk as a fundamental corporate process. In fact, the organization may have a good sense of business risks in general (competitors, supply-chain, market dynamics, etc.), but it may not have a comparable sense of the IT/security-related risks. The risk management team is accountable for deriving risk values to all risk exposures that an organization may face.

The risk management team is tasked with identifying if a possible issue applies to the organization's business critical assets; it is the team tasked with discovering issues on currently deployed systems. Artifacts generated by the team, such as but not limited to a risk assessment report, will provide a perspective into the state of the security for the particular organization and will provide critical information to all levels within the enterprise at large. A proper reporting structure is needed. In many organizations the expense associated with deploying these measures is considered an operating cost.

It is not advisable (or useful) for the risk management team to work in a vacuum. The risk management team needs to be positioned so it can present information security risks in a business context. The risk management team will typically work with the business units as well as have ties into every area of information technology in the organization. This can be accomplished by identifying key liaisons. The liaisons are critical to the risk assessment process, and it is important that defined roles and expectations are set. The risk management team will also distribute the processes that will be followed when a risk must be evaluated.

This team should be critical, clinical, and analytical in the decision-making processes when it is time to justify investments based on defined risk models. All too often an organization will have an incident, a security breach, or a poor audit review that influences an "impulse investment" into security technology and products. The risk management team will be able to ensure that all risks of the organization are viewed as a whole, and key stakeholders are motivated to spend on the priority risk items that remain open and that will provide the biggest security gain and align the organization with the risk posture they are trying to achieve.

Defining the set of policies, procedures, safeguards, tools, and mechanisms that are required, however, is not always a straightforward process. This is because the security discipline is still relatively immature and there is a need to continue to search for new policies, procedures, best practices, and technologies to ensure that the information security triad (confidentiality, integrity, and availability) is protected. Unfortunately, some practitioners may be looking for textbook cases or exercises that they may have learned in a rote way to prepare for some exam at some point in the past, rather than having an all-encompassing up-to-date view of the enterprise architecture and the organization's evolving information security requirements.

The issue with most information security professionals is that they are usually focused on protocol lacunae (abstract syntax, procedures, timeouts, issues), rather than fundamental risk assessment at the enterprise level. As an example, a top-of-the-class C++ programmer does not, in most cases, understand the overall business risk of an organization. A technician that has a decade of packet-level router configuration knowledge does not necessarily have business knowledge to decide the course of action of a Fortune 100 company at the enterprise level. It is true that most security professionals are able to use industry best practices to identify risks at a generic level, but it takes a specific information security skill set to be successful in identifying risks and properly managing them. Furthermore, organizations cannot afford to simply "Google" what other companies are doing and lift "best practices" that may or may not be best for the specific situation at hand. What is best for an advertisement company may not be best for an insurance company; what is best for a fashion company may not be best for a hospital; what is best for a university may not be best for a military agency; and what is best for a retailer may not be best for a national research laboratory. Also, organizations cannot afford to simply gather meta information from consulting companies, whether presented in triangular, quadrant, or pentagram form, and blindly apply these simplified two-dimensional views as "Best Practices" for their company, when everybody knows that far from being two-dimensional, the (security) world is conspicuously multidimensional.

One is aware that "certified engineers" (although not the only ones) can instantly recite the packet-level scripts of routers or firewalls, but the architectural and strategic planning skills are altogether a different thing. These packet engineers can be rationally integrated into a risk assessment team, along with other more expansive talent to comprise a high-power collaborative entity, the kind that we advocate in this book. Exposure to IT risk situations and predicaments over periods of several years can prepare staffers for the broad-scope architectural and strategic planning requirements of today's IT environments. An overnight course with cramming is less effective.

Refocusing internally, however, even the most technically trained security professional may have gaps in his or her skills, since security risks are inherent across all platforms. While the professional may have expertise in one or two platforms, he or she does not have a complete view. *This means that to properly assess risk, companies need to create a team of pooled talent that has deep knowledge in many areas* Other times, highly qualified individuals are ill-positioned in organizations that are poorly constructed in such a manner that these professionals are rendered ineffective.

Further complicating risk assessment is the fact that no matter how safe an organization is at any given point, the level of security assurance can change at any given moment. Organizations are exposed to new unexpected issues in software that is deployed. Information security risk exposures are always present and continually changing, therefore to help justify a risk management team it is critical to ensure that the risks within an organization are properly documented and reported. The fact of the matter is that information security risks are far too critical to be left up to an ad hoc assemblage of information security engineers or other low-level information technology professionals.

6.3.4 Priority-Oriented Rational Approach

Achieving perfect security and reducing all risk exposures is what every organization ought to strive to achieve; however, for each risk exposure that is mitigated there are costs associated. Therefore a prioritization is needed. Many corrective measures are often recommended because they are the best solution to minimize the risk. However, in many instances the best solution is more expensive than another potential "almost-as-good" solution. The additional level of security may not be worth the effort or investment compared to the other mitigating plans that can be implemented as well. The Risk Management team will be responsible for assessing all of the organizations' risks and making sure that these risks are suitably analyzed so that they may be properly handled.

Another way of stating the above is that one ought to rank all the risk exposures by the expected loss and then tackle first the ones with the highest risk (expected loss). An even better way follows. Recall that in Chapter 2 we defined the benefit $B(\Theta_j, A_i R_x)$ to be the cost difference between the reduction in risk due to the remediation R_x for threat Θ_j to asset A_i and the expense needed for remediation:

$$B(\Theta_j, A_i \oplus R_x) = \{\text{Risk}(\Theta_j, A_i) - \text{Risk}(\Theta_j, A_i \oplus R_x)\} - C(\Theta_j, A_i \oplus R_x).$$

Generally, one would like

$$C(\Theta_j, A_i \oplus R_x) < \text{Risk}(\Theta_j, A_i) - \text{Risk}(\Theta_j, A_i \oplus R_x),$$

namely,

$$B(\Theta_j, A_i \oplus R_x) > 0.$$

The prioritization process entails ranking all the benefits as defined here and then starting with the remediations with the highest benefit and continuing until funds run out. However, also as noted in Chapter 2, there may be instances where risk reduction is mandated by regulation, or there may be cases where the nonfinancial consequences are high or undesirable that the risk must be reduced regardless of cost. If there are multiple possible remediations, say R_k, with $k = 1,\ldots, r$, typically one would want to find R_o, such that

$$\text{Max } B_{k-1, \ldots, r}(\Theta_j, A_i \oplus R_r) = B_o(\Theta_j, A_i \oplus R_o).$$

When analyzing security issues, a well-positioned risk assessment team will follow qualitative and quantitative method(s) to ensure all applicable approaches are evaluated. The processes that the team follows will ensure that issues will not be bogged down by lack of technical information; furthermore, it will not invest excessive amounts of time to create extremely detailed statistics when they are not required or of limited use. However, by using proven methods as well as leveraging the information security industry, the team will able to provide grounded solutions.

The function and the subtending team must have the processes, tools, and procedures in place that allow them to successfully identify and uncover risk exposures, assess the severity of risk exposures, prioritize open risk exposures, determine mitigating strategies, and provide assurance that risks have been properly mitigated. Although each area has its own requirements, the one common factor among these areas is that there must be appropriate, calibrated, and timely information provided in a business format.

To expedite and streamline its core functions, the risk management team needs to create ready-to-go templates for the security professionals to apply to the risk exposures as they are reviewed. Creating a scorecard (commonly referred to as a dashboard) for each risk exposure can provide the communication foundation for each area. This dashboard not only allows security professionals to understand and prioritize workload, but also allows executive management of an organization to gauge current levels of exposure and monitoring progress. In addition, the dashboard will show executive management if the proper amount of resources is allocated to the task of protecting information assets.

The risk management team typically is best-positioned as a central clearinghouse enabling it to determine all IT-related risks within the organization. Because all data on information security risks will be stored in a centralized place under the auspices of the team, it will be easy for business and security professionals to understand priorities as well as gaps. This dashboard is where all of the risk assessment work that the team completes comes together to paint the big picture. Previously, risk management teams have only been generally responsible for running vulnerability scans against internal or external servers and reporting on issues found. The risk management team is well-positioned to provide much more value than just running a scan and reporting results.

Ideally, a risk coordinator or owner within each of the other information technology departments should be assigned in order to help the risk management team work effectively with other departments. Each operational support area is in the best position to provide critical information to the risk management team in order for a proper assessment to be made on any issues that arise. Typically, the teams within an organization that support the daily operations will be able to provide information on assets and also help with the dissection of complex vulnerabilities. Implementable processes and procedures to engage other departments must be defined in order for the risk management team to be successful.

The value that a risk management function and subtending team brings to an organization may not be immediately obvious to organizations that have grown accustom to the traditional security structure. However, as security issues continue to span an ever-increasing number of constituent IT elements and assets, it becomes clear that organizations need a specific internal team that handles the classification of issues an organization must address.

6.4 OVERVIEW OF PRAGMATIC RISK MANAGEMENT PROCESS

A synthesis of overall process discussed in Part 2 is depicted in Figure 6.6. As can be seen, there are two linked sections in this overall process: (1) the creation of a risk management team and adoption of methodologies and (2) the iterative procedure for ongoing risk management.

6.4.1 Creation of a Risk Management Team, and Adoption of Methodologies

What follows is "A Process in Five Basic Steps to Create a Risk Management Team and Define Methodologies":

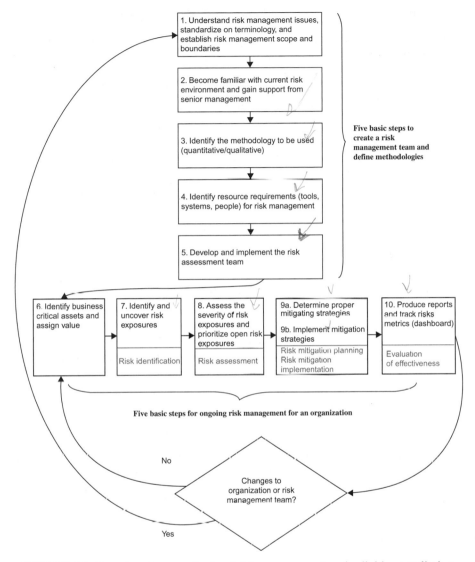

FIGURE 6.6. Ten steps to a synthesis of risk management and reliable remediation.

1. Understand risk management issues, standardize on terminology, and establish risk management scope and boundaries.
2. Become familiar with current risk environment and gain support from senior management.
3. Identify the risk management methodology to be used (quantitative/ qualitative).
4. Identify resource requirements (people, process, technology) for risk management.
5. Develop and implement the risk management team.

6.4.2 Iterative Procedure for Ongoing Risk Management

What follows is "A Process in Five Basic Iterative Steps for Ongoing Risk Management for an Organization":

6. Identify business critical assets and assign value.
7. Identify and uncover risk exposures (risk identification).
8. Assess the Severity of risk exposures and prioritize open risk exposures (risk assessment).
9. Determine proper mitigating strategies (risk mitigation planning and implementation).
10. Produce reports and track risks metrics (publish a dashboard) (evaluation of effectiveness).

6.5 ROADMAP TO PRAGMATIC RISK MANAGEMENT

Chapter 7 covers the first three steps to create a risk management team, namely,

- Understand risk management issues, standardize terminology, and establish risk management scope and boundaries.
- Become familiar with current risk environment and gain support from senior management.
- Identify the risk management methodology to be used (quantitative/qualitative).

Just like any IT process or new technology that is being introduced to an organization, the establishment of a risk management process may not be as simple as one would think. Prior to implementing any portions of a risk management program, it is important to undertake the following two tasks at a high level:

1. Assess the current state of risk management already implemented at the firm:
   - Does the organization have anything already in place? N o.
   - Is risk management done at each corporate team/department level or is there a central team responsible?
2. Assess the culture of the organization:
   - Are they open to change?
   - What is the level of support for information security?

Certain organizations are able to handle a lot of change and other organizations are not. It is critical to understand where the organization is currently in the process, and it is also important to understand how fast and how broadly the risk management processes can be implemented. Once there is an understanding of what is already in place and how the organization will support the implementation of a risk management program, one can proceed to the next steps.

Chapter 7 continues with a review of how to gain support from senior management, establish the management scope, and define acceptable risk for the enterprise. The value of a risk management program needs to be clearly articulated since many (if not most) organizations have not (officially) implemented such a process before, and they may believe that their business has been operating fine. Chapter 7 concludes with defining two critical elements that need to be implemented to support a successful risk management program:

- Waivers programs
- Selecting the organization's risk management methodology that will be used as the core of the program

Chapter 8 covers the last two steps required to create a risk management team, namely,

- Identify resource requirements (people, process, technology) for risk management
- Develop and implement the risk management team

It does take a fair amount of resources to properly implement an effective risk management team. It is important that the organization invest the time to understand the operating costs to support this program. An appreciation of the budget requirements and the creation of, and commitment for, such a budget enables the organization to define the mandate and scope of the information security risk management team. The scope of the risk management function will need to be commensurate with the budget that can be allocated. This chapter also covers staffing requirements, and the specialized skills that are required to run the team. We discuss different sourcing options that an organization can utilize to properly staff the risk management function in general as well as an in-house risk management team are presented in the chapter. A description of risk management tools and risk management services that may also be appropriate for the organization is provided.

At this stage in the program the risk management team is in place at the organization. Chapter 9 starts the discussion for a pragmatic implementation of the risk management process, as depicted in Figure 6.6. The first step involves identifying the organization's IT assets. It may be desirable to categorize assets according to the following (or similar) classes [AND200301]: (1) *Critical*—The organization cannot operate without this asset even for a short period of time; (2) *Essential*—The organization could work around loss of the information asset for days or perhaps a week, but eventually the information asset would have to be returned for use; (3) *Normal*—The organization can operate without this information asset for an extended (but finite) period of time, during which units or individuals may be inconvenienced and/or need to identify alternatives.

The identification of an organization's assets is part of the iterative process because new assets may be added over time; therefore, security managers need to ascertain that their horizon of operations captures all the deployed IT assets, both to protect them and to make sure that they understand the potential jump-off point to other types of exposures (for example, deploying Bluetooth-enabled peripherals may open the door to other injection/infection vectors). The chapter provides some guidelines on how an organization can determine which assets are critical and must be protected. Asset management systems can be put to use for risk management because these typically include asset ownership; they also embody a process to ensure that assets are updated appropriately. The chapter then discusses the type of risk exposures that an organization may face. There are two types of risk exposures discussed in the chapter: "foreseeable" risk exposure and "unforeseeable" risk exposure. These terms are defined *de novo* in order to help a real-world practitioner understand two classes of events that may occur and how the risk management team must be prepared to handle them.

As noted above, when implementing a new information security program most professionals start by creating a security policy. That policy constitutes the guiding principles and is the basis for making risk decisions within the organization. It will dictate and determine the actions that information security professionals at the organization will take. These days most practitioners are able to create a policy-based industry recommendations, as seen in Appendix 6A. However, once the security policy is in place, most practitioners struggle with what are the next steps to effectively deploy the policy as well as determining ongoing risk priorities. A successful risk management program will help guide, organize, and clarify what are (and where are) the most of important assets that need to be protected; the program will also assist with prioritization and identify the steps to implement controls. Chapter 9 discusses these issues and focuses on the following steps of the process:

- Identify and uncover risk exposures (risk identification).
- Assess the severity of risk exposures and prioritize open risk exposures (risk assessment).
- Determine proper mitigating strategies (risk mitigation planning and implementation).

Chapter 10 covers the final step in the iterative procedure for ongoing risk management, namely,

- Produce reports and track risks metrics (publish a dashboard) (evaluation of effectiveness).

Despite the acceptance of information security at many organizations as a worthwhile practice, most organizations are still not investing (sufficient) resources into implementing risk management at this point in time. Typically, this is driven by the fact that there are other initiatives that directly impact the bottom line for organizations and provide an immediate return on investment. In most cases, information security and a risk management program have been looked at as a limited investment to avoid some possibly large exposure-caused expenditure in the future. IT in general and information security in particular have been historically viewed as a cost center and not one that provides value to the organization beyond its core mandate of (safely) running business-support systems. Fortunately, in recent years, there have been business cases that have provided analyses that show that information technology is actually a driver for businesses. It is now accepted that IT can help to drive value of an organization instead of just being a cost center. Chapter 10 closes with a review on how information security and a risk management program can also provide this level of measurable value. We cover how to define and create a dashboard and truly determine the effectiveness of the risk management program as well as a review of executive reporting that is required.

Figure 6.6 also re-enforces the fact that the risk management procedure is iterative and situation-dependent: if there are changes to the organizations (for example, deployment of new systems, deployment of new networks, deployment of new assets, mergers and acquisitions, change in mission, and so on), then the risk management team needs to reassess the situation and make appropriate accommodations. Also, if there are changes to the risk management team (for example, loss of some key talent, reorganizations, and so on), it may be useful to repeat some of the steps, as shown in Figure 6.6.

REFERENCES

[BAN200701] M. Bandor, "Process and Procedure Definition: A Primer," SEPG 2007 – 26–29 March 2007, Software Engineering Institute (SEI), Carnegie Mellon University.

[BOL200701] M. Bolch, "Risk Management Staffing Isn't Always Part of IT," 7 June 2007, SearchCIO.com.

[ENI200801] European Network and Information Security Agency (ENISA), 2008.

[ITP200901] IT Policy Compliance Group, Managing Spend on Information Security and Audit for Better Results, February 2009, Managing Director, Jim Hurley.

[SAN200901] SANS, The SANS Security Policy Project, The SANS Institute, 8120 Woodmont Avenue, Suite 205, Bethesda, MD, 20814.

APPENDIX 6A: EXAMPLE OF A SECURITY POLICY

This appendix contains an illustrative example of a security policy. It is based directly on SANS documentation on the topic of Security Policies [SAN200901] (refer to the *SANS Institute* for extensive support in the area of policies).

6A.1 Purpose of Employee Internet Use Monitoring and Filtering Policy

The purpose of this policy is to define standards for systems that monitor and limit web use from any host within <Company Name>'s network. These standards are designed to ensure employees use the Internet in a safe and responsible manner, and ensure that employee web use can be monitored or researched during an incident.

6A.2 Scope

This policy applies to all <Company Name> employees, contractors, vendors, and agents with a <Company Name>-owned or personally owned computer or workstation connected to the <Company Name> network. This policy applies to all end-user-initiated communications between <Company Name>'s network and the Internet, including web browsing, instant messaging, file transfer, file sharing, and other standard and proprietary protocols. Server-to-server communications, such as SMTP traffic, backups, automated data transfers, or database communications are excluded from this policy.

6A.3 Policy

6A.3.1 Website Monitoring.
The Information Technology Department shall monitor Internet use from all computers and devices connected to the corporate network. For all traffic the monitoring system must record the source IP address, the date, the time, the protocol, and the destination site or server. Where possible, the system should record the user ID of the person or account initiating the traffic. Internet use records must be preserved for 180 days.

6A.3.2 Access to Website Monitoring Reports.
General trending and activity reports will be made available to any employee as needed upon request to the Information Technology Department. Computer Security Incident Response Team (CSIRT) members may access all reports and data if necessary to respond to a security incident. Internet use reports that identify specific users, sites, teams, or devices will only be made available to associates outside the CSIRT upon written or e-mail request to Information Systems from a Human Resources Representative.

6A.3.3 Internet Use Filtering System.
The Information Technology Department shall block access to Internet websites and protocols that are deemed inappropriate for <Company Name>'s corporate environment. The following protocols and categories of websites should be blocked:

- Adult/Sexually Explicit Material
- Advertisements & Pop-Ups

- Chat and Instant Messaging
- Gambling
- Hacking
- Illegal Drugs
- Intimate Apparel and Swimwear
- Peer-to-Peer File Sharing
- Personals and Dating
- Social Network Services
- SPAM, Phishing, and Fraud
- Spyware
- Tasteless and Offensive Content
- Violence, Intolerance and Hate
- Web-Based E-mail

6A.3.4 *Internet Use Filtering Rule Changes.* The Information Technology Department shall periodically review and recommend changes to web and protocol filtering rules. Human Resources shall review these recommendations and decide if any changes are to be made. Changes to web and protocol filtering rules will be recorded in the Internet Use Monitoring and Filtering Policy.

6A.3.5 *Internet Use Filtering Exceptions.* If a site is miscategorized, employees may request the site be unblocked by submitting a ticket to the Information Technology help desk. An IT employee will review the request and unblock the site if it is miscategorized.

Employees may access blocked sites with permission if appropriate and necessary for business purposes. If an employee needs access to a site that is blocked and appropriately categorized, they must submit a request to their Human Resources representative. HR will present all approved exception requests to Information Technology in writing or by e-mail. Information Technology will unblock that site or category for that associate only. Information Technology will track approved exceptions and report on them upon request.

6A.4 Enforcement

The IT Security Officer will periodically review Internet use monitoring and filtering systems and processes to ensure that they are in compliance with this policy. Any employee found to have violated this policy may be subject to disciplinary action, up to and including termination of employment.

6A.5   Definitions

Internet Filtering. Using technology that monitors each instance of communication between devices on the corporate network and the Internet and blocks traffic that matches specific rules.

User ID. User name or other identifier used when an associate logs into the corporate network.

IP address. Unique network address assigned to each device to allow it to communicate with other devices on the network or Internet.

SMTP. Simple Mail Transfer Protocol. The Internet protocol that facilitates the exchange of mail messages between Internet mail servers.

Peer-to-Peer File Sharing. Services or protocols such as BitTorrent and Kazaa that allow Internet-connected hosts to make files available to, or download files from, other hosts.

Social Networking Services. Internet sites such as Myspace and Facebook that allow users to post content, chat, and interact in online communities.

SPAM. Unsolicited Internet e-mail. SPAM sites are websites link to form unsolicited Internet mail messages.

Phishing. Attempting to fraudulently acquire sensitive information by masquerading as a trusted entity in an electronic communication.

Hacking. Sites that provide content about breaking or subverting computer security controls.

CHAPTER 7

ASSESSING ORGANIZATION AND ESTABLISHING RISK MANAGEMENT SCOPE

This chapter continues the description of the information security risk management process introduced in Chapter 6 by discussing the second and third procedural block in the flow (see Figure 7.1). The second block in the process covers (i) becoming familiar with the risk exposure environment and (ii) gaining support from senior management. The third block in the process covers selecting the risk management methodology that will be used by the organization as the core of the program. The chapter also covers waivers.

What follows is a checklist of activities to support these functions.

✔ Understanding current environment for typical organizations
✔ Soliciting support from senior management
✔ Establishing risk management scope and boundaries
✔ Defining acceptable risk for the organization
  • Determining organization's guiding risk principles
  • Determining organization's risk tolerance
✔ Risk management committee
  • Defining purpose
  • Defining approval authority
  • Recruiting members and create team
✔ Risk management process
  • Defining alerting processes
  • Defining communication goals
  • Defining engagement model

Information Technology Risk Management in Enterprise Environments: A Review of Industry Practices and a Practial Guide to Risk Management Teams, by Jake Kouns and Daniel Minoli
Copyright © 2010 John Wiley & Sons, Inc.

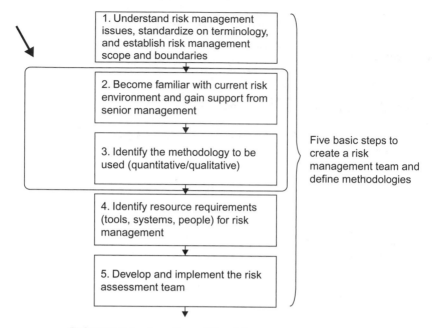

FIGURE 7.1. A section of the risk management process.

✔ Risk waivers program
- Defining process and procedures
- Defining review cycles

✔ Creating an organization-specific risk methodology
- Qualitative
- Quantitative
- Fuzzy-Set Theory Approach

7.1 ASSESSING THE CURRENT ENTERPRISE ENVIRONMENT

We discussed briefly in Chapter 2 the concept of architecture planning. One can certainly look at the establishment of a risk management program as being a subtask in the establishment of a security architecture, which in turn is a subelement of a comprehensive enterprise architecture. A set of design approaches have developed over the years describing how to define and implement an architecture. In architecture planning, one starts with an assessment of the "as is environment"; then under the guidance of "principles" and "requirements", one defines the "target architecture" (also called the "to be" environment.)

The observation that follows immediately herewith sounds like a tautology (and it is), but before initiating changes at any organization in regard to information security risk management, it is important to first understand the "as is" environment of that organization.

TABLE 7.1. Techniques to Establish the "As Is" Environment

Method	Advantages	Disadvantages
Documentation review	• Focused Information • Fast results (previous audits)	• Time-consuming • Documentation may not exist
Stakeholder interviews	• Expertise information	• Possibility exists to derive biased information based on stakeholders perception
Enterprise risk assessment	• Fact-based	• Complex • Expensive • Time Intensive

There are at least three ways to get a perspective of the organization (see Table 7.1):

1. Review current documentation and past audits
2. Interview key stakeholders
3. Perform enterprise risk assessment

Each of these methods has advantages and disadvantages, but the exercise is worth doing; in fact, the best approach is to use a combination or all of these techniques.

Obviously, there are many organizational structures according to several dimensions such as industry class (e.g., financial, petrochemical, consumer goods—as covered in Appendix 8A), company size (very large, large, medium, and small), the degree/type of global network connectivity, regulatory obligations, and so on. Therefore, both the information security approach in general and the risk management in particular need to be appropriately tailored. If the security policies/procedures do not fit the organization, they will not be successful. It is recommended, therefore, that an information security practitioner take the time to understand the current "as is" institutional environment, then define the target environment, and finally assess the best way to make requisite improvements to move toward that target. In order to be successful, the risk management planner should endeavor to understand the strengths and weaknesses of the organization's information security team and identify key skill sets and any gaps thereof.

The approach of "jumping in" to implement "some/any" risk management program is not the optimal way to proceed. Generally, staffers that either (i) have limited knowledge and/or have learned the craft recently, (ii) have never done this before and are eager to show that "they can do it," or (iii) have little "high-altitude" formal advanced training in the discipline and have learned the subject by informal balkanized training (for example, by starting out as a technician[29]

---

[29]A technician here is someone on call to react to a real-time problem sitting constantly in front of a computer screen trying to find a solution without reference to the broader discipline but focusing instead just on the specific environment of the firm.

and by being promoted to more analytical functions) have a tendency to indeed "just jump in." Such an approach is strongly discouraged. In general, it is best to find the right person that has undertaken a given task before, even if this means hiring a new person who is an expert in the true sense of the word.

For the "as is" assessment, one needs to establish, among other issues,

- Who is accountable for security and who is responsible for security at the organization?
- What kind of risk exposures are relevant (and/or have a probability of occurrence greater than some lower-bound value, say, greater than 0.001)?
- What are the IT assets and their value?
- What is the ultimate philosophy of management? That is, establish a risk management group that pays for itself (and, therefore, has an opex budget equal to the aggregate risk), or a group that is smaller (that is, the company effectively self-ensures), or a group that is larger (for example, for regulatory reasons)?
- What mechanisms are already in place?
- Which industry risk management model, if any, should we use.

7.1.1 Accountability versus Responsibility

Regulation and compliance often requires that an individual (or function) responsible for security be clearly and explicitly identified. If it is not clear who is responsible for security functions, it is generally impossible to actually secure a company. There needs to be clarity in defining information security roles and responsibilities. If it is not immediately clear who that individual is, then an assessment of the situation is needed. It may well be that after the assessment described here the person responsible in the "to be" environment is the same as in the "as is" environment; however, the assessment is (almost invariably) required.

In some environments, particularly where there are semiautonomous lines of business (LOBs) or subsidiaries, the security function may be handled in a decentralized manner. In fact, if an organization is very large or highly decentralized, then it may actually be advantageous to have decentralized security; this follows from the fact that the distributed staff may in principle have a better appreciation of the business imperatives, systems, operations, customer base, IT assets, and risk exposures affecting the LOB. However, if many answers start off with the qualifier "it depends" when referring to how security is handled in business units or divisions, this could be an indication of some latent problem in definitional clarity.

In the context of the first question posed above, "Who is *accountable* for security and who is *responsible* for security?", some people use these words interchangeably, but understanding the differences may be the key to a successful information security and risk management program. We define the terms next:

Having Accountability. This means being answerable to someone within the organization or for security activity within the organization. In many cases, there will be a department or individual that has accountability for security decisions but not necessarily responsible for security implementation. Typically, a Chief Information Security Officer (CISO) or Director of Information Security is accountable to the Chief Information Officer (CIO) for security.

Having Responsibility. This means being in charge of a security duty, obligation, or burden. An example of someone that is responsible for security is a Network Security employee that configures and manages firewalls.

An operative statement is that *information security is everyone's responsibility*. This originates from the fact that without having every employee or member of an organization taking responsibility, it is impossible to achieve an adequate level of security. This realization by employees is critical since often many (if not most) employees believe that there is a security department that handles all security issues. Considering that many of the high-risk security exposures occur at the end-user level, this personal ownership of the responsibility is important. Nonetheless, an organization must not only rely on this personal ownership to define roles and responsibility for information security: Publishing a loosely stated policy that asserts that information security is the responsibility of all users is not enough to ensure the integrity, confidentiality, and availability of data and assets. It is, therefore, critical that an organization explicitly determine and define who is responsible for carrying out specific information security directives.

Assigning accountability is not an effort directed at trying to offload security work on to executives, but is instead an attempt to ensure that they are engaged and understand the organizations security risks. Creating and defining this accountability is typically documented in the organization's enterprise information security policy.

The assertion "*I am accountable for all information security and risk management issues*" is typically a statement that is made by a security person that is in the policy and compliance area of the information security department within an organization. Senior management often looks for one person to be the individual to answer to and justify any security issue.

As discussed previously, defining the roles and responsibilities for information security tasks is a critical step in creating an information security and risk management program. Depending on the organization structure, information security may be handled in a centralized or decentralized environment. See Table 7.2. There are advantages and disadvantages to each structure, and the best fit depends on the organization structure and its culture.

TABLE 7.2. Information Security Implementation Options

Organization Structure	Advantages	Disadvantages
Centralized information security management	Consistent approach Economies of scale Simplify audit and compliance	Often security policies and standards do not fit across the board Security resources tend to focus on only larger issues and not provide specific attention if it were a ring fenced or dedicated resource
Decentralized information security management	Much closer to business alignment Dedicated resources to staff security needs	Many different levels of security in place Each individual security department or person responsible defines own security rules Often leads to audit and compliance issues
Hybrid information security management	Creates a balance between defining enterprise policies and responsibilities Provides dedicate resources onsite that understand users and business needs Provides structure and foundation for a consistent approach to security for the entire organization	Increased staffing is typical required (centralized department as well as security resources at each location) Roles and responsibilities can be easily confused Implementation can be difficult

7.2   SOLICITING SUPPORT FROM SENIOR MANAGEMENT

Because risk management is a form of an "insurance policy" against probabilistic events that may or may not have immediately visible quarterly financial returns (even for risk management teams that are staffed to be revenue neutral and/or self sustaining), there is a fundamental need to gain management support for this function and/or before attempting to enforce any type of risk management policy. Clearly, in order for security to be successful in any organization, it must be a priority within that organization. The only way to ensure that it is a priority is to acquire support from senior management. Without this support, security will always take a backseat to other issues and in many cases will come up short. If an organization does not want to secure their environment or make security a priority, there is very little one can do as an information security professional to ensure success. This is not to say security cannot be improved without direct management support, but it will eventually require their support for any substantive initiative to be fully and successfully implemented. As we noted in Chapter 6, there is a nontrivial cost associated with risk management staff (and also with tools and remediation capax/opex). This is a core reason why management support must be secured.

One area of concern with gaining management's support is the complexity involved with securing an organization. Information security issues are constantly changing and can be somewhat difficult to explain to executives in business terms; some executives may be looking for "black and white" answers when it comes to securing the business. Before attempting to gain support from management it is advisable, therefore, to determine what the communication strategy should be. In this context, we find that there are two kinds of professionals:

- Those who (hopefully without loss of generality) take *something complex and make it sound simple.* These are people who really know the craft, are self-confident, are interested in pedagogical teaching and team playing, communicate well, write whitepapers and articles, and make public presentations (these are the people that tend to eventually get promoted and eventually get make more money).

- Those who (needlessly) take *something simple and make it sound complex.* These are people who do not, in the end, really know the craft, who get lost in the weeds, who are latently not self-confident, who are interested in keeping information to themselves, absconding facts and designs, who do not communicate well, who hide behind an avalanche of acronyms, and who tend to be overprotective and do not opt to document (these are the people that are often stuck in positions forever and do not move ahead).

Clearly, we believe that the former cadre is better for an organization than the latter. Therefore, members of the risk management team should endeavor to explain issues in terms and parameters that their business counterparts can understand, making something complex simpler and clearer. However, it is important to note that this is not to say that complicated issues should be trivialized. Risk management professionals, security professionals, and IT people in general should never hide behind an avalanche of acronyms and undefined terms; otherwise they will never get true senior management support. Management may go along once or twice, but not provide support, in this predicament, on a sustained basis.

The dialogue with senior management may entail answering questions such as *"Are we secure?"* and *"What are the chances we could have a compromise?"* The answers need to take into account that the security threats and possible risk exposures a company may face are ever-changing: There is not as much volatility in other IT disciplines as there is in the security world, although there is a cyclical introduction of new technologies in the IT space every 3–5 years. In other areas of the business (e.g., manufacturing, logistics) the pace with which the trends and new technologies may need to be implemented is slower than is the case for information security. For example, when developing a business case for moving from a traditional voice network to a Voice over IP (VoIP) network, both the plan and the implementation can be made over time and can be properly planned. By comparing this example to the security world, we can see a difference: In security a situation often arises where there is a vulnerability that has been released in any one of the 100 applications that are present in the firm and one is required to upgrade and patch an extensive set of equipment, often immediately. In addition, these patches come unexpectedly at any given time. Other patches are released on a scheduled basis (monthly, quarterly) but require every piece of equipment from this particular vendor to be upgraded, even though one may just have done this exact thing a month earlier.

One way to address this issue is to follow the approach of example 2 in Appendix 8A, and thus explain to management. There we postulated the existence of a milieu of "cyber background noise" of constant exposure events, which, if left unmitigated, results in the loss of availability for a (sub)set of revenue-supporting systems and an ensuing loss of (a portion of the) revenue. While management might at first be skeptical that the loss of availability of a system from, say, 99.99% to 99.00% (that is, 86.7 hours a year) is an issue, that skepticism can easily be challenged by asking such manager to authorize, for the purpose of validating or debunking the hypothesis, that the firm simply turn off by decree such system for one-tenth of such interval—that is, 8.6 hours, say next Tuesday (and perhaps allow all the security people take a compensatory day off.) If a senior manager has any compunction about doing so, then that is the proof that a system unavailability is a business-critical and business-impacting resource that needs proper attention and care.

While it might appear that the business case to explain the value to the organization to move to a new IT technology can easily be quantified/qualified and explained in business language for executives to understand, explaining that resources must be invested for risk management of IT assets should be no more difficult than explaining why the company pays for insurance for their buildings, their plants, their goods while in transit, their workers, their truck fleet, their corporate jet, their officers (D&O), and so on. Risk mitigation offers business value against an array of probabilistically driven events, here specifically "to maintain where we are and protect the company from hackers." That *maintenance of the status quo* is intrinsic in any form of insurance.[30] No business person would argue, say, that "we don't need insurance on our buildings", or "we don't want security on our truck fleet"; this is because insurance of physical assets is a well-established stable practice that has developed long ago—on the other hand the idea of "insuring" IT assets by protecting them via risk mitigation is a relatively new concept, and so the potential for pushback. The risk management advocate needs to be able to argue the point in favor of intrinsic protection. Now, a firm may choose to go

---

[30]Even in personal life, one may spend 3–4% of one's income for home insurance, automobile insurance, umbrella insurance, life insurance, and other types of insurances.

strictly the "casualty way": pay someone else to compensate for an *incurred* business-loss infraction; or, it may, more wisely, choose to have an in-house capability to *handle the contingencies and even prevent them from happening*. In many cases the company has no choice because risk mitigation is mandated by applicable regulation.

It should be noted that the risk management team itself need not include all the personnel assets to undertake the function. As we know well at this juncture, risk management entails

1. (Ongoing) identification of threats, vulnerabilities, or (risk) events impacting the set of IT assets owned by the organization
2. Risk assessment
3. Risk mitigation planning
4. Risk mitigation implementation
5. Evaluation of the mitigation's effectiveness

The risk management team should really focus on tasks 1, 2, 3, and 5 and enlist all appropriate assistance from other corporate departments to implement a remediation (task 4). For example, if the risk management team determines that one should build out a more robust DMZ (demilitarized zone), it can rely on other people in the company (in IT) to do an industry survey of what firewall systems are available, to procure the firewall, to install the firewall (perhaps upgrading the power feed to a rack or closet), and to configure the firewall. Or, if the risk management team determines that one should use MultiProtocol Label Switching (MPLS) service instead of an Internet VPN-based service, it can rely on other people in the company to do an industry survey of what service flavors are available, to procure the service, and to configure the routers to support such service.

So, for example, a $2B insurance company subject to a medium probability of risk exposures could get away with one person dedicated to risk management (as we saw in passing in Chapter 6); on the other hand, if the risk management team also needs to know how (or expects) to configure routers, firewalls, switches, and servers (in three different OS flavors), select telecom services, understand service provider infrastructure, have hands-on familiarity with storage systems, and so on, naturally, then, the team will be understandably larger. But in this case the risk management team is not, prima facia, focusing on their core role.

Also, for example, if a company needs to have a 24×365 risk management operation, and each person in the perceived team structure of 30 staffers has 6 weeks of vacation a year, then that adds up to 180 staff-weeks of non-working time, or about 4 FTEs; if the vacation was only 2 weeks per person, the non-working time would be 60 weeks or, basically 1 FTE. Hence, the same work done by 30 people with 6 weeks vacations could be accomplished with 27 people, thereby saving about $0.5M/year in loaded salary.

For a given year y, define the total benefit of having a risk management function, T_y, as

$$T_y = \sum_{\text{all } j} \sum_{\text{all } i} B\left(\Theta_j, A_i \oplus R_{ji}\right),$$

where R_{ji} is the most cost-effective remediation for threat Θ_j to asset A_i. Then if $\chi_y(O)$ is the yearly operational cost of the risk management team for year y, the following criterion can be applied:

$$\chi_y(O) = \alpha \times T_y,$$

where

- $\alpha < 1$ (here the firm is trying to save money, and perhaps "cut a corner"— or, the team is so efficient and proficient that it more than pays for itself— or, the company is "self-insuring")
- $\alpha = 1$ (here the firm has completely self-funding team)
- $\alpha > 1$ (here the firm is being extra conservative and investing more than minimally needed)

(recall from Chapter 2 that that the benefit B is the difference between the risk and the cost to remediate it, but not including the operational cost of the risk management team itself).

For example, if the remediation of all issues had a benefit of \$1,000,000 and a team cost the company \$500,000, then we have $\alpha = 0.5$. Another way to look at this is define the risk management payback (RMP_y), for year y as

$$\text{RMP}_y = \alpha \times T_y - \chi_y(O)$$

For the example above, $\text{RMP}_y = \$500,000$. One wants RMP_y to be positive. If RMP_y is positive, the company has a team that is highly efficient and/or productive. If RMP_y is negative, the company either has an inefficient team ($\alpha \times T_y$ is low, namely low benefit, e.g., by picking an expensive remediation or a remediation that does not really reduce the risk) or is overspending for risk management ($\chi_y(O)$ is large, e.g., overpaying people, having too many people, or having a large staff because of regulatory requirements.) Or, the company may be "self-insuring" (this can be viewed as having an "inefficient staff," namely no staff at all—here $\alpha \times T_y$ is negative, although $\chi_y(O)$ is zero.)

Note that if the risk were zero (which never happens in real life), the benefit would also be zero (or negative) and RMP_y would be negative (that would say that in this case there was by definition zero risk, but the organization incurred the operational cost of maintaining the team.)

The advocate for the formation of the risk management team needs to be able to articulate these formulations to management. Such an advocate perhaps needs less in-depth academic book knowledge of obscure security issues and more knowledge of financial concepts (net present value, depreciated cash flows, weighted average cost of capital, internal rate of return, return on Investment, and so on) and of basic mathematics: The formulation given above, in Chapter 6 and in Chapter 2 (including approaches to approximate probabilities) is simple, direct, easily applicable, and to the point. If security certification programs do not teach these techniques, if they do not include basics about financial metrics, and if they do not have enough basic probability/risk/statistical tools, then the practitioner is strongly urged to acquire these core skills that go beyond learning the basic worm du jour, virus du jour, Trojan du jour, or vulnerability du jour and learn something that 20, 30, or 40 years into the future will still be valid.

Some have advocated the use of fear, uncertainty, and doubt (FUD)[31] as an approach to gain support to build out the risk management function. We strongly discourage this approach. Providing justification for information security decisions based solely on FUD can quickly lead to problems and lack of credibility. Enough information is available at this time in the industry and in the open (and online) press to be able to build a rational business model. Information security decisions cannot be based on FUD, which is all too often what seems to be communicated when trying to justify security and risk management at a high level. For example, if the question is

Why are we spending thousand dollars on this security product?

and the answers are

If we don't invest in this technology, we might get hacked
If we don't invest in this technology, we could fail the audit

then it is clear that the justification case is not really grounded in analytical facts. A security professional may be able to get away with using FUD to justify something once in a while, but not to advocate for the formation of a high-quality reliable risk management team. One manifestation of FUD is the dizzying exposition of (frankly unneeded) jargon used in the industry: CSO, CISO, CPO, CPSO, CCPO, CRO, CIRO, CISA, CISM, CGEIT, CISSP, ISSAP, ISSMP, ROSI, EF, SLE, ARO, ALE, and so on. Some may be lost in this acronym bonanza, but it seems that acronyms may be part of the FUD strategy of some people; perhaps an overall reduction of the overreliance on

---

[31]FUD typically is a scare tactic that is used as a marketing strategy to influence people into making the desired decision. It is largely believed that this term was first used in the 1970s when a large mainframe vendor was allegedly using FUD marketing campaigns to influence businesses not to purchase their competitors products.

acronyms-laden parlance in this industry would benefit the bottom line and actually improve enterprise security.

While incident frequencies are not always disclosed openly by firms trying to forestall embarrassment about infractions they suffer even after they may have hired expensive security personnel, the expert planner should be able to build, articulate, and justify plausible analytical models of threat probabilities based on reasoned common sense and/or following the principle of Maximum Likelihood Estimation. Maximum Likelihood Estimation is a statistical method allowing one to fit a mathematical model to data; for a set of data and underlying probability model, Maximum Likelihood Estimation picks the values of the model parameters that make the data "more likely" than any other values of the parameters would make them. Effectively this means that one can postulate the "most obvious' answer (rather than the universe of every possible answer), and then look to see if the data supports that conclusion. Applying this to risk management at a very coarse level, if a vendor recommends that software release y is needed to meet current security threats, the likelihood that software release y-5 is still safe is not a good bet. If 10 firms with product x version y have had an infraction, then it is very likely that a company in question also having product x version y will be impacted in similar fashion. If a company has not tested their Disaster Recovery Plan in 3 years, the likelihood that the plan is still safe is not a good bet. If a company had an infraction 2 years ago and after some initial fixes nothing else has been done since, the likelihood that the firm is still safe is not a good bet. What this says is that the planner need not "prove" that there is a probability of an issue, but instead just needs to state that the likelihood is reasonably high that if similar circumstances exist that such an issue will be of relevance.

What follows is possibly motivational material that can be used as part of a (non-FUD-based) conversation with senior management. The *IT Policy Compliance Group* conducts benchmarks that are focused on delivering fact-based guidance on the steps that can be taken to improve security. Ongoing benchmarks measure three key performance results occurring among organizations: (1) the loss or theft of customer data; (2) the incidence and extent of business downtime from failures and disruptions occurring in IT; and (3) deficiencies in IT that must be corrected to pass audit. In a press-time study they found the following [ITP200901]:

- The losses that organizations are willing to sustain are exceedingly low, and the returns for improving results are extraordinarily high.
- Loss of confidentiality, integrity, and availability are larger business and financial risks than are outsourced IT projects, systems, information, or delays to critical projects.
- Best-in-class firms delay the onset of data loss or theft to decades or longer while also reducing the magnitude of financial impact.

- Organizations with the best track records are spending between 35% and 52% less on audit fees and expenses annually.
- Organizations with the worst results and highest losses from the use of IT are actually spending the same amounts on information security as the firms with the lowest risks and best outcomes.

More specifically, the IT Policy Compliance Group found the following:

- *Worst Outcomes.* Approximately 2 in 10 organizations (19%) are experiencing the worst outcomes, the highest data losses of thefts, the most downtime from IT failures, and the largest problems with regulatory compliance. These firms are experiencing more than 15 losses or thefts of data each year, 80 or more hours of business downtime from failures occurring in IT, and more than 15 deficiencies in IT that must be corrected to pass audit.
- *Normative Outcomes.* Nearly 7 in 10 organizations (68%) are operating at the norm with data loss or theft rates that range from 3 to 15 each year, between 7 and 79 hours of business downtime, and between 3 and 15 compliance deficiencies in IT that must be corrected.
- *Best Outcomes.* Only about one in 10 organizations 13 percent—are consistently operating with the best results, including fewer than three losses or thefts of sensitive information, less than six hours of business downtime, and fewer than three deficiencies to correct to pass audit.

In conclusion, the IT Policy Compliance Group found that the financial outcomes being experienced by organizations are directly related to the outcomes being managed within IT. Organizations with the worst outcomes in IT are experiencing highest levels of financial exposure and loss than all others. However, it is the majority of organizations that are overspending on audit.

The three communication styles that may be used by the risk management advocate are as follows (see Table 7.3):

1. **High Level Communications.** A style that typically only provides high level technical information. This approach tries to avoid providing specific details in order to make technical information easier for non-information technology professionals to understand.
2. **Detailed Communications.** A style that aims to provides all of the technical information available. This approach tries to avoid leaving out specific details in order to ensure all information is evaluated before a decision is reached.
3. **Hybrid Communications.** A style that attempts to keep the majority of information at a very high level when referring to technical information. With this style, key points are identified and then all technical information is provided and reviewed.

TABLE 7.3. Communication Styles

Executive Communication Style	Advantages	Disadvantages
High–level communications	Should be easily understood by all executives. Allows executives to be informed but not overloaded with details.	Executive may feel many decisions appear to be based on FUD. Executives may feel that they are not being told all of the information they should be.
Detailed communications	All information is available for review. Requires executives that truly understand technology.	Many executives do not understand the technical details, and this can lead to issues. Too much information can lead to the perception that the information security department does not know what they are doing.
Hybrid communications	Provides a balanced combination of high level and detailed information as required.	Requires risk management professionals with mastery of communication skills. May have a tendency to lean toward providing too many details.

We reinforce the point that, before approaching senior management to solicit support, is important to determine the communication strategy. Each organization will have to determine the approach that best fits the level of detail that will be received from the executives. What style will be most successful depends on the culture, style, training, and technology background of the management in question. Once the communication style has been determined, the next step is to seek an audience with senior management to advise of the current state of security and seek support for the program. As implied earlier, security risk exposures need to be explained in a business-oriented language (for example, by using presentation charts, which often have the ability to crystallize issues).

The top-down approach to implement information security is the most successful strategy because this way the organization shows a commitment to security. In some cases, it can be difficult to gain this support. Even with all of the high-profile security cases, it may still be difficult to lock-in support when senior management becomes aware that to resolve systemic security risk exposure situations, one may have to change the culture of the organization: Anything that appears to affect the culture that is currently in place or slow the potential for revenues is likely to be very challenging to sell. Therefore, a persuasive argument must be made that, from a statistical perspective (the same science that allows one to predict who the next President of the United States will be hours before the polls close), it is less costly for the firm to adopt remediation measure than to go without such measures.

Even if one assumed that all remediations R_{ji} (slightly) reduced the revenue by R_y, management must be assured that net benefit, NB_y, is positive, namely

$$NB_y = RMP_y - R_y = \alpha \times T_y - \chi_y(O) - R_y > 0.$$

For example, continuing with the illustrative case introduced above, if the reduction of revenue (or say productivity) because of all the security measures was $200,000 per year, then

$$NB_y = \$1,000,000 - \$500,000 - \$200,000 = \$300,000.$$

Some organizations choose to accept the risk for a variety of reasons including "self-insuring". In this context, self-insuring means being willing to incur a loss in specific instances because the cost of that loss is assumed to be less than the accrued cost of staffing the risk management team and the cost of affecting the remediations. These companies may take a time window approach of, say, looking at the expected loss over year y and $y + 1$ (for example), along with associated costs, and postulate that they may use some external service company to handle the issues on a as-needed basis (even if at premium for those "few times they are really needed") and save the operational costs of staffing a team for year y and $y + 1$. Recall that the benefit $B(\Theta_j, A_i \oplus R_x)$ is the cost difference between the expense needed for remediation and the reduction in risk:

$$B(\Theta_j, A_i \oplus R_x) = \{Risk(\Theta_j, A_i) - Risk(\Theta_j, A_i \oplus R_x)\}, -C(\Theta_j, A_i \oplus R_x)$$

where $C(\Theta_j, A_i \oplus R_x)$ is the expenditure of remediating A_i against threat Θ_j. Self-insurance means that

$$B(\Theta_j, A_i \oplus R_x) = -Risk(\Theta_j, A_i)$$

since we take Risk $(\Theta_j, A_i \oplus R_x)$ to be undefined in this circumstance and $C(\Theta_j, A_i \oplus R_x)$ is zero since nothing is done on a routine basis. Then,

$$T_y = -\Sigma_{all\ j}\Sigma_{all\ i}Risk(\Theta_j, A_i).$$

Here $\chi_y(O) = 0$, and the payback is negative when looking at the expression

$$RMP_y = \alpha \times T_y$$

(say $= 1$ in this case).

However, the company may opt to pay a "one-time, as needed" expense to address some specific (serious) problem in year y, say χ_y; the idea would be that

$$(\chi_y(O) + \chi_{y+1}(O)) - \left(\chi_y + \chi_{y+1}\right) > 0.$$

Example. In year y the "one-time, as needed" expense is \$20,000; in year $y+1$ the "one-time, as needed" expense is \$40,000. Then the total expense in year y and $y+1$ is \$60,000, which is obviously smaller than having two people on staff dedicated to risk management for each year, say at \$100,000 each.

$$2 \times 100,000 + 2 \times 100,000 - (20,000 + 40,000) = \$340,000,$$

which, indeed, is greater that zero. This approach does require the organization to have very clear understanding of their potential worst-case loss. A large data breach of credit card information can cost an organization millions of dollars. As hinted above in passing, the increased government regulations and expanding compliance requirements in many countries can, in same cases, be sufficient reasons to support security within an organization. Some examples of regulation are (also see Appendix 7A)

- SOX (Sarbanes–Oxley)
- HIPAA (Health Insurance Portability and Accountability Act of 1996)
- US State Audits
- UK Data Privacy Act
- Basel-II

Regulatory considerations may also require a probabilistic approach: What is the probability of being found in noncompliance, and what is the anticipated remediation cost? Generally speaking, given the recent global financial debacle, companies can expect greater scrutiny, and increased regulation. Some call the probabilistic approach the FUD factor; for example, "if you not do the following security requirements, then the CEO or some officer could go to prison." This may not be as much fear as reality; for example, a March 2009 *Financial Times* story stated that Swiss private banks were banning their top executives from travelling abroad because of fears that they may be detained as part of a global crackdown on bank secrecy, thus the possibility of officers going to jail is nonzero.) Unfortunately, some executives may be just looking to get a checkmark next to each of the regulations and not fully looking at the real risk. In addition, a number of the regulations leave some of the security controls open to interpretation.

In some organizations, referencing government or other regulations may actually be enough to provide the motivation to ensure that the security is adequate. It is recommended that regardless, time be invested in explaining the risks and not rely just of the formulation to do something "because we need to comply." There will be times when an external auditor passes an organization for, say, SOX compliance, but in reality there may still be a nontrivial risk. Here the security practitioner needs to find a persuasive way to explain to senior management that there are still security issues that may cause the organization to be at risk of exposure or perhaps even to fail a follow-up SOX audit.

After determining the proper communications style that fits the organization, having successfully explained the need for security, and having gained approval for a risk management program from senior management, one needs to define accountability with the executives. Accountability can be one of the most difficult points to explain. In the end, most senior managers now understand the need to support security initiatives but may not understand the need for them to get directly involved. However, there are instances when senior management needs to make their own specific risk management decisions: for example, senior management must be involved when a certain security risk has been quantified, but the organization chooses to accept the risk for a variety of reasons, including "self-insuring."

Once the practitioner has gained the attention and approval of senior management within the organization it will be an ongoing task to ensure that they are properly and consistently updated. A scorecard may be implemented to provide a view to security posture of the organization and the progress being made from the "as is" architecture to the "to be" target architecture. Chapter 10 discusses scorecards and compliance in more details.

The discussion above is very revealing because it points out that the optimal staffer for risk management is one that simultaneously is able to communicate (e.g., develop business cases, prepare presentations, write white papers, develop financial models) and has security knowledge. The optimal staffer is not one with 100% background in security and 0% in business communication/ marketing, nor one with 100% background in business communication/ marketing and 0% in security, but one that is 50–50, 66–34, or 75–25 knowledgeable in security and business communication.

7.3 ESTABLISHING RISK MANAGEMENT SCOPE AND BOUNDARIES

There are many risk exposures that an organization faces; therefore it is important to establish risk management scope and boundaries. Information security issues affect all parts of any business, including people, processes, and technology. Appendix 2A in Chapter 2 included a long list of issues of relevance, classified in the following categories:

- Information Security Threats
- Information Security Vulnerabilities
- Information Security Impacts
- Information Security Risk Events
- Information Security Controls

As noted in Chapter 6, the foundation of a sound information security and risk management program is the organization's information security policy. This policy should define the overall security program and define accountability within the organization for its implementation and oversight. An enterprise information security policy needs to address security from a comprehensive view and help determine the areas that are key controls. Some of the issues that deserve attention include:

- How are security policies handled?
- What is already defined?
- Where are the gaps?

Even organizations that do not have formally documented security policies typically have informal security practices that are followed. In this instance, however, many of the employees of the company do not understand the reasons why things are done in a certain manner, and it is most likely not even repeatable.

7.4   DEFINING ACCEPTABLE RISK FOR ENTERPRISE

Risk exposures might be more tolerable or acceptable, depending on the type of business or organizational charter. It is important to ensure that the risk management team has a clear picture from the top down in order to align the business with the level of security desired.

It should be understood that

a. the risk may be may not be able to be driven to zero (namely, $\text{Risk}(\Theta_j, A_i) - \text{Risk}(\Theta_j, A_i \oplus R_x) > 0$ in all cases), or

b. the risk may be too expensive be driven to zero (namely, $C(\Theta_j, A_i \oplus R_x)$ exceeds the allocated budget for year y), or

c. the benefit of achieving a certain baseline value may not be compelling (namely, $B(\Theta_j, A_i \oplus R_x) = \{\text{Risk}(\Theta_j, A_i) - \text{Risk}(\Theta_j, A_i \oplus R_x)\} - C(\Theta_j, A_i \oplus R_x)$ may be small; another way of stating this is that the internal rate of return (IRR) for the project is low).

Note: IRR is the discount rate used in capital budgeting that makes the net present value of all cash flows from a particular project equal to zero. The higher a project's internal rate of return, the more desirable it is to undertake the project. To find the internal rate of return, one finds the value(s) of r that satisfies the following equation:

$$\text{NPV} = \sum_{t=0}^{N} \frac{C_t}{(1+r)^t} = 0,$$

where C_t is the cash flow at time t.

Note: $\text{Risk}(\Theta_j, A_i \oplus R_x)$ represents the residual risk caused by threat Θ_j on asset A_i after the remediation R_x is applied.

Before defining how security should be handled in an organization, it is important to gain upper management's input in terms of

- The level of risk that is acceptable (Acceptable risk (AR))
- The availability of funds
- The IRR that management expects on the remediation project (acceptable IRR (AI)[32])

In other words,

1. The risk management team needs to find what the acceptable risk $\text{AR}(\Theta_j, A_i)$ from threat Θ_j on asset A_i is. Specifically, the team needs to find $\text{AR}(\Theta_j, A_i)$ given by management such that

$$\text{Risk}(\Theta_j, A_i \oplus R_x) < \text{AR}(\Theta_j, A_i).$$

   After management specifies the AR, the only choice the team has is to pick R_x such that this expression is met.
2. Funds $C(\Theta_j, A_i \oplus R_x)$ will be needed to apply the remediation, hence one needs to establish that they are available.
3. The $\text{IRR}(\Theta_j, A_i, R_x)$ needs to be computed to show that it exceeds the acceptable IRR AI.

Note: We have been citing the risk as being a positive number, but in a typical *cash flow analysis* (as stated in Chapter 2) all three numbers $\text{Risk}(\Theta_j, A_i)$, $C(\Theta_j, A_i \oplus R_x)$, and $\text{Risk}(\Theta_j, A_i \oplus R_x)$ should formally be considered as negative. For example, assume that the risk to an asset is $\text{Risk}(\Theta_j, A_i) = -\$1000$, the cost to remediate it is $C(\Theta_j, A_i \oplus R_x) = -\$350$, and the residual risk

---

[32]We assume for simplicity that the acceptable IRR is not dependent on the specific asset, remediation, or threat, but it is given general value, say 10%.

after the remediation is $\text{Risk}(\Theta_j, A_i \oplus R_x) = -\$200$. One could say that the \$350 investment eliminated \$800 of risk. In the IRR calculation, one can use the $-\$350$ as an outlay and $+\$800$ as the outcome. Using the function in Microsoft Excel gives a value of 129% for this example. Using the numbers in the negative form, one gets

$$B(\Theta_j, A_i \oplus R_x) = \{\text{Risk}(\Theta_j, A_i) - \text{Risk}(\Theta_j, A_i \oplus R_x)\} - C(\Theta_j, A_i \oplus R_x)$$
$$= (-1000 + 200) - (-350)$$
$$= -\$450.$$

We noted above that the following parameters require definition:

- Acceptable risk for the organization
- The cost of the asset
- The cost of the countermeasures
- What level of protection is acceptable (namely, what is the residual risk)

Some organizations may feel that information security controls will impact their business model; some managers believe that if controls are placed on how the business operates, it will reduce their revenues. But there is always a tradeoff in the revenues that a company is willing/able to bring in. For example, perhaps the revenues might actually double if one quadrupled the size of the advertisement budget, but is the company doing that? Perhaps the revenues might actually go down 10% unless one doubled to size of the advertisement budget, but is the company doing that? Perhaps the revenues might actually double if one reduced the item's cost in half (say with a new but expensive manufacturing plant), but is the company doing that? Perhaps the revenues might actually go down 10% unless one reduced the item's cost in half, but is the company doing that? A commercial fishery could increase its catch (and revenue) if its fishermen ventured 20 miles farther, but are they willing to take the increased risk exposure? A mining concern could mine more coal by going deeper into a problematic shaft and be willing to take the increased risk exposure, but do they do that? In each such case the decision may well be made that revenue and risk exposure need to be balanced. The same argument should apply when it comes to information security. Also, as noted earlier, one still wants the net benefit (NB) to remain positive:

$$\text{NB}_y = \text{RMP}_y - \text{R}_y = \alpha \times T_y - \chi_y(O) - R_y > 0$$

There may in fact be situations where knowing that there are strong security/risk management mechanisms will in fact increase revenues. For example, as consumers we all would prefer to bring our online business to a firm that has strong data confidentiality rather than to an online retailer that has a reputation for not protecting credit card data and has experienced other data loss events.

Some observations on asset costs follow. We defined in Chapter 2 the damage $D(\Theta_j, A_i)$ to asset A_i as the total cost of restoral, including deployment of a replacement asset doing the same function at the same level of performance, if needed, and also any potential business revenue loss or other losses caused by an unmitigated threat Θ_j. Note that $D(\Theta_j, A_i)$ could be

- Less than the cost $K(A_i)$ of the asset in question—for example, for minor damage and/or low cost of restoral and/or no revenue loss
- Same as the cost $K(A_i)$ of the asset in question—for example, a comparable replacement of an item that is somewhat of a commodity (say a brand new laptop computer not yet configured or used was stolen and one has to replace it with a new one from inventory)
- Higher than the cost $K(A_i)$ of the asset in question—for example, when the replacement part is higher and/or there was a lot of labor (say for either wiring up a device or to configure the device in software using some labor-intensive process)

Generally, the damage is less at the physical level and more at the logical level (theft of data, corruption of configuration, denial of service, etc.) Therefore, there is usually only a weak correlation between the device cost $K(A_i)$ and the damage $D(\Theta_j, A_i)$.

7.5 RISK MANAGEMENT COMMITTEE

We have just highlighted that it is critical to understand the organization and determine just how much security is optimally needed and/or desired. Information security is often at the top of the list whenever executives are asked about areas of concerns, with companies being in the news with what seems to be daily with security breaches. When asked, many executives will unequivocally state that they want security, but they may not be immediately ready to make the necessary cultural and business processes changes to become truly secure. Examples of cultural changes may include: not (and/or no longer) allowing the use of the corporate computer over a public WiFi hotspot, not (and/or no longer) allowing a Bluetooth peripheral, not (and/or no longer) allowing people to use the corporate computer over their home network, not allowing employees to send unencrypted messages, not allowing employees to download freeware, requiring employees to use complex passwords and change regularly, and so on.

In order to ensure that the security department operates in a risk-optimized fashion, a risk management committee should be created to provide advocacy.

All organizations have business priorities; increase revenues, lower costs, and so on. Typically, while organizations clearly express that they want security, they, may not be so willing to invest the resources required. Many companies that have experienced a breach lose customers due to a lack of confidence, and some have even almost gone out of business. The purpose of creating a risk management committee is to help ensure that priorities are defined on how to tackle security issues while at the same time focusing on keeping security as one of the top priorities in the organization.

While many organizations understand the importance of information security, not all parties within an organization agree what security controls are required. For example, some subgroups within IT may become defensive when the security-oriented improvements are suggested. The risk management committee can facilitate this process.

Note: There are many considerations that should be undertaken when creating this team. It is outside the scope of this text to discuss, but the reader is advised to further research the subject.

7.6   ORGANIZATION-SPECIFIC RISK METHODOLOGY

Chapter 4 provided a survey of available information security risk management methods and tools. It was noted that there is a multitude of guides, methodical approaches, and support tools. Some methods are based on a national standard; other methods are based on an international standard; some methods are based on a de facto standard. Some organizations may opt to generate their own method where national or international standards are taken as a foundation while existing organization-specific security mechanisms, policies, and/or infrastructure are subsumed into the method. The challenge for the organization is that of all these approaches have a degree of complexity. As we noted in Chapter 4, methods can be quantitative or qualitative in nature; some methods combine both approaches, while other methods allow the firm to select what approach to use within the same method. Table 7.4 compares the two methods.

TABLE 7.4. Quantitative versus Qualitative Risk Management

Quantitative	Qualitative
Objective	Subjective
Dollar value is assigned to risk	No dollar value is assigned
Cost–benefit analyses	No cost–benefit analyses
Automated and complex	No automation, less complex
Less guess work, since most times it uses a mathematical formula.	More guess work, can be viewed as more of a intuitive call
Results easy to communicate, perhaps not easy for some to understand if the values do not relate to something meaningful	Result difficult to communicate, because it can be hard to justify the results

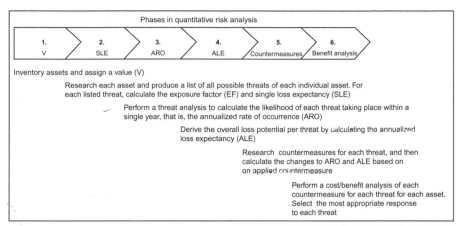

Modeled after James Michael Stewart, Ed Tittel, and Mike Chapple

FIGURE 7.2. Quantitative Analysis.

7.6.1 Quantitative Methods

Chapter 2 introduced the risk-theory analytical constructs and also defined the analytical measures for financial modeling, namely, return on security investment (ROSI); exposure factor (EF), single loss expectancy (SLE), annual rate of occurrence (ARO), and annual loss expectancy (ALE). Quantitative risk assessment is typically carried out in six steps, as shown in Figure 7.2.

A quick review follows (also see Table 7.5).

SLE is the cost attached to a threat/risk exposure to an asset, where damage is actually incurred; namely, it is the exact loss an organization will experience if the asset were damaged by a threat. It follows that

$$\text{SLE} = \text{Asset value} \times \text{Exposure factor} - V(A_i) \times \text{EF}.$$

ARO is the number of times that a risk exposure leading to actual damage is expected to occur during one year. Also seen as the normalized rate at which the risk exposure resulting in actual damage occurs during one (specified) year. ARO ranges from a value of 0.0 (the threat never materializes in damage) to 1.0 (the threat will result in damage during the year with certitude[33] once during the year) to N (for any N) (the threat will result in damage during the year with certitude N times during the year). ARO can be approximated from historical

[33]Some might argue that "nothing ever happens with certitude." Here is just one example to prove our point: leave a $3,000 laptop on a table at a busy coffee shop that has WiFi and go back a year later (a month later? a week-later? a day later?) and see if the laptop is still there waiting for its rightful owner...

TABLE 7.5. Key Quantitative Terms

Term	Formula
Exposure factor (EF)	%
Single loss expectancy (SLE)	SLE $=$ V $*$ EF
Annualized rate of occurrence (ARO)	# per year
Annualized loss expectancy (ALE)	ALE $=$ SLE $*$ ARO $=$ V $*$ EF $*$ ARO
Annual cost of the safeguard (ACS)	$ per year
Benefit of a safeguard	[Pre-countermeasure ALE − Post-countermeasure ALE] − ACS

data, by statistical inference on a recent sample, or by extrapolating data from another company (although this may be problematic).

ALE is the financial cost of a threat against a given asset. One has

$$ALE = SLE \times ARO.$$

For example if the SLE of an asset is \$9,000 and the ARO is 2.0 then the ALE is \$18,000. If the ARO is 20, then the ALE is \$180,000.

Calculation of these metrics are supported by the quantitative methods (including those listed in Chapter 4). Several tools automate the exercise and also typically create an asset inventory that incorporates ARO and $V(A_i)$ values. One also wants to be able to calculate the ALE for the (specific) asset A_i and the specific safeguard (control) R_x. This entails having the EF and ARO for those specific cases. As we have discussed a number of times the annual cost of the controls should not exceed the ALE. A quick check here is:

> ALE before safeguard − ALE after implementing the safeguard
> − Annual cost of safeguard $=$ value of the safeguard to the firm.

If the result of the left-hand side is negative, the control is effectively too expensive; if the number is positive, the deployment of the safeguard (remediation) accrues value to the firm.

For each specific risk exposure and/or threat, a number of controls (remediations) may be available. Each of these remediations must be priced out, and the benefit to the company must be assessed. We have already covered this topic at length in this text, and the basic principles are self-evident: Get the maximum benefit (e.g., maximum IRR) for the project. Cost factors associated with a remediation include but are not limited to: purchase cost of equipment/software; deployment cost of equipment/software; licensing costs of equipment/software; implementation, customization, and test-and-turn-up costs; opex costs associated with the equipment/software (operations, maintenance, administration, repair). Observers note that the annual savings or loss from a control should not be the only factor considered when making a decision about remediation. The issue of legal responsibility (including confidentiality of customer records) must be considered, especially in a litigious society. In some cases it is more prudent in the final analysis to "over-invest" in a remediation than to be exposed to legal liability if the asset or its content is compromised.

7.6.2 Qualitative Methods

Some companies may opt for a qualitative risk analysis. While in the quantitative method one assigned precise monetary values to the possible outcomes of risk exposures and then computed an expected value based on a probability distribution that such exposures resulted in actual damage, in the qualitative method one takes the approach of *ranking threats/exposure events on a scale*. Based on the scale, one evaluates the likelihood of occurrence, the costs, and the outcomes, based on judgment, experience, and situational awareness. Approaches that can be used for qualitative analysis include, but are not limited to, internal interviews, internal surveys, internal questionnaires, Delphi techniques, storyboarding, and internal Focus groups. The selection of the approach is based on the culture, environment, sophistication, and security savviness of the organization.

The Delphi approach is a systematic, interactive forecasting method that relies on interviewing and getting opinions from a group of (internal and/or external) experts.

A focus group (originally called "focused interviews" or "group depth interviews") can be defined as a group of interacting individuals having some common interest or characteristics, brought together by a moderator who uses the group and its interaction as a way to gain information about a specific or focused issue. A focus group is typically a dozen people or so who are unfamiliar with each other. The participants are selected because they have certain characteristics in common that relate to the topic of the focus group. The moderator or interviewer creates a permissive and nurturing environment that encourages different perceptions and points of view, without pressuring participants to vote, plan, or reach consensus. The group discussion is conducted several times with similar types of participants to identify trends and patterns in perceptions. Systematic analysis of the discussions provide clues and insights as to how a product, service, or opportunity is perceived by the group [MAR200901].

Storyboarding is the use of a series of pictures in separate frames to outline or brainstorm ideas about how to tell a story. It is a process of roughing out a subject matter, often in sketch form. Typically, this is done with a packet of sticky-notes. The process involves sketching or describing the most important steps in the process; these are referred to as key frames. A timeline is achieved by arranging the key frames in the sequence. See Figure 7.3 for a graphical perspective.

Picking up on the concept of ranking threats/exposure events on a scale, a simple chart to help the risk management committee review risks is shown in

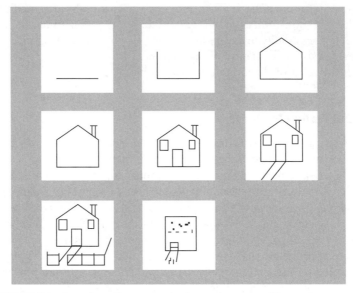

FIGURE 7.3. Storyboarding example: from plan to certificate of occupancy.

Figure 7.4. The first step is for the organization to define to the risk levels. Here is a starting point that could be used by the committee.

Likelihood of Occurrence:
- *Low:* Once every 5–10 years
- *Medium:* Once every 3–5 years
- *High:* Once a year

Impact of Risk:
- *Low:* Minor business interruption
- *Medium:* Significant business interruption/audit finding
- *High:* Potential to shutdown business or long-term affect

Each risk exposure that has been identified that applies to the organization's assets should go through this simple rating process. The qualitative descriptions can be defined as the organization sees fit to provide value in the process. For example, in regard to impact of risk, if defining a low risk as a minor business interruption is not helpful, then it should be modified to something more appropriate (i.e., $1000 to $5000). Once a rating is established for each risk exposure, one then needs to look at the controls that are in place.

An example follows.

Risk Exposure #1: Loss of organization's data center due to an environmental event (hurricane, flooding, etc.)

Impact of risk	High	Medium	High	High	Y axis - likelihood of impact of risk exposure
	Medium	Low	Medium	High	
	Low	Low	Low	Medium	
		Low	Medium	High	
		Likelihood of occurrence			

X axis - Likelihood of occurrence

FIGURE 7.4. Quantitative tool.

Risk Exposure #2: Breach of security in e-commerce environment

Risk Exposure #3: Breach of security that allow access to credit card information.

Some possible assignments are shown in Table 7.6.

7.6.3 Other Approaches

Another approach for dealing with uncertainty/lack-of-clarity is to use Fuzzy set theory, a concept developed by Zadeh and published in 1965[34] We briefly mention the techniques, but we do not apply the theory here; we encourage the reader to further research this topic.

At a general level the following uncertainty models are applicable:

- *Fuzziness:* Subjective, incomplete and imprecise data can be described and utilized with fuzzy sets, fuzzy functions, and fuzzy processes.
- *Randomness:* Random events that can be characterized with the mathematical theory of probability
- *Fuzzy randomness:* Simultaneously describing objective and subjective information as a fuzzy set of possible probabilistic models over some range of imprecision.

Fuzziness. Fuzzy set theory deals with sets or categories whose boundaries are "blurry" or "fuzzy." Fuzzy sets are sets whose elements have degrees of membership. The discipline enables the user to handle uncertainty when there is degree-vagueness, that is, having a property possessed by an object to varying degrees. For example, it may not be categorically clear a priori what the degree of threat to an organization might be: A threat may have a severe impact on PCs with company x (perhaps which has not kept up with the latest OS upgrades for the past 18 months), or a lesser impact on PCs with company y (perhaps which has not kept up with the latest OS upgrades for the past 6 months), or nearly no impact (or very small impact) on the PCs for company z that has totally kept up with the latest OS upgrades. Fuzzy logic is used in a

[34]L.A.Zadeh, "Fuzzy sets," *Information and Control* 1965, 8:338–353.

TABLE 7.6. Example of Qualitative Method

Risk Number	Risk Name	Risk Description	Risk Occurrence	Risk Impact	Risk Level	Controls	Mitigated Occurrence	Mitigated Impact	Mitigated Risk
1	Loss of datacenter	Total loss of datacenter due to environmental forces (hurricane, flood, etc.)	Low	High	Medium	None	Low	High	Medium
2	Security breach	Security breach in e-commerce environment	Medium	High	High	None	Medium	High	Medium
3	Privacy protection	Breach that allows access to credit cards information	Medium	High	High	-Hardening standards -PCI compliance vulnerability scans -Patching process	Low	High	Medium

large number of applications in engineering and computer science from bullet trains to washing machines to video cameras to video games [SMI200601].

If m_x represents the membership function of member x in a given set A, then in classical set theory m_x takes on only low values: 0 or 1. In Fuzzy set theory m_x takes on any value in the interval [0,1]. Hence, fuzzy set theory allows the gradual assessment of the membership of elements in a set as described by the membership function. One can then represent set A as

$$A = \{(x_1, m_1), (x_2, m_2), (x_3, m_3), \ldots\}.$$

For each element x, $m(x)$ is the grade of membership of x. If $A = \{x_1, \ldots, x_n\}$, the fuzzy set (A,m) can be denoted $\{m(x_1)/x_1, \ldots, m(x_n)/x_n\}$. An element mapping to the value 0 is not included in the fuzzy set, an element mapping to the value 1 describes a fully included member. The set is called the *support* of the fuzzy set (A,m) and the set is called the *kernel* of the fuzzy set (A,m). See Figure 7.5.

Randomness. As we already know and have defined in Chapter 2, randomness is described by *probability distribution functions* and *probability density functions*. Probability can be seen as being comprised of two related concepts [INS200901]:

- *Aleatory* probability, which represents the likelihood of future events whose occurrence is governed by some random physical phenomenon. This concept can be further divided into physical phenomena that are predictable, in principle, with sufficient information, and phenomena which are essentially unpredictable.
- *Epistemic* probability, which represents uncertainty about propositions when one lacks complete knowledge of causative circumstances. Such propositions may be about past or future events.

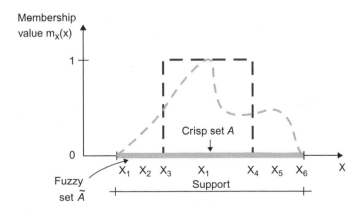

FIGURE 7.5. A Fuzzy set.

Fuzzy Randomness. Fuzzy randomness simultaneously describes objective and subjective information as a fuzzy set of possible probabilistic models over some range of imprecision. This generalized uncertainty model contains fuzziness and randomness as special cases. Objective uncertainty in the form of observed/measured data is modeled as randomness, whereas subjective uncertainty—for example, due to a lack of trustworthiness or imprecision of measurement results, of distribution parameters, of environmental conditions, or of the data sources—is described as fuzziness. The model fuzzy randomness then combines but do not mix objectivity and subjectivity; these are separately visible at any time. It may be understood as an imprecise probabilistic model, which allows for simultaneously considering all possible probability models that are relevant to describing the problem [INS200901].

7.7   RISK WAIVERS PROGRAMS

There will invariably be business needs that may directly conflict with information security policies and best practices. It is not a question of if, but more a question of how many and which ones are worth expanding political capital to correct.

Most security and risk management professionals take the stance that everything has to be corrected. While to a purist security professional this is the correct approach, if matters are handled in such a dogmatic way, the risk management program will not be successful. The security department is the key department advocating for security; however, security is not just an IT security department's issue. There must obviously be a partnership with the business side of the organization to describe and define the probability of damage/ARO of the risk exposure to the business asset. The aim for perfect security is not practical. This does not mean that an organization should stop making attempts to reach this desirable level; however, an organization does need to be realistic.

The main purpose of the waivers program is to force an organization to document the risk exposures and make a business decision related to how they are going to handle the issue. Organizations are forced to evaluate each risk exposure and choose from one of the four following options:

1. **Accept the Risk Exposure.** Management has reviewed the risk exposure and determined that the corrective action required does not make business sense. In this case, management recognizes the risk but chooses to accept it.
2. **Fully Correct the Risk Exposure.** Management has reviewed the risk exposure and determined that it is appropriate to invest in fully correcting the issue.
3. **Partially Mitigate the Risk Exposure.** Management has reviewed the risk exposure and determined that it will only partially correct the risk. There

may be some portions of the risk that can be easily addressed; however, a portion is not corrected.

4. **Insurance Against the Risk Exposure.** Management has reviewed the risk exposure and determined that formal insurance for this risk exposure should be obtained. In some cases all or a portion of the risk will be corrected as well as selecting the option to seek insurance.

The purpose of the waivers program is not to encourage management to avoid correcting and mitigating risk exposures; rather it can be an effective way to show compliance (internal or external audits) that one has made a business decision not to comply and not that the risk exposure was simply overlooked or ignored. There are valid reasons a certain risk exposure may be accepted, such as the costs to correct could be more than the value of the asset. In this case the organization would make a business decision not to correct the risk.

The system used to organize and manage waivers can range from a simplistic software system to a dedicated software system whose only purpose is to maintain and manage open risks. Here are some examples of what can be used to manage a waivers program:

1. **Microsoft Excel Spreadsheet.** Very simple and easy to get started tracking waivers. In most cases it will lack some functionality to help the risk management team maintain the waiver. Can also be challenging for the organization to submit waivers. Typically requires a form to be created to assist with information gathering.

2. **Microsoft Access Database.** Can still be somewhat easy to create; however, will take a resource with Access knowledge to create the system. May still lack some functionality; but being based on a lightweight database, there are opportunities for increased features. With proper configuration, it can be a bit easier for the organization to submit waivers electronically.

3. **Custom Developed Application.** May take substantial development efforts in order to get the wavier system started. Considering that the system will be custom developed, it will be designed to meet the organizations exact needs including the fields they would like to track. With this approach it would be very easy for an organization to submit waivers electronically typically using a web-based form. Costs range from low to moderate, based on resources within the organization.

4. **Commercially Developed Application.** Can be the easiest to implement within an organization and may include the ability to have support from a security vendor. Some applications are still able to be customized, and in most cases they have the most features and functionality for managing risks. Some features may include automatic notification of risks submitted and expirations. Also, it may include assistance for the risk management team as many tools are mapped to industry standards and

also assist by defining the risk to the organization of not correcting the issue.

The process to seek a waiver is straightforward and can easily be communicated to the organization. See below for the basic steps and additional points of consideration.

1. **Determine whether correcting risk is in conflict with business priorities.**
   - It is critical to have a way to handle this but remain in control.
   - Without waivers program it could kill the whole risk management program.
2. **Identify appropriate resources to submit waiver request.**
   - Typically, this is the team that is in violation of the security standard or policy.
   - This can create some conflict from time to time, and it may fall on the risk management team to submit the waivers on the team's behalf.
   - It is important to understand your organization and make the decision based on what one believes would fit the culture.
   - An advantage of the risk management team submitting the waivers would be that all of the risks that are open would be properly captured.
3. **Information security risk management team reviews the request and comments.**
   - A key step in the process is to ensure that the risk management team actually reviews the risks that are submitted.
   - In some cases, practitioners (not management) are willing to accept a large amount of risk. This may be for a number of reasons, but the number one reason tends to be the amount of time and resources it would take to correct the issue.
4. **Gain appropriate signoff from management for Waiver to be approved.**
5. **Ensure that there is proactive follow-up to manage open waivers.**

REFERENCES

[COO200901] N. R. Coons, Protect customer data with PCI standards, 25 Mar 2009, NetWorld Alliance, 13100 Eastpoint Park Blvd. Louisville, KY 40223.

[INS200901] Institute of Statics and Dynamics of Structures (TU Dresden), Fakultät Bauingenieurwesen, Institut für Statik und Dynamik der Tragwerke, Prof. Dr.-Ing. habil. B. Möller, 01062 Dresden, Germany.

[ITP200901] IT Policy Compliance Group, Managing Spend on Information Security and Audit for Better Results, February 2009, Managing Director, Jim Hurley. Founded in 2005, the IT Policy Compliance Group conducts benchmarks that are focused on delivering fact-based guidance on the steps that can be taken to improve results. Benchmark results are reported through www.itpolicycompliance.com for the benefit of members.

[MAR200901] M. Marczak and M. Sewell, Using Focus Groups For Evaluation, University Of Arizona at Tucson. Institute for Children, Youth and Families, P.O. Box 210033, Tucson, Arizona 85721–0033.

[MOT200401] J. Moteff, "Computer Security: A Summary of Selected Federal Laws, Executive Orders, and Presidential Directives," April 16, 2004, Congressional Research Service, The Library of Congress, Science and Technology Policy Resources, Science, and Industry Division.

[PCI200901] PCI Security Standards Council, LLC, 401 Edgewater Place, Suite 600, Wakefield, MA 01880, USA.

[SMI200601] M. Smithson, and J. Verkuilen, *Fuzzy Set Theory: Applications in the Social Sciences*, Sage, Thousand Oaks, CA, 2006.

APPENDIX 7A: SUMMARY OF APPLICABLE LEGISLATION

Not only is IT security the "right thing" to do, it is also the "mandated thing" to do. Risk management teams will need to have a basic understanding of the legislation that has evolved in the recent past. This appendix provides a highly abridged introductory treatment of this topic. While the U.S. federal government generally does not regulate the security of non-government computer systems at this time, it does require that sensitive information kept on non-government commercial systems be protected against unauthorized access and disclosure. The federal government does have an enforcement role: It investigates and prosecutes computer crimes; this is done both at the federal government level and at the state and local level (here federal government offers assistance to state and local law enforcement agencies in their investigation and prosecution of computer activities that are declared to be illegal at the state level). Also, the federal government funds R&D programs for the development of science in computer security. Some long-established U.S. government initiatives in the security and risk management arena include the Computer Security Act (CSA) of 1987, the Information Technology Management Reform Act of 1996, and the Government Information Security Reform Act of October 2000. Table 7A.1 lists some applicable government publications.

Up to now, regulation has been limited to medical information (Health Insurance Portability and Accountability Act of 1996) and to financial information (Gramm–Leach–Bliley Act); also relating to finances, the Sarbanes–Oxley Act of 2002 requires certain companies certify the accuracy of their internal financial controls. The Secretary of Health and Human Services has the authority to develop and enforce standards for medical information, while other agencies have the authority to develop and enforce standards for financial information (e.g., the Security Exchange Commission has authority to develop standards and enforce these regulations). As discussed in the Homeland Security Act of 2002, the Department of Homeland Security encourages

TABLE 7A.1. U.S. Government Publications of Interest to Risk Management (Partial List)

NIST Interagency Reports 4749. *Sample Statements of Work for Federal Computer Security Services: For Use In-House or Contracting Out*, December 1991.

NIST Special Publication (SP) 800-12. *An Introduction to Computer Security: The NIST Handbook*, October 1995.

Barbara Guttman, NIST Special Publication (SP) 800-14.

Generally Accepted Principles and Practices for Securing Information Technology Systems, September 1996.

NIST and Federal Computer Security Managers' Forum Working Group, NIST Special Publication (SP) 800-18. *Guide For Developing Security Plans for Information Technology Systems.*

NIST Special Publication 800-26, *Security Self-Assessment Guide for Information Technology Systems*, August 2001.

NIST Special Publication (SP) 800-27. *Engineering Principles for IT Security*, June 2001.

Gary Stoneburner, Alice Goguen, and Alexis Feringa, *Risk Management Guide for Information Technology Systems—Recommendations of the National Institute of Standards and Technology*, Special Publication 800-30, July 2002, Computer Security Division Information Technology Laboratory, National Institute of Standards and Technology Gaithersburg, MD 20899-8930.

Office of Management and Budget (OMB) Circular A-130. *Management of Federal Information Resources*, November 2000.

state and local government, academia, the private sector, and the general public to help protect the nation's information infrastructure (the role of the Department of Homeland Security is further elaborated in the Homeland Security Presidential Directive No. 7 and the National Strategy for Securing Cyberspace).

7A.1 Federal Computer Environments

The Federal Information Security Act of 2002 provides the basic statutory requirements for securing federal computer systems.[35] The Federal Information Security Act (FISMA) requires each agency to inventory its major computer systems, to identify and provide appropriate security protections, and to develop, document, and implement an agency-wide information security program. FISMA authorizes the National Institute of Standards and Technology (NIST) to develop security standards and guidelines for systems used by the federal government. It authorizes the Secretary of Commerce to choose which of these standards and guidelines to promulgate. FISMA authorizes the Director of the Office of Management and Budget (OMB) to oversee the

---

[35]This summary is loosely based on John Moteff's, "Computer Security: A Summary of Selected Federal Laws, Executive Orders, and Presidential Directives," April 16, 2004, Congressional Research Service, The Library of Congress, Science and Technology Policy Resource, Sciences, and Industry Division [MOT200401].

development and implementation of (including ensuring compliance with) these security policies, principles, standards, and guidelines. The Director of OMB is authorized to oversee the development of, and ensure compliance with, policies, principles, standards, and guidelines governing the security of all federal computer systems, except for national security computer systems. The Committee on National Security Systems has that authority over national security systems (which include both information and telecommunication systems). The Director of Central Intelligence has similar authority over computer systems that contain intelligence information. NIST has the responsibility for developing security standards and guidelines for all federal computer systems, except national security systems. The National Security Agency has that authority over national security systems.

7A.2 Private Computer Environments

As noted, there are currently no general federal requirements for private entities other than federal contractors operating systems for the federal government to secure their computer systems. However, there are requirements for entities that hold or process certain types of personal information to ensure the confidentiality of that information. To date, this includes financial information and medical information. There is also a federal requirement that certain firms that register with the Security and Exchange Commission (SEC) must include in the financial reports an assessment of their internal financial controls. To the extent that each of these types of information is held and/or processed electronically, the security of some private computer systems come under federal regulation.

Title V of the **Gramm–Leach–Bliley Act** requires financial institutions to protect the security and confidentiality of their customers' nonpublic personal information. The Act authorizes various federal regulatory agencies (the Comptroller of the Currency, the Security Exchange Commission, the Federal Deposit Insurance Corporation, et al.) to coordinate the development of regulations for meeting this requirement. Each of these federal agencies is authorized to enforce the regulations for those institutions in their jurisdiction. The regulations require financial institutions to develop, implement, and maintain a comprehensive information security program that contains appropriate administrative, technical, and physical safeguards. Such a program should include the designation of an employee to coordinate the program, risk assessments, regular tests and monitoring of safeguards, and a process for making adjustments in light of test results and/or changes in operations or other circumstances that may impact the effectiveness of the program.

The **Health Insurance Portability and Accountability Act of 1996** authorizes the Secretary of Health and Human Services to adopt standards that require health plans, health care providers, and health care clearinghouses to take reasonable and appropriate administrative, technical and physical safeguards to: ensure the integrity and confidentiality of individually identifiable health information held or transferred by them; to protect against any reasonably anticipated threats, unauthorized use or disclosure; and to ensure compliance with these safeguards by officers and employees. These security standards were adopted in 45 CFR Part 164, Subpart C. The Secretary assigned responsibility for enforcing these security standards to the Center for Medicare and Medicaid Services.

Besides these privacy-oriented rules, the **Sarbanes–Oxley Act of 2002** authorizes the Security Exchange Commission to prescribe regulations requiring entities that produce annual financial reports pursuant to sections 13(a) or 15(d) of the Securities Exchange Act of 1934 to contain a report on the firm's internal financial controls. The report must state the responsibility of management for establishing and maintaining an adequate internal control structure and procedures for financial reporting and assess the effectiveness of those structures and controls. External audits must attest to and report on management's assessments. "Internal control" is defined as a process that provides assurance regarding the reliability of financial reporting. It pertains to the maintenance of records that accurately reflect the transactions and dispositions of assets and prevents or detects unauthorized acquisition, use, or disposition of assets. The security of information technology (systems, software, applications) are critical element to assess.

7A.3   Industry-Specific Compliance Requirements

There are a number of industry-specific compliance directives, although many of these are strictly voluntary. We briefly discuss one highly criticized but de facto standard here that is a requirement for any organization that wishes to process credit card payments.

The **Payment Card Industry Data Security Standard (PCI DSS)** has been developed by a council of multiple financial institutions to enhance payment-account data security. It includes guidelines for user authentication, firewalls, encryption, anti-virus measures, and more. The PCI Security Standards Council is an open global forum for the ongoing development, enhancement, storage, dissemination, and implementation of security standards for account data protection. The PCI Security Standards Council's mission is to enhance payment account data security by driving education and awareness of the PCI Security Standards. The formation of the PCI council was announced in 2006 and comprises American Express, Discover Financial Services, JCB International, MasterCard Worldwide and Visa Inc. [COO200901, PCI200901]. The PCI DSS is a multifaceted security standard that includes requirements for security management, policies, procedures, network architecture, software design, and other critical protective measures. This comprehensive standard is intended to help organizations proactively protect customer account data.

The PCI Security Standards Council will enhance the PCI DSS as needed to ensure that the standard includes any new or modified requirements necessary to mitigate emerging payment security risks, while continuing to foster wide-scale adoption. Ongoing development of the standard will provide for feedback from the Advisory Board and other participating organizations. All key stakeholders are encouraged to provide input, during the creation and review of proposed additions or modifications to the PCI DSS. On October 1, 2008, version 1.2 of the PCI DSS requirements was released. The core of the PCI DSS is a group of principles and accompanying requirements, around which the specific elements of the DSS are organized:

Build and Maintain a Secure Network

Requirement 1: Install and maintain a firewall configuration to protect cardholder data.

Requirement 2: Do not use vendor-supplied defaults for system passwords and other security parameters.

Protect Cardholder Data

Requirement 3: Protect stored cardholder data.

Requirement 4: Encrypt transmission of cardholder data across open, public networks.

Maintain a Vulnerability Management Program

Requirement 5: Use and regularly update anti-virus software.

Requirement 6: Develop and maintain secure systems and applications.

Implement Strong Access Control Measures

Requirement 7: Restrict access to cardholder data by business need-to-know.

Requirement 8: Assign a unique ID to each person with computer access.

Requirement 9: Restrict physical access to cardholder data.

Regularly Monitor and Test Networks

Requirement 10: Track and monitor all access to network resources and cardholder data.

Requirement 11: Regularly test security systems and processes.

Maintain an Information Security Policy

Requirement 12: Maintain a policy that addresses information security.

CHAPTER 8

IDENTIFYING RESOURCES AND IMPLEMENTING THE RISK MANAGEMENT TEAM

This chapter continues the description of the information security risk management process introduced in Chapters 6 and 7 by discussing the fourth and fifth procedural block in the flow (see Figure 8.1). The fourth block in the process covers identifying the resource requirements (people, process, technology) for Risk Management. The fifth block in the process covers developing and implementing the Risk Management team.

The following is a checklist to support these activities:

- Operating costs to support risk management
- Organizational models
- Staffing requirements
  - Staff size requirements
  - Specialized skills required
  - Sourcing options
- Risk management tools
  - Evaluation, selection, and implementation
  - Organization usage
  - Commercial versus open source
- Risk management services
  - Alerting and analysis services
  - Assessments and audits
  - Project consulting
- Developing and implementing the risk management team
  - Creating security standards
  - Defining subject matter experts
  - Determining information sources

Information Technology Risk Management in Enterprise Environments: A Review of Industry Practices and a Practial Guide to Risk Management Teams, by Jake Kouns and Daniel Minoli Copyright © 2010 John Wiley & Sons, Inc.

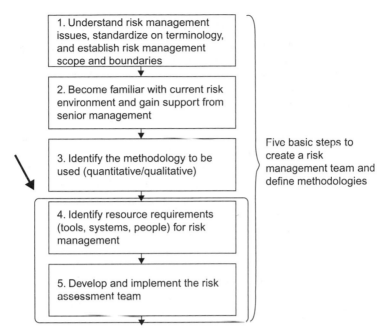

FIGURE 8.1. A section of the risk management process.

8.1 OPERATING COSTS TO SUPPORT RISK MANAGEMENT AND STAFFING REQUIREMENTS

Information security is a field that is still relatively immature, and even with the rapid improvements that organizations have been forced to make in recent years, there is still much to achieve. As is the case in many other information technology disciplines, it is critical that that the people, processes, and technology come together to be successful. Industry observers note that [PIR 200801]

Information security is the most challenging aspect of information processing because it is ever-changing and evolving. The simple reason for information security being so challenging is that the adversary only has to be right once, but the defender has to be right all of the time. The defender is plagued with a lack of investment, resources, time, and knowledge. The organization expects the defender to be able to prevent any damage to its information infrastructure, even with the limited resources and capabilities available to it. As soon as the defender creates and implements a control or set of controls to defend against an attack from an adversary, the adversary develops a new and more effective attack that forces the defender to develop yet another control. Ethics, laws, morals, lack of funding, and lack of resources do not restrict adversaries. The global communication capabilities that have grown as a result of the adoption of

Internet capabilities have allowed the adversary community to come together, without ever having a verbal or in-person conversation, to develop innovative attacks, share research and knowledge, and develop capabilities that far surpass what any one organization could achieve. The best chance the defender has to defeat the adversary is to take a risk management approach to information protection that facilitates the protection of the essential and critical elements using the available resources and capabilities.

A point to make note of is that success is achieved when there is a balance. All too often, security professionals may put too much credence in a technology-only solution, while management perhaps places too much trust on a confusing string of acronyms following peoples' names or expect that a process will automatically ensure that the sufficient controls are in place.

As we have seen, risk management is a systematic process for the identification, analysis, control and communication of risk events, and the implementation of controls to reduce risk to an acceptable level. Risk management methodologies support the making of informed decisions about the allocation of scarce resources appropriate to the risk exposure [AND200301]. As is the case with any corporate initiative, one starts out with requirements (what is needed to support a mission, in this case risk management), an assessment of what resources exist to successfully undertake the initiative, a gap analysis to establish what is required to reach the optimal level, and an estimation of the total and/or incremental cost to achieve the mission.

The issue of actual and potential financial loss to a firm has already been discussed in previous chapters, particularly in Table 6.2 and Figure 6.5; it was shown there that the business cost when risk management is not properly handled can be substantial. To address the matter, firms need to establish a working organizational structure for risk management and also build out an effective working team. We have already hinted at a number of issues regarding sizing of the risk management team in Chapters 6 and 7, but given its importance, some additional considerations are presented herewith.

The people, processes, and technology required to ensure that an organization is secured will require a financial investment on the part of the organization. Specifically, when a firm is building a risk management team from the ground up, the financial burden tends to be reviewed in a detailed manner. Once the team becomes operational, organizations tend to seek the right balance, but it has already gone past the decision to implement a team. It is important to set the proper expectation with management on what can be accomplished based on the amount of resources that will be invested.

At the RSA Security Conference in 2002, R. Clarke, the Special Adviser to the President on Cybersecurity, cited statistics that indicated that less than 0.0025% of corporate revenue on average is spent on information-technology security. He is famously quoted as follows: "If you spend more on coffee than on IT security, then you will be hacked . . . ." Current statistics show that the spending on information security has increased since 2002, but most executives

TABLE 8.1. Likelihood of Data Losses or Thefts

Size (Annual Revenue or Budget)	$50 million	$500 million	$5 billlion	$50 billion
Worst practices	1 in 9 years	1 in 5 years	1 in 2 years	1 in 1 years
Normal practices	1 in 23 years	1 in 14 years	1 in 6 years	1 in 3 years

Source: IT Policy Compliance Group, 2009.

still only see information security as a cost.[36] All too often, information security receives attention only when management must respond to a regulatory requirement. Well-publicized high-profile security incidents costing millions of dollars does get the attention of corporate managers. The TJ Maxx security breach that was reported in January 2007 exposed 94 million credit card numbers. TJ Maxx was forced to pay $41 million to Visa and $24 million to MasterCard to cover the replacement cost of new cards, as well as an $880,000 fine. The additional costs to TJ Maxx for legal fees (reportedly at $20 million), loss of sales, additional staff, and IT support still cannot be fully measured, but many have put the costs for this incident close to $4.5 billion dollars [WAR200901, GAU200701, COO200901]. Additional high-profile security breaches in 2009 such as Heartland Payment Systems, RBS WorldPay, and Hannaford Supermarkets have provided yet more evidence that suggests that security breaches are real and extremely costly. In most cases, organizations are not even capable of measuring the damage to their brand. The question, therefore, is "Are organizations truly spending the amount that is required to protect their assets?"

Firms with the best practices for managing confidentiality and integrity risks in IT are less likely to experience theft or loss of data. Based on the benchmarks with more than 2600 organizations, the IT Policy Compliance Group estimated the likelihood of underlying data loss and theft events having a negative financial impact for the organization to ranges from once every year to once in several years, as shown in Table 8.1. The total business downtime is also nontrivial, as shown in Table 8.2.

While some risk exposures have a low probability, the sum of the expected values across the entire organization over the year may be a good indication of what the budget for the department should be. The risk management advocate should endeavor to make a rough order of magnitude (ROM) estimate of these expected losses at his or her firm; then decide what fraction of the displaced expense should be channeled into creating the risk management team (this is the α value discussed in Section 7.2). For example, if the expected loss is $1M per year, the organization may opt to invest $1M per year into developing an in-house capability to handle the risk exposures; this assumes that the team

---

[36]The worldwide expenditure in security was $23.5B in 2008 and was forecast to increase to $44B in 2012 [DUN200901]. If we assumed, for simplicity, a sample space of 23,500 key firms worldwide, the per-company spending in 2008 would have been $1M/year. Noting that the global IT spending in 2006 was over $1 trillion [MIC200701], the security expenditures equate to 2%.

TABLE 8.2. Total Business Downtime from IT Failures and Disruptions

Size (Annual Revenue or Budget)	$50 million	$500 million	$5 billlion	$50 billion
Worst practices	93 hours	104 hours	132 hours	179 hours
Normative practices	8 hours	9 hours	12 hours	16 hours

would be able to drive the residual risk to zero. Or, some other values may be used. Or, if the expected loss is $1M per year and the residual risk is, say $250,000, then the organization may opt to invest $0.75 M per into developing an in-house capability to handle the risk exposures (or, again, some other values of α).

Another approach is to use a subset of all risk exposure to compute a ROM of the losses, and use this ROM directly, or employ some 'markup' factor. For example, assume that there were just three risk exposures as follows:

1. A virus will infect every desktop/laptop, eventually causing ½ day loss of productivity for each employee, with an average loaded salary of $750/ day. Say the probability that this will happen in a given year is 0.01.
2. Malware will infect the corporate CRM/service order database, which eventually requires 10 staff-days to rebuild and/or fix; IT staff costs the company $1250/day. Say the probability that this will happen in a given year is 0.03.
3. A keystroke logger enables an agent to eventually steal the employees HR records for past and present employees. The database has 10,000 entries. To remediate the issue, the company has to pay $100 per employee for a security alert service and also spend $10,000 in administrative/remediation costs (e.g., see [GAU200701]). Say the probability that this will happen in a given year is 0.02.

The expected losses for these risk exposures are: $7,500, $375, and $20,200, respectively, for a total of $28,075.

Yet another approach could be to allocate a fraction (say 0.1%) of the top line of the firm to IT risk management. As an example, consider a firm that has a $1B top line revenue and 2000 employees; a 0.1% allocation would mean a $1M/yr budget on Risk Management.

This example and the text above bring out some interesting observations:

- While the loss is nonzero, the loss may not justify a full-time person (not to say team) to manage/support the risk management function (because the loaded salary of such a person may be high, say $150,000 per year).
- The approach of dedicating a fraction of the top line, say 0.1%, may be "too generous" and/or an "overkill"; in the above example it would result in a $1M/year compensatory investment that exceeds the calculated risk. (An approach is to reduce the fraction, say to 0.01% of the top line, say

$100,000 in the above example, or, basically 1 FTE—full time equivalent resource.)

- Many organizations might struggle with determining expected losses for risk exposures that they face. It is however important that the risk management team can express this to management. For example, if TJ Maxx would have explained to management that an attack could cost them approximately $4.5 billion do you think they would have invested more in a proper risk management team?

Yet another approach is to use some generalized industry estimate for the ROM, (see, for example, Table 6.2 and Figure 6.5).

Appendix 8A provides a reference example. It looks at risk as a function of the company size. While the example is limited in scope, it can be inferred by additional work that the "sensitivity" to additional risk exposures is generally linear in nature and not quadratic or exponential. Some empirical/heuristic observations that can be made (without great loss of generality) are as follows:

- For low probability of risk exposure the company revenue must be at around $4B/year before one FTE dedicated to risk management is justified. For revenue of $16B/year, 2–3 FTEs are justified.
- For medium probability of risk exposure the company revenue must be at around $2B/year before one FTE dedicated to risk management is justified. For revenue of $16B/year, a team of 4–5 FTEs is justified.
- For a relatively high probability of risk exposure the company revenue must be at around $1B/year before one FTE dedicated to risk management is justified. For revenue of $16B/year, a team of 8–11 FTEs is justified.
- For high probability of risk exposure the company revenue must be at around $500M/year before one FTE dedicated to risk management is justified. For revenue of $16B/year, a team of 20–30 FTEs is justified.

While we have highlighted several (near-analytical) methods in this section, the message should be clear:

- Employ as much analytics as possible to arrive at a ROM of the expected losses.
- Decide what portion of the "displaced risk versus residual risk" should be channeled into the buildout of the risk management team.
- Decide on an organizational structure; also decide which steps of the entire risk management process are supported by the team; then determine what skillsets are needed, and then from there determine what the per FTE cost is, and consequently what the size of the team can be to stay on budget.

Take, for example, a $2B insurance company subject to a medium probability of risk exposures. To be "revenue-neutral" this company ought to have one person dedicated to risk management, or two people working 50% of the time on risk management; however, in some cases the number may be higher, for example, for regulatory-dictated reasons.

It must be said that the model of Appendix 8A is only to be used as a reference point. There is obviously an optimal number of staff that would be dedicated, and organizations that are smaller in size may require more to create the core of a team than the model suggests. The same goes for larger organizations as they may leverage economies of scale and be more efficient with their risk management practices. In addition, the models are attempting to indicate the number of employees that would be fully dedicated specifically to risk management. This is important as this does not include the other operational tasks or workload that may be grouped into an information security team. In most organizations, risk management functions tend to be grouped into other operational information security tasks.

8.2 ORGANIZATIONAL MODELS

We mentioned in the previous section the issue of organizational structure. It is important that there is responsibility and accountability for security and risk management within the organization. However, it is also important that the organization is not burdened with convoluted, complex structures, titles, matrixed approaches, or positions without explicit authority. Poor security management leads to organizations that [AND200301]

- Are not fully aware of the information security risks to their operations,
- Accept an unknown level of risk by default rather than consciously deciding what level of risk was tolerable,
- Have a false sense of security because they were relying on ineffective controls.
- Deal with security on an adhoc reactive basis,
- Cannot make informed judgments as to whether they were spending too little or too much of their resources on security, and/or
- Experience high losses due to breaches in corporate data confidentiality, integrity, and availability on a routine basis.

Some companies have a chief security officer (CSO) that handles all security-related matters. The CSO could have the chief information security officer (CISO), chief privacy officer (CPO), chief physical security officer (CPSO), chief compliance officer (CCO), and chief compliance and privacy officer (CCO), and chief compliance and privacy officer (CCPO) reporting to him or her. The CSO could report to the CEO, COO, or even senior vice president of HR. In other cases the CSO may have the CISO, CPO, and CCPO reporting to him or her and, in turn, report to the CIO; the CPSO may report to the senior vice president of HR.

The role of a chief risk officer (CRO) is emerging in risk-conscious organizations. The office of the CRO may report to the CEO (as depicted in Figure 8.2 bottom) or, more commonly, to the CIO, the director of IT, the CFO, or some other C-level executive. The CRO supports all functions related to communications for risk management and mitigation. Specifically, the CRO undertakes regular interaction with the management committee (typically the direct reports of the CEO) to provide guidance to the organization about the information-related risk exposures that arise in conjunction with business decisions, strategies and activities. Here the CISO, the CPO, CPSO, and the CCO are reporting to him or her.

The organization could also have a chief information risk officer (CIRO); CIRO is seen by some as the evolution for the role of the CSO and has overall ownership of the information risk management [PIR200801] (CIRO has risk management responsibilities as a CRO, but only focusing on IT—the CIRO would report to the CRO).

At a minimum an organization should have a CSO/CISO; in this case the CSO/CISO would likely report to the CIO (as depicted in Figure 8.2, top); the CISO is responsible for the day-to-day operations to ensure the confidentiality and integrity of IT assets. The addition of a CIRO or a management position focusing solely on risk management reporting to the CISO would be advantageous.

Studies have shown that a large majority (80%) of the organizations with a CSO/CISO in place are among the firms with the least financial risk and loss; by contrast, a large majority (60%) of the firms without a CSO/CISO tend to experiencing high financial risk and loss [ITP200901].

Members of the risk management team commonly work in a security office, rather than directly in the IT department. Companies often, but not invariably, augment a risk management team with a subgroup that handles IT-related assets such as the network, databases, desktops, and critical applications [BOL200701]. In mid-size companies, risk management is best positioned outside the IT department, because staffers who are implementing various technologies typically do not have the complete knowledge of security-related issues, regulatory compliance, and organizational policies. Figure 8.3 depicts a de-layered organizational model where information technology risk management reports reasonably close to the CEO of the organization

8.3 STAFFING REQUIREMENTS

Important factors related to staffing requirements have already been discussed in previous chapters. This section provides some additional observations and recommendations. We begin with the following assertions from some industry practitioners [BOL200701]:

It's a common mistake that companies make to think an IT risk management organization can be staffed by folks with industry certifications around security.

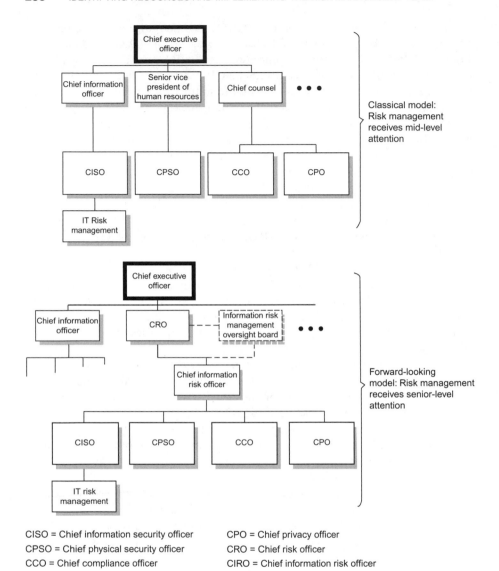

CISO = Chief information security officer   CPO = Chief privacy officer
CPSO = Chief physical security officer   CRO = Chief risk officer
CCO = Chief compliance officer   CIRO = Chief information risk officer

FIGURE 8.2. A classical and a progressive view of the CRO function.

In order to understand the ramifications of one or a series of events, one has to understand the business and the events in terms of potential lost revenue. And while understanding what occurred may require some technical acumen, one needs business know-how to interpret the outcome. An ideal risk manager should have an undergraduate degree in computer science and a master's degree in business administration to effectively manage a company's risk management plan.

IT shouldn't make risk decisions. . . . IT is there to deliver services to the business, while assessing risk requires a certain due diligence that's strategically focused on the business.

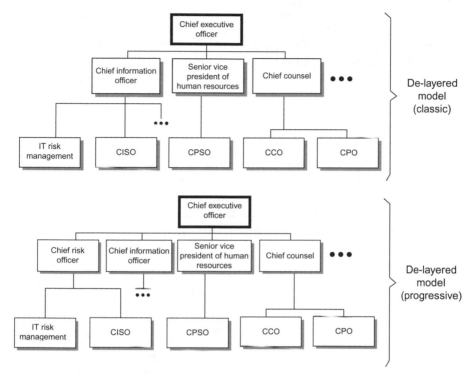

FIGURE 8.3. De-layered models for risk management.

People in those jobs need to be good communicators, technically savvy in multiple areas, business-sensitive, experienced in IT operations, focused on business security, and they should enjoy sleuthing and thrive on long hours.

The risk management activity cannot occur in isolation in the IT silo; it needs to entail on the business side and be conducted by people who speak business, understand business processes and can even help map them.

Before creating a risk management team, it is important to first establish what services the program plans to provide to the organization. For example, one needs to decide if the organization is seeking to

- Only pass audits
- Truly protect critical business assets
- Protect customer's personal information

Some of the related questions to address include the following: Are the teams just trying to provide technical scanning to uncover potential exposures, for example by scanning pre-production machines and/or production machines? Does the team only provide risk management consulting? Will there be a dedicated staff? Will there be virtual teams instead? Will there be a mixture of business and IT people?

Ideally there will be a dedicated staff of people that can handle all (except perhaps for implementation) of the risk management-related tasks, and with sufficient critical mass in terms of both the team size and the team's skill set, including business involvement.

8.3.1 Specialized Skills Required

Information security skills are not a commodity at this point in time, and it is even more challenging to ensure that security professionals have an understanding of risk management. A large percentage of information security professionals do not have the technical skillset required to be a security expert in *all* areas of IT. The information required to properly understand security risk exposures in technology is becoming more readily available but the body of knowledge is still is relatively immature.

As noted, risk management requires a blend of technical security skills as well as business skills. The typical base salary for information security management was approximately $120,000 at press time. When looking at the size of a staff that is required to support the risk management program at an organization, one can see that there will be a nontrivial investment to build out the team. An organization may also choose to staff the risk management team with a senior resource to provide guidance but then include a mix of mid-level professional as well. Even when an organization is able to hire the right people, it needs to make sure that the skills are up to date; this requires continued training.

In addition, in the information security field there are generalists as well as specialists that have expertise in focused areas of IT. Some have argued in favor of one breed, while others have argued in favor of the other breed. The reality is that both types are needed, in the correct mix. Generalists are able to see "the forest from the trees," are more open and ready to inject new technologies, and can offer a bridge from the "as is" to the "to be target" and/or from technology n to $n + 1$. Specialists are the hands-on people that can configure routers, systems, IDSs, OSs, and so on; however, they are usually quite embedded with the day-to-day mechanical production environment and are less able to jump to the "next best thing." Organizations cannot afford to have 100% of the people being complete super-specialists, nor 100% of the people being complete super-generalists. Perhaps a 30–70% mix of generalists and specialists is reasonable.

Many organizations find themselves in the situation where they are looking for the "playbook" on how to implement something securely. The fact is that in certain cases (even for some applications that have been around for nearly 15 years, such as how to securely implement an E-Commerce service, or for 25 years, such as how to securely implement an ATM banking network) the playbook or book solution is not available or, if available only covers most but not all cases or situations. Information security has been around for many years, but most times the information available on the topic just does not make it appear that way. It is not atypical that even an organization with a fully staffed risk management team will still require outside assistance with certain technologies, especially when these are very new (few people may be familiar with them) or very old (most people who knew such systems have long been retired).

8.3.2 Sourcing Options

Earlier in the previous chapter we discussed some of the options that can be used to staff a risk management team. The simple fact may be that even though there is a realization that addressing organization risk is important, a certain fraction of organizations are not going to want to spend the money that it would truly take to implement such a function in-house. However, outsourcing of information technology to the global market, particularly security, continues to be debated. Many companies believe that in a global economy all IT staff is a commodity and one should get the lowest price. Others believe that only specific information about the organization should be exposed to outside organizations. Clearly, transferring such work to another country raises the issues of the skill-set drain, ultimate economic security (in the English sense of the word), confidentiality of customer data, and national security. Furthermore, it is one thing to outsource basic IT functions (e.g., application development), but is altogether another matter to outsource information security and even risk management.

The current status is that while more companies are moving towards outsourcing, the outsourcing of security services is still being viewed with trepidation, especially when the outsourcing is to some far-away country. The benefits of security outsourcing include:

- More security knowledge
- Industry knowledge and understanding of risk
- Do not have to staff an in-house security team 24×365
- Can reduce expenditure based on service
- Can advise on best course of action
- Can take an independent view

For example, a 2008 report published by Verizon Business indicated that 75% of the data breaches that it studied were discovered by a third party, rather than a user or IT staffer inside the organization [WIL200901].

Some drawbacks of security outsourcing include:

- Opening up potential data loss
- Depending on the service it can be expensive
- Security service may not advise best solution
- Does not fully understand organization

- Typically recommends to correct all risk exposures
- Not all risk exposures may be an issue of concern for the specific firm

Consider an example where there is a team of three security engineers to handle risk assessment and scan servers; assume that the salaries (not fully loaded with benefits) are

#1 Engineer—$90,000 (senior)

#2 Engineer—$70,000 (intermediate)

#3 Engineer—$50,000 (mid/entry)

The total yearly salary is $210,000. Depending on the firm and the size of its operations, this cost can be relatively high. There are some security organizations that can perform external and internal vulnerability scans for a "reasonable" cost. In a worst-case scenario, if one has to contract with a security provider to perform vulnerability scans at $100K per year, the firm would lower its costs by 50%. This is just an example, but this logic should be applied to all functions that are planned to be offered by the security and risk management team.

Press-time surveys were showing that between 10% and 15% of companies were outsourcing security functions and that about 40% of large North American and European enterprises were planning to hire a third-party consultant to help them with security assessments [DUN200901]. Outsourcing of security functions is still being viewed with skepticism, although some practitioners have been advocating it for a number of years: Giving control of IT security to an outside firm—specifically to maintain equipment, monitor for attacks, perform scans, collect logs, or update security software—is not yet accepted practice. According to proponents, outsourcing security affords the in-house staff an opportunity to be freed up from mundane tasks to deal with more strategic security and risk management matters. Tasks such as patch and vulnerability management or antivirus support can consume a lot of staff time that might be better used in strategic risk-management operations for online business goals with partners and customers, for instance. Others worry that outsourcing implies losing sight of security risk exposures. The question of whether outsourcing is cost-effective is also not always answered in unambiguous terms. Some firms have subscribed to firewall monitoring, vulnerability assessment, and other functions, but have brought the functions back in-house using purchased tools [MES200801]. Figure 8.4 and Table 8.3 depict some areas where companies have sought outside outsourced support. Technologies broadly supported include threat protection (antivirus, antispam, antipharming/antiphishing), web filtering, vulnerability scanning, authentication, unified threat management, email archiving, encryption, firewall, VPN, intrusion detection and prevention (IDS/IPS), network monitoring and log review, penetration testing/compliance review, backup and storage, and business continuity [WIL200901, DUN200901]. Typical service support in the area of

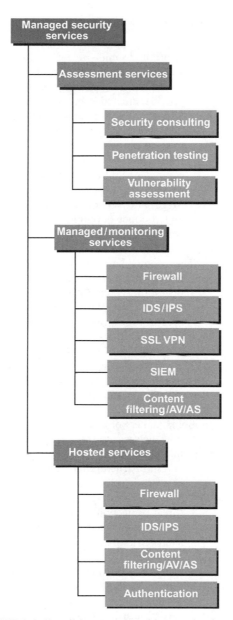

FIGURE 8.4. Possible outsourceable security functions.

risk management include assessment, remediation, design, and implementation of technical security solutions, such as penetration testing, identity management, and applications control and code reviews.

There are drawbacks in using consultants for security and/or risk management functions, as noted above. The operative questions are: "Is the firm getting high-quality security analysis? Is it truly a quality service?" A firm would not want to

TABLE 8.3. Security Outsourcing Companies

Pure-play managed security service providers (MSSPs)	Companies that provide out-sourced security services, primarily to mid-size enterprises and SMBs. They support all off the-shelf security components and are responsible for the safety of the clients' data. Press-time providers included but are not limited to Integralis, Perimeter eSecurity, SecureWorks, and Solutionary.
Network service providers or ISPs	Companies that typically offer services "in the cloud," using their own networks. Some also offer (a) virtual private network services based on customer premises equipment and/or (b) professional services. Press-time providers included but are not limited to AT&T, BT, MegaPath Networks, Savvis, and Verizon. Acquisitions and product development have allowed these companies to offer security on top of their network-based services.
Traditional IT outsourcing providers	These companies may take the on IT administration and/or hosting of an entire organization, including security operation centers (SOC) and network operations centers (NOC). These players typically cater to large organizations, providing custom security implementations. Press-time providers included but are not limited to CompuCom, EDS, HP, and IBM.
Established security management players	Best-of-breed security providers include IBM ISS, Symantec, and VeriSign, which provide professional security for staff augmentation and consulting components.
Software as a service (SaaS) providers	Some makers of traditional security software have moved into the security services space, targeting primarily midmarket customers looking to offload security costs and infrastructure requirements to ease their internal network loads. SaaS services eliminate the need for licensing structures and provide customers with real-time threat protection delivered through the cloud. Press-time providers included but are not limited to CA, Symantec, Trend Micro, and smaller pure-play providers such as Perimeter eSecurity,
Penetration testing and security audit services	Pen testing, aka ethical hacking, is a subset of outsourced services and attempts to breach IT systems from the outside via electronic methods to test the strength of clients' security postures. Security auditing determines activities by system users to rate the effectiveness of security controls and policies and verify compliance requirements. This category of services includes a slew of players, as well as larger network service providers that now fold in these capabilities as part of their outsourced offerings.

Source: Based in part after C. Dunlap [DUN200901].

be paying a consultant a high price just to scan the firm's network with a freely available open source product and report that the firm has some open ports at the perimeter. The firm should expect that the analysis is done properly and that the consultants bring value to the exercise.

Prior to contracting with any security provider, the firm should develop a Statement of Work that states clearly what the service is going to be and ensure that the service is not just "a point and click." Considerations such as the following (example for vulnerability scanning) need to be taken into account:

- How with they handle change control processes?
- Is there a possibility of crashing servers by accident?
- Is there a possibility of overloading (DoS) servers?
- Can they provide off hours services?

Note the following in reference to the costs for a risk assessment services/consultant services:

- Typically, most organizations bill at a very high rate.
- If one is not paying market rates, then he or she is probably getting average service.

Some cost figures are as follows [DUN200901]: vulnerability assessment scanning services are typically priced at $1 to $2 per IP address; pricing for web and e-mail security is based on volume, ranging from $1 to $6 per IP address, depending on the size of the rollout. Consulting services range from $125 to $275 per hour, while packages of basic security offerings, including penetration services, run from $7,000 to $25,000 per month. MSSP services usually cost between $100 and $4000 a month for SMEs, and they cost as much as $250,000 a month for some large enterprises.

Given that the salary rates/per hour are typically $125 to $275 (costs per day range from $1200 to $2000/day; costs per week range from $6000 to $10,000), if a firm required a high-powered security consultant to review a critical system that requires at least 12 months of support, the costs are very high; it would make more sense to hire and bring on their own staff that could provide the same service. This simple example shows that it is critical to look at all parts of the organization and the services provided to determine what makes sense to keep in-house and what is a prime example to contract with a service provider.

8.4 RISK MANAGEMENT TOOLS

The amount of information risks that must be managed is massive; organizing and reviewing risk exposures can be a daunting task. Not only is it challenging to understand what the appropriate questions are, but it is also challenging to manage all of the data.

Organizations need to determine the best way to manage risks (the repository that contains all the security information):

- Risks needs to be managed in a life cycle.
- Identifying the risk is not the only part of the process.
- Many risks needs to be followed-up on, and so on.

There are thousands of open source security packages available. A number of these open-source security tools provide sufficient capabilities to be useful to the CISO/CIRO. Table 8.4 identifies a small set of popular open source security tools [HIN200701].

8.5   RISK MANAGEMENT SERVICES

There are a number of companies that provide comprehensive solutions for corporate information compliance and provide solutions and services to manage internal IT compliance audits, Sarbanes–Oxley (SOX) compliance, data privacy law, IT governance, regulatory compliance, and risk management and assessment. These companies include, but are not limited to, CA Inc., Capgemini, Deloitte & Touche, Ernst & Young LLP, IBM, KPMG LLP, and Microsoft.

8.5.1   Alerting and Analysis Services

Some outfits provide alerting and analysis services. However, most alerting is related to managing risks that are tied to product vulnerabilities; most vendors provide free alerts (as we have seen in earlier sections of this book, critical vulnerabilities can give rise to nontrivial risk). These companies include, but are not limited to, Microsoft, Oracle, and Cisco. Free vulnerabilities services are provided by OSVDB and Secunia, among others. Other vulnerability databases include Security Tracker, French Security Incident Response Team (*FrSIRT*), ISS, CVE, and NVD. Vulnerability sharing services include VeriSign's iDefense and TippingPoint's ZDI (Zero Day Initiative).

8.5.2   Assessments, Audits, and Project Consulting

In many cases the skills required for a comprehensive review of a firm's risk are not always easily available (in-house skills may not be available), or, even if available, not easily accessible (individuals may be too busy with other development projects.) To deal with this, firms should note that some consulting outfits (for example, the ones listed at the opening of this section) provide risk assessment services, not just vulnerabilities and virus/worm

TABLE 8.4. Popular Open-Source Security Tools

Bro	A network IDS developed by the Lawrence Berkeley National Laboratory of the Department of Energy and is used in federal, military, and research labs. Bro is an open source, Unix-based NIDS that passively monitors network traffic and looks for anomalous traffic behavior. This tool works by first extracting the application layer of packets and then executes event-oriented analyzers comparing the patterns with signatures that have been identified as malicious data. Although Bro is a signature-based detection engine, it can detect attacks through changes in traffic patterns and predefined activities.
Nagios	A host and network monitoring tool that informs enterprise users of system or network outages before clients and users are affected by them. This tool is modular, allowing for extended functionality through Nagios plugins that return status information back to Nagios. The tool supports several out-of-band alerting functions including e-mail, instant message, and SMS. It offers a portfolio of monitoring capabilities, including the availability of network services such as SMTP, POP3, HTTP, NNTP, and PING.
Nessus	Vulnerability scanner that has become the de facto standard in enterprise environments and for vendors selling vulnerability management tools and services for actively assessing the risks inherent in a company's mission-critical devices and applications. Nessus risk assessments are powered by a database of vulnerability checks called Nessus Attack Scripting Language (NASL) scripts. NASL is a scripting language for writing security checks for Nessus to perform. The vulnerability database is updated daily.
Nikto	Nikto is an open-source (GPL) web server scanner that performs comprehensive tests against web servers for multiple items, including over 3500 potentially dangerous files/CGIs, versions on over 900 servers, and version-specific problems on over 250 servers. Scan items and plugins are frequently updated and can be automatically updated (if desired).
OSSEC HIDS	Open-source host intrusion detection and prevention system. Major operating system platforms are supported including Windows, MacOSX, HP-UX, Solaris, FreeBSD, OpenBSD, and Linux. OSSEC is capable of using the local system's firewall to dynamically block attack attempts on a mission-critical server. The OSSEC HIDS agent can add attacking IP addresses to the /etc/hosts.deny file, or it can block packets to and from them using the host's firewall. Firewalls that OSSEC currently supports include IPtables on Linux, pf on OpenBSD and FreeBSD, ipsec for AIX, ipfilter for Solaris, FreeBSD, and NetBSD, and ipfw for FreeBSD.
OSSIM	(*Open-Source Security Information Management.*) Its goal is to provide a comprehensive compilation of tools which, when working together, grant a network/security administrator with a detailed view over each and every aspect of his networks/hosts/physical access devices/server/etc.
Snort	A widely deployed open source tool for network intrusion detection and prevention. Some main capabilities include: stateful inspection, pattern matching through an advanced rules language, and protocol anomaly detection.

Source: Based in part on [HIN200701].

announcements. They can perform onsite reviews and perform an overall organization assessment. In many cases this can be to address regulatory or specific compliance requirements such as SOX, PCI/DSS, or HIPAA (as briefly discussed in Chapter 7). These outfits can undertake risk management/assessments of complex internal applications, servers, and networks.

8.6   DEVELOPING AND IMPLEMENTING THE RISK MANAGEMENT/ASSESSMENT TEAM

At this juncture it is assumed that the organization has made the decision to develop an in-house capability, has secured management approvals, and has a budget available.

Two approaches may be followed in terms of establishing the leadership function:

1. First hire a proven leader and then ask the leader to proceed with building out the team; or
2. Start building out the team with some key working-level personnel, and then later hire the leader. The leader would then round out the team.

Each approach has some pros and cons. The best course of action is to use firm-specific pragmatics on how to proceed.

Three approaches may be followed in terms of establishing the team itself:

1. Hire an entire team from the outside.
2. Transfer appropriate people already with the company (say in IT) to the team.
3. Use a combination of both.

In most cases the third approach is the best.

Figure 8.5 depicts one possible organization structure for a (reasonably large) team of 16 staffers. This particular organization is comprised of three subteams: a basic risk management/assessment subfunction, a security subfunction, and a business-support subfunction. The function can be built out starting from left to right, possibly "borrowing" some people (and/or support) from an existing security function and eventually establishing self-sufficiency.

It is critical to have standards and subject matter experts that can help a firm define acceptable risk. We briefly discuss these two topics next.

8.6.1   Creating Security Standards

In Chapter 6 we alluded to fact the that in addition to security policies there typically is a need for company-specific technical security standards (also called hardening standards), these being specific technical configuration items that define settings for applications, operating systems, databases, networks, and

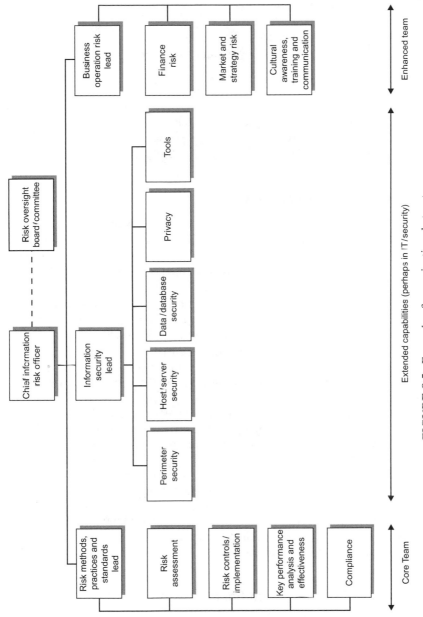

FIGURE 8.5. Example of organizational structure.

other software/hardware assets of the organization. One of the tasks of the risk management team could include a review and hardening of such company-specific standards.

The risk management team should

- Define hardening standards, if not already available
- Determine gaps in available hardening standards
- Explain the reasons for standards

For example, no software (build or buy) should be on the network (in production) without a security hardening standard.

Standards are typically where the real risk exposures can be found. Policies, most times, are so high level that they are not able to help remove risk exposures.

8.6.2 Defining Subject Matter Experts

One of the most interesting parts about information security is that everyone typically expects the security staffer to know everything about all aspects; most times this is just not possible. Figure 8.5, in effect, provides a taxonomy of requisite capabilities. Even then this may be an incomplete view of the world. For example, just looking at the network, one may be an expert in LANs, but maybe not in WANs, or in extranets, or in wireless/mobile networks (including Wi-Fi, WiMax, Bluetooth, ZigBee, 3/4G, and so on), or in multimedia/video networks. The same would be true of platform/Operating System expertise: typically a Microsoft Windows guru may not be a Linux guru or a VMware guru.

For hiring managers and firms, the challenge remains how to staff their organizations. In 1994 one of these authors wrote [MIN199501]

> A decade ago, what was important (at the time of an interview) was what one knew. . . . Today what is more important, in our view, is **how quickly one can learn something new**. . . . Since the technology is changing every 1 to 3 years, what one knew four or five years ago is of little use. A college graduate who left school 6 years ago may be in the same predicament, in terms of being out of date as someone who left college 20 years ago, but has kept up through reading and education.

This remains true today, particularly given the fast-paced nature of the security field, also as noted earlier in this chapter; some of the issues and technologies change drastically every 3–12 months.

8.6.3 Determining Information Sources

An organization can make the decision that they want to be secure, but they still must know and understand what changes must be implemented to reach that desired level of security. Some organizations will have little issues when it comes to defining security hardening standards and performing security analysis, however, it is more commonplace for organizations to struggle as to where they should start. It should be clear to any organization that in most cases they do not need to reinvent the wheel. There are numerous organizations that can empower firms with open security information. There are also several government agencies that freely provide information and advice. Some ways to keep abreast of developments in security is by

- Joining advocacy organizations and security mailing lists
- Meeting with other security professionals in the area
- Attending security conferences
- Continuing further reading/research on specific topics

REFERENCES

[AND200301] A. D. Andrews, Jr., "Security Program Management and Risk," GIAC Security Essentials Certification Practical Assignment Version 1.4b, March 23, 2003, SANS Institute. InfoSec Reading Room.

[BOL200701] M. Bolch, "Risk Management Staffing Isn't Always Part of IT," 7 June 2007, SearchCIO.com

[COO200901] N. R. Coons, "Protect Customer Data with PCI Standards," 25 March 2009, NetWorld Alliance, 13100 Eastpoint Park Blvd. Louisville, KY 40223

[DUN200901] C. Dunlap, "Making the security outsourcing decision," April 2009, *Information Week*, Information Week Analytics, DarkReading.

[GAU200701] S. Gaudin, "Estimates put T.J. Maxx security fiasco at $4.5 billion—The data breach at the major retailer will cost the company $100 per lost record, according to database security firm IPLocks," *Information Week*, May 2, 2007.

[HIN200701] E. Hines, "Top 5 Open Source Security Tools in the Enterprise," Applied Watch Technologies, LinuxWorld.com, 3/12/07.

[ITP200901] IT Policy Compliance Group, "Managing Spend on Information Security and Audit for Better Results, February 2009, Managing Director, Jim Hurley.

[MES200801] E. Messmer, "Outsourcing security tasks brings controversy," *Network World*, 03/20/2008.

[MIC200701] Micro Focus, "The Financial Value of IT Assets," Press Release, Wednesday, Oct 3, 2007, The Lawn, 22-30 Old Bath Road, Newbury, Berkshire RG14 1QN, UK.

[MIN199501] D. Minoli, *Analyzing Outsourcing—Reengineering Information and Communications Systems*, McGraw-Hill, New York, 1995.

[PIR 200801] J. P. Pironti, "Key elements of an information risk management program: Transforming information security into information risk management," 2008 Information Systems Audit and Control Association, *Information Systems Control Journal*, Volume 2, 2008.

[WAR200901] S. Wartenberg, "Credit-card Criminals often strike from afar," *The Columbus Dispatch*, March 8, 2009.

[WIL200901] T. Wilson, "How to Make the right Choice about Security Outsourcing," April 1, 2009, Information Week Business Technology, DarkReading.com.

APPENDIX 8A: SIZING EXAMPLE FOR RISK MANAGEMENT TEAM

This appendix contains two heuristic models to size up the risk management team for an environment where management expects a "self-paid model," followed by some additional observations. Generally, other models lead to comparable solutions. Some empirical observations are as follows:

- For low probability of risk exposure the company revenue must be at around $4B/year before one FTE dedicated to risk management is justified. For revenue of $16B/year, 2–3 FTEs are justified.
- For a relatively high probability of risk exposure the company revenue must be at around $1B/year before one FTE dedicated to risk management is justified. For revenue of $16B/year, a team of 8–11 FTEs is justified.
- For fairly high probability of risk exposure the company revenue must be at around $500M/year, before one FTE dedicated to risk management is justified. For revenue of $16B/year, a team of 20–30 FTEs is justified.

Reference Example 1

Table 8A.1 depicts an example of the risk as a function of the company size using Model 1 defined next.

- **Risk Event RE#1:** A virus will infect every desktop/laptop, eventually causing ½ day loss of productivity for each employee, with an average loaded salary of $750/day.
- **Risk Event RE#2:** Malware will infect the corporate CRM/service order database, which eventually requires 'Rev/100,000,000' staff-days to rebuild and/or fix; IT staff costs the company $1250/day.
- **Risk Event RE#3:** A keystroke logger enables an agent to eventually steal the employees HR records for past and present employees. The database has "5 × employees" entries. To remediate the issue, the company has to pay $100 per employee for a security alert service and also spend $10,000 in administrative/remediation costs.

Reference Example 2

Table 8A.2 depicts an example of the risk as a function of the company size using Model 2 defined next.

TABLE 8A.1. Reference Example Model 1

		Revenue (M)					
		$500	$1,000	$2,000	$4,000	$8,000	$16,000
Employees		1,000	2,000	4,000	8,000	16,000	32,000
p (RE#1)	0.01	$3,750	$7,500	$15,000	$30,000	$60,000	$120,000
p (RE#2)	0.01	$63	$125	$250	$500	$1,000	$2,000
p (RE#3)	0.01	$5,100	$10,100	$20,100	$40,100	$80,100	$160,100
"low"	Total Risk	$8,913	$17,725	$35,350	$70,600	$141,100	$282,100
	FTE ($100K)	0.09	0.18	0.35	0.71	1.41	2.82
p (RE#1)	0.02	$7,500	$15,000	$30,000	$60,000	$120,000	$240,000
p (RE#2)	0.02	$125	$250	$500	$1,000	$2,000	$4,000
p (RE#3)	0.02	$10,200	$20,200	$40,200	$80,200	$160,200	$320,200
"medium"	Total Risk	$17,825	$35,450	$70,700	$141,200	$282,200	$564,200
	FTE ($100K)	0.18	0.35	0.71	1.41	2.82	5.64
p (RE#1)	0.04	$15,000	$30,000	$60,000	$120,000	$240,000	$480,000
p (RE#2)	0.04	$250	$500	$1,000	$2,000	$4,000	$8,000
p (RE#3)	0.04	$20,400	$40,400	$80,400	$160,400	$320,400	$640,400
"high"	Total Risk	$35,650	$70,900	$141,400	$282,400	$564,400	$1,128,400
	FTE ($100K)	0.36	0.71	1.41	2.82	5.64	11.28
p (RE#1)	0.08	$30,000	$60,000	$120,000	$240,000	$480,000	$960,000
p (RE#2)	0.08	$500	$1,000	$2,000	$4,000	$8,000	$16,000
p (RE#3)	0.08	$40,800	$80,800	$160,800	$320,800	$640,800	$1,280,800
"fairly high"	Total Risk	$71,300	$141,800	$282,800	$564,800	$1,128,800	$2,256,800
	FTE ($100K)	0.71	1.42	2.83	5.65	11.29	22.57

Note: For simplicity, all probabilities taken to be equal; clearly, these can be any appropriate value.

TABLE 8A.2. Reference Example Model 2

Revenue (M)			$500	$1,000	$2,000	$4,000	$8,000	$16,000
p (RE#1)	"low"	0.01	$6,000	$12,000	$24,000	$48,000	$96,000	$192,000
	Total Risk		$6,000	$12,000	$24,000	$48,000	$96,000	$192,000
	FTE ($100K)		0.06	0.12	0.24	0.48	0.96	1.92
p (RE#1)	"medium"	0.02	$12,000	$24,000	$48,000	$96,000	$192,000	$384,000
	Total Risk		$12,000	$24,000	$48,000	$96,000	$192,000	$384,000
	FTE ($100K)		0.12	0.24	0.48	0.96	1.92	3.84
p (RE#1)	"high"	0.04	$24,000	$48,000	$96,000	$192,000	$384,000	$768,000
	Total Risk		$24,000	$48,000	$96,000	$192,000	$384,000	$768,000
	FTE ($100K)		0.24	0.48	0.96	1.92	3.84	7.68
p (RE#1)	"fairly high"	0.08	$48,000	$96,000	$192,000	$384,000	$768,000	$1,536,000
	Total Risk		$48,000	$96,000	$192,000	$384,000	$768,000	$1,536,000
	FTE ($100K)		0.48	0.96	1.92	3.84	7.68	15.36
p (RE#1)	"very high"	0.16	$96,000	$192,000	$384,000	$768,000	$1,536,000	$3,072,000
	Total Risk		$96,000	$192,000	$384,000	$768,000	$1,536,000	$3,072,000
	FTE ($100K)		0.96	1.92	3.84	7.68	15.36	30.72
p (RE#1)	"extremely high"	0.32	$192,000	$384,000	$768,000	$1,536,000	$3,072,000	$6,144,000
	Total Risk		$192,000	$384,000	$768,000	$1,536,000	$3,072,000	$6,144,000
	FTE ($100K)		1.92	3.84	7.68	15.36	30.72	61.44
p (RE#1)	"almost certain"	0.64	$384,000	$768,000	$1,536,000	$3,072,000	$6,144,000	$12,288,000
	Total Risk		$384,000	$768,000	$1,536,000	$3,072,000	$6,144,000	$12,288,000
	FTE ($100K)		3.84	7.68	15.36	30.72	61.44	122.88

- **Risk Event RE#1:** The revenue stream of a company originates equally from five sources supported by five distinct IT systems. It is assumed that the revenue is accrued uniformly over the 8750 hours during the year. It is assumed that in the absence of a risk management team, a set of vulnerabilities, security infractions, denial of service, and other security issues result in a reduction of the availability of the system to 99.00 for one of the systems with a certain probability p and that the 60% of the business that would have accrued during the (system) working hours is lost forever.

Application of Models

Table 8A.3 is a *synthetically* developed table, with no input at all from the companies shown. It just intends to illustrate how the risk management function *could* be staffed out at a company in a way that it is "revenue neutral" (or pays for itself) by making the cost of staffing the team equal to the (potential) expected loss incurred by the company. While some of the exposure events (used in the above model) may not occur every year, there likely would be different events of concern with every new year. And, additionally, the team could be enlarged or shrunk yearly based on perceived/anticipated/forecasted needs for that specific year.

Data on Number of Employees

Tables 8A.4, 8A.5, and 8A.6 provide some supplementary information on the number of employees of a company as compared with the revenue of the company (this parameter was used in Model 1).

Additional Observations

In Chapter 6 we included some press-time data on financial losses experienced by companies because of security infractions. These data (Table 6.2) were quite astonishing. If one were to use this loss data to calculate the size of the risk management team, it would be quite large. Table 8A.7 depicts some results (we are not suggesting that these team sizes be used, but just that one considers what the implications are). In the first block of rows we calculate what the team could be if they were to be revenue neutral at $100K/year (namely establishing a team such that they eliminated all the loss, but spent as much on themselves as it originally was the loss). The second block of rows shows the same, if the team cost was $200K/year. The third block of rows make the equivalence that if the loss was $x\%$ of the total revenue, then size of the team would be $x\%$ of the total number of employees. The fourth block of rows assumes that each member of the team must contribute the equivalent revenue (here revenue saved) as every other employee, which is taken to be $0.5M/year. The last set of rows shows the sizing based on Model 1 above. As can be seen, the size of the team would be

TABLE 8A.3. Synthetically Developed Table Depicting How the Risk Management Function Could Be Staffed Out at a Company in a way that it is 'Revenue Neutral' (Fortune 500 Companies)

Company	Revenues ($ millions) (for 2007)	Hypothetical Size of Risk Management Team, if One Were to Apply Above Model, at Low Probability of Exposure—Model 1	Hypothetical Size of Risk Management Team, if One Were to Apply Above Model, at Medium Probability of Exposure—Model 1	Hypothetical size of Risk Management Team, if One Were to Apply Above Model, at Low Probability of Exposure—Model 2	Hypothetical size of Risk Management Team, if One Were to Apply Above Model, at Medium Probability of Exposure—Model 2
Wal-Mart Stores	351,139.0	61.9	123.8	42.1	84.3
Exxon Mobil	347,254.0	61.2	122.4	41.7	83.3
General Motors	207,349.0	36.5	73.1	24.9	49.8
Chevron	200,567.0	35.3	70.7	24.1	48.1
ConocoPhillips	172,451.0	30.4	60.8	20.7	41.4
General Electric	168,307.0	29.7	59.3	20.2	40.4
Ford Motor	160,126.0	28.2	56.4	19.2	38.4
Citigroup	146,777.0	25.9	51.7	17.6	35.2
Bank of America Corp.	117,017.0	20.6	41.2	14.0	28.1
American Intl. Group	113,194.0	20.0	39.9	13.6	27.2
J.P. Morgan Chase & Co.	99,973.0	17.6	35.2	12.0	24.0
Berkshire Hathaway	98,539.0	17.4	34.7	11.8	23.6
Verizon Communications	93,221.0	16.4	32.9	11.2	22.4
Hewlett-Packard	91,658.0	16.2	32.3	11.0	22.0
Intl. Business Machines	91,424.0	16.1	32.2	11.0	21.9
Valero Energy	91,051.0	16.0	32.1	10.9	21.9
Home Depot	90,837.0	16.0	32.0	10.9	21.8
McKesson	88,050.0	15.5	31.0	10.6	21.1
Cardinal Health	81,895.1	14.4	28.9	9.8	19.7
Morgan Stanley	76,688.0	13.5	27.0	9.2	18.4
UnitedHealth Group	71,542.0	12.6	25.2	8.6	17.2
Merrill Lynch	70,591.0	12.4	24.9	8.5	16.9
Altria Group	70,324.0	12.4	24.8	8.4	16.9
Goldman Sachs Group	69,353.0	12.2	24.4	8.3	16.6
Procter & Gamble	68,222.0	12.0	24.0	8.2	16.4

TABLE 8A.3. (Continued)

Company	Revenues ($ millions) (for 2007)	Hypothetical Size of Risk Management Team, if One Were to Apply Above Model, at Low Probability of Exposure—Model 1	Hypothetical Size of Risk Management Team, if One Were to Apply Above Model, at Medium Probability of Exposure—Model 1	Hypothetical Size of Risk Management Team, if One Were to Apply Above Model, at Low Probability of Exposure—Model 2	Hypothetical size of Risk Management Team, if One Were to Apply Above Model, at Medium Probability of Exposure—Model 2
Kroger	66,111.2	11.7	23.3	7.9	15.9
AT&T	63,055.0	11.1	22.2	7.6	15.1
Boeing	61,530.0	10.8	21.7	7.4	14.8
AmerisourceBergen	61,203.1	10.8	21.6	7.3	14.7
Marathon Oil	60,643.0	10.7	21.4	7.3	14.6
State Farm Insurance Cos	60,528.0	10.7	21.3	7.3	14.5
Costco Wholesale	60,151.2	10.6	21.2	7.2	14.4
Target	59,490.0	10.5	21.0	7.1	14.3
Dell	57,095.0	10.1	20.1	6.9	13.7
Wellpoint	56,953.0	10.0	20.1	6.8	13.7
Johnson & Johnson	53,324.0	9.4	18.8	6.4	12.8
MetLife	53,275.0	9.4	18.8	6.4	12.8
Sears Holdings	53,012.0	9.3	18.7	6.4	12.7
Pfizer	52,415.0	9.2	18.5	6.3	12.6
Dow Chemical	49,124.0	8.7	17.3	5.9	11.8
Wells Fargo	47,979.0	8.5	16.9	5.8	11.5
United Technologies	47,829.0	3.4	16.9	5.7	11.5
United Parcel Service	47,547.0	8.4	16.8	5.7	11.4
Walgreen	47,409.0	8.4	16.7	5.7	11.4
Lowe's	46,927.0	8.3	16.5	5.6	11.3
Wachovia Corp.	46,810.0	8.3	16.5	5.6	11.2
Time Warner	44,788.0	7.9	15.8	5.4	10.7
Microsoft	44,282.0	7.8	15.6	5.3	10.6
Freddie Mac	44,002.0	7.8	15.5	5.3	10.6
CVS/Caremark	43,813.8	7.7	15.4	5.3	10.5

(Continued)

TABLE 8A.3. (Continued)

Company	Revenues ($ millions) (for 2007)	Hypothetical Size of Risk Management Team, if One Were to Apply Above Model, at Low Probability of Exposure—Model 1	Hypothetical Size of Risk Management Team, if One Were to Apply Above Model, at Medium Probability of Exposure—Model 1	Hypothetical size of Risk Management Team, if One Were to Apply Above Model, at Low Probability of Exposure—Model 2	Hypothetical size of Risk Management Team, if One Were to Apply Above Model, at Medium Probability of Exposure—Model 2
Motorola	43,739.0	7.7	15.4	5.2	10.5
Sprint Nextel	43,531.0	7.7	15.3	5.2	10.4
Medco Health Solutions	42,543.7	7.5	15.0	5.1	10.2
Caterpillar	41,517.0	7.3	14.6	5.0	10.0
Safeway	40,185.0	7.1	14.2	4.8	9.6
Lockheed Martin	39,620.0	7.0	14.0	4.8	9.5
Caremark Rx	36,750.2	6.5	13.0	4.4	8.8
Archer Daniels Midland	36,596.1	6.5	12.9	4.4	8.8
Sunoco	36,081.0	6.4	12.7	4.3	8.7
Allstate	35,796.0	6.3	12.6	4.3	8.6
Intel	35,382.0	6.2	12.5	4.2	8.5
PepsiCo	35,137.0	6.2	12.4	4.2	8.4
Walt Disney	34,285.0	6.0	12.1	4.1	8.2
Sysco	32,628.4	5.8	11.5	3.9	7.8
Prudential Financial	32,488.0	5.7	11.5	3.9	7.8
Johnson Controls	32,413.0	5.7	11.4	3.9	7.8
FedEx	32,294.0	5.7	11.4	3.9	7.8
Honeywell Intl.	31,367.0	5.5	11.1	3.8	7.5
Ingram Micro	31,357.5	5.5	11.1	3.8	7.5
Alcoa	30,896.0	5.4	10.9	3.7	7.4
Best Buy	30,848.0	5.4	10.9	3.7	7.4
Northrop Grumman	30,304.0	5.3	10.7	3.6	7.3
DuPont	28,982.0	5.1	10.2	3.5	7.0
Hess	28,720.0	5.1	10.1	3.4	6.9
Federated Dept. Stores	28,711.0	5.1	10.1	3.4	6.9
Cisco Systems	28,484.0	5.0	10.0	3.4	6.8
New York Life Insurance	28,365.1	5.0	10.0	3.4	6.8

TABLE 8A.3. (Continued)

Company	Revenues ($ millions) (for 2007)	Hypothetical Size of Risk Management Team, if One Were to Apply Above Model, at Low Probability of Exposure—Model 1	Hypothetical Size of Risk Management Team, if One Were to Apply Above Model, at Medium Probability of Exposure—Model 1	Hypothetical size of Risk Management Team, if One Were to Apply Above Model, at Low Probability of Exposure—Model 2	Hypothetical size of Risk Management Team, if One Were to Apply Above Model, at Medium Probability of Exposure—Model 2
American Express	27,145.0	4.8	9.6	3.3	6.5
TIAA-CREF	26,756.8	4.7	9.4	3.2	6.4
Washington Mutual	26,561.0	4.7	9.4	3.2	6.4
Hartford Financial Services	26,500.0	4.7	9.3	3.2	6.4
Delphi	26,392.0	4.7	9.3	3.2	6.3
Comcast	25,700.0	4.5	9.1	3.1	6.2
Aetna	25,568.6	4.5	9.0	3.1	6.1
Tyson Foods	25,559.0	4.5	9.0	3.1	6.1
HCA	25,477.0	4.5	9.0	3.1	6.1
News Corp.	25,327.0	4.5	8.9	3.0	6.1
Travelers Cos.	25,090.0	4.4	8.8	3.0	6.0
Mass. Mutual Life Insurance	24,863.4	4.4	8.8	3.0	6.0
Countrywide Financial	24,444.6	4.3	8.6	2.9	5.9
General Dynamics	24,212.0	4.3	8.5	2.9	5.8
International Paper	24,186.0	4.3	8.5	2.9	5.8
Coca-Cola	24,088.0	4.2	8.5	2.9	5.8
Liberty Mutual Ins. Group	23,520.0	4.1	8.3	2.8	5.6
Raytheon	23,274.0	4.1	8.2	2.8	5.6
3M	22,923.0	4.0	8.1	2.8	5.5
Deere	22,768.9	4.0	8.0	2.7	5.5
Merck	22,636.0	4.0	8.0	2.7	5.4
Halliburton	22,576.0	4.0	8.0	2.7	5.4
AMR	22,563.0	4.0	8.0	2.7	5.4
Abbott Laboratories	22,476.3	4.0	7.9	2.7	5.4
Plains All Amer. Pipeline	22,444.4	4.0	7.9	2.7	5.4

(*Continued*)

Company	Revenues ($ millions) (for 2007)	Hypothetical Size of Risk Management Team, if One Were to Apply Above Model, at Low Probability of Exposure—Model 1	Hypothetical Size of Risk Management Team, if One Were to Apply Above Model, at Medium Probability of Exposure—Model 1	Hypothetical size of Risk Management Team, if One Were to Apply Above Model, at Low Probability of Exposure—Model 2	Hypothetical size of Risk Management Team, if One Were to Apply Above Model, at Medium Probability of Exposure—Model 2
Nationwide	22,253.0	3.9	7.8	2.7	5.3
Weyerhaeuser	22,250.0	3.9	7.8	2.7	5.3
Lyondell Chemical	22,228.0	3.9	7.8	2.7	5.3
Publix Super Markets	21,819.7	3.8	7.7	2.6	5.2
McDonald's	21,586.4	3.8	7.6	2.6	5.2
Tech Data	21,446.1	3.8	7.6	2.6	5.1
Humana	21,416.5	3.8	7.5	2.6	5.1
Electronic Data Systems	21,337.0	3.8	7.5	2.6	5.1
Northwestern Mutual	20,726.2	3.7	7.3	2.5	5.0
Wyeth	20,350.7	3.6	7.2	2.4	4.9
Goodyear Tire & Rubber	20,258.0	3.6	7.1	2.4	4.9
Emerson Electric	20,133.0	3.5	7.1	2.4	4.8
J.C. Penney	19,903.0	3.5	7.0	2.4	4.8
Supervalu	19,863.6	3.5	7.0	2.4	4.8
Coca-Cola Enterprises	19,804.0	3.5	7.0	2.4	4.8
Constellation Energy	19,446.1	3.4	6.9	2.3	4.7
UAL	19,340.0	3.4	6.8	2.3	4.6
Apple	19,315.0	3.4	6.8	2.3	4.6
AutoNation	19,314.4	3.4	6.8	2.3	4.6
U.S. Bancorp	19,109.0	3.4	6.7	2.3	4.6
Occidental Petroleum	19,029.0	3.4	6.7	2.3	4.6
Sara Lee	18,539.0	3.3	6.5	2.2	4.4
Staples	18,160.8	3.2	6.4	2.2	4.4
Whirlpool	18,080.0	3.2	6.4	2.2	4.3
Tesoro	18,002.0	3.2	6.3	2.2	4.3
Bristol-Myers Squibb	17,914.0	3.2	6.3	2.1	4.3

TABLE 8A.3. (Continued)

Company	Revenues ($ millions) (for 2007)	Hypothetical Size of Risk Management Team, if One Were to Apply Above Model, at Low Probability of Exposure—Model 1	Hypothetical Size of Risk Management Team, if One Were to Apply Above Model, at Medium Probability of Exposure—Model 1	Hypothetical size of Risk Management Team, if One Were to Apply Above Model, at Low Probability of Exposure—Model 2	Hypothetical size of Risk Management Team, if One Were to Apply Above Model, at Medium Probability of Exposure—Model 2
Lear	17,838.9	3.1	6.3	2.1	4.3
Manpower	17,786.5	3.1	6.3	2.1	4.3
Express Scripts	17,660.0	3.1	6.2	2.1	4.2
TJX	17,516.4	3.1	6.2	2.1	4.2
Rite Aid	17,271.0	3.0	6.1	2.1	4.1
Loews	17,227.6	3.0	6.1	2.1	4.1
Delta Air Lines	17,171.0	3.0	6.1	2.1	4.1
Kimberly-Clark	16,746.9	3.0	5.9	2.0	4.0
Bear Stearns	16,551.4	2.9	5.8	2.0	4.0
Cigna	16,547.0	2.9	5.8	2.0	4.0
Dominion Resources	16,524.0	2.9	5.8	2.0	4.0
Paccar	16,454.1	2.9	5.8	2.0	3.9
Lennar	16,256.7	2.9	5.7	2.0	3.9
Duke Energy	15,967.0	2.8	5.6	1.9	3.8
Gap	15,943.0	2.8	5.6	1.9	3.8
Xerox	15,895.0	2.8	5.6	1.9	3.8
Anheuser-Busch	15,717.1	2.8	5.5	1.9	3.8
United States Steel	15,715.0	2.8	5.5	1.9	3.8
FPL Group	15,710.0	2.8	5.5	1.9	3.8
Eli Lilly	15,691.0	2.8	5.5	1.9	3.8
Exelon	15,654.0	2.8	5.5	1.9	3.8
Union Pacific	15,578.0	2.7	5.5	1.9	3.7
Kohl's	15,544.2	2.7	5.5	1.9	3.7
Centex	15,465.1	2.7	5.5	1.9	3.7
Capital One Financial	15,191.0	2.7	5.4	1.8	3.6

(*Continued*)

311

TABLE 8A.3. (Continued)

Company	Revenues ($ millions) (for 2007)	Hypothetical Size of Risk Management Team, if One Were to Apply Above Model, at Low Probability of Exposure—Model 1	Hypothetical Size of Risk Management Team, if One Were to Apply Above Model, at Medium Probability of Exposure—Model 1	Hypothetical size of Risk Management Team, if One Were to Apply Above Model, at Low Probability of Exposure—Model 2	Hypothetical size of Risk Management Team, if One Were to Apply Above Model, at Medium Probability of Exposure—Model 2
D.R. Horton	15,051.3	2.7	5.3	1.8	3.6
Office Depot	15,010.8	2.6	5.3	1.8	3.6
Burlington No. Santa Fe	14,985.0	2.6	5.3	1.8	3.6
Nike	14,954.9	2.6	5.3	1.8	3.6
Progressive	14,786.4	2.6	5.2	1.8	3.5
DIRECTV Group	14,755.5	2.6	5.2	1.8	3.5
Nucor	14,751.3	2.6	5.2	1.8	3.5
Texas Instruments	14,630.0	2.6	5.2	1.8	3.5
Computer Sciences	14,623.6	2.6	5.2	1.8	3.5
AFLAC	14,616.0	2.6	5.2	1.8	3.5
CBS	14,479.1	2.6	5.1	1.7	3.5
CHS	14,383.8	2.5	5.1	1.7	3.5
Oracle	14,380.0	2.5	5.1	1.7	3.5
Southern	14,356.0	2.5	5.1	1.7	3.4
Murphy Oil	14,307.4	2.5	5.0	1.7	3.4
Pulte Homes	14,274.4	2.5	5.0	1.7	3.4
Amgen	14,268.0	2.5	5.0	1.7	3.4
Avnet	14,253.6	2.5	5.0	1.7	3.4
ConAgra Foods	14,171.9	2.5	5.0	1.7	3.4
Fluor	14,078.5	2.5	5.0	1.7	3.4
Illinois Tool Works	14,055.0	2.5	5.0	1.7	3.4
Chubb	14,003.0	2.5	4.9	1.7	3.4
Enterprise GP Holdings	13,991.0	2.5	4.9	1.7	3.4
Qwest Communications	13,923.0	2.5	4.9	1.7	3.3
Arrow Electronics	13,577.1	2.4	4.8	1.6	3.3
USAA	13,416.4	2.4	4.7	1.6	3.2

TABLE 8A.3. (Continued)

Company	Revenues ($ millions) (for 2007)	Hypothetical Size of Risk Management Team, if One Were to Apply Above Model, at Low Probability of Exposure—Model 1	Hypothetical Size of Risk Management Team, if One Were to Apply Above Model, at Medium Probability of Exposure—Model 1	Hypothetical size of Risk Management Team, if One Were to Apply Above Model, at Low Probability of Exposure—Model 2	Hypothetical size of Risk Management Team, if One Were to Apply Above Model, at Medium Probability of Exposure—Model 2
Waste Management	13,363.0	2.4	4.7	1.6	3.2
Eastman Kodak	13,274.0	2.3	4.7	1.6	3.2
SunTrust Banks	13,260.4	2.3	4.7	1.6	3.2
Huntsman	13,148.2	2.3	4.6	1.6	3.2
TRW Automotive Holdings	13,144.0	2.3	4.6	1.6	3.2
Continental Airlines	13,128.0	2.3	4.6	1.5	3.2
Sun Microsystems	13,068.0	2.3	4.6	1.5	3.1
National City Corp.	12,952.7	2.3	4.6	1.6	3.1
Health Net	12,908.4	2.3	4.6	1.5	3.1
Masco	12,833.0	2.3	4.5	1.5	3.1
Pepsi Bottling	12,730.0	2.2	4.5	1.5	3.1
American Electric Power	12,622.0	2.2	4.4	1.5	3.0
Edison International	12,622.0	2.2	4.4	1.5	3.0
Textron	12,591.0	2.2	4.4	1.5	3.0
Northwest Airlines	12,568.0	2.2	4.4	1.5	3.0
PG&E Corp.	12,539.0	2.2	4.4	1.5	3.0
L-3 Communications	12,476.9	2.2	4.4	1.5	3.0
Eaton	12,370.0	2.2	4.4	1.5	3.0
Public Service Enterprise Group	12,288.0	2.2	4.3	1.5	2.9
Colgate-Palmolive	12,237.7	2.2	4.3	1.5	2.9
Kinder Morgan	12,208.0	2.2	4.3	1.5	2.9
Toys "R" Us	12,206.0	2.2	4.3	1.5	2.9
Marriott International	12,160.0	2.1	4.3	1.5	2.9
Consolidated Edison	12,137.0	2.1	4.3	1.5	2.9

(Continued)

TABLE 8A.3. (Continued)

Company	Revenues ($ millions) (for 2007)	Hypothetical Size of Risk Management Team, if One Were to Apply Above Model, at Low Probability of Exposure—Model 1	Hypothetical Size of Risk Management Team, if One Were to Apply Above Model, at Medium Probability of Exposure—Model 1	Hypothetical size of Risk Management Team, if One Were to Apply Above Model, at Low Probability of Exposure—Model 2	Hypothetical size of Risk Management Team, if One Were to Apply Above Model, at Medium Probability of Exposure—Model 2
United Auto Group	12,109.9	2.1	4.3	1.5	2.9
Phelps Dodge	12,090.2	2.1	4.3	1.5	2.9
Marsh & McLennan	12,069.0	2.1	4.3	1.4	2.9
ONEOK	11,906.8	2.1	4.2	1.4	2.9
Bank of New York Co.	11,891.0	2.1	4.2	1.4	2.9
Sempra Energy	11,850.0	2.1	4.2	1.4	2.8
Williams	11,812.9	2.1	4.2	1.4	2.8
FirstEnergy	11,726.0	2.1	4.1	1.4	2.8
General Mills	11,640.0	2.1	4.1	1.4	2.8
Aramark	11,621.2	2.0	4.1	1.4	2.8
Circuit City Stores	11,597.7	2.0	4.1	1.4	2.8
US Airways Group	11,557.0	2.0	4.1	1.4	2.8
Smithfield Foods	11,506.8	2.0	4.1	1.4	2.8
Viacom	11,466.5	2.0	4.0	1.4	2.8
Visteon	11,418.0	2.0	4.0	1.4	2.7
Omnicom Group	11,376.9	2.0	4.0	1.4	2.7
Cummins	11,362.0	2.0	4.0	1.4	2.7
Medtronic	11,292.0	2.0	4.0	1.4	2.7
American Standard	11,208.2	2.0	4.0	1.3	2.7
EMC	11,155.1	2.0	3.9	1.3	2.7
Entergy	11,066.6	2.0	3.9	1.3	2.7
PPG Industries	11,037.0	1.9	3.9	1.3	2.6
Genworth Financial	11,029.0	1.9	3.9	1.3	2.6
KB Home	11,003.8	1.9	3.9	1.3	2.6
Reliant Energy	10,985.4	1.9	3.9	1.3	2.6
Sanmina-SCI	10,955.4	1.9	3.9	1.3	2.6

Company	Revenues ($ millions) (for 2007)	Hypothetical Size of Risk Management Team, if One Were to Apply Above Model, at Low Probability of Exposure—Model 1	Hypothetical Size of Risk Management Team, if One Were to Apply Above Model, at Medium Probability of Exposure—Model 1	Hypothetical size of Risk Management Team, if One Were to Apply Above Model, at Low Probability of Exposure—Model 2	Hypothetical size of Risk Management Team, if One Were to Apply Above Model, at Medium Probability of Exposure—Model 2
PNC Financial Services Group	10,939.0	1.9	3.9	1.3	2.6
Kellogg	10,906.7	1.9	3.8	1.3	2.6
Anadarko Petroleum	10,904.0	1.9	3.8	1.3	2.6
TXU	10,856.0	1.9	3.8	1.3	2.6
World Fuel Services	10,785.1	1.9	3.8	1.3	2.6
Unum Group	10,718.8	1.9	3.8	1.3	2.6
Amazon.com	10,711.0	1.9	3.8	1.3	2.6
Progress Energy	10,702.0	1.9	3.8	1.3	2.6
Devon Energy	10,696.0	1.9	3.8	1.3	2.6
Limited Brands	10,670.6	1.9	3.8	1.3	2.6
Google	10,604.9	1.9	3.7	1.3	2.5
Schering-Plough	10,594.0	1.9	3.7	1.3	2.5
Solectron	10,560.7	1.9	3.7	1.3	2.5
Genuine Parts	10,457.9	1.8	3.7	1.3	2.5
Baxter International	10,378.0	1.8	3.7	1.2	2.5
Dean Foods	10,339.0	1.8	3.6	1.2	2.5
Aon	10,311.0	1.8	3.6	1.2	2.5
Ashland	10,007.0	1.8	3.5	1.2	2.4
YRC Worldwide	9,918.7	1.7	3.5	1.2	2.4
Principal Financial	9,870.0	1.7	3.5	1.2	2.4
Xcel Energy	9,847.8	1.7	3.5	1.2	2.4
Echostar Communications	9,818.5	1.7	3.5	1.2	2.4
ArvinMeritor	9,810.0	1.7	3.5	1.2	2.4
Harrah's Entertainment	9,780.7	1.7	3.4	1.2	2.3

(*Continued*)

TABLE 8A.3. (Continued)

Company	Revenues ($ millions) (for 2007)	Hypothetical Size of Risk Management Team, if One Were to Apply Above Model, at Low Probability of Exposure—Model 1	Hypothetical Size of Risk Management Team, if One Were to Apply Above Model, at Medium Probability of Exposure—Model 1	Hypothetical size of Risk Management Team, if One Were to Apply Above Model, at Low Probability of Exposure—Model 2	Hypothetical size of Risk Management Team, if One Were to Apply Above Model, at Medium Probability of Exposure—Model 2
Dana	9,724.0	1.7	3.4	1.2	2.3
Alltel	9,723.3	1.7	3.4	1.2	2.3
Guardian Life of America	9,693.7	1.7	3.4	1.2	2.3
Tenet Healthcare	9,622.0	1.7	3.4	1.2	2.3
TEPPCO Partners	9,612.2	1.7	3.4	1.2	2.3
Danaher	9,596.4	1.7	3.4	1.2	2.3
CSX	9,566.0	1.7	3.4	1.1	2.3
Yum Brands	9,561.0	1.7	3.4	1.1	2.3
State St. Corp.	9,525.0	1.7	3.4	1.1	2.3
Fidelity National Financial	9,436.1	1.7	3.3	1.1	2.3
BB&T Corp.	9,414.8	1.7	3.3	1.1	2.3
Parker Hannifin	9,407.6	1.7	3.3	1.1	2.3
Norfolk Southern	9,407.0	1.7	3.3	1.1	2.3
S&C Holdco 3	9,350.0	1.6	3.3	1.1	2.2
H.J. Heinz	9,331.4	1.6	3.3	1.1	2.2
CenterPoint Energy	9,319.0	1.6	3.3	1.1	2.2
R. R. Donnelley & Sons	9,316.6	1.6	3.3	1.1	2.2
Automatic Data Proc.	9,263.2	1.6	3.3	1.1	2.2
Dollar General	9,169.8	1.6	3.2	1.1	2.2
Applied Materials	9,167.0	1.6	3.2	1.1	2.2
Air Products & Chem.	9,158.8	1.6	3.2	1.1	2.2
Southwest Airlines	9,086.0	1.6	3.2	1.1	2.2
Lincoln National	9,062.9	1.6	3.2	1.1	2.2
Baker Hughes	9,034.1	1.6	3.2	1.1	2.2
DTE Energy	9,024.0	1.6	3.2	1.1	2.2
OfficeMax	8,965.7	1.6	3.2	1.1	2.2

TABLE 8A.3. (Continued)

Company	Revenues ($ millions) (for 2007)	Hypothetical Size of Risk Management Team, if One Were to Apply Above Model, at Low Probability of Exposure—Model 1	Hypothetical Size of Risk Management Team, if One Were to Apply Above Model, at Medium Probability of Exposure—Model 1	Hypothetical size of Risk Management Team, if One Were to Apply Above Model, at Low Probability of Exposure—Model 2	Hypothetical size of Risk Management Team, if One Were to Apply Above Model, at Medium Probability of Exposure—Model 2
Liberty Media	8,948.0	1.6	3.2	1.1	2.1
Lucent Technologies	8,796.0	1.6	3.1	1.1	2.1
Avon Products	8,763.9	1.5	3.1	1.1	2.1
SLM	8,751.2	1.5	3.1	1.1	2.1
Sonic Automotive	8,706.4	1.5	3.1	1.0	2.1
Nordstrom	8,560.7	1.5	3.0	1.0	2.1
BJ's Wholesale Club	8,524.2	1.5	3.0	1.0	2.0
Reynolds American	8,510.0	1.5	3.0	1.0	2.0
First American Corp.	8,499.1	1.5	3.0	1.0	2.0
Pepco Holdings	8,362.9	1.5	2.9	1.0	2.0
Praxair	8,324.0	1.5	2.9	1.0	2.0
Rohm & Haas	8,308.0	1.5	2.9	1.0	2.0
Apache	8,288.8	1.5	2.9	1.0	2.0
Fortune Brands	8,255.0	1.5	2.9	1.0	2.0
ITT	8,185.9	1.4	2.9	1.0	2.0
Hilton Hotels	8,162.0	1.4	2.9	1.0	2.0
Ameriprise Financial	8,140.0	1.4	2.9	1.0	2.0
SAIC	8,127.0	1.4	2.9	1.0	2.0
Fifth Third Bancorp	8,108.0	1.4	2.9	1.0	1.9
Assurant	8,070.6	1.4	2.8	1.0	1.9
Hertz Global Holdings	8,058.4	1.4	2.8	1.0	1.9
Gannett	8,033.4	1.4	2.8	1.0	1.9
Smurfit-Stone Container	7,944.0	1.4	2.8	1.0	1.9
Mohawk Industries	7,905.8	1.4	2.8	0.9	1.9
Winn-Dixie Stores	7,878.2	1.4	2.8	0.9	1.9

(*Continued*)

TABLE 8A.3. (Continued)

Company	Revenues ($ millions) (for 2007)	Hypothetical Size of Risk Management Team, if One Were to Apply Above Model, at Low Probability of Exposure—Model 1	Hypothetical Size of Risk Management Team, if One Were to Apply Above Model, at Medium Probability of Exposure—Model 1	Hypothetical size of Risk Management Team, if One Were to Apply Above Model, at Low Probability of Exposure—Model 2	Hypothetical size of Risk Management Team, if One Were to Apply Above Model, at Medium Probability of Exposure—Model 2
Energy Transfer Equity	7,859.1	1.4	2.8	0.9	1.9
Dillard's	7,849.4	1.4	2.8	0.9	1.9
Boston Scientific	7,821.0	1.4	2.8	0.9	1.9
Sherwin-Williams	7,809.8	1.4	2.8	0.9	1.9
Starbucks	7,786.9	1.4	2.7	0.9	1.9
Campbell Soup	7,778.0	1.4	2.7	0.9	1.9
Regions Financial	7,756.4	1.4	2.7	0.9	1.9
Coventry Health Care	7,733.8	1.4	2.7	0.9	1.9
Terex	7,647.6	1.3	2.7	0.9	1.8
MGM Mirage	7,588.0	1.3	2.7	0.9	1.8
Commercial Metals	7,555.9	1.3	2.7	0.9	1.8
Qualcomm	7,526.0	1.3	2.7	0.9	1.8
Owens-Illinois	7,523.5	1.3	2.7	0.9	1.8
KeyCorp	7,507.0	1.3	2.6	0.9	1.8
NiSource	7,495.9	1.3	2.6	0.9	1.8
Eastman Chemical	7,450.0	1.3	2.6	0.9	1.8
Jacobs Engineering Grp.	7,421.3	1.3	2.6	0.9	1.8
Monsanto	7,344.0	1.3	2.6	0.9	1.8
Smith International	7,333.6	1.3	2.6	0.9	1.8
Chesapeake Energy	7,325.6	1.3	2.6	0.9	1.8
KeySpan	7,181.6	1.3	2.5	0.9	1.7
Dover	7,179.6	1.3	2.5	0.9	1.7
Crown Holdings	7,140.0	1.3	2.5	0.9	1.7
Land O'Lakes	7,102.3	1.3	2.5	0.9	1.7
Clear Channel Communications	7,099.4	1.3	2.5	0.9	1.7

TABLE 8A.3. (Continued)

Company	Revenues ($ millions) (for 2007)	Hypothetical Size of Risk Management Team, if One Were to Apply Above Model, at Low Probability of Exposure—Model 1	Hypothetical Size of Risk Management Team, if One Were to Apply Above Model, at Medium Probability of Exposure—Model 1	Hypothetical size of Risk Management Team, if One Were to Apply Above Model, at Low Probability of Exposure—Model 2	Hypothetical size of Risk Management Team, if One Were to Apply Above Model, at Medium Probability of Exposure—Model 2
First Data	7,076.4	1.2	2.5	0.8	1.7
VF	7,033.5	1.2	2.5	0.8	1.7
National Oilwell Varco	7,025.8	1.2	2.5	0.8	1.7
Integrys Energy Group	6,979.2	1.2	2.4	0.8	1.7
CIT Group	6,927.7	1.2	2.4	0.8	1.7
PPL	6,904.0	1.2	2.4	0.8	1.7
Northeast Utilities	6,897.4	1.2	2.4	0.8	1.7
American Family Ins. Grp.	6,893.1	1.2	2.4	0.3	1.7
Ameren	6,880.0	1.2	2.4	0.3	1.7
Liberty Global	6,812.9	1.2	2.4	0.8	1.6
CMS Energy	6,810.0	1.2	2.4	0.8	1.6
CDW	6,785.5	1.2	2.4	0.8	1.6
Newell Rubbermaid	6,709.5	1.2	2.4	0.8	1.6
Calpine	6,705.8	1.2	2.4	0.8	1.6
IAC/InterActiveCorp	6,684.2	1.2	2.4	0.8	1.6
Celanese	6,668.0	1.2	2.4	0.8	1.6
Virgin Media	6,637.4	1.2	2.3	0.8	1.6
Ball	6,621.5	1.2	2.3	0.8	1.6
C.H. Robinson Worldwide	6,556.2	1.2	2.3	0.8	1.6
MeadWestvaco	6,530.0	1.2	2.3	0.8	1.6
Enbridge Energy Partners	6,509.0	1.1	2.3	0.8	1.6
Estée Lauder	6,508.9	1.1	2.3	0.8	1.6
Omnicare	6,493.0	1.1	2.3	0.8	1.6
Realogy	6,492.0	1.1	2.3	0.8	1.6
Owens Corning	6,461.0	1.1	2.3	0.8	1.6

(Continued)

TABLE 8A.3. (Continued)

Company	Revenues ($ millions) (for 2007)	Hypothetical Size of Risk Management Team, if One Were to Apply Above Model, at Low Probability of Exposure—Model 1	Hypothetical Size of Risk Management Team, if One Were to Apply Above Model, at Medium Probability of Exposure—Model 1	Hypothetical size of Risk Management Team, if One Were to Apply Above Model, at Low Probability of Exposure—Model 2	Hypothetical size of Risk Management Team, if One Were to Apply Above Model, at Medium Probability of Exposure—Model 2
Black & Decker	6,447.3	1.1	2.3	0.8	1.5
Yahoo	6,425.7	1.1	2.3	0.8	1.5
Mellon Financial Corp.	6,395.0	1.1	2.3	0.8	1.5
Family Dollar Stores	6,394.8	1.1	2.3	0.8	1.5
Synnex	6,343.5	1.1	2.2	0.8	1.5
Federal-Mogul	6,326.4	1.1	2.2	0.8	1.5
Ryder System	6,306.6	1.1	2.2	0.8	1.5
Safeco	6,289.9	1.1	2.2	0.8	1.5
Quest Diagnostics	6,272.3	1.1	2.2	0.8	1.5
CarMax	6,260.0	1.1	2.2	0.8	1.5
McGraw-Hill	6,255.1	1.1	2.2	0.8	1.5
Dole Food	6,219.3	1.1	2.2	0.7	1.5
Interpublic Group	6,190.8	1.1	2.2	0.7	1.5
Harley-Davidson	6,185.6	1.1	2.2	0.7	1.5
Thrivent Financial for Lutherans	6,164.6	1.1	2.2	0.7	1.5
NVR	6,156.8	1.1	2.2	0.7	1.5
Atmos Energy	6,152.4	1.1	2.2	0.7	1.5
Hovnanian Enterprises	6,148.2	1.1	2.2	0.7	1.5
NCR	6,142.0	1.1	2.2	0.7	1.5
Toll Brothers	6,123.5	1.1	2.2	0.7	1.5
Autoliv	6,118.0	1.1	2.2	0.7	1.5
Group 1 Automotive	6,083.5	1.1	2.1	0.7	1.5
AK Steel Holding	6,069.0	1.1	2.1	0.7	1.5
Allied Waste Industries	6,028.8	1.1	2.1	0.7	1.4
Cablevision Systems	6,006.7	1.1	2.1	0.7	1.4
Starwood Hotels & Rsrts.	5,979.0	1.1	2.1	0.7	1.4

Company	Revenues ($ millions) (for 2007)	Hypothetical Size of Risk Management Team, if One Were to Apply Above Model, at Low Probability of Exposure—Model 1	Hypothetical Size of Risk Management Team, if One Were to Apply Above Model, at Medium Probability of Exposure—Model 1	Hypothetical size of Risk Management Team, if One Were to Apply Above Model, at Low Probability of Exposure—Model 2	Hypothetical size of Risk Management Team, if One Were to Apply Above Model, at Medium Probability of Exposure—Model 2
Brunswick	5,971.3	1.1	2.1	0.7	1.4
eBay	5,969.7	1.1	2.1	0.7	1.4
AutoZone	5,948.4	1.0	2.1	0.7	1.4
Ryerson	5,908.9	1.0	2.1	0.7	1.4
Molson Coors Brewing	5,902.8	1.0	2.1	0.7	1.4
Agilent Technologies	5,891.0	1.0	2.1	0.7	1.4
W.W. Grainger	5,883.7	1.0	2.1	0.7	1.4
Charles Schwab	5,880.0	1.0	2.1	0.7	1.4
Goodrich	5,878.3	1.0	2.1	0.7	1.4
Asbury Automotive Group	5,863.1	1.0	2.1	0.7	1.4
Becton Dickinson	5,834.8	1.0	2.1	0.7	1.4
Performance Food Group	5,826.7	1.0	2.1	0.7	1.4
NRG Energy	5,812.0	1.0	2.0	0.7	1.4
Pitney Bowes	5,811.2	1.0	2.0	0.7	1.4
USG	5,810.0	1.0	2.0	0.7	1.4
Bed Bath & Beyond	5,809.6	1.0	2.0	0.7	1.4
Freeport-McMoRan Cpr. & Gld	5,790.5	1.0	2.0	0.7	1.4
Boise Cascade Holdings	5,779.9	1.0	2.0	0.7	1.4
Unisys	5,757.2	1.0	2.0	0.7	1.4
Foot Locker	5,750.0	1.0	2.0	0.7	1.4
Reliance Steel & Alum.	5,748.4	1.0	2.0	0.7	1.4
Hormel Foods	5,745.5	1.0	2.0	0.7	1.4
Darden Restaurants	5,720.6	1.0	2.0	0.7	1.4
Avis Budget Group	5,689.0	1.0	2.0	0.7	1.4

(Continued)

TABLE 8A.3. (Continued)

Company	Revenues ($ millions) (for 2007)	Hypothetical Size of Risk Management Team, if One Were to Apply Above Model, at Low Probability of Exposure—Model 1	Hypothetical Size of Risk Management Team, if One Were to Apply Above Model, at Medium Probability of Exposure—Model 1	Hypothetical size of Risk Management Team, if One Were to Apply Above Model, at Low Probability of Exposure—Model 2	Hypothetical size of Risk Management Team, if One Were to Apply Above Model, at Medium Probability of Exposure—Model 2
Mattel	5,650.2	1.0	2.0	0.7	1.4
Advanced Micro Devices	5,649.0	1.0	2.0	0.7	1.4
Kelly Services	5,639.0	1.0	2.0	0.7	1.4
Charter Communications	5,613.0	1.0	2.0	0.7	1.3
Blockbuster	5,611.3	1.0	2.0	0.7	1.3
Whole Foods Market	5,607.4	1.0	2.0	0.7	1.3
Avery Dennison	5,583.1	1.0	2.0	0.7	1.3
Tribune	5,582.6	1.0	2.0	0.7	1.3
Temple-Inland	5,581.0	1.0	2.0	0.7	1.3
Ross Stores	5,570.2	1.0	2.0	0.7	1.3
Rockwell Automation	5,561.4	1.0	2.0	0.7	1.3
Triad Hospitals	5,537.9	1.0	2.0	0.7	1.3
Owens & Minor	5,533.7	1.0	2.0	0.7	1.3
Leggett & Platt	5,505.4	1.0	1.9	0.7	1.3
Beazer Homes USA	5,462.0	1.0	1.9	0.7	1.3
AGCO	5,435.0	1.0	1.9	0.7	1.3
Stryker	5,405.6	1.0	1.9	0.6	1.3
W.R. Berkley	5,394.8	1.0	1.9	0.6	1.3
Affiliated Computer Svcs.	5,353.7	0.9	1.9	0.6	1.3
Wesco International	5,320.6	0.9	1.9	0.6	1.3
GameStop	5,318.9	0.9	1.9	0.6	1.3
Mosaic	5,305.8	0.9	1.9	0.6	1.3
Timken	5,301.5	0.9	1.9	0.6	1.3
Micron Technology	5,272.0	0.9	1.9	0.6	1.3
Barnes & Noble	5,261.3	0.9	1.9	0.6	1.3

TABLE 8A.3. (Continued)

Company	Revenues ($ millions) (for 2007)	Hypothetical Size of Risk Management Team, if One Were to Apply Above Model, at Low Probability of Exposure—Model 1	Hypothetical Size of Risk Management Team, if One Were to Apply Above Model, at Medium Probability of Exposure—Model 1	Hypothetical size of Risk Management Team, if One Were to Apply Above Model, at Low Probability of Exposure—Model 2	Hypothetical size of Risk Management Team, if One Were to Apply Above Model, at Medium Probability of Exposure—Model 2
Peabody Energy	5,256.3	0.9	1.9	0.6	1.3
Pilgrim's Pride	5,235.6	0.9	1.8	0.6	1.3
Hexion Specialty Chemicals	5,233.0	0.9	1.8	0.6	1.3
Energy East	5,230.7	0.9	1.8	0.6	1.3
UGI	5,221.0	0.9	1.8	0.6	1.3
Pantry	5,211.2	0.9	1.8	0.6	1.3
Pacific Life	5,201.9	0.9	1.8	0.6	1.2
Henry Schein	5,191.0	0.9	1.8	0.6	1.2
Corning	5,174.0	0.9	1.8	0.6	1.2
Avaya	5,148.0	0.9	1.8	0.6	1.2
Marshall & Ilsley Corp.	5,127.9	0.9	1.8	0.6	1.2
Lexmark International	5,108.1	0.9	1.8	0.6	1.2
Longs Drug Stores	5,097.1	0.9	1.8	0.6	1.2
Auto-Owners Insurance	5,090.1	0.9	1.8	0.5	1.2
Franklin Resources	5,050.7	0.9	1.8	0.6	1.2
Peter Kiewit Sons'	5,049.0	0.9	1.8	0.6	1.2
Newmont Mining	5,039.0	0.9	1.8	0.6	1.2
Emcor Group	5,021.0	0.9	1.8	0.6	1.2
El Paso	5,011.0	0.9	1.8	0.6	1.2
Graybar Electric	5,009.1	0.9	1.8	0.6	1.2
Liz Claiborne	4,994.3	0.9	1.8	0.6	1.2
Host Hotels & Resorts	4,958.0	0.9	1.7	0.6	1.2
Hershey	4,944.2	0.9	1.7	0.6	1.2
Anixter International	4,938.6	0.9	1.7	0.6	1.2
Allegheny Technologies	4,936.6	0.9	1.7	0.6	1.2

(Continued)

TABLE 8A.3. (Continued)

Company	Revenues ($ millions) (for 2007)	Hypothetical Size of Risk Management Team, if One Were to Apply Above Model, at Low Probability of Exposure—Model 1	Hypothetical Size of Risk Management Team, if One Were to Apply Above Model, at Medium Probability of Exposure—Model 1	Hypothetical size of Risk Management Team, if One Were to Apply Above Model, at Low Probability of Exposure—Model 2	Hypothetical size of Risk Management Team, if One Were to Apply Above Model, at Medium Probability of Exposure—Model 2
BlueLinx Holdings	4,899.4	0.9	1.7	0.6	1.2
Ecolab	4,895.8	0.9	1.7	0.6	1.2
DaVita	4,880.7	0.9	1.7	0.6	1.2
H&R Block	4,872.8	0.9	1.7	0.6	1.2
Western & Southern Financial	4,838.1	0.9	1.7	0.6	1.2
MDC Holdings	4,801.7	0.8	1.7	0.6	1.2
Frontier Oil	4,796.0	0.8	1.7	0.6	1.2
Erie Insurance Group	4,785.5	0.8	1.7	0.6	1.1
Shaw Group	4,781.4	0.8	1.7	0.6	1.1
Level 3 Communications	4,778.0	0.8	1.7	0.6	1.1
RadioShack	4,777.5	0.8	1.7	0.6	1.1
Ryland Group	4,757.2	0.8	1.7	0.6	1.1
Aleris International	4,748.8	0.8	1.7	0.6	1.1
Big Lots	4,743.0	0.8	1.7	0.6	1.1
Jones Apparel Group	4,742.8	0.8	1.7	0.6	1.1
SPX	4,723.0	0.8	1.7	0.6	1.1
Wm. Wrigley Jr.	4,686.0	0.8	1.7	0.6	1.1
Tenneco	4,685.0	0.8	1.7	0.6	1.1
Mirant	4,684.0	0.8	1.7	0.6	1.1
Clorox	4,660.0	0.8	1.6	0.6	1.1
Nash-Finch	4,631.6	0.8	1.6	0.6	1.1
Expeditors Intl. of Washington	4,626.0	0.8	1.6	0.6	1.1
Advance Auto Parts	4,616.5	0.8	1.6	0.6	1.1
Sovereign Bancorp	4,612.0	0.8	1.6	0.6	1.1
Constellation Brands	4,603.4	0.8	1.6	0.6	1.1

TABLE 8A.3. (Continued)

Company	Revenues ($ millions) (for 2007)	Hypothetical Size of Risk Management Team, if One Were to Apply Above Model, at Low Probability of Exposure—Model 1	Hypothetical Size of Risk Management Team, if One Were to Apply Above Model, at Medium Probability of Exposure—Model 1	Hypothetical size of Risk Management Team, if One Were to Apply Above Model, at Low Probability of Exposure—Model 2	Hypothetical size of Risk Management Team, if One Were to Apply Above Model, at Medium Probability of Exposure—Model 2
BorgWarner	4,585.4	0.8	1.6	0.6	1.1
XTO Energy	4,576.0	0.8	1.6	0.5	1.1
SCANA	4,563.0	0.8	1.6	0.5	1.1
Cincinnati Financial	4,550.0	0.8	1.6	0.5	1.1
United Stationers	4,546.9	0.8	1.6	0.5	1.1
Fiserv	4,544.2	0.8	1.6	0.5	1.1
Comerica	4,539.0	0.8	1.6	0.5	1.1
Chiquita Brands Intl.	4,499.1	0.8	1.6	0.5	1.1
Mutual of Omaha Ins.	4,497.6	0.8	1.6	0.5	1.1
Northern Trust Corp.	4,473.0	0.8	1.6	0.5	1.1
Global Partners	4,472.4	0.8	1.6	0.5	1.1
Western Union	4,470.2	0.8	1.6	0.5	1.1
Conseco	4,467.4	0.8	1.6	0.5	1.1
Community Health Sys.	4,369.9	0.8	1.5	0.5	1.0
BJ Services	4,367.9	0.8	1.5	0.5	1.0
M&T Bank Corp.	4,359.9	0.8	1.5	0.5	1.0
Kindred Healthcare	4,355.9	0.8	1.5	0.5	1.0
Western Digital	4,341.3	0.8	1.5	0.5	1.0
Sealed Air	4,327.9	0.8	1.5	0.5	1.0
SunGard Data Systems	4,323.0	0.8	1.5	0.5	1.0
Total Risk Management Professionals (when each entry is rounded up a whole number)		2012	3748	1400	2629

Note: With the working assumption that the Total Risk Management Professionals figure represents one-third of all Corporate America, the number of IT risk management professionals in the United States is in the 6000–12,000 (using Model 1). Assuming that the United States is 50% of the global base, the global number of IT risk management professionals is in the 12,000–24,000 range.

325

TABLE 8A.4. Number of Employees of a Company as Compared with the Revenue of the Company, Sorted by Company Revenue

Company	Employees	Revenues ($M) (2006)	Revenue/Employee ($M)	Industry
Wal-Mart Stores	1,800,000	315,654.0	0.175363	General Merchandisers
Royal Dutch Shell	109,000	306,731.0	2.814046	Petroleum Refining
BP	96,200	267,600.0	2.781705	Petroleum Refining
General Motors	335,000	192,604.0	0.574937	Motor Vehicles & Parts
Chevron	59,000	189,481.0	3.211542	Petroleum Refining
DaimlerChrysler	382,724	186,106.3	0.486268	Motor Vehicles & Parts
Toyota Motor	285,977	185,805.0	0.64972	Motor Vehicles & Parts
Ford Motor	300,000	177,210.0	0.5907	Motor Vehicles & Parts
ConocoPhillips	35,600	166,683.0	4.682107	Petroleum Refining
General Electric	316,000	157,153.0	0.49732	Diversified Financials
Total	112,877	152,360.7	1.349794	Petroleum Refining
ING Group	115,300	138,235.3	1.198918	Insurance: Life, Health (stock)
Citigroup	303,000	131,045.0	0.432492	Banks: Commercial and Savings
AXA	78,800	129,839.2	1.647706	Insurance: Life, Health (stock)
Allianz	177,625	121,406.0	0.683496	Insurance: P & C (stock)
Volkswagen	344,902	118,376.6	0.343218	Motor Vehicles & Parts
Fortis	54,245	112,351.4	2.071184	Banks: Commercial and Savings
Crédit Agricole	136,848	110,764.6	0.809399	Banks: Commercial and Savings
American Intl. Group	97,000	108,905.0	1.122732	Insurance: Life, Health (stock)
Assicurazioni Generali	61,561	101,403.8	1.647208	Insurance: Life, Health (stock)
Siemens	461,000	100,098.7	0.217134	Electronics, Electrical Equipment
Sinopec	730,800	98,784.9	0.135174	Petroleum Refining
NTT	199,113	94,869.3	0.47646	Telecommunications
Carrefour	440,479	94,454.5	0.214436	Food & Drug Stores
HSBC Holdings	284,000	93,494.0	0.329204	Banks: Commercial and Savings
ENI	72,258	92,603.3	1.281565	Petroleum Refining
Aviva	54,791	92,579.4	1.689683	Insurance: Life, Health (stock)
	7,444,100	4,036,599.00	0.542255	

TABLE 8A.5. Number of Employees of a Company as Compared with the Revenue of the Company, Sorted by Revenue per Employee

Company	Employees	Revenues ($M) (2006)	Revenue/Employee ($M)	Industry
Sinopec	730,800	98,784.9	0.135174	Petroleum Refining
Wal-Mart Stores	1,800,000	315,654.0	0.175363	General Merchandisers
Carrefour	440,479	94,454.5	0.214436	Food & Drug Stores
Siemens	461,000	100,098.7	0.217134	Electronics, Electrical Equipment
HSBC Holdings	284,000	93,494.0	0.329204	Banks: Commercial and Savings
Volkswagen	344,902	118,376.6	0.343218	Motor Vehicles & Parts
Citigroup	303,000	131,045.0	0.432492	Banks: Commercial and Savings
NTT	199,113	94,869.3	0.47646	Telecommunications
DaimlerChrysler	382,724	186,106.3	0.486268	Motor Vehicles & Parts
General Electric	316,000	157,153.0	0.49732	Diversified Financials
General Motors	335,000	192,604.0	0.574937	Motor Vehicles & Parts
Ford Motor	300,000	177,210.0	0.5907	Motor Vehicles & Parts
Toyota Motor	285,977	185,805.0	0.64972	Motor Vehicles & Parts
Allianz	177,625	121,406.0	0.683496	Insurance: P & C (stock)
Crédit Agricole	136,848	110,764.6	0.809399	Banks: Commercial and Savings
American Intl. Group	97,000	108,905.0	1.122732	Insurance: Life, Health (stock)
ING Group	115,300	138,235.3	1.198918	Insurance: Life, Health (stock)
ENI	72,258	92,603.3	1.281565	Petroleum Refining
Total	112,877	152,360.7	1.349794	Petroleum Refining
Assicurazioni Generali	61,561	101,403.8	1.647208	Insurance: Life, Health (stock)
AXA	78,800	129,839.2	1.647706	Insurance: Life, Health (stock)
Aviva	54,791	92,579.4	1.689683	Insurance: Life, Health (stock)
Fortis	54,245	112,351.4	2.071184	Banks: Commercial and Savings
BP	96,200	267,600.0	2.781705	Petroleum Refining
Royal Dutch Shell	109,000	306,731.0	2.814046	Petroleum Refining
Chevron	59,000	189,481.0	3.211542	Petroleum Refining
ConocoPhillips	35,600	166,683.0	4.682107	Petroleum Refining

TABLE 8A.6. Number of Employees of a Company as Compared with the Revenue of the Company, Sorted by Industry

Company	Employees	Revenues ($M) (2006)	Revenue/Employee ($M)	Industry	Revenue/ Emp ($M)
Citigroup	303,000	131,045.0	0.432492	Banks: Commercial and Savings	0.552794
Fortis	54,245	112,351.4	2.071184	Banks: Commercial and Savings	
Crédit Agricole	136,848	110,764.6	0.809399	Banks: Commercial and Savings	
HSBC Holdings	284,000	93,494.0	0.329204	Banks: Commercial and Savings	
General Electric	316,000	157,153.0	0.49732	Diversified Financials	0.217134
Siemens	461,000	100,098.7	0.217134	Electronics, Electrical Equipment	
Carrefour	440,479	94,454.5	0.214436	Food & Drug Stores	
Wal-Mart Stores	1,800,000	315,654.0	0.175363	General Merchandisers	0.183045
ING Group	115,300	138,235.3	1.198918	Insurance: Life, Health (stock)	
AXA	78,800	129,839.2	1.647706	Insurance: Life, Health (stock)	
American Intl. Group	97,000	108,905.0	1.122732	Insurance: Life, Health (stock)	
Assicurazioni Generali	61,561	101,403.8	1.647208	Insurance: Life, Health (stock)	
Aviva	54,791	92,579.4	1.689683	Insurance: Life, Health (stock)	
Allianz	177,625	121,406.0	0.683496	Insurance: P & C (stock)	1.18338
General Motors	335,000	192,604.0	0.574937	Motor Vehicles & Parts	
DaimlerChrysler	382,724	186,106.3	0.486268	Motor Vehicles & Parts	
Toyota Motor	285,977	185,805.0	0.64972	Motor Vehicles & Parts	
Ford Motor	300,000	177,210.0	0.5907	Motor Vehicles & Parts	
Volkswagen	344,902	118,376.6	0.343218	Motor Vehicles & Parts	0.521716
Royal Dutch Shell	109,000	306,731.0	2.814046	Petroleum Refining	
BP	96,200	267,600.0	2.781705	Petroleum Refining	
Chevron	59,000	189,481.0	3.211542	Petroleum Refining	
ConocoPhillips	35,600	166,683.0	4.682107	Petroleum Refining	
Total	112,877	152,360.7	1.349794	Petroleum Refining	
Sinopec	730,800	98,784.9	0.135174	Petroleum Refining	
ENI	72,258	92,603.3	1.281565	Petroleum Refining	1.048126
NTT	199,113	94,869.3	0.47646	Telecommunications	0.47646

TABLE 8A.7. Team Size Calculations Using Financial Loss Data

Annual Revenue or Budget	Average Annualized Financial Loss Rates—Data Loss-Theft and Downtime (in percentage)		
	Worst Practices	Normative Practices	Best Practices
$50 million	$1.5 million	$240,000	$20,500
$500 million	$19 million	$3.3 million	$211,000
$5 billion	$329 million	$60 million	$2.25 million
$50 billion	$5 billion	$1.2 billion	$25 million
$50 million	0.03%	0.48%	0.04%
$500 million	0.038%	0.66%	0.04%
$5 billion	6.58%	1.20%	0.05%
$50 billion	10.00%	2.40%	0.05%

Annual Revenue or Budget	Nominal Employees	Size of Risk Management Team	Worst Practices	Normative Practices	Best Practices
$50 million		By revenue neutrality, based on revenue loss ($100K/FTE)	15	2.4	.2
$500 million			190	33	2.1
$5 billion			3,290	600	22.5
$50 billion			50,000	12,000	260
$50 million		By revenue neutrality, based on revenue loss ($200K/FTE)	8	1	0.1
$500 million			95	17	1
$5 billion			1,645	300	11
$50 billion			26,000	6,000	125

TABLE 8A.7. (Continued)

Annual Revenue or Budget	Nominal Employees	Size of Risk Management Team	Worst Practices	Normative Practices	Best Practices
$50 million	100	By Equivalent % of employees against total when looking at revenue loss	3	0.5	0.04
$500 million	1,000		38	6.6	0.4
$5 billion	10,000		658	120	5
$50 billion	100,000		10,000	2,400	50
$50 million		By requiring that each risk management employee generate equivalent of $500k/yr	3	0.5	0.04
$500 million			38	6.6	0.4
$5 billion			658	120	5
$50 billion			10,000	2,400	60
$50 million		By Model 1 above		0.09	
$500 million				0.9	
$5 billion				1.8	
$50 billion				18	

fairly large if the financial loss data cited in the study [ITP200901] was used to perform the calculations.

APPENDIX 8B: EXAMPLE OF VULNERABILITY ALERTS BY VENDORS AND CERT

This appendix, taken it its entirety from the **US CERT (United States Computer Emergency Readiness Team)** web page (http://www.us-cert.gov/current/), is included to provide to the reader an example of (press time) vulnerability alerts and show their impact. The US-CERT Current Activity web page is a regularly updated summary of the most frequent, high-impact types of security incidents currently being reported to the US-CERT. The reader will find this web page resource of great value.

April 3, 2009 Microsoft Releases Security Advisory 969136

March 30, 2009 Conficker Worm Targets Microsoft Windows Systems

March 30, 2009 Mozilla Foundation Releases Firefox 3.0.8

March 26, 2009 Sun Releases Updates for Java SE

March 26, 2009 OpenSSL Releases Security Advisory

March 25, 2009 Cisco Releases Multiple Security Advisories for IOS Vulnerabilities

March 23, 2009 Sun Releases Alert for Java System Identity Manager Vulnerabilities

March 18, 2009 Adobe Releases Security Bulletin

March 18, 2009 Autonomy KeyView SDK Vulnerability

March 17, 2009 Waledac Trojan Horse Spam Campaign Circulating

Microsoft Releases Security Advisory 969136

added April 3, 2009 at 08:47 am

Microsoft has released security advisory 969136 to address reports of a vulnerability in Microsoft Office PowerPoint. By convincing a user to open a specially crafted Office file, a remote attacker may be able to gain access to the affected system with the same rights as the user running PowerPoint.

US-CERT encourages users and administrators to review Microsoft Security Advisory 969136 and implement the suggested workarounds listed in the advisory to help mitigate the risks.

Conficker Worm Targets Microsoft Windows Systems

added March 29, 2009 at 08:18 pm | updated March 30, 2009 at 03:06 pm

US-CERT is aware of public reports indicating a widespread infection of the Conficker/Downadup worm, which can infect a Microsoft Windows system from a thumb drive, from a network share, or directly across a corporate network, if the network servers are not patched with the MS08-067 patch from Microsoft.

Home users can apply a simple test for the presence of a Conficker/Downadup infection on their home computers. The presence of a Conficker/Downadup infection may be detected if a user is unable to surf to their security solution website or if they are unable to connect to the websites, by downloading detection/removal tools available free from those sites:

http://www.symantec.com/norton/theme.jsp?themeid = conficker_worm&
inid = us_ghp_link_conficker_worm

http://www.microsoft.com/protect/computer/viruses/worms/conficker.mspx

http://www.mcafee.com

If a user is unable to reach any of these websites, it may indicate a Conficker/ Downadup infection. The most recent variant of Conficker/Downadup interferes with queries for these sites, preventing a user from visiting them. If a Conficker/Downadup infection is suspected, the system or computer should be removed from the network or unplugged from the Internet—in the case for home users.

Instructions, support, and more information on how to manually remove a Conficker/Downadup infection from a system have been published by major security vendors. Please see below for a few of those sites. Each of these vendors offers free tools that can verify the presence of a Conficker/Downadup infection and remove the worm:

Symantec:

http://www.symantec.com/business/security_response/writeup.jsp?docid = 2009-011316-0247-99

Microsoft:

- http://support.microsoft.com/kb/962007
- http://www.microsoft.com/protect/computer/viruses/worms/
conficker.mspx
- Microsoft PC Safety hotline at 1-866-PCSAFETY, for assistance.

US-CERT encourages users to prevent a Conficker/Downadup infection by ensuring all systems have the MS08-067 patch (see http://www.microsoft.com/ technet/security/Bulletin/MS08-067.mspx), disabling AutoRun functionality (see http://www.us-cert.gov/cas/techalerts/TA09-020A.html), and maintaining up-to-date anti-virus software.

Mozilla Foundation Releases Firefox 3.0.8

added March 30, 2009 at 09:25 am

Mozilla Foundation has released Firefox 3.0.8 to address two vulnerabilities. Exploitation of these vulnerabilities may allow an attacker to execute arbitrary code or cause a denial-of-service condition. The Mozilla Foundation Security Advisories also indicate that one of these vulnerabilities also affects SeaMonkey.

US-CERT encourages users and administrators to review the following Mozilla Foundation Security Advisories and update to Firefox 3.0.8 to help mitigate the risks:

- Mozilla Foundation Security Advisory 2009-12
- Mozilla Foundation Security Advisory 2009-13

Sun Releases Updates for Java SE

added March 26, 2009 at 08:54 am

Sun has released updates for Java SE to address multiple vulnerabilities. These vulnerabilities may allow an attacker to execute arbitrary code, cause a denial-of-service condition, or operate with escalated privileges.

US-CERT encourages users to review the Sun Java SE 6 Update Release Notes and upgrade to Java SE version 1.6.0_13 to help mitigate the risks.

OpenSSL Releases Security Advisory

added March 26, 2009 at 08:36 am

OpenSSL has released a security advisory to address multiple vulnerabilities. These vulnerabilities may allow an attacker to cause a denial-of-service condition or bypass security restrictions in affected applications.

US-CERT encourages users and administrators to review the OpenSSL security advisory. Because OpenSSL is widely redistributed, users should check for updates from their operating system vendors and vendors of other products using OpenSSL. Users of OpenSSL from the original source distribution should upgrade to OpenSSL 0.9.8k.

Cisco Releases Multiple Security Advisories for IOS Vulnerabilities

added March 25, 2009 at 03:41 pm

Cisco has released multiple security advisories to address vulnerabilities in IOS Software. These vulnerabilities may allow an attacker to cause a denial-of-service condition, interfere with network traffic, or operate with escalated privileges.

US-CERT encourages users and administrators to review the following Cisco security advisories and apply any necessary workarounds or updates to help mitigate the risks.

- cisco-sa-20090325-udp: Cisco IOS Software Multiple Features Crafted UDP Packet Vulnerability
- cisco-sa-20090325-tcp: Cisco IOS Software Multiple Features Crafted TCP Sequence Vulnerability
- cisco-sa-20090325-ip: Cisco IOS Software Multiple Features IP Sockets Vulnerability
- cisco-sa-20090325-webvpn: Cisco IOS Software WebVPN and SSLVPN Vulnerabilities
- cisco-sa-20090325-mobileip: Cisco IOS Software Mobile IP and Mobile IPv6 Vulnerabilities
- cisco-sa-20090325-scp: Cisco IOS Software Secure Copy Privilege Escalation Vulnerability
- cisco-sa-20090325-sip: Cisco IOS Software Session Initiation Protocol Denial of Service Vulnerability
- cisco-sa-20090325-ctcp: Cisco IOS cTCP Denial of Service Vulnerability

Sun Releases Alert for Java System Identity Manager Vulnerabilities

added March 23, 2009 at 12:24 pm

Sun Microsystems has released an alert to address multiple vulnerabilities in the Java System Identity Manager. These vulnerabilities may allow an attacker to execute arbitrary commands, conduct cross-site scripting attacks, modify configuration settings, or obtain sensitive information.

US-CERT encourages users and administrators to review Sun Alert 253567 and apply any necessary patches.

Adobe Releases Security Bulletin

added March 18, 2009 at 04:39 pm

Adobe has released security bulletin APSB09-04 to address multiple vulnerabilities, one of which is the JBIG2 vulnerability originally addressed in security advisory APAA09-01 and security bulletin APSB09-03. These vulnerabilities may allow an attacker to execute arbitrary code or cause a denial-of-service condition.

US-CERT encourages users to review Adobe security bulletin APSB09-04 and apply any necessary updates. Additional information regarding the JBIG2 vulnerability can be found in the Vulnerability Notes Database.

Autonomy KeyView SDK Vulnerability

added March 18, 2009 at 09:13 am

US-CERT is aware of reports of a vulnerability that affects the Autonomy KeyView SDK wp6sr.dll library. This library is used by certain products, including Lotus Notes and Symantec, to support the handling of Word Perfect documents. By convincing a user to open a specially crafted Word Perfect document with an application using the affected Autonomy KeyView SDK library, a remote attacker may be able to execute arbitrary code.

US-CERT encourages users and administrators to do the following to help mitigate the risks:

- IBM Lotus Notes users should review the IBM Flash Alert and implement the listed fixes or workarounds.
- Symantec users should review Symantec Security Advisory SYM09-004 and implement the listed fixes or workarounds.
- Registered Autonomy users should review the related Autonomy alert (login required).

Waledac Trojan Horse Spam Campaign Circulating

added March 17, 2009 at 09:08 am

US-CERT is aware of public reports of malicious code circulating via spam e-mail messages related to bogus terror attacks in the recipient's local area. These messages use subject lines implying that a fatal bomb attack has occurred near the recipient and contain a link to "breaking news." Users who click on the link will be taken to a site posing as a Reuters news article that contains a bogus news story about the fatal bomb attack. The systems serving the bogus news story check a visiting user's IP address to obtain a geographical location to insert a nearby placename into the bogus article. The articles also contain links to video content, claiming that the latest Flash Player is required to view the video. If users attempt to update or install the Flash Player from the link provided in the article, their systems may become infected with malicious code.

US-CERT encourages users and administrators to take the following preventative measures to help mitigate the security risks:

- Install antivirus software, and keep the virus signatures up to date.
- Do not follow unsolicited links and do not open unsolicited email messages.
- Use caution when visiting untrusted websites.
- Use caution when downloading and installing applications.
- Obtain software applications and updates directly from the vendor's website.

APPENDIX 8C: EXAMPLES OF DATA LOSSES—A ONE-MONTH SNAPSHOT

The Open Security Foundation's DataLossDB (http://www.datalossdb.org) maintains a chronology of data breaches resulting in the disclosure of private data. Table 8C.1 provides a snapshot of such data (asset) exposure *for two months* (March and April 2009, around the time this chapter was being written). The reader can easily see the trends; also consult this website for an up-to-date and complete view including a key for breach types if interested. The point worth noting is the chronic risk exposure to which firms are subjected to.

TABLE 8C.1. Sixty Days Worth of Reported Data Loss Incidents

Date	Name	Country	BreachType	Records Affected
March 1, 2009	City of Muskogee	US	Lost Media	4,500
March 2, 2009	Wiltshire County Council	GB	Lost Media	1,385
March 4, 2009	Elk Grove Unified School District	US	Lost Document	520
March 4, 2009	New York City Police Department	US	Stolen Tape	80,000
March 4, 2009	St. Rita's Medical Center	US	Stolen Document	242
March 4, 2009	Jackson Memorial Hospital	US	Stolen Drive	200,000
March 5, 2009	Landlord's Source Centre	CA	web	1,393
March 5, 2009	Rental Research Services, Inc.	US	FraudSe	318
March 6, 2009	Bottle Domains	AU	Hack	60,000
March 6, 2009	Federal Emergency Management Agency	US	Stolen Laptop	50
March 6, 2009	Idaho National Laboratory	US	Snail Mail	59,000
March 6, 2009	New York City Office of Payroll Administration	US	Lost Document	3,470
March 8, 2009	New Forest District Council	GB	web	2,000
March 8, 2009	DeZonia Group, Inc.	US	Stolen Computer	Unknown
March 9, 2009	Sonoma County Sheriff	US	Stolen Laptop	1,000
March 9, 2009	Pentel of America Ltd	US	Hack/Web	2,076
March 11, 2009	Gwent Police	GB	Lost Media	2,300
March 11, 2009	Coleman for Senate	US	web	4,716
March 12, 2009	Wiltshire County Council	GB	web	146
March 16, 2009	University of Toledo	US	Stolen Computer	24,450
March 17, 2009	Shell Oil	NZ	Hack/Web	5,900
March 17, 2009	Penn State University	US	Virus	1,000
March 18, 2009	Central Ohio Transit Authority	US	Unknown	900
March 18, 2009	University of West Georgia	IT	Stolen Laptop	1,300
March 18, 2009	Walgreens	US	Email	28,000
March 18, 2009	New York City Housing Authority	US	Disposal_Document	Unknown
March 18, 2009	Huron University College	CA	Hack	25,000
March 19, 2009	Metropolitan Nashville Public Schools	US	Disposal_Document	21
March 20, 2009	Suffolk Coastal District Council	GB	Stolen Laptop	3,000
March 21, 2009	Solano Community College	US	Disposal_Document	Unknown

TABLE 8C.1. (Continued)

Date	Name	Country	BreachType	Records Affected
March 24, 2009	Massachusetts General Hospital	US	Lost Document	66
March 30, 2009	Sprint Nextel	US	FraudSe	Unknown
March 31, 2009	Palo Alto Medical Foundation	US	Stolen Laptop	1,000
April 1, 2009	State of Maryland	US	Snail Mail	8,000
April 1, 2009	Massey University	NZ	web	200
April 1, 2009	University of Washington	US	Hack	6,000
April 2, 2009	Wigan Borough Council	GB	Stolen Laptop	33,000
April 2, 2009	Fujitsu Consulting Inc.	US	Snail Mail	3,410
April 3, 2009	Town of Culpeper	US	web	7,845
April 3, 2009	Policy Studies, Inc	US	FraudSe	1,600
April 7, 2009	Richmond Dermatology Specialists, PC	US	Disposal_Document	Unknown
April 8, 2009	Hawaii Department of Transportation	US	Stolen Laptop	1,892
April 8, 2009	Metropolitan Nashville Public Schools	US	web	18,000
April 8, 2009	Northeast Rehabilitation Hospital	US	Stolen Laptop	Unknown
April 9, 2009	North Carolina Department of Motor Vehicles	US	Unknown	13
April 9, 2009	Fox Entertainment Group	US	FraudSe	Unknown
April 9, 2009	Inct Interactive	US	Hack	9,561
April 10, 2009	Vavrinek, Trine, Day and Co.	US	Stolen Laptop	Unknown
April 10, 2009	Penn State Erie, The Behrend College	US	Virus	10,868
April 10, 2009	Gexa Energy	US	Hack	Unknown
April 10, 2009	Oklahoma Employment Security Commission	US	Stolen Drive	5,534
April 11, 2009	Peninsula Orthopaedic Associates	US	Stolen Tape	100,000
April 12, 2009	CBIZ Medical Management Professionals	US	Stolen Computer	Unknown
April 13, 2009	VHA Inc.	US	Stolen Laptop	14,380
April 21, 2009	FairPoint Communications	US	Lost Media	4,400
April 22, 2009	Marian Medical Center	US	Stolen Media	3,200
April 23, 2009	Aberdeen Royal Infirmary	GB	Stolen Laptop	1,392
April 23, 2009	Oklahoma Department of Human Services	US	Stolen Laptop	1,000,000
April 24, 2009	Warrior Express	US	Disposal_Document	Unknown
April 28, 2009	Centaurus Financial	US	Hack	1,400
April 29, 2009	Bradford Teaching Hospital NHS Foundation Trust	GB	Lost Media	5,650
April 29, 2009	Addenbrooks Hospital	GB	Lost Media	741
April 29, 2009	West Virginia State Bar	US	Hack/Web	Unknown
April 29, 2009	Illinois Department on Aging	US	web	170
April 30, 2009	Oklahoma Housing Finance Agency	US	Stolen Laptop	225,000
April 30, 2009	Brooke Auto Insurance Company	US	Disposal_Document	Unknown

Source: Courtesy of Open Security Foundation / DataLossDB.org.

CHAPTER 9

IDENTIFYING ASSETS AND ORGANIZATION RISK EXPOSURES

At this juncture in the risk management program, a risk management team will have been deployed and is assumed to start its work. Naturally, no organizational environment is ever a complete "Greenfield" situation where work starts at "Square 1"; in reality, some of the risk management efforts may have been done over time, but perhaps in a piecemeal fashion. This chapter covers three process blocks (see Figure 9.1): (i) identification of business-critical assets and assignment of value, (ii) identification of risk exposures (risk identification), and (iii) assessment of severity of risk exposures (risk assessment) and prioritization of risk exposures to be remediated.

The following is a checklist of activities:

- ✔ Importance of asset identification and management
- ✔ Enterprise architecture
- ✔ Types of critical assets
- ✔ Asset ownership
- ✔ Process for asset information updates
- ✔ Vulnerability identification/classification
- ✔ Threat analysis
- ✔ Type of risk exposures
  - Foreseeable risk exposures
  - Unforeseeable risk exposures
  - Internal team programs (to uncover risk exposures)

9.1 IMPORTANCE OF ASSET IDENTIFICATION AND MANAGEMENT

The importance of asset management cannot be understated, nor can the relationship and impact that it has on risk management. It is well documented

Information Technology Risk Management in Enterprise Environments: A Review of Industry Practices and a Practial Guide to Risk Management Teams, by Jake Kouns and Daniel Minoli
Copyright © 2010 John Wiley & Sons, Inc.

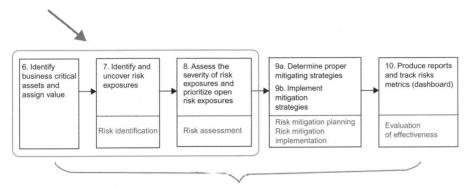

Five basic steps for ongoing risk management for an organization

FIGURE 9.1. Risk management process steps covered in Chapter 9.

and an obvious statement that in order to understand how to protect something, one must first define what an organization has to protect. It is critical that the business side of the organization is part of the process, and this cannot be an IT only function. The business needs to identify the functions (processes and technology) that are required to operate the business. Once we are able to identify the critical business applications, we are then able to prioritize the approach and risk management: this will be discussed later in this chapter. At a high level, it is important that one understand the basic premise that it is possible that one could spend hours and a great deal of resources assessing the risk on a particular asset and then come to find out that it is of little importance.

Proper asset identification and management is one of the most important steps; but in most organizations, information security and risk management professionals tend to overlook this and in fact spend the least amount of time. Unfortunately, even if the importance is understood by an organization, actually implementing an IT asset management program has not typically been an easy task. Getting the business to clearly define what are their most important assets and the value to the organization can be almost impossible. If this portion of the process works, the next hurdle is ensuring that IT Security practitioners are able to overcome their challenges as well. Many security practitioners, depending on past experience, find it difficult to make recommendations that are tailored to the value of specific assets. Security policies and standards are typically defined on purpose to be something that can be either implemented or not. Given this nature, security recommendations can be extremely black or white. To a security practitioner, it is either secure or not. Officers and managers may struggle with the question of "how much security is enough?" Since this question can be a challenge to answer, security practitioners will tend to push to implement more than typically required to protect the asset, including implementing all best practice security standards. Proper understanding of assets is the core of risk management.

There are some clear-cut situations that will require specific compliance and security implementations such as dealing with the protection of credit card information under PCI/DSS as referred to in Appendix 7A.3. There are other controls that are required that will be easy to evaluate such as when dealing with medical information such as HIPAA or Social Security Numbers. It may also even be clear for many organizations when dealing with critical business plans and strategy or protecting the patent information for a product.

9.2 ENTERPRISE ARCHITECTURE

We introduced briefly the concept of enterprise architecture (EA) in Chapter 2. A number of firms have deployed some sort of enterprise architecture framework (AF) that typically provides a layered organized view of the IT assets. Each of these layers needs to be protected. Layered frameworks and models for enterprise architecture have proven useful because layering has the advantage of defining contained, nonoverlapping partitions of the environment. Most frameworks contain four basic domains, as follows: (i) *Business architecture*: documentation that outlines the company's most important business processes; (ii) *Information architecture*: identifies where important blocks of information, such as a customer record, are kept and how one typically accesses them; (iii) *Application system architecture*: a map of the relationships of software applications to one another; and (iv) *Infrastructure technology architecture*: a blueprint for the gamut of hardware, storage systems, and networks. IT assets at all four of these layers can suffer risk exposure and be impacted by threats, vulnerabilities, and risk events. Therefore, IT assets at all four of these layers require risk management.

Next we define a simple enterprise architecture model that we have used in recent years, as depicted in Figure 9.2. This decomposition of the enterprise is modeled after TOGAF and is as follows:

Top Layer

- **Business Function:** A description of the all business elements and structures in that are covered by the enterprise.
- **Business Architecture:** An architectural formulation of the business function.

Next Layer

- **Information Function**: A comprehensive identification of the data, the data flows, and the data interrelations required to support the business function. The identification, systematization, categorization, and inventory/storage of information are always necessary to run a business, but these are essential if the data-handling functions are to be automated.
- **Information Architecture**: An architectural formulation of the information function via a data model.

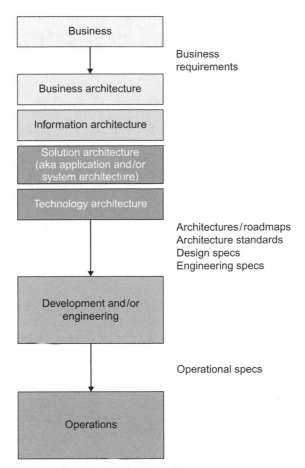

FIGURE 9.2. Enterprise architecture model, also showing architecture artifacts.

Next Layer

- **(Systems/Application) Solution Function**: The function that aims at delivering/supplying computerized IT system(s) required to support the plethora of specific functions needed by the Business function.
- **(Systems/Application) Solution Architecture**: An architectural definition of the (systems/application) solution function.

Bottom Layer

- **Technology Infrastructure Function**: The complete technology environment required to support the information function and the (systems/application) solution function.
- **Technology Infrastructure Architecture**: An architectural formulation (description) of the technology infrastructure function.

These architecture sublayers are clearly related to each other via well-definable relations; integration of these sublayers is a necessity for a cohesive and effective enterprise architecture design. These layers are hierarchical only in the weak sense; hence, they can also be seen as *domain* (rather than layers per se).

Note: Most AFs do not currently address security in an intrinsic manner; therefore, when organizations make use of an AF, the security "architecture" has to be overlaid onto the AF.

Figure 9.3 partitions the IT space from an architectural perspective into logical resources, physical resources, and management resources. Physical resources in the technology layer provide the environment and services for executing applications; these resources encompass platforms (mainframe and mid-range processors) along with hardware and operating systems (OSs) classifications; storage; desktops; and networks (covering eight subcomponents). The operations and management layer is a combination of processes and tools required to support the entire IT environment. It covers detection of faults and outages, configuration, administrative accounting, performance, and security. Figure 9.4 shows how the key components of an architecture-enabled environment relate to each other.

Looking at the top layer (business layer), as mentioned in the previous section, key business processes also need to be protected from risk events. To reduce the risk, the corporate stakeholder needs to have knowledge of the major business processes that use IT assets and of the IT assets themselves. If a threat incapacitated an order processing process, or a payroll process, or a service delivery process, it may be very costly for an organization to recover from the ensuing liabilities. Table 9.1 shows some typical business processes (and example of systems supporting these processes.) Of course, most business processes will be specific to the organization.

The next layer (information layer) encompasses all the data elements of an organization. Data elements may include customers' name, credit card information, business secrets, employee data, inventory information, company secrets, formulas, product specifications, and so on. Clearly, these data need to be protected from risk exposure.

The next layer (information systems layer) covers systems that support the processes of the business function, as well as IT-specific processes. Both the Information systems and the IT processes are generally deemed critical/ essential. For example, if a system (server) supporting a business process such as order processing is incapacitated or degraded, the business process function (in this example, order processing) is also undermined. The same may be true about e-mail, company intranet, central-license office applications such as word processing, financial tools, and so on. Table 9.2 identifies some typical IT processes that require consideration in the context of risk management (recall that we consider a process that either makes use of an IT system, or an IT process itself, also an IT asset).

Finally, the technology layer includes all discrete hardware in the networking, platform (servers and mainframes), and storage systems of the

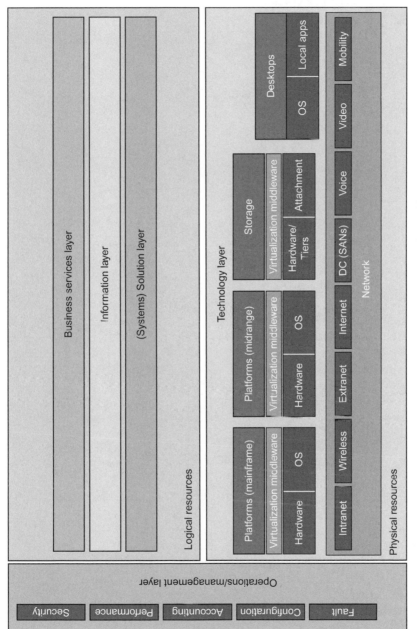

FIGURE 9.3. A layered model of the enterprise architecture.

343

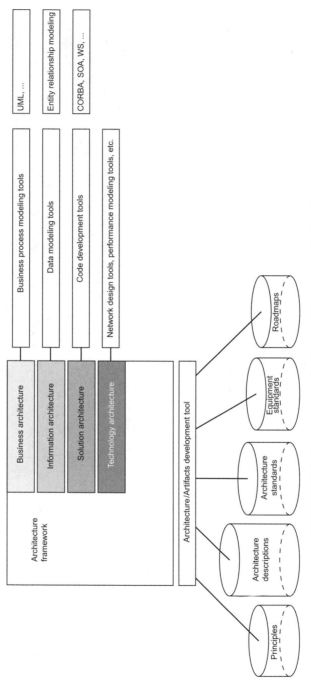

FIGURE 9.4. Key components of an architecture-enabled environment.

TABLE 9.1. Example of Business Processes for a Medium-Size Firm

- Financial system (A/P, billing, general ledger, vendor management, and so on) (e.g., SAP)
- Customer relationship management (CRM) (e.g., Siebel)
- Email and collaborative databases (e.g., Lotus Notes, Outlook)
- Support of mobile email services for all PDA devices (e.g., Blackberry)
- External corporate website
- Payroll system

Note: Different organizations will have their own organization-specific business processes.

organization, such as routers, processors, blade servers, data warehousing systems, and so on. If these elements are compromised, all layers above the technology layer are impacted.

In summary, (virtually) all IT assets deployed by an organization require risk management. An EA (e.g., as illustrated in Figures 9.2–9.4) provides a classification of resources into "affinity classes"[37]; also see Figure 9.5. This classification may assist the organization's information security stakeholders assign responsibility based on subject-matter expertise on a per-layer basis. The use of an organization-wide EA will also reduce the number of discrete technologies/approaches used, thereby decreasing the set of unique capabilities,

---

[37]This is another example of grouping of IT assets into layers, where the upper layers depend on the lower ones [MAR200601]:

Layer 1: **The environment**: assets that are needed to guarantee the following layers:
- Equipment and supplies: power, air-conditioning, communications.
- Personnel: management, operations, development, etc.
- Others: buildings, furniture, etc.

Layer 2: **The information system** itself:
- Computer equipment (hardware)
- Applications (software)
- Communications
- Information media: discs, tapes, etc.

Layer 3: **The information**:
- Data
- Meta-data: structures, indicators, encryption keys, etc.

Layer 4: **The functions of the organization**, which justify the existence of the information system and give it purpose:
- Objectives and mission
- Goods and services produced

Layer 5: **Other** assets:
- Credibility or good image
- Accumulated knowledge
- Independence of criterion or action
- The privacy of persons
- The physical well-being of persons

TABLE 9.2. Typical IT Processes

Manage Infrastructure
- Network infrastructure—care, feed, restore
- Phone service availability
- Network infrastructure configuration

Manage Data
- Data redundancy
- Data sizing and allocation

Ensure Continuous Service
- PC availability
- PC infrastructure configuration

Ensure Systems Security
- Ensure infrastructure security (manage infrastructure, intrusion detection, and so on)
- Update security patches

Manage Service Desk and Incidents
- Service desk incident management

Manage Third-Party Services
- Management of third party (e.g., consultants)
- Renewal process for software and technologies

Manage Performance and Capacity
- Use of performance monitoring tools and measurement of compliance of external vendors
- Analysis of data
- Reporting

tools, and mitigation strategies required. Certainly, one can undertake a network vulnerability assessment (NVA) as some in the industry advocate [PEL200301], but firms are highly encouraged to also take a host vulnerability assessment (HVA), a system vulnerability assessment (SVA), a storage vulnerability assessment (StVA), and so on—in fact, a vulnerability assessment for all the elements contained at all layers of the EA.

9.3   IDENTIFYING IT ASSETS

This portion of the risk management exercise is comprised of two steps:

1. Identify all assets
2. Assign value to the asset

The first activity is known formally as IT asset management (ITAM). Generally, IT assets are classified as

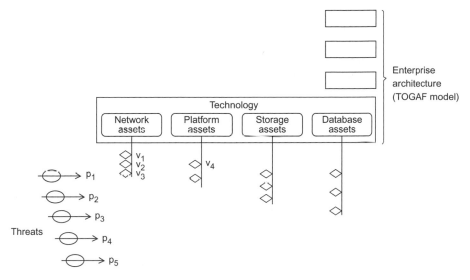

p_i = probability threat i is launched against enterprise v_i = Vulnerability i

FIGURE 9.5. Assets as components of an architecture-enabled environment.

- Physical assets (including hardware)
- Logical assets (including software and data)
- Services (e.g., ability to operate a certain business process)
- Intangible assets (e.g., reputation, brand)
- Human assets (knowledgeable staffers)

Assets of interest clearly include systems, networks, applications, and business data. Appendix 9A provides an example of an asset inventory. Additional considerations related to assets include: the complexity of the technology used in the construction of the asset; the level to which information relating to the technology is public; and the life expectancy of the asset [ETSI200301].

Unless the company already has an asset management system, the risk management team may find that asset data are spread across multiple departments and sources. The team may need to aggregate and analyze, data from purchasing, finance, IT, facilities, security, operations, and others sources. They may find data in spreadsheets, financial systems, text documents, or schematics. At least some portion of the asset identification phase may possibly be automated. Two types of automated tools exist, at least for the asset identification portion of the "value assignment" exercise [WAL200001]:

- **Asset Tracking Tools** ("Auto-discovery" Tools). Software systems that gather data about IT assets over the intranet. The tool can discover data about the desktop itself, as well as data about the software installed on the desktop. The emphasis of tracking tools is on getting "live" data from the enterprise in order to have the timeliest information about the state of the infrastructure.

- **Asset Repository Tools.** A database tool that unifies asset data including, but not limited to, ownership, location, version, serial numbers, and so on. The emphasis of repository tools is on statically defining what the enterprise should be and on serving as a point of reference against the tracking tool's "live" data to identify deviance from standard.

These tools enable the organization to optimize service and asset costs, mitigate security and compliance risks, and increase efficiency and effectiveness. Asset management facilitates the following tasks, among others:

- Inventory control
- Total cost of ownership management
- Software license compliance
- Operational monitoring and control
- Decision-making about IT resource deployment, including risk management and business continuity/disaster recovery planning
- Rapid new employee provisioning
- Standardization and compliance

Tools range from open-source freely available software to high-end systems that optimize asset tracking by consolidating assets and each configuration item into a central repository—for example, an ITIL (IT Infrastructure Library)-based configuration management database (CMDB). There are several tools available, but one illustrative example of such a tool is HP AssetCenter. HP AssetCenter goes beyond asset tracking by providing complete and fully integrated life-cycle IT asset management, following ITIL best practices[38] and empowered by configuration management capabilities that establish a CMDB. AssetCenter drives IT operations and decision-making by doing the following [HP200901]:

Optimizing Service and Asset Costs

- Effectively manages contracts, leases, license agreements, and warranties
- Avoids potential penalties by using license management automation
- Extends hardware life cycles
- Completes asset and project expense audit tracking
- Enables fixed asset and invoice reconciliation

---

[38]IT Infrastructure Library (ITIL) is a set of best practices with its roots in the 1980s in British Civil Service; more recently it has flourished in other world regions as the most visible resource for best practices in what it defines as IT Service Management (ITSM). ITIL 3.0 includes service life-cycle management, which provides recommendations for processes and enabling technologies for managing IT services throughout their life cycle from inception to retirement [ENT200701].

Mitigating Security and Compliance Risk

- Quantifies and measures financial compliance risks of IT infrastructure
- Prepares for software audits by using standards and automated processes
- Enforces software and hardware standards to improve system security and continuity
- Builds baseline for physical security

The press-time trend for ITAM is an evolution toward a more cohesive, dynamic, and integrated functionality closely aligned to service management, change management, and capacity planning, in an effort to recognize that asset investments as dynamic contributors rather than merely passive objects to be managed according to traditional mechanisms [ENT200701].

Table 9.3 provides a press time listing of asset management software. These systems typically support facility, IT asset management and automated maintenance management. These tools variably embody a number of functions such as

- Hardware and software inventory and asset tracking
- Control of IT infrastructure by monitoring all IT assets across the firm
- Integrated solution enabling IT staff to deploy software and track hardware and software configurations
- Customizable Web-based asset management solution
- Combined enterprise asset database and service management capabilities into a single Web-based architecture
- Support of asset, inventory, depreciation and PC audit tracking
- PC life-cycle management, to deploy, update, and manage software and/or security
- Enterprise asset and maintenance management tools with ITIL-based help desk incorporating customer, contract, and queue management
- Support of maintenance, purchasing and inventory functions
- Discovery, inventory, usage, software license compliance and life-cycle management
- Ability to automate the process of proving compliance

Once assets are identified, it is important that an organization has a process to ensure that they are continually updated. Certainly, automated tools facilitate this process. This includes the process of adding and removing assets as well as reevaluating the value as required. To ensure that this happens, an organization must define asset ownership, and the implementation of a data governance or data stewardship program can enable this to happen. Data governance is a topic that is now getting a large amount of coverage and is considered important to information technology organizations. If one does not have clear ownership of

TABLE 9.3. Press-Time List of Asset Tracking Software

Absolute Software
Accuware
AdventNet
Airframe Business Software
Aleier
AlphaPoint Technology
Altiris
Applied Innovation Management
Apptio
Asentrix Systems
AssetSmart
Attachmate
Automation Centre
Avantis
Avexus
BDNA
Black Duck
Blue Mountain Quality Resources
BMC Remedy
BMC Service Desk Express
Centennial Software
Centromeric
Clear Rock
Codima
Cogep
Compco
Computerized Inventory Systems Specialists
Corrigo
CrossTec
Crow Canyon Software
CWorks Systems
DataSplice
Dell
Dot Com Infoway
Dynaprice.com
E-Innovative Services Group
eam2go
Eden Communications
eMaint Enterprises
ePlus
Eracent

TABLE 9.3. (Continued)

eTeklogics
Everdream
Express Metrix
FasTrak SoftWorks
fixIQ
Fluensee
Fractal Solutions
FrontRange Solutions
Great Lakes Software
Hardcat
HP AssetCenter
IBM
Indus International
Infor
infraWise
Innovation Asset Group
InQuest Technologies
INSYSTEK
Intasoft
Intelliset
Kwok Systems
LANDesk Software
Liberty Street Software
LicenseWatch
Lime Software
Link It Software
Mainsaver Software
ManageSoft
MIS Utilities
MSoft eSolutions
Nero Global Tracking
NetFuzion
NetSupport
Novell
Novo Solutions
Numara Software
Oracle
Paradigm Business Systems
Paradigm Designs Software
PMI Software

TABLE 9.3. (Continued)

PS'Soft
PurchasingNet
QMS Software
Real Asset Management
RedBeam
RevelationData
SAManage
Sassafras Software
SchoolDude.com
ScienceLogic
SeeControl
Sightwave
SingleTusk Solutions
Smartpath
SolveDirect
Spiceworks
Sunflower Systems
Technology Management Solutions
TEKLYNX
Third City Solutions
Tideway
UTS Global
Valogix
Vector Networks
Velocity Integrations Software
Verian Technologies
Verifichi
Wasp Barcode Technologies
WiseTrack Software
xAssets

assets within an organization it becomes very challenging to determine what levels of control should be placed on those assets even with a proper risk management committee implemented as discussed in Chapter 7. In many cases the business themselves or the business practice and practitioners themselves do not understand the value of the assets in which they work with on a daily basis. The concept of data governance ensures that management has clear ownership of assets and must provide controls at all levels of the organization.

- Data stewards provide approval to those needing to access the data.
- Data stewards are responsible for updating the value of data.

9.4 ASSIGNING VALUE TO IT ASSETS

After having developed an inventory of assets, the next step is assigning a value to the assets. Unfortunately, according to observers organizations generally do not know nor measure the value of their IT assets (and, in turn, the contribution those assets make to the business). A recent study by Micro Focus found that[39] [MIC200701]

- Less than half of CIOs and CFOs ever try to quantify the financial value of their IT assets.
- Nearly two-thirds (60%) do not know the size of their core software assets.
- One-third do not know what they spend on their software assets.
- More than half (56%) think the real financial value of core software assets is ignored or poorly evaluated compared against brand, property, and intellectual property values.

Obviously this predicament is not conducive to proper risk management.

Some of the factors to consider when determining an IT asset's value include [WIT200401]

- Original development costs, licensing, infrastructure, and other standard tangible costs
- Costs to replace, acquire, or reengineer the asset
- Operational costs to support and execute the asset
- Business value retained by the successful operation of the asset
- Costs related to the operational impact when the asset is unavailable
- Value of the asset to the competition
- Value of the intellectual property associated with the asset
- Litigation costs associated with the unavailability of the asset
- Loss of competitive advantage, sales, goodwill, and market share due to asset unavailability
- What is the value if a system supported legacy components in other operational systems?

---

[39]Results of research carried out amongst CIOs and CFOs across five countries (France, Germany, Italy, United Kingdom, and United States) highlight how the size and value of IT assets are being ignored by the world's leading companies, compared to other regularly measured corporate assets such as cash, brand, property, and intellectual property. Micro Focus research, carried out in companies with revenues from $100M up to over $1B, shows that less than half of all CIOs & CFOs (48%) ever try to quantify the financial value of their IT assets. Only 37% of CIOs have tried, compared to 60% of finance heads. Less than one-third of all respondents (29%) from both groups ever try to quantify the contribution that all their IT assets make to the business' performance. The research found that nearly two-thirds (60%) of CFOs and CIOs do not know the size of their core software assets, whereas one-third (29%) do not know what they spend on their core software assets each year. Even more concerning is that this figure comprises one-third (29%) of finance heads [MIC200701].

Identifying and defining the potential value loss of each exposure is a basic step in security risk analysis; this starts with the assessment of the asset's value. We discussed in earlier chapters that $V(A_i) = \beta \times K(A_i)$ for some unbounded β, $0 < \beta < \infty$, where $K(A_i)$ is the cost of asset A_i. Intrinsic asset costs include acquisition, maintenance, and replacement/retirement costs, as follows [PAR200801]:

- *Initial acquisition costs*, including asset purchase, required peripheral or supporting devices, operating system and software, and service contracts. These data will generally be obtained from purchase orders; some of these data may need to be calculated as a pro-rata share of a bulk purchase or license agreement.
- *Ongoing maintenance costs*, including annual service contracts, upgrade or replacement parts, and the costs associated with service desk incidents for each device. Ideally this information is collected at the time of purchase/ service and is immediately attached to the asset's service history record.
- *Replacement costs* for hardware, software, and infrastructure elements. One also needs to include both disposal costs for existing assets and install/ deployment costs for new assets. For commodity items such as end-user hardware (desktop, laptop) and software, these costs should be predictable within a range and will tend to be updated once a year as new contracts are negotiated. For high-impact or high-value items the cost of purchase may only be a small part of the total costs, and those costs may be difficult to estimate.

If the organization has conducted work in the area of business continuity, it is advised to review the material produced. A properly conducted business impact analysis (BIA) can provide detailed insight into the values of assets. While this is out of scope for this book, the reader is suggested to research the topic further.

9.5 VULNERABILITY IDENTIFICATION/CLASSIFICATION

As we noted in Chapter 2, a vulnerability is a weakness in a system that can potentially be exploited by an attacker, and a threat is an exogenous (inimical) action that has a probability > 0 of causing damage to an asset; a threat is any potential danger to information or the systems in the environment. The risk presented by that vulnerability is based on the likelihood that an attacker will take advantage of that vulnerability. This requires both a vulnerability analysis and a threat analysis. As we noted in Chapter 1, the number of entry points into the intranet is increasing due to factors such as technologies such as Wireless and Bluetooth, the use of e-commerce technologies, the use of Web Services and/or cloud computing, IPv6, and worker mobility (where users may use a laptop outside the perimeter, thereby allowing access to the laptop's

C-drive and/or reinjecting a virus/Trojan when the laptop rejoins the corporate network).

A vulnerability analysis (also called vulnerability assessment) is a detailed study of the security infrastructure of an organization's systems. It covers every piece of the information systems infrastructure in order to provide a comprehensive and consistent evaluation of the current state of the information security environment. A vulnerability assessment covers every IT asset of an organization: from a user workstation to the operating systems, databases, firewalls, and Internet routers. Automated tools are generally used to assist in the evaluation process [ENT 200901].

Some of the techniques used for penetration testing in support of a vulnerability analysis include network penetration tests, application penetration tests, and social engineering tests [ENT200901]:

- Network penetration tests can be external or internal. An external penetration test seeks to establish the security posture of the firm's systems that are accessible over the Internet, while an internal penetration test simulates attacks that may arise from the inside (e.g., a disgruntled employee, a naive/untrained user causing involuntary problems, or an attacker who has been able to bypass perimeter defenses). Some of the techniques that can be used to provide a comprehensive security assessment include war-dialing, war-driving, and Blue-Snarfing [ENT200901]. War-dialing penetration testing simulates the methods used by a hacker to potentially identify phone numbers that can successfully connect to a modem. Bluetooth Discovery and Blue-Snarfing penetration testing represent methods of evaluating Bluetooth devices, including cell phones and PDAs; these are important because of the sensitive information that they contain. War-driving penetration testing is the process of discovering wireless access (Wi-Fi) points to the firm's intranet and rouge devices.
- Application penetration tests aim at testing the security of standalone and web-based applications, specifically to identify vulnerabilities such as flow injections, buffer overflows, and cross-site scripting. It can also be used to detect issues such as improper error handling, insecure configuration management, credential pre-detection, and file path abuse.
- Social engineering tests aim at discovering weaknesses related to the human aspect of IT, which is often the weakest link in a security infrastructure. Rather than performing a sophisticated technical analysis, a potential attacker could simply convince employees through e-mails or telephone conversations to find out, for example, what applications are being used, the naming scheme for users, and so on.

Vulnerability analysis and assessment entail developing a comprehensive list of all known vulnerabilities that can be used against those assets that require some level of protection [CAR200901]. There are tools that can be used to determine what some of the vulnerabilities are; however, these tools provide an incomplete picture at best. For example, there are software diagnostic systems that provide a server scanning service that can test a server's operating software, its operating system, database system, web server software, and other middleware for known system vulnerabilities. Also, as noted in previous chapters, there are several vulnerability alert subscription services available, including but not limited to

- IBM Internet Security Systems X-Force
- National Vulnerability Database (NVD)
- Open Source Vulnerability Database (OSVDB)
- Secunia
- Security Focus Bugtraq
- Security Tracker
- Verizon's Risk Intelligence Security Solutions

In addition to becoming aware of what general and/or possibly relevant vulnerabilities are described in the open "press" and/or industry (e.g., Internet Explorer Version x has vulnerability y and z), a firm needs to become cognizant, at every point in time, about the company-specific vulnerabilities. Among other techniques to assess these, vulnerability identification studies can make use of footprinting, scanning, and enumeration.

- *Footprinting* is the method of indirect probing (interrogating) hosts on the Internet for information about a firm's systems, without actually *touching* them. If a firm undertook this on its own behalf, it would be able to discover what a potential attacker can also discover without the firm's knowledge.
- *Scanning* is the method of interrogating a firm's systems for available services, resource sharing, software version information, user account information, and other exploitable conditions. Specifically, port scanning is the process of testing some, or all, of the Transmission Control Protocol (TCP) and User Datagram Protocol (UDP) ports to determine which are open and what services are being provided through those open ports. A port is, in effect, a "door" into a computer. On the outside of the port is the network that the host is connected to; on the inside of the port there is a program monitoring that port and (generally) ready to respond by providing its specific service. There are 65,535 possible TCP ports and 65,535 UDP ports. The first 1023 ports are considered well known, meaning that there is general agreement on which services will be provided through which ports (e.g., web servers provide their service through TCP Port 80, DNS servers through UDP Port 53 and TCP Port 53). If a port has a program actively monitoring, then that port is considered open, otherwise it is considered closed. Penetration testing provides an assessment of exposures to both internal and external intrusions; tests typically include

- Network penetration tests
- Application penetration tests
- Social engineering tests
- *Enumeration* is the method where a firm directly interrogates its own systems searching for the detailed data and information that an intruder would be able use to perpetrate an attack.

Broadband access to the Internet has facilitated the deployment of mobile endpoints making Internet connections with no intervening enterprise-level firewalls and security policies to mediate access; these devices can pose a potential threat to enterprise IT assets when the devices reconnect to the corporate network. Another area of possible concern is the area of "cloud computing", now receiving some attention in the industry. IT areas and technologies that should be investigated to determine what vulnerabilities may be particularly applicable include but are not limited to [DRO200901]

- HTTP and HTML
  - HTTP traffic analysis
  - HTTP message
  - OPTIONS and TRACE
  - Forms and frames security
  - JavaScript and the DOM
  - Dynamic HTML
- Cross-Site Request Forgeries (CSRF)
  - CSRF in a GET request
  - GET CSRF
  - POST to GET
  - CSRF in a POST
  - POST CSRF
- SQL Injection
  - SQL syntax
  - SQL SELECT
  - Accessing data
  - SQL injection
  - Bypassing authentication
  - Discovery and prevention
- Web Applications
  - web servers
  - web application servers
  - Frameworks

- Databases securing
- Database connections
- web services, SOAP, XML
- Web 2.0 Security
  - MySpace Worm
  - AJAX Security
  - Adobe Flash/Flex
  - Client reverse engineering
  - Mash up security
  - Securing web services
  - SOAP SQL injection
- Authorization
  - Authorization failures
  - Forceful browsing
  - Parameter manipulation
  - Authorization enforcement
- Cross-Site Scripting
  - Stored XSS
  - Reflected XSS
  - DOM-based XSS
  - XSS Impact
  - Discovery and prevention
- Session Management
  - Cookies and flags
  - Cookie eavesdropping
  - Predicting session IDs
  - Session case studies
  - Leaking session IDs
- Input Handling
  - Input validation
  - White versus black list
  - Encodings
  - Input versus output encoding
  - Dark side of encoding
- Data from the Client, Partners, and Vendor
  - Hidden field tampering
  - web developer extension
  - Hidden field tampering
  - Bypassing client controls

- Other Vulnerabilities
  - Header injection
  - Malicious file execution
  - URL redirection
  - Cache control
  - Content type
  - Denial of service
  - Command injection
  - Buffer overflows
  - Cloud computing
- Networks
  - Intranet
  - Extranet
  - Wireless networks (WiFi)
  - Personal area networks (PANs, such as Bluetooth, ZigBee)
  - 3G/4G Cellular/mobile e-mail (e.g., WiMAX, LTE)
  - Voice networks
  - Video/videoconferencing networks

There may be a variety of issues to consider; these issues arise not only from the sheer number of vulnerabilities for a given system (e.g., Outlook, Internet Explorer, and so on), but also because many firms may allow non-standard devices to be used. These non-standard devices may not get the full attention of IT, thereby proving a possible access path for an intruder (an intruder may seek the weakest link to penetrate). For example, a firm may have 20,000 PCs operating under Microsoft Windows, but the graphics department may opt to use 100 Macs. These 100 devices may not get the same level of IT attention from a security perspective and thus may become a weak link in the chain.

There is interest in being able to get some sort of analytical measure of vulnerability severity. At press time most software vendors released security vulnerabilities in their products with their own severity ratings. Considering that organizations have numerous software packages, this makes it very difficult for a risk management team to correlate across difference assets. The Common Vulnerability Scoring System (CVSS) is a vendor-neutral, industry standard that conveys vulnerability severity and helps determine urgency and priority of response, developed by the National Infrastructure Advisory Council (NIAC). It solves the problem of multiple, incompatible scoring systems and is usable and understandable by anyone. CVSS is currently maintained by the Forum of Incident Response and Security Teams (FIRST) and was a combined effort involving organizations such as, but not limited to, CERT/CC, Cisco Systems, DHS/MITRE, eBay, Microsoft, and Symantec. The CVSS model is designed to provide end users with an overall composite score representing the severity and risk of a vulnerability. It is derived from metrics and formulas. The metrics are in three distinct categories that can be quantitatively or qualitatively measured. Base metrics contain qualities that are intrinsic to any given vulnerability; these qualities do not change over time or in different environments. Temporal metrics contain characteristics of a vulnerability that evolve over the lifetime of the vulnerability. Environmental metrics contain characteristics of a vulnerability that are related to an implementation in a specific user's environment [CIS200901].

The parameterizations that follow are used to calculate a specific threat/vulnerability's CVSS score. There are three sets of parameters: base parameters, temporal parameters, and environmental parameters.

9.5.1   Base Parameters

Once discovered, analyzed, and catalogued, there are certain aspects of a vulnerability that do not change, assuming the initial information is complete and correct. These immutable characteristics will not change over time, nor in different environments. The base metric group captures the access to and impact on the target.

Access Vector

Local (L). A vulnerability exploitable with only local access requires the attacker to have either physical access to the vulnerable system or a local (shell) account. Examples of locally exploitable vulnerabilities are peripheral attacks such as Firewire/USB DMA attacks, and local privilege escalations.

Adjacent Network (A). A vulnerability exploitable with adjacent network access requires the attacker to have access to either the broadcast or collision domain of the vulnerable software. Examples of local networks include local IP subnet, Bluetooth, IEEE 802.11, and local Ethernet segment.

Network (N). A vulnerability exploitable with network access means that the vulnerable software is bound to the network stack and the attacker does not require local network access or local access. Such a vulnerability is often termed "remotely exploitable." An example of a network attack is an RPC buffer overflow.

Access Complexity

High (H). Specialized access conditions exist. For example: In most configurations, the attacking party must already have elevated privileges or spoof additional systems in addition to the attacking system (e.g., DNS hijacking). The attack depends on social engineering methods that would be easily detected by knowledgeable people. For example, the victim must perform several suspicious or atypical actions. The vulnerable configuration is seen very rarely in practice. If a race condition exists, the window is very narrow.

Medium (M). The access conditions are somewhat specialized; the following are examples: The attacking party is limited to a group of systems or users at some level of authorization, possibly untrusted. Some information must be gathered before a successful attack can be launched. The affected configuration is non-default and is not commonly configured (e.g., a vulnerability present when a server performs user account authentication via a specific scheme, but not present for another authentication scheme). The attack requires a small amount of social engineering that might occasionally fool cautious users (e.g., phishing attacks that modify a web browser's status bar to show a false link, having to be on someone's "buddy" list before sending an IM exploit).

Low (L). Specialized access conditions or extenuating circumstances do not exist. The following are examples: The affected product typically requires access to a wide range of systems and users, possibly anonymous and untrusted (e.g., Internet-facing web or mail server). The affected configuration is default or ubiquitous. The attack can be performed manually and requires little skill or additional information gathering. The "race condition" is a lazy one (i.e., it is technically a race but easily winnable).

Authentication

Multiple (M). Exploiting the vulnerability requires that the attacker authenticate two or more times, even if the same credentials are used each time. An example is an attacker authenticating to an operating system in addition to providing credentials to access an application hosted on that system.

Single (S). The vulnerability requires an attacker to be logged into the system (such as at a command line or via a desktop session or web interface).

None (N). Authentication is not required to exploit the vulnerability.

Confidentiality Impact

None (N). There is no impact to the confidentiality of the system.

Partial (P). There is considerable informational disclosure. Access to some system files is possible, but the attacker does not have control over what is obtained, or the scope of the loss is constrained. An example is a vulnerability that divulges only certain tables in a database.

Complete (C). There is total information disclosure, resulting in all system files being revealed. The attacker is able to read all of the system's data (memory, files, etc.)

Integrity Impact

None (N). There is no impact to the integrity of the system.

Partial (P). Modification of some system files or information is possible, but the attacker does not have control over what can be modified, or the scope of what the attacker can affect is limited. For example, system or application files may be overwritten or modified, but either the attacker has no control over which files are affected or the attacker can modify files within only a limited context or scope.

Complete (C). There is a total compromise of system integrity. There is a complete loss of system protection, resulting in the entire system being compromised. The attacker is able to modify any files on the target system.

Availability Impact

None (N). There is no impact to the availability of the system.

Partial (P). There is reduced performance or interruptions in resource availability. An example is a network-based flood attack that permits a limited number of successful connections to an Internet service.

Complete (C). There is a total shutdown of the affected resource. The attacker can render the resource completely unavailable.

9.5.2 Temporal Parameters

As a vulnerability ages, certain intrinsic characteristics will change with time. In many cases, when a vulnerability is first discovered, the number of vulnerable systems will be at or close to its peak, while the availability of exploit and remedial information will be at its lowest point. As time progresses, patch information will become more available and more systems will be fixed as more exploits occur, driving the need for the fix. Eventually, the number of vulnerable systems will reach its low point as remedial information reaches its high point. The CVSS temporal metrics group captures these characteristics of a vulnerability that change over time.

Exploitability

Unproven (U). No exploit code is available, or an exploit is entirely theoretical.

Proof-of-Concept (POC). Proof-of-concept exploit code or an attack demonstration that is not practical for most systems is available. The code or technique is not functional in all situations and may require substantial modification by a skilled attacker.

Functional (F). Functional exploit code is available. The code works in most situations where the vulnerability exists.

High (H). Either the vulnerability is exploitable by functional mobile autonomous code, or no exploit is required (manual trigger) and details are widely available. The code works in every situation, or is actively being delivered via a mobile autonomous agent (such as a worm or virus).

Not Defined (ND). Assigning this value to the metric will not influence the score. It is a signal to the equation to skip this metric.

Remediation Level

Official Fix (OF). A complete vendor solution is available. Either the vendor has issued an official patch, or an upgrade is available.

Temporary Fix (TF). There is an official but temporary fix available. This includes instances where the vendor issues a temporary hotfix, tool, or workaround.

Workaround (W). There is an unofficial, non-vendor solution available. In some cases, users of the affected technology will create a patch of their own or provide steps to work around or otherwise mitigate the vulnerability.

Unavailable (U). There is either no solution available or it is impossible to apply.

Not Defined (ND). Assigning this value to the metric will not influence the score. It is a signal to the equation to skip this metric.

Report Confidence

Unconfirmed (UC). There is a single unconfirmed source or possibly multiple conflicting reports. There is little confidence in the validity of the reports. An example is a rumor that surfaces from the hacker underground.

Uncorroborated (UR). There are multiple non-official sources, possibly including independent security companies or research organizations. At this point there may be conflicting technical details or some other lingering ambiguity.

Confirmed (C). The vulnerability has been acknowledged by the vendor or author of the affected technology. The vulnerability may also be "confirmed" when its existence is confirmed from an external event such as publication of functional or proof-of-concept exploit code or widespread exploitation.

Not Defined (ND). Assigning this value to the metric will not influence the score. It is a signal to the equation to skip this metric.

9.5.3 Environmental Parameters

Different user environments can have an immense bearing on how (or if) a vulnerability affects a given information system and its stakeholders. The CVSS environmental metrics group captures characteristics of vulnerabilities that are tied to system distribution and network environment.

Collateral Damage Potential

None (N). There is no potential for loss of life, physical assets, productivity, or revenue.

Low (L). A successful exploit of this vulnerability may result in slight physical or property damage. Or, there may be a slight loss of revenue or productivity to the organization.

Low-Medium (LM). A successful exploit of this vulnerability may result in moderate physical or property damage. Or, there may be a moderate loss of revenue or productivity to the organization.

Medium-High (MH). A successful exploit of this vulnerability may result in significant physical or property damage or loss. Or, there may be a significant loss of revenue or productivity.

High (H). A successful exploit of this vulnerability may result in catastrophic physical or property damage and loss. Or, there may be a catastrophic loss of revenue or productivity.

Not Defined (ND). Assigning this value to the metric will not influence the score. It is a signal to the equation to skip this metric.

Target Distribution

None (N). No target systems exist, or targets are so highly specialized that they only exist in a laboratory setting. Effectively 0% of the environment is at risk.

Low (L). Targets exist inside the environment, but on a small scale. Between 1% and 25% of the total environment is at risk.

Medium (M). Targets exist inside the environment, but on a medium scale. Between 26% and 75% of the total environment is at risk.

High (H). Targets exist inside the environment on a considerable scale. Between 76% and 100% of the total environment is considered at risk.

Not Defined (ND). Assigning this value to the metric will not influence the score. It is a signal to the equation to skip this metric.

Confidentiality Requirement

Low (L). Loss of confidentiality is likely to have only a limited adverse effect on the organization or individuals associated with the organization (e.g., employees, customers).

Medium (M). Loss of confidentiality is likely to have a serious adverse effect on the organization or individuals associated with the organization (e.g., employees, customers).

High (H). Loss of confidentiality is likely to have a catastrophic adverse effect on the organization or individuals associated with the organization (e.g., employees, customers).

Not Defined (ND). Assigning this value to the metric will not influence the score. It is a signal to the equation to skip this metric.

Integrity Requirement

Low (L). Loss of integrity is likely to have only a limited adverse effect on the organization or individuals associated with the organization (e.g., employees, customers).

Medium (M). Loss of integrity is likely to have a serious adverse effect on the organization or individuals associated with the organization (e.g., employees, customers).

High (H). Loss of integrity is likely to have a catastrophic adverse effect on the organization or individuals associated with the organization (e.g., employees, customers).

Not Defined (ND). Assigning this value to the metric will not influence the score. It is a signal to the equation to skip this metric.

Availability Requirement

Low (L). Loss of availability is likely to have only a limited adverse effect on the organization or individuals associated with the organization (e.g., employees, customers).

Medium (M). Loss of availability is likely to have a serious adverse effect on the organization or individuals associated with the organization (e.g., employees, customers).

High (H). Loss of availability is likely to have a catastrophic adverse effect on the organization or individuals associated with the organization (e.g., employees, customers).

Not Defined (ND). Assigning this value to the metric will not influence the score. It is a signal to the equation to skip this metric.

An example of a CVSS evaluation is shown in Figure 9.6

While CVSS has several flaws, it can be useful for when trying to prioritize a large amount of issues such as findings from a network vulnerability scan. However, there also are concerns with CVSS:

- The process by design requires an organization to provide metrics to get the real ratings. Many organizations overlook this set and only use the base scores that are provided.
- Many organizations struggle with using CVSS to convey the issues to an IT organization or the business. For example, the latest Oracle quarterly

Samba unauthorized root file system access vulnerability

Vulnerability alert   Powered by IntelliShield

Threat type:	**Intrusion: Unauthorized access**
IntelliShield ID:	**17348**
Version:	**4**
First published:	**January 05, 2009 02:25 PM EST**
Last published:	**April 03, 2009 05:51 PM EDT**
Vector:	**Network**
Authentication:	**Single**
Exploit:	**Proof-of-concept**
Port:	**Not available**
CVE:	**CVE-2009-0022**
BugTraq ID:	**33118**

Urgency:	**Weakness**	1
Credibility:	**Confirmed**	5
Severity:	**Mild damage**	3
CVSS base:	**6.0**	**CVSS Calculator**
CVSS temporal:	**4.7**	CVSS version 2

Description

Samba versions 3.2.0 through 3.2.6 contain a vulnerability that could allow an authenticated, remote attacker to access files on the root file system.
The vulnerability is due to an error in Samba that allows authenticated users to gain unauthorized access to the root file system of the affected Samba server. The user could exploit the vulnerability to disclose information that should otherwise be restricted.

Proof-of-concept code is publicly available.

Samba confirmed the vulnerability and released updated software.

Warning Indicators

Samba versions 3.2.0 through 3.2.6 are vulnerable if the attacker connects to the share by using a version of the smbclient prior to 3.0.28.

IntelliShield Analysis

To exploit the vulnerability, an attacker must be authenticated. Furthermore, the attacker must connect to the share using an older version of the smbclient. The system must also have registry shares enabled, which includes the following non-default settings:
registry shares = yes
include = registry
config backend = registry

Vendor Announcements

Samba has released a security advisory at the following link: CVE-2009-0022
Mandriva has released a security advisory at the following link: MDVSA-2009:042
Slackware has released a security advisory at the following link: SSA:2009-005-01
Ubuntu has released a security notice at the following link: USN-702-1

Impact

An authenticated, remote attacker could exploit the vulnerability to gain unauthorized access to the root file system of the affected Samba server.

Technical Information

The vulnerability exists when an authenticated user attempts to connect to a share using a version of the smbclient prior to 3.0.28. If the user attempts to connect by using an empty string in the name field, they could gain remote access to the root file system of the affected Samba server.
The registry shares option was a feature that was added to Samba servers in version 3.2.0; this option is disabled in default installations. When a user attempts to connect to a share, the *load_registry_service()* function of source/smbd/service.c compares the supplied name to the available shares. The user-controlled servicename argument that is submitted by the user is compared to the GLOBAL_NAME parameter, and a path is created and sent to the authenticated user. A null servicename argument causes the *load_registry_service()* function to return a path to the root directory, granting the user access to the root file system of the affected Samba server.

Safeguards

Administrators are advised to apply the appropriate updates.
Administrators are advised to restrict access to trusted users.
Administrators may consider disabling registry shares, which is the **registry shares = no** setting.

Patches/Software

Samba has released updated software at the following link: Samba 3.2.7 or later
Mandriva products can be updated automatically using **MandrivaUpdate.**
Slackware packages can be updated using the **upgradepkg command.**
Ubuntu has released updated packages; users can install the updates using **Update Manager.**

FIGURE 9.6. Example of a CVSS evaluation.

critical patches were rated a 4.3. What does a 4.3 mean? What if it was 4.7 or 7.0? Does that change the response the organization should implement?

Organizations should move toward a repeatable process that enables the business to be successful without disruption (or minimize). In some cases, the best approach for example is to implement a monthly or bi-monthly patching program that regardless of the severity of the patches that are released, they are implemented. The complexity associated with implementing a scoring and rating system that matches the organization can in some cases lead a risk management team to create their own internal severity rating.

9.6 THREAT ANALYSIS: TYPE OF RISK EXPOSURES

Next, one wants to looks at threats that may exploit the vulnerabilities identified during the previous step. Threat analysis deals with identifying the source of the threats, determining the types of threats, assessing the threat likelihood (factors affecting threat likelihood), and establishing threat levels.

Threat analysis aims to create a list of known exploits and determine the likelihood of a potential threat arising from each one. An exploit is a means that may be utilized by a threat to make use of a vulnerability in one's environment. A list of the top threat agents in an organization's environment is required to perform a proper threat analysis. A threat agent is the person or process attacking the network through a vulnerable port on the firewall, or a process used to access data in a way that violates your security policy [CAR200901]. As part of this exercise, one can also assess the exposures factor (EF), namely, determining the percentage of asset loss caused by each identified threat.

The risk management process seeks to classify threats depending on their probability (likelihood) of occurrence, their possible impact upon the targeted system, and the infraction costs that they may give rise to. The probability of a threat typically depends on the motivation for an attacker to carry out an attack associated to the threat in relation to the difficulties that must be resolved by the attacker in order to conduct such an attack. The risk associated to a threat is a function of its likelihood and the consequences (loss) on the system if the threat successfully achieves its objective. A threat can be ranked as [ETSI200301]

- Minor when it is unlikely to happen or when its impact is low;
- Major when its likelihood is possible and its impact is medium; or
- Critical when it is likely to happen and its impact either medium or high; or when its likelihood is possible and its impact is high

See Figure 9.7 Figure 9.8 depicts the microcosms of risk exposure and consequences.

Threat modeling is a technique a risk management team can use to identify threats, attacks, vulnerabilities, and countermeasures in the context of a specific application scenario. Threat modeling is performed to identify when and where more effort should be applied. There are many possible vulnerabilities, threats, and exploits; it is unlikely that an application will encounter all of them. It is also unlikely that a company would need to address all of them. Threat modeling helps the risk management team identify where the organization

Risk evaluation function   **Likelihood of a threat**

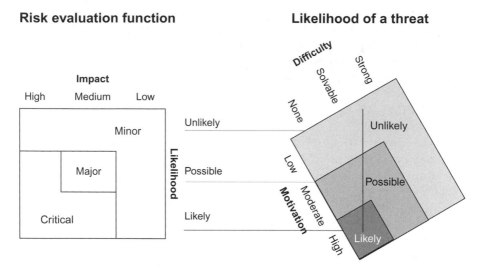

FIGURE 9.7. Dimensions of risk evaluation.

needs to apply effort. In the *patterns & practices* threat modeling approach one incrementally organizes vulnerabilities in a more systematic and repeatable manner [MEI200501]. Two tools can be used for threat modeling, among others: (i) pattern-based information model and (ii) incremental rendering. Pattern-based information modeling allows one to identify the patterns of repeatable problems and solutions and organize them into categories; thereafter one can use these categories for additional analysis to identify vulnerabilities of a given application associated with each category. Incremental rendering makes note of the concept that threat modeling is an iterative process; one iterates by increasing the detail of the model whenever new environmental facts become known, and/or through the application lifetime as (new) uses and configurations of the application appear.

9.6.1   Type of Risk Exposures

Depending upon whom one asks, and as seen in the first section of the book, there can be many different ways to describe what a risk exposure is; perhaps the definition of risk exposure is not properly being used at the firm at this point in time. There are two key risk exposures when you get right down to the practitioners version of risk assessment: (1) foreseeable risk exposures and (2) an unforeseeable risk exposures.

   Foreseeable Risk Exposures. A foreseeable risk exposure is one that the organization is able to plan in advance to handle. This allows the company to make the decision on the risk exposure in a timeline that suits the organization. For example, a project or new product launch

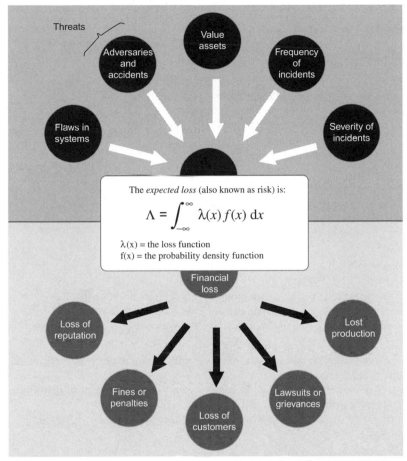

The *expected loss* (also known as risk) is:

$$\Lambda = \int_{-\infty}^{\infty} \lambda(x)\, f(x)\, \mathrm{d}x$$

$\lambda(x)$ = the loss function
$f(x)$ = the probability density function

Modeled after P. Engel [ENG200901]

FIGURE 9.8. A microcosms of risk exposure and consequences.

or service for an organization is a type of exposure that we are referring to here. This allows the company to assign resources and the time to do the assessment and then determine the level of risk that is acceptable for moving forward with launching the product or service to address foreseeable risk exposures.

Unforeseeable Risk Exposures. An unforeseeable risk exposure is one where the organization does not have sufficient notice and is not able to plan and implement based on their own timeframe. An example of this type of risk exposure is a vulnerability announcement in a piece of software that is critical to the organization's infrastructure. In this particular case, the announcement is made that there is an issue and the organization needs to respond as soon as possible based on the level of risk and if the assets are affected. An organization needs to develop the following:

TABLE 9.4. Vulnerability Identification, Threat Analysis, and Remediation Planning

Vulnerability Identification

Goal:

  Identify weaknesses before it can be exploited

Process:

  Continually scan for new vulnerabilities
  Continually scan for rogue technology devices
  Keep up to date on vulnerability alerts
  Carry out compliance testing
  Carry out operational availability analysis

Technologies

  Scanners
  Vulnerability assessment tools
  Penetration testing tools
  New vulnerability alert subscription

Threat Analysis

Goal:

  Identify threat agents that can exploit identified vulnerabilities
  Measure the efficiency of current controls and countermeasures
  Minimize downtime due to threat activity and other negative ramifications

Process:

  Classify new vulnerabilities based on probability of success of exploitation and potential damage
  Classify vulnerable asset by role in company and business impact of disruption
  Align threats with business impact and develop proper mediation steps
  Use results of incidents to improve preventive measures

Technologies:

  Vulnerability management automated tools
  Intrusion detection and prevention systems
  Event correlation
  Content filtering
  Antivirus

Remediation

Goal:

  Reduce business downtime and business impact
  Contain and mitigate damages
  Respond effectively and efficiently to incident

Process:

  Roll out temporary fix
  Test and implement permanent fix
  Carry out proper configuration management
  Report activities to affected business units and personnel
  Document change to environment

TABLE 9.4. (Continued)

Technologies:
  Patch management
  Configuration and software deployment tools
  Vulnerability management automated tools

---

  a. A process to address unforeseen risk exposures
  b. A process for alerting and monitoring
    • Vendor Security Alerts
    • Public available lists to watch for vulnerabilities: OSVDB, NVD, CERT
    • Paid services

9.6.2 Internal Team Programs (to Uncover Risk Exposures)

We have discussed in depth the staffing of a risk management team in previous chapters. With a properly staffed team in place it is now important to determine the process and uncover risk exposures. There are two main ways that this can be approached by looking at (1) an organization's projects and (2) assets on the network. The following observations are noteworthy:

- Security needs to be built into the project management life cycle (PMLC)
- Security needs to be built into all projects, not bolted on afterwards
- Each project that an organization embarks on increases the potential revenues but at the same time can have serious security issues and introduce risk exposures
- Security needs to be built into the systems development life cycle (SDLC)
- Each organization has implemented (hopefully) some type of PMLC and SDLC; given this, it is hard to specifically state where the security checkpoints are required but must be incorporated.

9.7 SUMMARY

In summary, the risk management team should conduct vulnerability identification and threat analysis, and prepare for remediation planning. Table 9.4 provides a snapshot of related activities, as discussed in [HAR200801].

REFERENCES

[CAR200901] Carolina IT Consulting, Inc. (CITC), North Carolina, 3902 Alden Street, Indian Trail, NC 28079. http://www.citconline.com/services/security.htm

[CIS200901] Cisco Systems, "Common Vulnerability Scoring System (CVSS)," San Jose, CA.

[DRO200901] DROISYS Corporation, 4800 Patrick Henry Drive, Santa Clara, CA, 95054.

[ENG200901] P. Engel, Security Reference Guide, CDW, Flyer 59323AB. 2009.

[ENT200701] Enterprise Management Associates, Inc., "Enabling IT to Act Like a Business Using Next, Generation IT Asset Management", a white paper prepared for Hewlett-Packard, 2007. 2585 Central Avenue, Suite 100, Boulder, CO 80301.

[ENT 200901] Enterprise Risk Management Inc., "Vulnerability Assessments," 800 Douglas Road, North Tower, Coral Gables, FL 33134

[ETSI200301] ETSI, "ETSI Threat Vulnerability and Risk Analysis (TVRA) Method," TS102 165-1, V4.1.1, 2003.

[HAR200801] S. Harris, "Vulnerability Management Lifecycle (Part 1 of 2)," February 1, 2008. Also, "Vulnerability Management Lifecycle (Part 2 of 2)," February 3, 2008, http://cisspblog.logicalsecurity.com/2008/02/03/ulnerability-management-lifecycle-part-2-of-2/

[HP200901] HP, A Foundation for Value, HP Whitepaper, http://h41112.www4.hp.com/promo/asset-management/uk/en/pdf/WP-AM-linchpin_4AA0-5584EEE.pdf

[MAR200601] MARGERIT – Version 2: Methodology for Information Systems Risk Analysis and Management. Book I – The Method, Published by MINISTERIO DE ADMINISTRACIONES PÚBLICAS, Madrid, 20 June 2006 (v 1.1), NIPO: 326-06-004-8.

[MEI200501] J. D. Meier, A. Mackman, and B. Wastell, "Threat Modeling Web Applications," Patterns & Practices Library, Microsoft Corporation, May 2005.

[MIC200601] Microsoft Solutions for Security and Compliance and Microsoft Security Center of Excellence, *The Security Risk Management Guide*, Microsoft Corporation, Redmond, WA, 2006.

[MIC200701] Micro Focus, The financial Value of IT Assets, Press Release, Wednesday Oct 03, 2007, The Lawn, 22-30 Old Bath Road, Newbury, Berkshire RG14 1QN, UK.

[PEL200301] T.R. Peltier, J. Peltier, J.A. Blackley, *Managing a Network Vulnerability Assessment*, CRC Press, New York, NY, 2003.

[PAR200801] S. Parkin, "A Pragmatist's Guide to Structuring IT Asset Data," January 2008, www.fastiis.org/resources/Publications/Download/id/102/

[WAL200001] W. Waltner, "Collect and Manage Data on Your IT Assets," April 18, 2000, http://articles.techrepublic.com.com/5100-1087811-1028415.html

[WIT200401] S. Withrow, "Putting Value on IT Assets," Business Applications TechGuides, Builder.com, September 22, 2004.

APPENDIX 9A: COMMON INFORMATION SYSTEMS ASSETS

This appendix, drawn from *Microsoft Solutions for Security and Compliance and Microsoft Security Center of Excellence, The Security Risk Management Guide, 2006*, lists information system assets commonly found in organizations of various types [MIC200601]. It is not intended to be comprehensive, and it is unlikely that this list will represent all of the assets present in an organization's unique environment. Therefore, it is important that an organization customizes the list during the risk assessment phase of the project.

TABLE 9A.1. Common Information Systems Assets

Asset Class	Overall IT Environment	Asset Name	Asset Rating
Tangible	Physical infrastructure	Data centers	5
Tangible	Physical infrastructure	Servers	3
Tangible	Physical infrastructure	Desktop computers	1
Tangible	Physical infrastructure	Mobile computers	3
Tangible	Physical infrastructure	PDAs	1
Tangible	Physical infrastructure	Cell phones	1
Tangible	Physical infrastructure	Server application software	1
Tangible	Physical infrastructure	End-user application software	1
Tangible	Physical infrastructure	Development tools	3
Tangible	Physical infrastructure	Routers	3
Tangible	Physical infrastructure	Network switches	3
Tangible	Physical infrastructure	Fax machines	1
Tangible	Physical infrastructure	PBXs	3
Tangible	Physical infrastructure	Removable media (tapes, floppy disks, CD-ROMs, DVDs, portable hard drives, PC card storage devices, USB storage devices, and so on)	1
Tangible	Physical infrastructure	Power supplies	3
Tangible	Physical infrastructure	Uninterruptible power supplies	3
Tangible	Physical infrastructure	Fire suppression systems	3
Tangible	Physical infrastructure	Air conditioning systems	3
Tangible	Physical infrastructure	Air filtration systems	1
Tangible	Physical infrastructure	Other environmental control systems	3
Tangible	Intranet data	Source code	5
Tangible	Intranet data	Human resources data	5
Tangible	Intranet data	Financial data	5
Tangible	Intranet data	Marketing data	5

(Continued)

TABLE 9A.1. (Continued)

Asset Class	Overall IT Environment	Asset Name	Asset Rating
Tangible	Intranet data	Employee passwords	5
Tangible	Intranet data	Employee private cryptographic keys	5
Tangible	Intranet data	Computer system cryptographic keys	5
Tangible	Intranet data	Smart cards	5
Tangible	Intranet data	Intellectual property	5
Tangible	Intranet data	Data for regulatory requirements (GLBA, HIPAA, CA SB1386, EU Data Protection Directive, and so on)	5
Tangible	Intranet data	U.S. Employee Social Security numbers	5
Tangible	Intranet data	Employee drivers' license numbers	5
Tangible	Intranet data	Strategic plans	3
Tangible	Intranet data	Customer consumer credit reports	5
Tangible	Intranet data	Customer medical records	5
Tangible	Intranet data	Employee biometric identifiers	5
Tangible	Intranet data	Employee business contact data	1
Tangible	Intranet data	Employee personal contact data	3
Tangible	Intranet data	Purchase order data	5
Tangible	Intranet data	Network infrastructure design	3
Tangible	Intranet data	Internal websites	3
Tangible	Intranet data	Employee ethnographic data	3
Tangible	Extranet data	Partner contract data	5
Tangible	Extranet data	Partner financial data	5
Tangible	Extranet data	Partner contact data	3
Tangible	Extranet data	Partner collaboration application	3
Tangible	Extranet data	Partner cryptographic keys	5
Tangible	Extranet data	Partner credit reports	3
Tangible	Extranet data	Partner purchase order data	3

Asset Class	Overall IT Environment	Asset Name	Asset Rating
Tangible	Extranet data	Supplier contract data	5
Tangible	Extranet data	Supplier financial data	5
Tangible	Extranet data	Supplier contact data	3
Tangible	Extranet data	Supplier collaboration application	3
Tangible	Extranet data	Supplier cryptographic keys	5
Tangible	Extranet data	Supplier credit reports	3
Tangible	Extranet data	Supplier purchase order data	3
Tangible	Internet data	web site sales application	5
Tangible	Internet data	web site marketing data	3
Tangible	Internet data	Customer credit card data	5
Tangible	Internet data	Customer contact data	3
Tangible	Internet data	Public cryptographic keys	1
Tangible	Internet data	Press releases	1
Tangible	Internet data	White papers	1
Tangible	Internet data	Product documentation	1
Tangible	Internet data	Training materials	3
Intangible	Reputation		5
Intangible	Goodwill		3
Intangible	Employee moral		3
Intangible	Employee productivity		3
IT Services	Messaging	E-mail/scheduling (for example, Microsoft Exchange)	3
IT Services	Messaging	Instant messaging	1
IT Services	Messaging	Microsoft Outlook® Web Access (OWA)	1
IT Services	Core infrastructure	Active Directory® directory service	3
IT Services	Core infrastructure	Domain name system (DNS)	3
IT Services	Core infrastructure		3

(Continued)

375

TABLE 9A.1. (Continued)

Asset Class	Overall IT Environment	Asset Name	Asset Rating
IT Services	Core infrastructure	Dynamic host configuration protocol (DHCP)	3
IT Services	Core infrastructure	Enterprise management tools	3
IT Services	Core infrastructure	File sharing	3
IT Services	Core infrastructure	Storage	3
IT Services	Core infrastructure	Dial-up remote access	3
IT Services	Core infrastructure	Telephony	3
IT Services	Core infrastructure	Virtual private networking (VPN) access	3
IT Services	Core infrastructure	Microsoft Windows® Internet Naming Service (WINS)	1
IT Services	Other infrastructure	Collaboration services (for example, Microsoft SharePoint®)	

CHAPTER 10

REMEDIATION PLANNING AND COMPLIANCE REPORTING

This chapter covers the last two functional blocks of the risk management method discussed in this book: planning mitigation strategies, and compliance reporting. Remediation is the process of correcting a fault or deficiency in the IT environment to reduce or bound a risk to an acceptable level. Tools and manual penetration testers do a reasonably good job of discovery; however, it is common knowledge that firms are finding it challenging to remediate security issues in complex applications and systems. As a result, organizations sometimes delay the remediation process. This is clearly not a desirable predicament to be in. This chapter addresses this critical issue. Figure 10.1 depicts graphically the topics covered in the chapter. The following is a checklist of activities:

✔ Determining risk value and severity of risk exposures
✔ Remediation approaches
✔ Prioritizing remediations
✔ Determining mitigating timeframes
✔ Compliance monitoring, metrics, and reporting

10.1 DETERMINING RISK VALUE

Figure 10.2 provides a way to summarize the discussion of previous chapters. Vulnerability analysis and threat modeling covered in Chapter 9 led to an intermediary "strategizing" stage where risk mitigation prioritization, risk mitigation strategy, and implementation roadmaps are developed. At that point the remediation tasks can be implemented and project-managed to completion. Risk mitigation prioritization will depend on the benefit to be

Information Technology Risk Management in Enterprise Environments: A Review of Industry Practices and a Practial Guide to Risk Management Teams, by Jake Kouns and Daniel Minoli
Copyright © 2010 John Wiley & Sons, Inc.

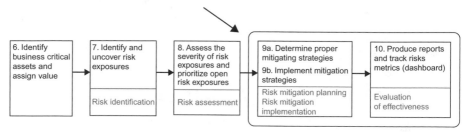

FIGURE 10.1. Risk management process steps covered in Chapter 10.

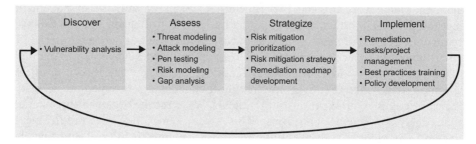

FIGURE 10.2. From risk exposure discovery to remediation implementation.

derived by the set of activities; as discussed in previous chapters, this entails calculating the risk and the remediation costs and focusing on those projects that have the highest payback. This entails a cost–benefit analysis to determine cost-effectiveness.

We have discussed the topic of determining risk value at length in previous chapters. One approach is to endeavor to follow a quantitative approach. This approach has the advantage that it can support the budgeting process in a direct way. The drawback of this approach is that the threat probabilities may be hard to determine. To deal with this last issue, one may estimate the probabilities by postulating some intuitive values (using, for example, the Maximum Likelihood Estimation concepts discussed in Chapter 7; for example, if a vendor recommends that software release y is needed to meet current security threats, the likelihood that software release y-5 is still safe is not a good bet). As covered in Chapter 2, the benefit $B(\Theta_j, A_i \oplus R_x)$ is the cost difference between the expense needed for remediation of asset A_i to a threat Θ_j, and the reduction in risk due to the remediation R_x:

$$B\left(\Theta_j, A_i \oplus R_x\right) = \left\{\text{Risk}\left(\Theta_j, A_i\right) - \text{Risk}\left(\Theta_j, A_i \oplus R_x\right)\right\} - C\left(\Theta_j, A_i \oplus R_x\right).$$

Generally, one would like

$$C\left(\Theta_j, A_i \oplus R_x\right) < \text{Risk}\left(\Theta_j, A_i\right) - \text{Risk}\left(\Theta_j, A_i \oplus R_x\right)$$

or

$$B\left(\Theta_j, A_i \oplus R_x\right) > 0.$$

If there are multiple possible remediations, say R_k, with $k = 1, \ldots, r$, typically one would want to find R_o such that

$$\text{Max } B_{k=1 \ldots r}\left(\Theta_j, A_i \oplus R_r\right) = B_o\left(\Theta_j, A_i \oplus R_o\right).$$

The other approach is to use qualitative methods.

As we have seen, companies can use the mechanisms of an Enterprise Architecture to organize their entire IT operation. In the previous chapter we discussed classifying IT assets by the layers of the architecture model. In turn, one can also classify remediation plans using, for convenience, the same layers. Remediation is the process of correcting a fault or deficiency; specifically, it is the process of adding controls at all layers of the enterprise architecture.

- **Business Architecture:** An architectural formulation of the business function. This includes business processes, and documentation.
- **Information Architecture**: An architectural formulation of the information function via a data model. This includes the data schema as well as the database and the data itself.
- **(Systems/Application) Solution Architecture**: An architectural definition of the (systems/application) solution function. This includes all the systems used by the organization. Company-developed systems as well as off-the-shelf shrink-wrapped (commercial off the shelf—COTS) software.
- **Technology Infrastructure Architecture**: An architectural formulation (description) of the Technology Infrastructure Function. This includes the platforms (server hardware, mainframes), networks (data, voice, video, wireless), and storage of the firm. This also includes the operating systems and the software release for all elements (routers, firewalls, PBXs, ACDs, etc.)

Obviously, it must be recognized that patching alone does not secure an organization. There are various types of remediations: technical remediations, regulatory remediations, and process remediations.

Technical remediations include, among others:

- Hosts/servers/clients/storage/endpoint security
- Software, application systems, office applications, OSs

- Networks/perimeter, including extranets and wireless networks
- "Nodal" elements (PBXs, ACDs, switches, and so on)

Regulatory remediation include, among others:

- SOX compliance
- HIPAA compliance
- ISO 27001 compliance
- PCI compliance

Process remediations include, among others:

- Developing and communicating a security policy
- Documenting security standards and processes performed within the IT security area
- Deployment of new security schemes
- Developing a security management plan, to incorporate best security practices,
- Strengthening object/application authority scheme
- Re-architecting user authorities, implementing "least privilege access"
- Developing and implementing role-based access
- Revising processes to meet security policy/standards/requirements
- Educating organizations on security best practices
- Investigating the need for third-party network access control
- Investigating the security of business partners connected via extranets (or even just connected via traditional, non-electronic means to share sensitive data)
- System clean-up of unused libraries, user profiles, authority scheme, etc.

Regardless of the approach or asset (and/or asset layer), the risk management team is responsible for the remediation prioritization process. Table 10.1 depicts one possible approach modeled after the process used by CERT to assess vulnerabilities.

10.2 REMEDIATION APPROACHES

Remediation can include, but is not limited to, installing patches, tracking corrective actions, and validating that the actions undertaken by the risk management team (or the internal/external group engaged by the team to implement a solution) actually corrected the problem, namely reduced probability of damage, specifically with $q(\Theta_l, A_i \oplus R_x) < p(\Theta_l, A_i)$. Remediation

TABLE 10.1. Remediation Process Modeled after the Process used by CERT

Collection	Identify vulnerability reports by monitoring public sources of vulnerability information and processing discovery. Vulnerabilities can be catalogued.
Analysis	Determine general severity, considering factors such as the number of affected systems, impact, and attack scenarios. Based on severity and other attributes, a firm may select some vulnerabilities for further analysis. This can be a prioritization step based on the absolute value of the risk involved.
Coordination	Work with vendors to address vulnerabilities, if necessary. The firm may maintain an "open issue list" with the vendor. Newer products tend to have more issues. If the firm has a leverage position with the vendor, a good, two-way communication environment may be created. Generally, this approach works for larger firms with a lot of buying power; smaller firm may have to wait on general release of patches.
Disclosure	The risk management team may opt to notify critical stakeholders about the vulnerabilities. At the same time the team should produce accurate technical information focused on solutions and mitigation techniques.

also occasionally involves performing forensics analysis to determine the cause of the infraction and also to attempt to recover any lost data.

The remediation approach clearly depends on which layer of the architecture and which technology within each layer one is considering. In effect, the remediation approach depends on the asset A_i and threat Θ_j. For software business applications, operating systems, office applications, and software controlled elements, patching and/or updating software is usually an effective and well-recognized approach to remove vulnerabilities. Making configuration and/or architecture changes are yet another way to correct for vulnerabilities; clearly, architecture changes are more complex to undertake than configuration changes.

At a broad level, one has four approaches:

- In-house automated vulnerability remediation
- In-house manual vulnerability remediation
- In-house hybrid approach
- Reliance on an outside firm providing a service (as discussed in Chapter 8)

Automated vulnerability remediation tools are available, but generally apply to only a subset of vulnerabilities. Some software systems and some network perimeters are amenable to automated remediation; however, tools now on the market still require, and rightly so, a manual oversight process to oversee the remediation implementation. Some products may incorporate some level of automatic vulnerability remediation, especially in terms of uploading patches and fixes. For example, many intrusion prevention systems (IPSs) proactively protects servers from malicious attacks while supporting compliance needs. To combat threats, an IPS combines several protection technologies into a single, multilayered agent. Typically, host protection systems provide intrusion prevention signatures in addition to a local firewall; these signatures work similarly to antivirus signatures and are effective against threats that are known (they are not effective against threats that are unknown). Firms benefit from preemptive protection by having vulnerability protection built in to all of the network, server, and desktop products. The following IPS features are noted herewith to provide the reader a small sense of what is possible in this arena.

- Protects servers against known and unknown attacks without requiring patches. Vulnerability-centric intrusion prevention blocks network worms and other exploits to known vulnerabilities, while buffer overflow exploit prevention blocks attacks against unknown buffer overflow exploits.
- Audits server applications. Audit applications that are running and accessing the network before establishing an application or network lock-down policy.
- Enforces service and application policy. Ensures that only authorized services and applications are running on servers. Prevents unauthorized programs from being installed.
- Enforces network access policy. Ensures that only authorized applications are accessing the network and sets port and IP restrictions for inbound and outbound server traffic.

A hybrid approach where one automatically scans the environment for known vulnerabilities and then makes the data available to the risk management team to decide which vulnerabilities to address first is a recommended approach to follow. The risk management committee (discussed in Chapter 7) may meet on a periodic basis, say monthly or quarterly, and review a list of vulnerabilities or other risk exposures that the firm needs to address from a technical perspective. The committee will typically identify those threats or vulnerabilities they deem critical for their business environment. In some cases, reviewing vulnerabilities is not appropriate to have the risk management committee review because it is too far "down in the weeds." Some organizations have opted to administer the actual remediation process in a distributed manner, to reach the asset owner which does not necessarily reside in the IT/network or security groups.

Most companies still take a manual approach. Manual remediation involves two steps:

1. Manual (or perhaps automatic) vulnerability analysis (for example, using the techniques discussed in Chapter 9 such as footprinting, scanning, and enumeration, among others)
2. Manual remediation, which is dependent on the layer of the enterprise architecture where the vulnerability has been identified or the specific technology within a given layer

For example, when looking at possible company-specific vulnerabilities of the company's network, with the goal of identifying remediations, the first step may entail port scanning. Port scanning can reveal several things about hosts on the network—for example [BEL200101],

- Whether a host is online and reachable. If a system is offline, a port scan will report that the system could not be reached.
- Port scanning can help identify the types of services the study subject offers. For example, if TCP 80 is open, it is likely a web server.
- If a firewall exists between the scanning point and the target host. Port scanning will report which ports, if any, are being filtered by a firewall or similar device.
- Many services respond to a port scan's query by replying with their "banner," which usually contains the name, version, manufacturer, and other information about the service ("banner grabbing").

While a remediation that involves a change to a set of firewalls to close some ports can be done both manually and in a semi- or totally automatic manner, certain remediations have to be handled manually. For example, one may determine that because VoIP is deployed one needs to have a stateful firewall with Deep Packet Inspection instead of a more basic firewall. Obviously the upgrade of the firewall infrastructure and the deployment of several such routers at the perimeter will require manual intervention.

Contracted remediation services aim at enhancing existing security controls or adding new controls to a firm's environment which are identified during the assessment phase. Typical services include, but are not limited to,

- Security policy and procedures enhancements
- Secure network architectures deployment
- Security technologies strengthening, including:
  - Virtual private networks (VPN)
  - Public key infrastructure (PKI)
  - Intrusion detection systems (IDS)
  - Content filtering
  - Firewalls
- Deployment of assessment tools
- Authentication and authorization
- Encryption

Table 10.2 depicts some basic remediations, as discussed in [BEL200101].

CERT recommends that to reduce the security risks posed by software vulnerabilities, developers should strive to address both the number of

TABLE 10.2. Basic Remediations

Anti-virus Systems	Install antivirus protection systems on servers (focusing on files), end systems, and post offices (focusing on in and outbound e-mail and attachments), and keep them current.
Backups	Maintain full and reliable backups of all data, log files, and configurations. Archive all software upgrades, and patches offline so that they can be reloaded when necessary.
Enable and Monitor Logging and Auditing	Log events that either alert the firm to problems or help the firm manage security issues.
Scan Systems Regularly	Such scans allow the firm to determine if the systems have been compromised.
Software Updates to be Current	Operating systems and client or servers applications benefit from running recent versions of the software. All relevant updates should be applied as soon as reasonable.
Unnecessary Accounts Should Be Removed	If a local administrator/guest account has a trivial password, an intruder can, from a remote host, *connect to* that system using its local administrator account and exercise administrative privileges on that machine and its resources (disks, files, printers, programs, etc.). Just disabling an account is not sufficient to guard against an intruder abusing it; a threat approach is to enter a system through one account, re-enable a disabled account (preferably with greater privilege, or the potential of escalating its privilege), and continue the intrusion using that account.

vulnerabilities in software that are being developed and the number of vulnerabilities in software that are already deployed. Related to the first item, CERT seeks to help engineers understand how vulnerabilities are created and discovered: With education, engineers will learn how detect and elim-inate—and eventually avoid—vulnerabilities in software products before the products are shipped. Most organizations that rely on vendor-provided soft-ware are at the mercy of the software vendor and hence need to ensure that they are alerted of any identified security issues.

10.3 PRIORITIZING REMEDIATIONS

There are going to be more security risks than a security practitioner or organization can handle. Therefore it is important to be able to focus on the critical risks to the critical assets. In the previous chapter we discussed how the assets can be identified and values can be assigned. This exercise also intrinsically supports the prioritization mechanism. The prioritization process should be such that the aggregate benefit (as defined in this book) is optimized.

Recall the discussion of Chapter 2:

$$\text{Total firm benefit from remediation} = \sum_{i=1,\dots,z} B_o\left(\Theta_j, A_i \oplus R_o\right)$$

and review the optimization process discussed there.

If the practitioner does not want to work out the combinatorial optimization analysis, the practitioner should make use of the following heuristics.

Parkinson's Law. Work expands so as to fill the time available for its completion.

- If allowed, security work will "expand so as to fill the time."
- Need to ensure that the team focuses on meaningful work.

Pareto Principle. The Pareto principle (also known as the "80–20 rule," "the law of the vital few," and the "principle of factor scarcity") states that, for many events, roughly 80% of the effects come from 20% of the causes.

- Need to ensure that the security team does not get caught up trying to solve risks with little value.
- Twenty percent of the risks will have the largest positive impact if addressed.
- Need to ensure that there is a mechanism to select the largest risks and ensure focus.

The prioritization of risks need to be handled within the subcategories of risk exposures discussed in the previous chapter:

- Unforeseeable (unanticipated) risk exposures
- Foreseeable (anticipated) risk exposures

As mentioned, CVSS can be used to help address numerous vulnerabilities that are uncovered in a routine vulnerability scan. However, using a framework like CVSS does not typically help an organization prioritize all open risks. An organization should look to implement (or use an already existing process) to prioritize the workload.

10.4   DETERMINING MITIGATING TIMEFRAMES

Just as the prioritization of risk exposures need to be handled within the subcategories of risks discussed in the previous chapter, likewise one needs to make that distinction when determining mitigation timeframes as well.

Unforeseeable (Unanticipated) Risk Exposures

- Most of these types of risks affect assets that are already in production.
- Timeframes should be adjusted depending on the asset and function (internal LAN, DMZ, perimeter, e-commerce, and so on).
- Internal resources assumed to be protected by additional controls, maybe having more time to deploy a remediation; in contrast to an external resource, for example, a web server that is available on the Internet would need to be corrected in an accelerated timeframe.
- Timeframes set for requiring corrective actions (patch deployed, etc.) need to properly communicated and tracked.

Foreseeable (Anticipated) Risk Exposures

- As mentioned, risks in this category are typically project-based.
- The business is able to make decisions as to what level of risk to accept prior to implementation into a production state.
- For any risk that is uncovered or is part of the project process, there needs to be a detailed compliance action plan.

A Compliance Action Plan (CAP) must be completed. A CAP describes

- What is going to be done to correct an open issue?
- Based on guiding principles defined previously, how much risk is acceptable?
- What is the agreed to solution, because there is more than one way to solve an issue (important to understand)?
- When is it enough in terms of a security solution or corrective action?
- When will the corrective actions be implemented?

Creating a solid CAP is critical so that security compliance does not turn into pushing paper and relying on waivers:

- Waivers are important in allowing a business to accept risks.
- Waivers cannot be a way to allow the business to just avoid doing security work required.
- Need to focus on results.
- Do not want CAP to drag on and on.

A number of mitigation strategies (more related to unforeseeable risk exposures) need to be repeatable processes. Examples include installing patches to address system vulnerabilities. These processes will occur on a monthly, quarterly, or even ad hoc fashion, based on when patches are released. The process should be well known and established to test and implement.

10.5   COMPLIANCE MONITORING AND SECURITY METRICS

Even the most mature organizations are going to identify numerous risk exposures through the processes as defined in the previous chapters. If there were no risks at all being identified, there is perhaps something wrong with the discovery phase. It is to be expected that any given organization is going to have a number of vulnerability/exposures/mitigations actively being managed. There may be some risk exposures that will be documented and potentially never fully closed out, based on the business tolerance for risk, or what is acceptable risk for the organization. Regardless, a successful program needs to track the risks and be able to speak towards the effort at any given point. If the firm's CIO or internal/external auditor asks for a status of an open risk exposure, it is important to give an updated and accurate report.

Compliance is the part of the risk management program that pulls everything together. A way to think about compliance is the following statement: "Are we doing what we say we are (or think we are)?" An organization that has made an investment in a risk management program and a risk management team needs to have the assurance that what they believe is happening is truly implemented. This is where a compliance program comes into place.

Compliance monitoring is part of the broader topic of security metrics. The establishment of IT security metrics enables the organization to analyze the performance of IT's technical, operational, and management controls.

IT security metrics support the monitoring of security goals and objectives by quantifying the level of implementation of the security controls and the effectiveness and efficiency of the controls, analyzing the adequacy of security activities, and identifying possible improvement actions. For example, as we saw in passing in Chapter 3, the National Institute of Standards and Technology (NIST) released the Revision 1 of their "Special Publication 800-55" in July 2008 entitled "Performance Measurement Guide for Information Security," which focuses on security metrics. Publication 800-55 is a guide to assist in the development, selection, and implementation of measures to be used at the information system and program levels. These measures indicate the effectiveness of security controls applied to information systems and supporting information security programs. Such measures are used to facilitate decision-making, improve performance, and increase accountability through the collection, analysis, and reporting of relevant performance-related data thereby providing a way to tie the implementation, efficiency, and effectiveness of information system and program security controls to an agency's success in achieving its mission. The performance measures development process described in this guide will assist agency information security practitioners in establishing a relationship between information system and program security activities under their purview and the agency mission, helping to demonstrate the value of information security to their organization. The document identifies 17 IT security topics of relevance, ranging from risk management and security controls assessment to personnel security, training, and awareness to incident response capability and audit trails [AKS200901]:

- Risk management measurements quantify the number of conducted system risk assessments and the degree of managerial involvement in the risk assessments procedures. Security plan metrics quantify the percentage of systems with approved system security plans and the percentage of current system security plans. Security control metrics determine the efficiency of closing significant system weaknesses by evaluating the existence, the timeliness, and effectiveness of a process for implementing corrective actions.
- Personnel security metrics quantify the percentage of users with special access to systems who have undergone background evaluations. Security awareness metrics are concerned with the percentage of employees with significant security responsibilities who have received specialized training.
- Data integrity metrics quantify the percentage of systems with automatic virus definition updates and automatic virus scanning and the percentage of systems that perform password policy verification. Logical access control metrics are concerned with the number of users with access to security software that are not security administrators. To ensure that personnel with access to security software have the appropriate skill sets and have undergone appropriate screening, no person should be allowed such access unless he or she is designated as a security administrator. These metrics also include the percentage of systems running restricted protocols and the percentage of websites with a posted privacy policy (if an organization runs websites with public access).
- Contingency planning measurements include the percentage level of critical data files and operations with an established backup frequency as well as the percentage of systems that have a contingency plan. Incident response capability metrics quantify the percentage of agency components with incident handling and response capability and the number of incidents reported to FedCIRC, NIPC, and local law enforcement.
- System development life-cycle metrics quantify the percentage of systems that are in compliance with the OMB requirement for integrating security costs into the system life cycle. Audit trails metrics quantify the percentage of systems on which audit trails provide a trace of user actions.

The IT security metrics also include authentication, authorize processing, physical and environmental protection, hardware and systems software maintenance, input/output controls and documentation measurements.

The specific interest here is risk management measurements. The need to measure IT security performance in general and risk management performance in particular is driven by regulatory as well as financial factors. A number of existing laws, rules, and regulations cite IT security performance measurements as a requirement. Metrics can also be used as a way to provide positive press on the work the security teams are doing.

Compliance also ensures that the visibility of the actions required to correct the risk is maintained. Many organizations that have tried to implement a proper risk program do a decent job of identifying the risks that need to be corrected; however, they appear to struggle with actually implementing controls to reduce the risk exposure to the organization's critical assets. Organizational audits may enable an organization to produce a risk register that shows what the issues are, yet the organization may be unable to show that any change was actually introduced as part of the risk management program. The operative goal is not to create a hollow risk management team that is not empowered or able to properly affect the organization and move toward better security.

As implied above, some of the metrics that need to be tracked include patches and technical hardening standards. With the use of an enterprise architecture (EA) framework, one has a structure that defines a view of the organization IT environment. A layered framework helps to ensure that controls are in place when required. Therefore, the risk management practitioner needs to create a view focused on a security architecture model that maps to the EA. There has been relatively little work to date on security architectures (SA), but some models have evolved. Some of the more well-known SAs include the following [AME200501]:

- **International Standard (IS) ISO 7498-2, the Security Architecture.** ISO 7498-2 provides a general description of security services and related mechanisms, that can be ensured by the security reference model, and of the positions within the reference model where the services and mechanisms may be provided. This framework extends the field of application of ISO 7498, open systems interconnection reference model, to cover secure communications between open systems. It adds to the concepts and principles included in ISO 7498 but does not modify them. Is no implementation specification, nor a basis for assessing the conformance of actual implementations.
- **Moriconi, Xiaoleiand, and Riemenschneider Methodology.** This SA is formalized in terms of common architectural abstractions; then the SA is refined into specialized architectures where each one is suitable for implementation under different security assumptions. The methodology permits proofs to be constructed to see if every implementation satisfies the intended security policy.
- **Whitman & Mattord Methodology.** This SA also makes use of architectural layers as follows: physical, personal, operations, communications, network, and information security layers. The functions of these layers are as follows:
  - The physical security layer addresses the protection of physical items, objects or areas from unauthorized access and misuse.

- The personal security layer addresses the protection of the individual or a group of individuals who are authorized to access the organization and its operation.
- The operations security layer focuses on the protection of detail of a particular operation or series of activities.
- The communications security layer encompasses the protection of the organization's communication media, content, and technology.
- The network security layer protects the network components, connections, and contents.
- The information security layer is concerned with protecting the information, the systems and hardware that use, store and transmit that information.
- **NIST Special Publication 800-27, Security Principles and Practices.** The NSTISSC model is a comprehensive model for information security (INFOSEC) and an evaluation standard. It includes:
  - The lattice model is a mathematical structure of elements organized by a relation among them.
  - The Bell–La Padula confidentiality model identifies allowable communication paths
  - The Biba integrity model defines integrity levels in terms of the Bell–La Padula sensitivity levels.

10.6   COMPLIANCE REPORTING

There are three focus areas where compliance reporting needs to be focused:

1. Practitioners
2. Management
3. Executives

Practitioners are the key individuals that are able to reduce risk exposures in an organization. Most IT practitioners want to be secure and do the right thing, but are perhaps unclear of what that actually means. Standards and policies can be created, distributed, and explained to all practitioners, but there could still be issues of noncompliance. Practitioners will be more willing to assist with helping to implement controls if they are provided the information before that is shared with management. When the compliance reports make their way to management with outstanding issues, it typically comes across as putting a spotlight on the fact that an IT practitioner or team is not doing their job. The goal would to be able to provide the information to this group first to allow them to correct the situation and feel a part of the process.

Management reports provide the oversight to ensure that the IT practitioners actually implement and address the issues that are raised. Monthly compliance reporting tends to work very well with this group.

Executive reporting typically has no direct impact over IT (except for the CIO function), yet these executives do in fact have a stake in the controls that are implemented, especially from a regulatory perspective. The risk management team needs to determine who is appropriate to receive this information; the risk management committee should certainly be included. The team needs to decide the frequency of the report issuance (e.g., quarterly, semiannually). The report will need to be concise and not require detailed reading, perhaps with icons red, yellow, and green flags on various remediation activities either just completed or underway.

REFERENCES

[AME200501] S. Amer, J. W. Humphries, and J. A. Hamilton, "Survey: Security in the System Development Life Cycle," White paper, 2005, Auburn Information Assurance Laboratory, Information Assurance Laboratory, Computer Science & Software Engineering, 107 Dunstan Hall, Auburn University, AL 36849–5347.

[AKS200901] AKS-Labs, "IT Balanced Scorecard—IT Security Metrics," 2501 Blue Ridge Road, Suite 150, Raleigh, NC 27607.

[BEL200101] B. J. Bellamy, Jr., "Vulnerability Identification and Remediation Through Best Security Practices," SANS Institute Security Reading Room, December 7, 2001.

BASIC GLOSSARY OF TERMS USED IN THIS TEXT

Acceptable risk: The level of residual risk that has been determined by management to be a reasonable level of potential loss for a given asset.

Accountability: The property that ensures that the actions of an entity may be traced uniquely to the entity. This may cover nonrepudiation, deterrence, fault isolation, intrusion detection and prevention, and after-action recovery and legal action [ENI200801].

Action: An act taken against an asset by a threat agent. Requires first that contact occur between the asset and threat agent [JON200501].

Annual loss expectancy (ALE): ALE is the total amount of money that an organization will lose in one year if nothing is done to mitigate the risk [MIC200601]. ALE is obtained by multiplying the SLE by the ARO. ALE provides a budgeting number that can be used to establish controls or safeguards to prevent this type of damage. The information security community has widely adopted the approach of calculating annualized loss expectancy.

Annual rate of occurrence (ARO): The number of times that a risk is expected to occur during one year [MIC200601]. Also seen as the normalized rate at which the risk exposure resulting in actual damage occurs during one year. One can get a heuristic estimate of the ARO based on past experience, but past performance is no guarantee of future results.

Applications service provider (ASP): An organization that offers (typically browser-based) services that can be accessed by consumers of the service over a network. Consumers of these services are often small businesses looking to reduce the need for internal support of applications as well as an acknowledgment that the ASP may have specialized tools and expertise in a particular field. By externalizing application access, companies are

---

Information Technology Risk Management in Enterprise Environments: A Review of Industry Practices and a Practial Guide to Risk Management Teams, by Jake Kouns and Daniel Minoli
Copyright © 2010 John Wiley & Sons, Inc.

potentially at a greater information security risk. The organization must be careful in the selection and compliance program for ASPs to ensure that they are meeting the (consumer) company's security requirements.

Architecture (e.g., enterprise architecture): "The fundamental organization of a system, embodied in its components, their relationships to each other and the environment, and the principles governing its design and evolution" (ANSI/IEEE) Std 1471-2000.

Assessment of risk: An evaluation of the information security vulnerabilities for system or solution, using as much analytics as possible. The security assessment should be done both in a quantitative manner (for example, computing the expected loss, the expected cost, the variance of the outcomes), as well as in a qualitative manner (what alternative scenarios are possible, what risk mediation techniques are available, and so on).

Assets (IT assets): Anything of value to an organization, such as hardware and software components, data, people, and documentation. Something of value that requires protection. The value of an asset may be monetary or nonmonetary. For example, a computer system clearly has a monetary value that may be expressed in terms of its cost of acquisition or replacement. Data, however, is an asset that may have a monetary value (the cost to acquire), a nonmonetary value (loss of public confidence regarding data accuracy), or both [NIS199801].

Assurance: Measure of confidence that the security features, practices, procedures, and architecture of an information system accurately mediates and enforces the security policy [HAY200301].

Attack: An attempt to gain unauthorized access to an information system's services, resources, or information, or the attempt to compromise an information system's confidentially, integrity, or availability [NIC200001]. An action taken that utilizes one or more vulnerabilities to realize a threat. An inimical agent following through on a threat or exploiting a vulnerability.

Audit: The process of examining the history of a transaction to find out what happened. An operational audit can be an examination of ongoing activities to determine what is happening. It can also be an independent review and examination [NIC200001].

Availability: Maintaining unimpeded access 100% of the time to all IT assets. The protection against blockage, limitation, or diminution of benefit from an asset that is owed. Availability is one of the basic characteristics of a secure system. A breach of availability occurs when an authorized user is prevented from timely, reliable access to data or a system. An example of this is a denial of service (DoS) attack.

Backup: Activities related to the creation and testing of disaster recovery and continuity of operations plans as well as preparation of copies of data files that are stored "out of harm's way" [NIS199801].

Broad-spectrum risk analysis: Any analysis that accounts for the risk from multiple threat communities against a single asset [JON200501].

Business continuity planning: A (written) plan describing the procedures the company takes in case of potentially disruptive events short of a disaster (for which the Disaster Recovery Plan is applicable) to ensure that the operations of the company can continue unimpeded.

Certification body: An accredited certification body is a third-party organization that assesses/certifies the IT environment (or more specifically an information security management system) against a given standard—for example, BS7799-2/ISO 27001.

Changes to the organization's risk profile: A description of how the vulnerabilities, threats, and assets have changed over time.

Commercial and federal chief information officers: Managers that ensure the implementation of risk management for agency IT systems and the security provided for these IT systems.

Common threats—catastrophic incidents: These threats include (among others): fire; flood; earthquake; severe storm; terrorist attack; civil unrest/riots; landslide; avalanche; and industrial accident.

Common threats—Malicious persons: These threats include (among others): hacker, cracker; computer criminal; industrial espionage; government sponsored espionage; social engineering; disgruntled current employee; disgruntled former employee; terrorist; negligent employee; dishonest employee (bribed or victim of blackmail); and malicious mobile code.

Common threats—Mechanical failure: These threats include (among others): power outage, hardware failure, network outage, environmental controls failure, and construction accident.

Common threats—Nonmalicious persons: These threats include (among others) uninformed employees and uninformed users.

Compromise: Disclosure of information to unauthorized persons or a violation of the security policy of a system in which unauthorized intentional or unintentional disclosure, modification, destruction, or loss of an object may have occurred [NIC200001].

Confidentiality: The protection of any corporate data from being divulged to a party that does not have legal right to that data. The protection against unauthorized access, appropriation, or use of assets. A breach of confidentiality occurs, for example, when a person knowingly accesses a computer without authorization or exceeding authorized access.

Consequence: Outcome of an event or change in circumstances affecting the achievement of objectives. Note that: (i) There can be more than one consequence from one event. (ii) Consequences can range from positive to negative. (iii) Consequences can be expressed qualitatively or quantitatively. A consequence may be certain or uncertain and can have positive or negative effects on objectives [ENI200801, GUI200701].

Contact: Occurs when a threat agent establishes a physical or virtual (e.g., network) connection to an asset [JON200501].

Contingency plan: A plan for emergency response, backup operations, and post-disaster recovery in a system, as part of a security program, to ensure availability of critical system resources and facilitate continuity of operations in a crisis [ENI200801]. (see Business continuity planning)

Control components: The major elements of the internal control process. For example, the Basel Committee on Banking Supervision identifies the following control components that integrate internal control into the management process:

- Management oversight and control culture
- Risk recognition and assessment
- Control activities and segregation of duties
- Information and communications
- Monitoring activities and correcting deficiencies

Control documentation: Formal documentation of a firm's internal control such as policies, procedures, standards, and so on.

Control objectives: The primary goals of an internal control system—for example, safeguarding of assets, compliance with regulations, and data integrity.

Control Objectives for Information and Related Technology (Cobit): An IT governance framework, defined by the IT Governance Institute (ITGI). This framework can be used in ensuring proper control and governance over information and the systems that create, store, manipulate, and retrieve it. Effective IT governance helps ensure that IT supports business goals, maximizes business investment in IT, and appropriately manages IT-related risks and opportunities [COB200901]. COBIT is increasingly gaining momentum as a leading tool for IT governance. ITGI is a research think tank established in 1998 in recognition of the increasing criticality of information technology to enterprise success. In many organizations, success depends on the ability of IT to enable achievement of business goals; in such an environment, governance over IT is as critical a board and management discipline as corporate governance or enterprise governance. Effective IT governance helps ensure that IT supports business goals, maximizes business investment in IT, and appropriately manages IT-related risks and opportunities. By conducting original research on IT governance and related topics, ITGI helps enterprise leaders understand and have the tools to ensure effective governance over IT within their enterprise.

Control strength (CS): The strength of a control as compared to a standard measure of force.

Control(s): Also known as safeguards or countermeasures. An organizational, procedural, or technological means of managing risk. Means and mechanisms of managing risk, including policies, procedures, guidelines, practices, or organizational structures, which can be administrative, technical, management or legal in nature.

Corrective action: An action intended to reduce or eliminate a known weakness or gap in a security environment.

Cost–benefit analysis: An assessment of the cost of providing protection or security commensurate with the risk and magnitude of asset loss or damage. An estimate and comparison of the relative value and cost associated with each proposed control so that the most effective are implemented [MIC200601].

Countermeasures/controls: Procedures and techniques used to prevent the occurrence of a security incident, detect when an incident is occurring or has occurred, and provide the capability to respond to or recover from a security incident. Countermeasures, controls, and safeguards are terms that are often used synonymously. A safeguard may be a password for a user identifier, a backup plan that provides for offsite storage of copies of critical files, audit trails that allow association of specific actions to individuals, or any of a number of other technical or procedural techniques [NIS199801].

Crisis management: A firm's response to a severe event that could impair its function—for example, a major, publicly disclosed security infraction.

Data availability: The state where data are accessible and services are operational [ENI200801].

Decision support: Prioritization of risk based on a cost–benefit analysis. The cost for the security solution to mitigate a risk is weighed against the business benefit of mitigating the risk [MIC200601].

Defense-in-depth: The approach of using multiple layers of security to guard against failure of a single security component [MIC200601].

Definition of scope: Process for the establishment of global parameters for the performance of risk management within an organization. Within the definition of scope for risk management, internal and external factors have to be taken into account [ENI200801].

Denial of service: The result of any action or series of actions that prevents any part of an information system from functioning [NIC200001].

Detective control: Control introduced to discover events that have occurred or to test the effectiveness of preventive control.

Disaster recovery planning: A (written) plan describing the steps company would take to restore computer operations in the event of a disaster containing four components: the emergency plan, the backup plan, the recovery plan, and the test plan [INF200701]. The process of restoring a system to full operation after an interruption in service, including equipment repair/replacement, file recovery/restoration [ENI200801].

Enterprise architecture: A plan-of-record, a blueprint of the recommended structure, arrangement, configuration, functional groupings/partitioning, interfaces, data, protocols, logical functionality, integration, technology, of an IT resource needed to support a corporate business function. Typically, resources that need architectural formulations include applications, security subsystems, data structures, networks, hardware platforms, storage, and desktop systems, to name just a few. The following are considered part of the enterprise architecture:

- The enterprise architecture description (of the current or target state)
- The enterprise standards set
- The enterprise approved equipment list
- The roadmap along with (migration) strategies

Enterprise risk management (ERM): A structured and disciplined risk management approach that takes into account strategy, process, people, technology and knowledge with the purpose of continually evaluating and managing risks to business strategies and objectives on an enterprise-wide basis. A process, effected by an entity's board of directors, management and other personnel, applied in strategy setting and across the enterprise, designed to identify potential events that may affect the entity, and manage risk to be within its risk appetite, to provide reasonable assurance regarding the achievement of entity objectives [COS200401]. It is more encompassing than IT risk management, although IT risk management could be considered to be part of it.

Enumeration: The method where a firm directly interrogates its own systems searching for the detailed data and information that an intruder would be able use to perpetrate an attack.

Evaluation of mitigation's effectiveness: Monitoring the environment for effectiveness against the previous set of threats, vulnerabilities, or events and determining if new/different threats, vulnerabilities, or events results from the modifications made to the environment.

Event: Occurrence of a particular set of circumstances. The event can be certain or uncertain. The event can be a single occurrence or a series of occurrences [ENI200801].

Exploit: A means of using a vulnerability in order to cause a compromise of business activities or information security [MIC200601]. An attempt to gain unauthorized access to an information system's services, resources, or information, or the attempt to compromise an information system's confidentially, integrity, or availability [NIC200001]. An action taken that utilizes one or more vulnerabilities to realize a threat. An inimical agent following through on a threat or exploiting a vulnerability.

Expose to Risk: A state of uncertainty where some of the possibilities involve a loss, catastrophe, or other undesirable outcome. An environment exposed to risk events, threats, and/or vulnerabilities.

Exposure: The potential loss to an area due to the occurrence of an adverse event. A threat action whereby sensitive data are directly released to an unauthorized entity (RFC 2828). The Microsoft security risk management process narrows this definition to focus on the extent of damage to a business asset [MIC200601].

Exposure factor (EF): The percentage of loss that a realized threat could have on a certain asset. It is the percentage of damage (loss) that an organization would experience if a given asset were in fact compromise by a threat/exposure.

Footprinting: A method of accumulating information about a specific host or network environment typically for the purpose of finding ways to attack a system. Footprinting typically consists more of indirect methods that help to reveal system vulnerabilities. Indirect information gathering such as searching the Internet for information about a firm's systems, networks, and employees, without actually *touching* the systems directly. If a firm undertook this on its own behalf, it would be able to discover what a potential attacker can also discover without the firm's knowledge.

Fraud: Computer-related crimes involving deliberate misrepresentation or alteration of data in order to obtain something of value [INF200701].

Fraud discovery: Mechanisms and processes to identify fraud.

Fraud interdiction: actions to recover from and/or prevent future fraud.

Fuzzy randomness: Fuzzy randomness simultaneously describes objective and subjective information as a fuzzy set of possible probabilistic models over some range of imprecision. This generalized uncertainty model contains fuzziness and randomness as special cases.

Fuzzy set theory: Mathematical set theory that deals with sets or categories whose boundaries are "blurry" or "fuzzy." Fuzzy sets are sets whose elements have degrees of membership. The discipline enables the user to handle uncertainty when there is degree-vagueness—that is, having a property possessed by an object to varying degrees.

Gramm–Leach–Bliley Act: Legislation that requires financial institutions to protect the security and confidentiality of their customers' nonpublic personal information. The regulations require financial institutions to develop, implement, and maintain a comprehensive information security program that contains appropriate administrative, technical, and physical safeguards. Such a program should include the designation of an employee to coordinate the program, risk assessments, regular tests and monitoring of safeguards, and a process for making adjustments in light of test results and/or changes in operations or other circumstances that may impact the effectiveness of the program.

Guidelines: In the context of a corporate setting and security policy, these are general statements, recommendations, or administrative instructions designed to achieve the policy's objectives by providing a framework within which to implement procedures. A guideline can change frequently based on the environment and should be reviewed more frequently than standards and policies. A guideline is not mandatory, rather a suggestion of a best practice. Hence "guidelines" and "best practice" are interchangeable [GUE200701].

Hackers/crackers: The term "hacker" was originally coined to apply to individuals who focused on learning all they could about IT, often to the exclusion of many other facets of life. A "cracker" is any individual who uses advanced knowledge of networks or the Internet to compromise network security. Typically, when the traditional hacker compromised the security of an IT system, the objective was academic (i.e., a learning exercise), and any resulting damage or destruction was unintentional. Currently, the term hacker is being more widely used to describe any individual who attempts to compromise the security of an IT system, especially those whose intention is to cause disruption or obtain unauthorized access to data. Hacker/cracker activity generally gets high press coverage even though more mundane security incidents caused by unintentional actions of authorized users tend to cause greater disruption and loss [NIS199801].

Hoax: Usually an e-mail that gets sent in chain-letter mode describing some devastating, but highly unlikely, virus. Hoaxes are detectable as having no file attachment, and no reference to a third party who can validate the claim, as well as by the general tone of the message.

Impact: The result of an unwanted incident. The overall business loss expected when a threat exploits a vulnerability against an asset.

Impact analysis: The identification of critical business processes and the potential damage or loss that may be caused to the organization resulting from a disruption to those processes. Business impact analysis identifies [ENI200801] (i) the form the loss or damage will take, (ii) how that degree of damage or loss is likely to escalate with time following an incident, (iii) the minimum staffing, facilities, and services needed to enable business processes to continue to operate at a minimum acceptable level, and (iv) the time for full recovery of the business processes.

Impacts: Adverse consequences or outcomes on the individual, organization, or community at large resulting from information security incidents [CIS200701].

Incident: An event having an actual or potentially adverse effect on the security or performance of a system.

Independent evaluations: Reviews of a firm's system of internal control or risk management by internal or external entities.

Information asset: Information an organization must have to conduct its mission or business. That is, actual data elements, records, files, software (application) system and so on.

Information risk management: A security service that typically includes risk assessment and risk mitigation.

Information security (also INFOSEC, infosecurity): The protection of information systems against unauthorized access to or modification of information—whether in storage, processing, or transit—and against the denial of service to authorized users or the provision of service to unauthorized users, including those measures necessary to detect, document, and counter such threats [GOV200801].

Information security (infosecurity) risks: The coincidence of threats acting on vulnerabilities to cause impacts.

Information security management system (ISMS): A set of policies concerned with information security management (the term is used in the ISO/IEC 27001 context). A management system for dealing with information security risk exposures; namely, a framework of policies, procedures, and physical, legal, and technical security controls forming part of the organization's overall risk management processes. A (computerized) system that is used to manage (administratively) said policies.

Information systems (IS): The collection of assets used to support computer-based data acquisition, storage, processing, distribution, and so on. Synonym: IT system. The term "IT system" refers to a general support system (e.g., mainframe computer, mid-range computer, local area network, agency-wide backbone) or a major application that can run on a general support system and whose use of information resources satisfies a specific set of user requirements [STO200201].

Information technology (IT) asset (ITA): The universe of IT assets that are employed by an enterprise (organization, firm) to conduct its business, including the hardware (e.g., servers, routers, switches, storage units), the media, the communications elements, and the actual environment.

INFOSEC: Information systems security

Inherent risk: The risk before considering the beneficial effect of any risk mitigation or control.

Integrity: The state where information and/or data is retained in its original uncorrupted form. The property that data has not been altered or destroyed in an unauthorized manner (ISO 7498-2). The protection against unauthorized manipulation, modification, or loss of assets. A breach of integrity occurs when a system or data has been accidentally or maliciously modified, altered, or destroyed without authorization.

Intelligent threat: A circumstance in which an adversary has the technical and operational capability to detect and exploit a vulnerability and also has the demonstrated, presumed, or inferred intent to do so [SHI200001].

Internal audit: *(financial term)* Mechanisms to validate control solution effectiveness. An ongoing appraisal of the financial health of a company's operations by its own employees.

Internal control: A process put in place by senior management intended to provide reasonable assurance regarding things such as safeguarding of assets, compliance with regulations, and integrity/reliability of data.

Intrusion: A threat action whereby an unauthorized entity gains access to sensitive data by circumventing a system's security protections. This includes physical trespass, penetration, reverse engineering, and cryptoanalysis [SHI200001].

Joke: A harmless program that causes various benign activities to display on the computer (for example, an unexpected screen saver).

Liabilities: Risk exposures, risk events, vulnerabilities; consequences of these.

Likelihood: The chance of something happening. This can be a mathematically well-defined probability or a subjective estimate, say in terms of general descriptors (such as rare, unlikely, likely, almost certain).

Loss event: Occurs when a threat agent's action (threat event) is successful in negatively affecting an asset [JON200501].

Loss event frequency (LEF): The probable frequency, within a given timeframe, that a threat agent will inflict harm upon an asset [JON200501].

Measurement of risk: A set of possibilities each with quantified probabilities and quantified losses.

Measurement of uncertainty: A set of probabilities assigned to a set of possibilities (specifically risk events, threats, and/or vulnerabilities).

Misappropriation: A threat action whereby an entity assumes unauthorized logical or physical control of a system resource via theft of service, theft of functionality, or theft of data [SHI200001].

Misuse: A threat action that causes a system component to perform a function or service that is detrimental to system security. Misuses may come in the form of tampering, malicious logic, or violation of permissions [SHI200001]. The term is sometimes used to describe an attack that originates from the internal network, while intrusion is used to describe attacks from the outside [LEH200601].

Mitigation: Limitation of any negative consequence of a particular event. Addressing a risk exposure by taking actions designed to counter the underlying threat [MIC200601].

Mitigation plan: The set of actions intended to improve control to mitigate identified risk(s).

Mitigation solution: The implementation of a control, which is the organizational, procedural, or technological control put into place to manage a security risk [MIC200601].

Monitor and review: A process for measuring the efficiency and effectiveness of the organization's Risk Management processes is the establishment of an ongoing monitor and review process. This process makes sure that the specified management action plans remain relevant and updated. This process also implements control activities including reevaluation of the scope and compliance with decisions [ENI200801].

Multilevel risk analysis: Any analysis that accounts for the risk from a single threat community against a layered set of assets (e.g., defense in depth) [JON200501].

Office of Management and Budget (OMB) Circular A-130: Management of Federal Information Resources. November 2000. U.S. Government Publications of Interest to Risk Management.

OPSEC (operations security): A systematic and proved process by which an organization and its supporting contractors (or other activity/organization) can deny to potential adversaries information about capabilities and intentions by identifying, controlling, and protecting generally unclassified evidence of the planning and execution of sensitive activities [INF200701].

Penetration testing (also pentesting): Attempting to penetrate a system's security layers in order to demonstrate security risk. This type of test typically is aimed to simulate a real-world attack.

Physical access: Direct access to systems or networks, allowing passive or active intrusion.

Policies (security context): Rules and practices that specify or regulate how a system or organization provides security services to protect sensitive and critical system resources. A formal, brief, and high-level statement or plan that embraces an organization's general beliefs, goals, objectives, and acceptable procedures for a specified subject area. Policy attributes include the following: require compliance (mandatory); failure to comply will result in disciplinary action; focus on desired results, not on means of implementation; further defined by standards and guidelines [GUE200701].

Preventive Control: Risk control established to prevent an event from occurring.

Probability: A measure of how likely it is that some event will occur.

Probability, in the *frequentist* view, which is the most common view (particularly in scientific environments), is the frequency of an experiment that is repeated infinitely many times.

Perform a certain well-defined experiment N times, and look at the times the outcome A fits a specified criterion; let this number be n. The observed frequency is freq(A) $= n/N$.

$$p[A] = \lim_{N\to\infty} [n/N] = \lim_{N\to\infty} freq(A).$$

Subjective probability view—Bayesian statistics—is where the probability is interpreted as the *"degree of belief"* in a stated proposition.

Probable loss magnitude (PLM): The probable magnitude of loss resulting from a loss event [JON200501].

Procedure (generic context): Documentation that defines "how" to do the task and usually only applies to a single role. A written description of a course of action to be taken to perform a given task.

Process (generic context): A well-defined sequence of actions directed to some end. A process defines "what" needs to be done and which roles are involved. A systematic set of activities which uses resources to transform inputs to outputs. A process consists of the following [BAN200701]:

- Roles and responsibilities of the people (roles) assigned to do the work
- Appropriate tools and equipment to support individuals in doing their jobs
- Procedures and methods defining "how" to do the tasks and relationships between the task

Qualitative risk management: An approach to risk management in which the participants assign relative values to the assets, risks, controls, and impacts [MIC200601].

Quantitative risk management: An approach to risk management in which participants attempt to assign objective numeric values (for example, monetary values) to the assets, risks, controls, and impacts [MIC200601].

Regulatory compliance: Measures, procedures, mechanisms, actions, and audit trails that enable an organization to meet the rules and regulations identified in applicable legislation.

Reputation: The opinion that people hold about an organization; most organizations' reputations have real value even though they are intangible and difficult to calculate.

Residual risk: The portion of risk remaining after security measures have been applied [NIC200001]. The risk that remains after mitigation (countermeasures) has been applied.

Return on security investment (ROSI): The total amount of money that an organization is expected to save in a year by implementing a security control [MIC200601].

Review of security controls: The routine evaluation, assessment, audit, or review of the security controls placed on an information technology system. The type and depth of the reviews should be commensurate with the acceptable level of risk established for given IT asset.

Risk (exposure) perception: Way in which a stakeholder views a risk exposure, based on a set of values or concerns.

Risk (singular): The expected loss resulting from risk events, threats, and vulnerabilities. The expected (financial) loss due to the probability that a threat will materialize—Namely, the aggregation (summation) of the possibilities, their probabilities, and the loss associated with each possibility.

Risk is the net (negative) impact of the exercise of a vulnerability, considering both the probability and the impact of occurrence [STO200201]. Risk comes about because of the (nonzero) probability that a vulnerability may be exploited or that a threat may become harmful [NIC200001]. The potential for loss as a consequence of endogenous or exogenous events. An expectation of the loss expressed as the expected value of the probabilistic distribution that a particular threat will exploit a particular vulnerability with a particular harmful result.

The combination of the probability of an event and its consequence (ISO Guide 73).

Risk management is the process of identifying risk, assessing risk, and taking steps to reduce risk to an acceptable level.

Risk acceptance: An informed decision to accept the possibility that a given threat will exploit vulnerabilities of an asset or group of assets and thereby cause harm to the organization.

Risk analysis (aka risk assessment): Process of analyzing a given environment and the relationships of its risk-related attributes. The analysis should identify threat vulnerabilities, associate these vulnerabilities of affected assets, identify the potential nature of an undesirable result, and identify and evaluate risk-reducing countermeasures [TIP200001]. Systematic use of information to identify sources and to estimate the risk. Risk analysis provides a basis for risk evaluation, risk treatment, and risk acceptance [ENI200801].

Risk assessment (aka risk analysis): A study of vulnerabilities, threats, probabilistic likelihood, impact or loss, and theoretical effectiveness of security measures. The process of evaluating threats and vulnerabilities, known and postulated, to determine expected loss and establish the degree of acceptability to system operations [INF200701].

The assignment of value to assets, threat frequency (annualized), consequence (that is, exposure factors), and other elements of chance. The reported results of risk analysis can be said to provide an assessment or measurement of risk, regardless of the degree to which quantitative techniques are applied. The term "risk assessment" is used to characterize both the process and the results of analyzing and assessing risk [TIP200001].

The process of analyzing threats to and vulnerabilities of an information system and the potential impact the loss of information or capabilities of a system would have on national security. The resulting analysis is used as a basis for identifying appropriate and cost-effective countermeasures [NIC200001]. The process of evaluating threats and vulnerabilities, known and postulated, to determine expected loss and establish the degree of acceptability to system operations.

The process of calculating quantitatively the potential damage and/or monetary cost caused by a threat, a vulnerability, or by an event impacting the set of IT assets owned by the organization. Identification of the potential damage to the IT assets and/or to the business processes based on previous internal and external events, input from subject matter experts, and audits. Specifically, this entails (a) quantifying the potential damage and (b) quantifying the probability that damage will occur.

A process that systematically identifies valuable system resources and threats to those resources, quantifies loss exposures (i.e., loss potential) based on estimated frequencies and costs of occurrence, and (optionally) recommends how to allocate resources to countermeasures so as to minimize total exposure. The analysis lists risks in order of cost and criticality, thereby determining where countermeasures should be applied first. It is usually financially and technically infeasible to counteract all aspects of risk, and so some residual risk will remain, even after all available countermeasures have been deployed. A study of vulnerabilities, threats, probabilistic likelihood, impact or loss, and theoretical effectiveness of security measures.

Assessment where management identifies the potential risks to business strategy and objectives based on internal and external historical risk events, input from subject matter experts, audit reports, and its own understanding of the internal and external business environment.

Risk assessment process: Process for the identification and evaluation of risks and risk impacts, as well as for the recommendation of risk-reducing measures.

Risk assessment team (RAT) (aka risk management and remediation team): Corporate/institutional team responsible for comprehensive risk management (identification, assessment, containment) and security assurance.

Risk avoidance: Decision not to become involved in, or action to withdraw from, a risk exposure situation.

Risk communication: A process to exchange or share information about risk between the decision-maker and other stakeholders [ENI200801].

Risk control: Actions implementing risk management decisions.

Risk criteria: Terms of reference by which the significance or risk is assessed. Risk criteria can include associated cost and benefits, legal and statutory requirements, socioeconomic aspects, the concerns of stakeholders, priorities, and other inputs to the assessment [ENI200801].

Risk deficiencies: Gaps in control structures that expose a firm to unacceptable risks.

Risk estimation: Process used to assign values to the probability and consequences of a risk.

Risk evaluation: Process of comparing the estimated risk against given risk criteria to determine the significance of risk [ENI200801].

Risk evaluation process: Ongoing (repeatable) processes for environment evaluation leading to a high-assurance risk management program.

Risk event: The actual occurrence of something that generates a loss by materializing the risk.

Risk exposure (also liability): A state of uncertainty where some of the possibilities (also colloquially called "risks") involve a loss, catastrophe, or other undesirable outcome. An environment exposed to risk events, threats, and/or vulnerabilities.

Risk financing: Provision of funds to meet the cost of implementing risk treatment and related costs.

Risk governance: Processes addressing accountability, ownership, roles and responsibilities for risk management. Risk governance reflects the required structure and information flow and reporting, and it describes the rules and process for making risk-related decisions.

Risk identification: The process of identifying threats, vulnerabilities, or events (malicious or nonmalicious, deterministic/planned or random) impacting the set of IT assets owned by the organization.

Risk impact: The effect a risk would have on a firm's ability to achieve its mission if the risk occurred.

Risk limits: (aka risk threshold and risk tolerance) The boundaries for acceptable risk taking.

Risk management (aka risk management and control): The process of identifying risk, analyzing and assessing risk, and taking steps to reduce risk to an acceptable level. The process of determining an acceptable level of risk, assessing the current level of risk, taking steps to reduce risk to the acceptable level, and maintaining that level of risk. Entails

- (Ongoing) identification of threats, vulnerabilities, or (risk) events impacting the set of IT assets owned by the organization
- Risk assessment
- Risk mitigation planning
- Risk mitigation implementation
- Evaluation of the mitigation's effectiveness

The process established to identify, control, and minimize the impact of uncertain events [INF200701]. The process concerned with the identification, measurement, control, and minimization of security risks in information systems to a level commensurate with the value of the assets protected [NIC200001]. The practices, processes, and activities that enable a firm to make informed risk-considering decisions.

Risk management, when properly practiced, positions an organization to accomplish its mission(s) by (1) better securing the IT systems that store, process, or transmit organizational information; (2) enabling management to make well-informed risk management decisions to justify the expenditures that are part of an IT budget; and (3) assisting management in authorizing (or accrediting) the IT systems on the basis of the supporting documentation resulting from the performance of risk management [STO200201].

Term characterizes the overall process of risk mitigation. The first phase, risk assessment, includes identification of the assets at the risk and their value, risks that threaten a loss of that value, risk-reducing measures, and the budgetary impact of implementing decisions related to the acceptance, mitigation, or transfer of risk. The second phase of risk management includes the process of assigning priority to, budgeting, implementing, and maintaining appropriate risk-reducing measures [TIP200001].

Assessment of the probability (likelihood) of occurrence various risks and the potential impact such an event could have for the company. The process established to identify, control, and taking steps to minimize the impact of uncertain events.

Risk map: The pictorial representation of risk (which has been identified through a risk assessment process). This pictogram often takes the form of a two-dimensional grid with likelihood of occurrence on one axis, and severity on the other axis. The risk map is used as follows: The risks that fall in the high-frequency/high-severity quadrant are given priority risk management attention.

Risk metrics: Metrics that can be used to assess the occurrence of risk events or establish the probability of future risk events.

Risk mitigation: Techniques and principles to address risk and either eliminate it or minimize it. Techniques to ascertain that future reoccurrences of the same event will result in no or less damage. Methods to increase security assurance. Involves risk identification, risk analysis, risk assessment, and risk management.

Risk mitigation implementation: Deploying and placing in service equipment solution identified during the risk mitigation planning phase, or actuating new corrective processes.

Risk mitigation planning: Process for controlling and mitigating IT risks. It typically includes cost–benefit analysis and the selection, implementation, test, and security evaluation of safeguards. This overall system security review considers both effectiveness and efficiency, including impact on the mission and constraints due to policy, regulations, and laws [STO200201].

Risk mitigation process: Process for prioritizing, implementing, and maintaining the appropriate risk-reducing measures identified from the risk assessment process.

Risk optimization: Process related to a risk exposure to minimize the negative and to maximize the positive consequences and their respective probabilities [ENI200801].

Risk prioritization: The ranking of significant risk by frequency and/or severity. This ranking information drives to the understanding of the overall risk exposure and prioritization.

Risk profile: A view of the overall set of risks, along with their degree of magnitude or significance.

Risk reduction: Actions taken to lessen the probability or the negative consequences, or both, associated with a risk.

Risk response: A response strategy and action plan for mitigating risks that are determined to exceed desired risk limits. Additional mitigation activities may be appropriate for risks that are above desired risk limits if there is an appropriate cost benefit associated with those activities.

Risk retention: Acceptance of the burden of loss, or benefit of gain, from a particular risk. Risk retention includes the acceptance of risks that have not been identified. Risk retention does not include treatments involving insurance, or transfer by other means [ENI200801].

Risk retirement: Eliminating risk. Complete risk elimination is usually impossible; hence, one of the goals of risk management is risk reduction, risk minimization, or, indeed "management" in the common sense of the word.

Risk self-assessment: The process by which an organization identifies, assesses, and determines the appropriate course of action for addressing risks that exceed acceptable limits.

Risk treatment: Process of selection and implementation of measures to modify risk.

Risk, acceptable limits: Risk limits acceptable to an organization.

Risk, cause: A condition that allowed a risk exposure to occur. Causes include internal problems or external matters.

Risk, control: The process of comparing actual performance with planned performance, analyzing variances, evaluating possible alternatives, and taking appropriate corrective action as needed.

Risk, effect: The consequence that a risk exposure has to a firm. The effect can be measured qualitatively (low, moderate, high, extreme) or quantitatively (dollar amount) terms. The total financial value at risk because of a nefarious event. Exposure also deals with the degree to which a firm's reputation is at risk. Exposure relates to the possibility of loss without regard to the probability of actually experiencing the event.

Risk, net risk: The level of risk considering the effect of existing risk control.

Risk-adjusted measures: Metrics that incorporate the net impact of risks related to the objective that the metric supports.

Risk-exposing event (also called risk event): Any changes in the state of the environment that have the potential of creating a new state where there is nonzero risk.

Risks (plural) (colloquial): Individual possibilities (risk events) that are encountered with risk exposures.

Safeguards: (also known as controls, this being a more widely used term; also a synonym of countermeasure) Risk-reducing measures that act to detect, prevent, or minimize loss associated with the occurrence of specified threat or category of threats. Safeguards are also often described as controls or countermeasures [TIP200001]. Practices, procedures, controls or mechanisms that reduce risk. An organizational, procedural, or technological means of managing risk. Means and mechanisms of managing risk, including policies, procedures, guidelines, practices, or organizational structures, which can be administrative, technical, management, or legal in nature.

Scanning: The method of interrogating a firm's systems for available services, resource sharing, software version information, user account information, and other exploitable conditions. Port scanning is the process of testing some, or all, of the Transmission Control Protocol (TCP) and User Datagram Protocol (UDP) ports to determine which are open and what services are being provided through those open ports.

Security: All activities related to defining, achieving, and maintaining data confidentiality, integrity, and availability.

Security architecture development: A company-wide blueprint that describes the target multi-tiered security plan for the organization.

Security risk scorecard: A scorecard that illustrates the organization's current risk profile.

Security risks: Exposure to infraction, penetration, theft, compromise, or inappropriate disclosure. Typical security risks can include (but are not limited to) [LES200501]:

- Inappropriate access to, or disclosure of, information or loss of data integrity through inadequately secured physical facilities;
- Loss of accessibility and data integrity because of nonexistent or inadequate business continuity or disaster recovery policies and procedures;
- Inappropriate disclosure through inadequate screening of personnel, resulting (in extreme cases) in extortion, fraud attempts or terrorist uses; and
- Inappropriate access to, or disclosure of, information by reason of formal or informal government access (such as law enforcement or national security requests, or economic or political espionage).

  Significant legal risks arising from security risks include violation of data protection and intellectual property laws (through the disclosure of third-party proprietary data), export and defense trade control laws, and notice statutes (requiring notification of security breaches to the individuals) [LES200501].

Significant risk exposure: A risk event, or a combination of risk events, to which a firm is exposed, where the cost of an infraction or the probability of an infractions are high. Such risk exposure requires attention because of the probability of occurrence or the severity of impact or a combination of the two. Such exposure could have a material (quantitative or qualitative) adverse effect on a firm's earnings, reputation, and so on.

Single loss expectancy (SLE): SLE is the total amount of revenue that is lost from a single occurrence of the risk. It is a monetary amount that is assigned to a single event that represents the company's potential loss amount if a specific threat exploits a vulnerability. One calculates the SLE by multiplying the asset value by EF.

Social engineering: Obtaining information from individuals by trickery. A euphemism for nontechnical or low-technology means—such as lies, impersonation, tricks, bribes, blackmail, and threats—used to attack information systems [SHI200001].

Standard (corporate): In the context of a corporate setting and security policy, a mandatory action or rule designed to support and conform to a policy. A standard should make a policy more meaningful and effective. A standard must include one or more accepted specifications for hardware, software, or behavior [GUE200701].

Strategic imperatives: High-level objectives that set the direction of a company.

Strategic objectives: An organization's goals or activities to address competitiveness, business advantages, or change.

Strategic planning: A process for long-term goal-setting, determining priorities, and making decisions.

Threat: An event or activity that has the potential to cause harm to the information systems. Term defines an event (tornado, theft, or computer virus infection) the occurrence of which could have an undesirable impact [NIC200001]. Situations that might deliberately or accidentally exploit vulnerabilities causing information security incidents [CIS200701]. A potential cause of an unwanted impact to a system or organization (ISO 13335-1).

A potential for violation of security, which exists when there is a circumstance, capability, action, or event that could breach security and cause harm. A threat is a possible danger that might exploit a vulnerability. The means through which the ability or intent of a threat agent to adversely affect an automated system, facility, or operation can be manifest. A threat can be either "intentional" (i.e., intelligent; e.g., an individual cracker or a criminal organization) or "accidental" (e.g., the possibility of a computer malfunctioning, or the possibility of an "act of God" such as an earthquake, a fire, or a tornado). In some contexts the term is used narrowly to refer only to intelligent threats [SHI200001].

Threat action: An assault on system security.

Threat agent: Any agent (e.g., object, substance, human, etc.) that is capable of acting against an asset in a manner that can result in harm [JON200501].

Threat analysis: An analysis of the probability of occurrences and consequences of damaging actions to a system [SHI200001].

Threat capability (Tcap): The probable level of force that a threat agent is capable of applying against an asset [JON200501].

Threat community: A subset of the overall threat agent population that shares key characteristics [JON200501].

Threat consequence: A security violation that results from a threat action. Includes disclosure, deception, disruption, and usurpation.

The following subentries describe four kinds of threat consequences, and they also list and describe the kinds of threat actions that cause each consequence.

Threat actions that are accidental events are marked by an asterisk (*) [SHI200001]:

- *(Unauthorized) Disclosure (A Threat Consequence)*: A circumstance or event whereby an entity gains access to data for which the entity is not authorized. The following threat actions can cause unauthorized disclosure:
  - *Exposure*: A threat action whereby sensitive data is directly released to an unauthorized entity. This includes deliberate exposure, scavenging, * human error, and * hardware/software error.
  - *Interception*: A threat action whereby an unauthorized entity directly accesses sensitive data traveling between authorized sources and destinations. This includes theft, wiretapping (passive), and emanations analysis.
  - *Inference*: A threat action whereby an unauthorized entity indirectly accesses sensitive data (but not necessarily the data contained in the communication) by reasoning from characteristics or byproducts of communications. This includes traffic analysis and signals analysis.
  - *Intrusion*: A threat action whereby an unauthorized entity gains access to sensitive data by circumventing a system's security protections. This includes trespass, penetration, reverse engineering, and cryptanalysis.
- *Deception (a threat consequence)*: A circumstance or event that may result in an authorized entity receiving false data and believing it to be true. The following threat actions can cause deception:
  - *Masquerade*: A threat action whereby an unauthorized entity gains access to a system or performs a malicious act by posing as an authorized entity. This includes spoof and malicious logic.
  - *Falsification*: A threat action whereby false data deceives an authorized entity. This includes substitution and insertion.
  - *Repudiation*: A threat action whereby an entity deceives another by falsely denying responsibility for an act. This includes false denial of origin and false denial of receipt.

- *Disruption (a threat consequence)*: A circumstance or event that interrupts or prevents the correct operation of system services and functions. The following threat actions can cause disruption:
  - *Incapacitation*: A threat action that prevents or interrupts system operation by disabling a system component. This includes malicious logic, physical destruction, * human error, * hardware or software error, and * natural disaster.
  - *Corruption*: A threat action that undesirably alters system operation by adversely modifying system functions or data. This includes tamper, malicious logic, * human error, * hardware or software error, and * natural disaster.
  - *Obstruction*: A threat action that interrupts delivery of system services by hindering system operations. This includes interference and overload.
- *Usurpation (a threat consequence)*: A circumstance or event that results in control of system services or functions by an unauthorized entity. The following threat actions can cause usurpation:
  - *Misappropriation*: A threat action whereby an entity assumes unauthorized logical or physical control of a system resource. This includes theft of service, theft of functionality, and theft of data.
  - *Misuse*: A threat action that causes a system component to perform a function or service that is detrimental to system security. This includes tamper, malicious logic, and violation of permissions.

Threat event frequency (TEF): The probable frequency, within a given timeframe, that a threat agent will act against an asset [JON200501].

Threat modeling: A technique that a risk manager can use to identify threats, attacks, vulnerabilities, and countermeasures in the context of a specific application scenario.

Trojan horse: A program that neither replicates nor copies itself, but causes damage or compromises the security of the computer. Typically, an individual e-mails a Trojan horse to a recipient (it does not e-mail itself), and it may arrive in the form of a joke program or software of some sort.

Uncertainty: The lack of complete certainty, that is, the existence of more than one possibility. The "true" outcome/state/result/value is not known.

Usurpation: A circumstance or event that results in control of system services or functions by an unauthorized entity. The following threat actions can cause usurpation [SHI200001]:

- *Misappropriation*: A threat action whereby an entity assumes unauthorized logical or physical control of a system resource.
- *Theft of Service*: Unauthorized use of service by an entity.
- *Theft of Functionality*: Unauthorized acquisition of actual hardware, software, or firmware of a system component.

- *Theft of Data*: Unauthorized acquisition and use of data.
- *Misuse*: A threat action that causes a system component to perform a function or service that is detrimental to system security.
- *Tamper*: In the context of misuse, deliberate alteration of a system's logic, data, or control information to cause the system to perform unauthorized functions or services.
- *Malicious Logic*: In the context of misuse, any hardware, software, or firmware intentionally introduced into a system to perform or control execution of an unauthorized function or service.
- *Violation of Permissions*: Action by an entity that exceeds the entity's system privileges by executing an unauthorized function.

Virus: A program or code that replicates itself. A virus infects another program, boot sector, partition sector, or document that supports macros, by inserting itself or attaching itself to that medium. Most viruses only replicate, although many do a large amount of damage as well.

Vulnerability: A weakness in an information system (in the procedures, hardware design, internal controls, or software) that can be exploited [NIC200001]. Any weakness, administrative process, or act or physical exposure that makes an information asset susceptible to exploit by a threat. A lack of a safeguard, which may be exploited by a threat, causing harm to the information systems. A software flaw that permits an exogenous agent to use a computer system without authorization or use it with authorization in excess of that which the system owner specifically granted said agent. A flaw in a system's security procedures, design, implementation, or internal controls (for example, lack of or inadequate physical, logical, procedural, or legal protection of information assets) that could be exploited and result in a security breach, violation of the system security policy or other impact [CIS200701].

Waivers: Exception. Purpose of the waivers program is to force an organization to document the risk exposures and make a business decision related to how they are going to handle the issue.

Worm: A program that makes copies of itself—for example, from one disk drive to another, or by copying itself using e-mail or another transport mechanism. The worm may do damage and compromise the security of the computer; it may arrive in the form of a joke program or software of some sort.

REFERENCES

[BAN200701] M. Bandor, "Process and Procedure Definition: A Primer," SEPG 2007, 26–29 March 2007, Software Engineering Institute (SEI), Carnegie Mellon University.
[CIS200701] CISSPforum and ISO27k Implementer's Forum, "Top Information Security Risks for 2008," White Paper, Dec. 2007.

[COB200901] IT Governance Institute, 3701 Algonquin Road, Suite 1010, Rolling Meadows, IL 60008, USA.

[COS200401] Enterprise Risk Management—Integrated Framework, Executive Summary, White Paper of the Committee of Sponsoring Organizations of the Treadway Commission (COSO), September 2004.

[ENI200801] European Network and Information Security Agency (ENISA), 2008.

[GOV200801] U.S. National Information Systems Security Glossary.

[GUE200701] M. D. Guel, A Short Primer for Developing Security Policies, 2007, The SANS Institute, 8120 Woodmont Avenue, Suite 205, Bethesda, Maryland 20814

[GUI200701] ISO TMB WG on Risk Management, Committee Draft ISO/IEC CD Guide 73, Risk management—Vocabulary, 2007.

[HAY200301] M. V. Hayden, National Information Assurance (IA) Glossary, CNSS Instruction No. 4009, revised May 2003, Committee on National Security Systems, CNSS Secretariat (I42), National Security Agency, 9800 Savage Road, STE 6716, Ft Meade, MD, 20755-6716. Tel. (410) 854-6805. UFAX: (410) 854-6814, nstissc@radium.ncsc.

[INF200701] Infosec@UGA, The University of Georgia, Office of Information Security, Athens, GA, 30602-1911.

[JON200501] J. A. Jones, "An Introduction to Factor Analysis of Information Risk (FAIR)," 2005, http://www.riskmanagementinsight.com.

[LEH200601] D. Lehmann, Siemens CERT, http://www.sans.org/resources/idfaq

[LES200501] M. Lesk, M. R. Stytz, and R. L. Trope, "Averting Security Missteps in Outsourcing," IEEE Computer Society, 1540-7993/05, IEEE Security & Privacy.

[MIC200601] Microsoft Solutions for Security and Compliance and Microsoft Security Center of Excellence, The Security Risk Management Guide, Microsoft Corporation, Redmond, WA, 2006.

[NIC200001] R. K. Nichols, D. J. Ryan, and J. J. C. H. Ryan, Defending Your Digital Assets, McGraw-Hill, New York, 2000.

[NIS199801] NIST SP 800-16 Information Technology Security Training Requirements: A Role- and Performance-Based Model, M. Wilson, D. E. de Zafra, S. I. Pitcher, J. D. Tressler, and J. B. Ippolito, editors, NIST, April 1998.

[SHI200001] R. Shirey, Internet Security Glossary, RFC 2828, May 2000, Copyright © The Internet Society, 2000. All Rights Reserved. This document and translations of it may be copied and furnished to others, and derivative works that comment on or otherwise explain it or assist in its implementation may be prepared, copied, published and distributed, in whole or in part, without restriction of any kind, provided that the above copyright notice and this paragraph are included on all such copies and derivative works.

[STO200201] G. Stoneburner, A. Goguen, and A. Feringa, "Risk Management Guide for Information Technology Systems—Recommendations of the National Institute of Standards and Technology," Special Publication 800-30, July 2002, Computer Security Division Information Technology Laboratory, National Institute of Standards and Technology Gaithersburg, MD 20899-8930. [This document may be used by nongovernmental organizations on a voluntary basis. It is not subject to copyright.]

[TIP200001] H. F. Tipton, and M. Krause, Information Security Management Handbook, fourth edition, Auerbach, Boca Raton, FL, 2000.

Information Technology Risk Management in Enterprise Environments: A Review of Industry Practices and a Practial Guide to Risk Management Teams, by Jake Kouns and Daniel Minoli
Copyright © 2010 John Wiley & Sons, Inc.